DESIGNING LIBRARIES FOR THE 21ST CENTURY

H. THOMAS HICKERSON,
JOAN K. LIPPINCOTT,
and LEONORA CREMA, editors

Association of College and Research Libraries
A division of the American Library Association
Chicago, Illinois 2022

The paper used in this publication meets the minimum requirements of American National Standard for Information Sciences–Permanence of Paper for Printed Library Materials, ANSI Z39.48-1992. ∞

Library of Congress Control Number: 2022943709

Printed in the United States of America.

26 25 24 23 22 5 4 3 2 1

Dedication

To the late Susan Nutter:
partner, inspiration, visionary

Contents

intro

INTRODUCTION

TOM HICKERSON
JOAN K. LIPPINCOTT
LEONORA CREMA
Coeditors

Designing libraries for the 21st century encompasses many aspects, ranging from conceptualizing a compelling, aesthetically pleasing, and sustainable structure with a striking and functional interior to developing staff positions and expertise that will be commensurate with the capabilities of the facility when it opens. A technology infrastructure that will allow the building to change with a rapidly evolving technical environment and programming spaces to enhance the research and learning mission of the university are also key elements of the 21st-century library. Envisioning ways to highlight the library's print and digital collections and identifying strategies to support diversity, equity, and inclusion in the library will be integral to the success of the project for its constituencies. Often major building projects focus almost entirely on the physical facility, but in this volume, we make the case for looking at a building project in a more holistic fashion.

For the past two decades or more, we have seen a transformational shift in the design of college and research libraries, moving away from buildings designed primarily to house collections of books and journals. While many library expansions were still driven by the need for added stack space well into the 21st century, the increasing urgency to develop new learning spaces, incorporating new technologies and collaborative spaces for students, led libraries to change. Visionary librarians, planners, and university leaders began thinking about library buildings in new ways, centered more on people than on collections. The need for openness to let in natural light, rather than windowless spaces for protecting books, and flexibility to accommodate rapidly changing technologies were widely recognized. This book provides guidance, principles, good practice, and typical processes for designing contemporary libraries. We intend for it to be both practical and inspirational.

The dramatic changes in the conceptualization of library buildings in the past 20 years have been driven by changes in the core functions of universities and colleges. In research, all disciplines rely on digital tools and content. In teaching and learning, technologies have been incorporated into pedagogy, and the active and social aspects of learning have been increasingly emphasized. In many institutions, there is a renewed emphasis on inclusion and community engagement. Today, all new buildings and renovations seek to address these and other developments and are designed with the expectation of continuous and rapid change. The flexible, permeable spaces developed in contemporary libraries have enabled libraries to pivot and adjust to conditions as they have developed, notably during the many months of the coronavirus pandemic.

In this volume, we seek to explore major trends and identify promising strategies to prepare libraries for the future. An impressive array of authors, largely drawn from past presenters at the Designing Libraries for the 21st Century Conferences, will provide their big-picture perspectives and practical advice.

We begin with a selection of chapters that provide context for the trends in contemporary libraries, which reflect developments in scholarship, research, and learning—core elements of the academic enterprise—along with emphasis on community and inclusion. We then present several chapters that provide insight into how major projects seek to align their vision with institutional mission and priorities. Next, we highlight different perspectives, including those of library leaders, campus planners, and architects, on the architectural aspects of buildings and the planning process, including how to ensure effective communication among these groups. A section on key planning elements offers ideas for incorporating collections, technologies, responsive user services, and accessible design in contemporary libraries. Next, several well-developed partnerships are described, illuminating the opportunities and challenges of such relationships as well as the process used at several institutions to achieve collaborations. The convergence of a variety of cultural heritage organizations, including libraries, museums, and archives, is also explored. In the following section, we have the views of some leaders who have practical experience with change management. New library spaces require robust organizational capacity to realize their fullest potential. This includes ensuring that staff are supported and equipped to implement changes in operations and programs. Development of new types of expertise in staff is a critical element in the realization of the potential of 21st-century libraries. Finally, exemplary programs for a wide variety of library users, which take full advantage of the affordances of new or renovated facilities and help to realize an inclusive environment, are presented. Planning with synergy between users, programs, services, technologies, and new developments in research, teaching, and learning should provide a foundation for the 21st-century library. This section highlights a variety of innovative programs and services for students, faculty, staff, and the broader community.

Our book focuses primarily on academic libraries in North America, although we also include chapters on the Calgary Public Library and the National Library of Qatar, two projects with exceptional physical facilities and outstanding programming for their user communities. Academic libraries can learn much from facilities outside academia.

Our intention is for this book to serve a broad audience of individuals and teams who are involved in a planning process for a significant renovation, expansion, or new build of a library facility. Many of our authors have been very candid about what they would do differently in hindsight or how they have made needed changes in their facility after the building was opened. We anticipate that an entire institutional planning group will use this book as background for their work and as the basis for discussions on each aspect of their project. We also suggest that librarians might use particular chapters with faculty and institutional leaders to assist in their understanding of contemporary libraries or to expose them to trends in specific aspects of a project, such as digital collections and new technologies. The book can also be a valuable tool for those working on fundraising and communications, assisting with crafting messages about what 21st-century libraries are and can be. In addition, we hope the book will be used by library and information science students who are taking academic library classes to help prepare them for their professional roles.

It is clear that during the many months of the pandemic, students greatly missed opportunities for collaborative learning, access to technologies that they do not own themselves, and opportunities to feel part of a community. Lack of physical access to institutional libraries during the pandemic led to real losses in learning and in research productivity for many students and faculty. Twenty-first-century libraries are designed to foster active learning and research supported by digital tools and staff expertise, and we believe that there will be a renewed appreciation for "library as place." Our intention is for this book to assist campuses in developing a robust planning process through its emphasis on pragmatic models informed by important trends in higher education, learning, research, and design.

The Designing Libraries for the 21st Century Conferences

While a relatively small number of entirely new academic library buildings have been erected in the 21st century, this new concept of libraries was realized in the construction of the Taylor Family Digital Library at the University of Calgary and the James B. Hunt Jr. Library at North Carolina State University (NCSU). Profession-wide, there was great interest in these new libraries, giving rise to the first Designing Libraries for the 21st Century Conference, held at the University of Calgary in the spring of 2012, with conferences subsequently held at Calgary, NCSU, and the Georgia Institute of Technology.

The conference was not initially envisioned as ongoing, but it quickly became apparent that the event generated rich discourse among the people in the room—librarians, architects, planners, scholars, academic administrators—and an exchange of ideas and plans between and among the institutions represented. Many came as teams from their institution when they had a project underway. The momentum of these conversations, held in the setting of remarkable new library spaces, launched the continuing series. And it has stimulated us, the editors, to share this discourse with a wider audience by bringing together insights from past Designing Libraries conferences in this volume.

Now planning for its ninth installment at Temple University, Designing Libraries for the 21st Century has emerged as the premier North American conference focused specifically on this new generation of academic libraries. The conference draws an international audience combining visionary thinking, panels and group discussions, tours, and tactical planning for real-life building projects. Its particular success has been in going beyond the standard elements and checklists for designing or renovating facilities to address the reimagining of roles for libraries made possible by new uses of space. The value of flexible, open, and permeable design has been a key emphasis, currently being illustrated by the requirements necessitated by the COVID pandemic, with libraries re-crafting their spaces in ways that fulfill new health and safety requirements. While a number of authors address the pandemic to some degree in their chapters, this is not a focus of the book. In the long run, we believe the trajectory libraries are on—building active, social, technology-rich spaces—will prevail.

We hope that this book will inspire all readers to expand their vision of libraries, reconceive how their libraries contribute to the institutional mission, and explore the possibilities waiting to be discovered. In the words of Tom Hickerson, founder of the Designing Libraries series, in what has become the conference tagline and mantra: "Design for the Library You Know, Design for the Library You Can Imagine, and Design for the Library You Cannot Yet Imagine."

Acknowledgments

The editors thank all of the authors in this volume for their valuable contributions, their insight, and their desire to pass along what they have learned to others. We also thank the staff members who participated in or supported the Designing Libraries conferences at University of Calgary, North Carolina State University, and Georgia Tech. Special thanks to the late Susan Nutter and Greg Raschke of North Carolina State University, Catherine Murray-Rust of Georgia Tech, and Joe Lucia of Temple University.

The Coalition for Networked Information (CNI) has been a cosponsor of each Designing Libraries conference, and executive director Clifford Lynch was especially supportive of the investment of staff time in their planning. Thanks also to CNI's Diane Goldenberg-Hart for her assistance.

We appreciate the guidance and support of the Association of College and Research Libraries (ACRL), especially our publisher, Erin Nevius; copyeditor Judith Lauber; designer Dawn Mueller; and the New Publications Advisory Board.

SECTION I

21ST-CENTURY ACADEMIC LIBRARIES IN AN EVOLVING ENVIRONMENT

1

CHAPTER ONE

PERMEABLE THINKING AND DESIGN

Libraries and the Changing Knowledge Ecosystem

TOM HICKERSON

The roles and practices of libraries are symbiotically related to the nature of architectural design and space use in libraries. Therefore, it is not surprising that for centuries the structure and appearance of academic libraries reflected the primacy of the collection and the structure of the bookstacks housing that collection. This continued through the 20th century with the construction of new buildings and expansions largely driven by the growth in collections and their management. But the underlying fundamentals of academic libraries have changed dramatically in the last 50 years and continue to change at a pace necessitating permeable thinking and design.

During these last 50 years, beginning in the early 1970s, fundamental changes began with the introduction and distribution of machine-readable cataloging that reduced the need for cataloging staff and led to the introduction of computer terminals into spaces with few electrical outlets. This change soon enabled online public access catalogs and led to the widespread removal of card catalogs in the 1980s. The 1980s also saw the first introduction of electronic databases and journals, a change that would later be transformative.

The early 1990s saw widespread digitization as a preservation means, and increasingly in teaching as these images became available in digital form. The internet was beginning to be used, principally among scientists, when the World Wide Web was invented in 1989, followed by the development of Mosaic in 1993, the first popularly used graphical web browser. This development changed the information ecosystem and dramatically changed libraries.

With the web in place, library users could access library information from anywhere, and using powerful search engines they could access information of all kinds. The internet also made possible the establishment in 1991 of arXiv.org by Paul Ginsparg. Developed at the Los Alamos National Laboratory and later moving to Cornell University, this important harbinger of the open access movement made physics preprints freely available worldwide.[1]

The arrival of the World Wide Web initiated a sense of crisis in libraries, raising the question "Why will we need libraries?" a concern illustrated by the article "The Deserted Library," appearing in the *Chronicle of Higher Education* in November 2001.[2] Both students and faculty began to leave the library. Students soon came back, but faculty did not.

The return of students was stimulated by a new vision for student learning, best characterized by a study conducted by Scott Bennett, *Libraries Designed for Learning*, published in 2003.[3] This influential work stressed that user space should be shaped by both the educational and the social needs of students, supporting knowledge creation as well as access to information.

Realized through information and learning commons, including individual computer workstations and cafés, this led to a need for a very different footprint within libraries, which challenged existing architecture and was increasingly made possible by the transfer of significant portions of the book and journal collection to off-site storage.

Libraries in a Time of Institutional Change

With the arrival of the 21st century, a transformative vision driven by new learning space priorities began evolving. Research itself was also changing, driven by the need to address societal "Grand Challenges" through multidisciplinary, multi-institutional, and community-based collaboration. Research began to employ new media and analytical tools in rich combinations. Geospatial analysis and visualization are increasingly applied in many fields, from medicine to the humanities. Spaces for cutting-edge technologies and collaborative research endeavors have become critical. Through these evolutions, library interiors have been further transformed.

The library footprint on campus was also changing. As universities began reducing and combining discipline-based academic units, and with more resources accessible online and independent of physical space, the number of branch libraries decreased.

Today, in an age of open access, open data, and open science, the physical housing of books and journals has lost its previous relevance. Instead, library-based functional capacities are discipline-agnostic and are provided as a constellation serving multiple fields and achieving economies of scale. The designing of library space in synergistic combination with associated campus programs is also growing.

Academic institutions are in a period of redefinition, and the pace of change in institutional mission and goals necessitates capacity for realignment in all of the principal elements of the academy. Major developments include

- declining societal confidence in the effectiveness and cost-efficiency of higher education,
- perceptions of higher education as contributing to elitist divisions and inequality,
- expectations of an enlarged public role in addressing community and societal concerns,
- changes in public funding and in access to publicly funded research,
- expanded commercial, governmental, and community partnerships,
- increasing disciplinary realignment,
- increased interest and investment in STEM (science, technology, engineering, and mathematics) fields, further augmented by the pandemic,
- changes in research methods, employing new models, new media, and new technologies,
- efforts to sustain the vitality of the humanities and the arts through enhanced relevance to current cultural concerns, and
- an expanding role of universities as repositories of artistic and diverse cultural heritage.

In this environment, libraries must align both with the evolving needs of their students and scholars and with the changing mission and goals of their institutions. Increasingly, they are focused on demonstrating their contributions to the expanded public role of their universities and being viewed as critical partners for campus and community collaborative initiatives.

Professionally, libraries embody a service ethos and a commitment to equity and inclusion. Supporting this, their buildings are frequently large, technology-rich, and increasingly permeable, and they are accustomed to welcoming a diverse range of users, often 24 hours a day. As universities and colleges seek to consolidate existing activities while also expanding into new areas, libraries are outstanding institutional assets. In combination, these changes are transforming the organizational and professional model and the spatial and architectural design of libraries.

Permeability: A New Model for Campus Planning and Design

What is permeability? Most importantly, permeability reflects the way humans use a space, and it includes how they perceive a space and how the space connects with them. It is not the way to design the perfect library. In many ways, it is the opposite of perfection or permanence. It is likely that before construction of any new building is completed, a need to make adjustments will be recognized. Permeability is based on an expectation of ongoing changes, some of which were foreseen and some that were not yet imagined. And while some changes will be based on the user or staff experience, others will be university-based or arise in the world beyond the campus. Permeable thinking gives us the capacity to recognize such changes; permeable design enables us to make those changes.

As an architectural concept, permeability is not limited to libraries. It is applicable to all types of institutional design. Permeable design approaches and construction and engineering techniques are being widely applied. They are usually described as open and flexible approaches generating spatial flexibility.

Flexibility is certainly a critical aspect, but permeability also incorporates humanness. While there is broad awareness of the nature of exponential technological change, we should remember that the first Apple iPhone was developed in 2004–2006 and publicly announced in January 2007, barely a dozen years after the announcement of Netscape Mosaic. Reviewing the changes in the following 12 years, and citing the work of Ray Kurzweil,[4] Jim Gibson suggests that in every dozen years we will see the combining of "eight or more different technologies that have never been connected, let alone existed before." He warns that we are entering a time in which the human capacity to apprehend and make sense of this landscape is being challenged.[5]

In today's environment, attention tends to focus on the "Innovation of Things," but Gibson suggests that it is imperative that we also address an "Innovation of Ways."[6] This is where we must focus in current planning and design. Libraries are ideal places in which to create a balancing of the advances of technological development with the fundamental needs of humanness, spaces that are consistently supportive of human nurturing and equality.

Catalyst for Connection, Creativity, and Innovation

Permeability is particularly applicable for academic libraries and other university buildings. University campuses are a complex of related buildings serving a common set of users. In the past, some campuses strove for architectural uniformity obscuring the uniqueness of the programs within. Such buildings sometimes seemed unwelcoming. Today, architectural design should seek to provide easily discernible understanding of the nature and purpose of a facility and welcome those entering. Permeable spaces are

- open and transparent from within and from the outside in—intentionally creating connections between their interior and their exterior,
- spaces in which those entering can exercise a sense of relationship and ownership enabling them to shape the use of the space,
- creative spaces responsive to their users and where "the architecture" does not dictate practice, and
- enabled by cutting-edge technologies balanced by the humanness of their users.

Design features of permeable spaces include

- first floors that create a sense of openness and accessibility for the entirety of a building,
- cafés and other areas that catalyze informal socializing, that are not someone's personal space and can be used as one chooses (figure 1.1),

fig 1.1

Café in the Taylor Family Digital Library, University of Calgary.

(Credit: Photo by Dave Brown/University of Calgary.)

- atria providing important visual connection between floors and spaces,
- open walls and staircases connecting people and helping them to "read" activities in the building (figure 1.2),

fig 1.2

Energy, Environment, and Experiential Learning Building, University of Calgary.

(Credit: Courtesy of the University of Calgary.)

- versatile furnishings to address a diversity of purposes,
- accessible and supportive spaces for all users, supporting both collaboration and quiet study and reflection,
- instructional spaces that can be enlarged or reduced in size as needed,
- transparent spaces enabling diverse use and putting interaction on display (figure 1.3),

fig 1.3

Taylor Institute for Teaching and Learning, University of Calgary.

(Credit: Photo by Dave Brown/University of Calgary.)

- collision spaces where people can come together to brainstorm, collaborate, and disrupt, breaking down silos to foster interdisciplinary thinking and action,
- multifaceted labs that support research partnerships, student projects, and public engagement, purposefully collaborative and community-building (figure 1.4),

fig 1.4

"Student-owned" collaborative space, Taylor Family Digital Library, University of Calgary.

(Credit: Photo by Dave Brown/University of Calgary.)

- environmental architecture, materials, and engineering that address climate sustainability and human health, and
- technological infrastructure that enables diverse capabilities throughout and offers expandable capacity (figure 1.5).

fig 1.5

Visualization Studio, Taylor Family Digital Library, University of Calgary.

(Credit: Photo by John Brosz/ University of Calgary.)

"Fostering flow, creating connectivity, promoting creative solutions": this is the way in which Jeanne L. Narum, principal of the Learning Spaces Collaboratory, and her colleagues characterize permeable design and its applicability in a diverse array of campus construction. Such buildings reflect the concept of permeability in strikingly different ways, making the case for a new language, new approaches, and new visions. Narum and colleagues identify three examples as being illustrative of the diverse ways in which permeability is being realized: the Watt Family Innovation Center at Clemson University, the Leach Teaching Gardens at Texas A&M University, and the Taylor Family Digital Library at the University of Calgary.[7]

WATT FAMILY INNOVATION CENTER

The mission of the Watt Family Innovation Center (figure 1.6) is to create an environment in which collaboration among students, faculty, and leaders from industry and government generates ideas and solves complex problems. Architecturally, external and internal glass walls provide abundant natural light and transparency to the outside and between rooms. Demountable walls, raised flooring, power-over-Ethernet, and connected lighting enable efficient and economical changes to room sizes and space configurations. All furniture is on wheels, permitting easy spatial reconfigurations.

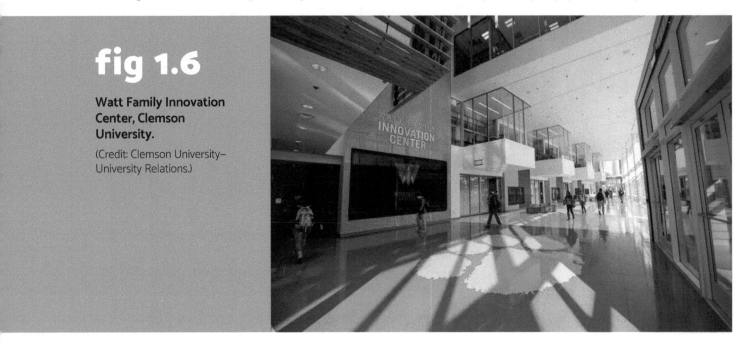

fig 1.6

Watt Family Innovation Center, Clemson University.

(Credit: Clemson University–University Relations.)

Audiovisual and information technology systems also advance permeability. A 209-foot-by-24-foot Media Lights display outside the building advertises events being held there. Within the building, more than 200 touch screens support presentations and distance communication. All screens are centrally controlled, allowing content to be selectively distributed throughout the building and to external locations.

Architecturally, the Watt Center is a model of permeability aligning effectively with its organizational mandate to serve and integrate all disciplines and to foster diverse corporate connections. In addition to its other roles, it is the administrative home of Clemson's Creative Inquiry program connecting undergraduates to industry-supported research preparing them for life beyond the campus.[8]

LEACH TEACHING GARDENS OF THE COLLEGE OF AGRICULTURE AND LIFE SCIENCES

The Leach Teaching Gardens (figure 1.7) are a prime example of Texas A&M University's Campus Master Plan, updated in 2017. The update sought to reimagine the campus physical environment and sense of place, aligning with academic priorities while enhancing intellectual, emotional, and physical wellness for the university community and for the community at large. Guiding principles include

- an open space network as a basis for enriched campus experiences,
- the campus as an incrementally holistic and integrated whole versus a series of isolated hubs,
- campus forums that provide exposure to a wide range of perspectives and generate encounters and interactions that lead to new insights and discovery,
- mobility planning that prioritizes pedestrian connections over vehicular access, and
- a campus identity of fluid engagement.

fig 1.7

Leach Teaching Gardens, Texas A&M University.

(Credit: Ed Rhodes, Texas A&M AgriLife.)

The Leach Teaching Gardens, completed in 2018, are an exemplary application of these guidelines and a model of permeability. These public gardens include 21 themed gardens, an outdoor classroom, an event lawn, a demonstration area, and a pavilion. The gardens experientially connect students and the public to the world of horticulture and food production. They also serve as a peaceful sanctuary where everyone can relax, enjoy, and learn.[9]

Realizing Permeability in Library Design: The Taylor Family Digital Library

Initial planning had been underway for several years, and extensive interviews with library staff regarding space needs had been conducted by an outside consultant when, in the summer of 2006, design planning for a new central library at the University of Calgary began in earnest. The province of Alberta had allocated initial funding in the spring of 2006, and a substantial private gift was received later in the year. In addition to the new library, the $205 million (CAD) project included an off-campus storage facility and the redesign of the adjacent central quadrangle. The Taylor Family Digital Library (TFDL) would formally open in September 2011.

A new university provost and project executive (Alan Harrison) and a new university librarian and programmatic design lead (Tom Hickerson) had both arrived in the summer of 2006, almost simultaneously. Their immediate challenge was to develop a guiding vision for the project. They shared a common commitment to creating a building focusing on student learning, emerging technologies, and knowledge creation. It was agreed that the physical collection would be largely housed elsewhere and that the building would include the university museum and the university press. This broad cultural mission was formally enunciated through the naming of Hickerson as vice provost for libraries and cultural resources (LCR) and university librarian in the fall of 2006.

The name Taylor Family Digital Library was formally enunciated by the president of the University of Calgary (Harvey Weingarten) in agreement with the principal donors (Don and Ruth Taylor). For some, the phrase *digital library* suggested a narrower concept that libraries had seized on a decade earlier as a means of indicating that they were adapting to the impact of the internet. But through the process of elaborating the vision for the new building, the realization became clear that every aspect of the creation, dissemination, and preservation of information in 21st-century libraries rests upon digital technologies. Libraries must fully embrace this reality as a way of understanding, organizing, and designing their future.

As the vision evolved, it came to include the following principal elements:

- Libraries are now in a state of continuous transformation, and the design and construction should enable and advance ongoing spatial and programmatic change.
- Access to information is now ubiquitous; design instead for knowledge creation by both students and scholars.
- Focus on social spaces designed for student learning, spaces "owned by students."
- Today's research is enabled by the combination of digital media and analytical tools; focus on the research experience, not on research resources.
- Libraries, archives, and museums reflect a convergence of knowledge and culture, and these cultural assets are increasingly important in teaching, scholarship, and community engagement.
- Environmental sustainability and user accessibility are vital elements in all campus construction.

The provost and the vice provost were supported by a diverse array of planning professionals led by the associate vice president for facilities development (Stephen Dantzer) and by numerous library staff, led by the project director (Jackie Bell, and later Claudette Cloutier) and the technology lead (Shawna Sadler). The architectural team from Kasian Architecture and Design, was led by architect Bill Chomik and interior designer Lois Wellwood, and the construction manager and principal contractor was CANA Construction. The Schematic Design document was accepted and signed by the university in February 2008, and the project was underway.

Designing for Change

In 2011, principal architect Bill Chomik would describe the TFDL as having been "designed and built to not only reflect the digital revolution in education and the resulting new ways of learning of recent years, but also with the flexibility to accommodate the twists and turns of future educational requirements—and new technologies."[10] Fundamental to realizing this vision was comprehensive installation of raised flooring throughout the six-floor, 265,000-square-foot building. Raised flooring significantly increased construction costs but insured ubiquitous electrical and network connectivity and energy-efficient and healthy heating and cooling. In combination with extensive use of demountable walls (non-load-bearing), raised flooring has fostered effective, ongoing repurposing of space throughout the building and easy adaptation to evolving accessibility and universal design imperatives (figure 1.8).

fig 1.8

Installing raised flooring and underfloor HVAC and electrical and network connections, Taylor Family Digital Library, University of Calgary.

(Credit: Photo by Dave Brown/University of Calgary.)

Underfloor heating and cooling, in combination with the construction of a small pond in the redesigned quadrangle enabling recirculation of water from the building, contributed to LEED Gold certification. The University of Calgary is a leader in LEED certified construction. This reflects the critical value of a holistic approach in all aspects of campus design.

Experiencing the TFDL

Welcoming users into the building is a broad passageway from the Taylor Quadrangle (figure 1.9). This passage, equipped with minimal security constraints, proceeds directly through the building, providing effective transit for over 10,000 individuals daily. A guiding principle was ease of access and interflow between indoor and outdoor space, including addressing user mobility challenges. As described by Loraine Fowlow, professor of architecture at the University of Calgary:

> The TFDL provides seamless integration of building entrance with its homogeneously surfaced exterior hardscaping. Variations in surrounding topography are handled through gentle sloping of the ground plane, so as to link between neighbouring buildings without the need for stairs. The main plaza flows directly into the west entrance of the building, which has a low-profile door threshold that provides completely barrier-free access. The east entrance is accessed via a ramp from a pedestrian and service vehicle mall, a sequence that is entirely curb-free. The ground plane surrounding the TFDL is one continuous uninterrupted surface that does away entirely with the need for providing alternative barrier-free access routes: through the simple means of not including barriers in the first place.[11]

fig 1.9

West view of the Taylor Family Digital Library from the Taylor Quadrangle, University of Calgary.

(Credit: Photo by Dave Brown/University of Calgary.)

Upon entering, one is able to discern a broad spectrum of spatial and programmatic attributes, including a café, dual-monitor workstations, collaborative workrooms, an information desk, a stairway to the second-floor learning commons, elevators, automated checkout machines, and the lower gallery of the university art museum. Adjacent to the museum is Gallery Hall, a large space for library town halls, scholarly presentations, small conferences, student and community activities, exhibition openings, and celebratory receptions. Walls of the passageway include paintings on one side and a large media wall promoting library programs and collections on the other. This multifaceted view immediately provides both users and those passing through with a clear sense of both the scope and the specifics of the TFDL experience.

The building also offers well-lit space, vistas, and adjacency to green space, long recognized as benefits in human-centered architectural design.[12] The curtain-wall construction exterior of the building consists largely of glass panels. Most panels are clear glass, allowing a great deal of natural light into the building, but some panels are fritted or opaque, based on space use within. Most student learning spaces allow easy exterior views, and most such spaces are on the west side of the building, offering views of the open quadrangle. From the upper floors, one can gaze beyond the campus toward the western prairies and see the snow-capped peaks of the Canadian Rockies.

On the lower two floors, the two-floor glass expanse is shielded by a stainless-steel, transparent grid diminishing heat and the glare on computer screens from the incoming sunlight. The combination of internal openness and exterior landscapes affords users a comfortable awareness of space and place, and the interior walls on all floors feature distinctive paintings from the museum's collections. At night, the lighted floors provide a lively beacon in the heart of the campus.

Instructional spaces on the third flour include computer lab type settings, as well as spaces for small group interaction. All walls include multiple media displays that can be controlled independently. Most importantly, the large space seating 152 can be quickly divided into two spaces or four by lowering soundproof curtains from the ceiling. When not being employed for instruction, these spaces and technologies can be used by students for individual study or collaboratively.

Cutting-edge technologies are incorporated into all aspects of the building, and multi-surface computing was introduced into the planning early on after project team visits led by the provost to IBM and HP research centers in New York and California. The Visualization Studio includes a high-resolution visualization wall (35 million pixels). The selection of the visualization technology was conducted by a multidisciplinary faculty team. Ensuring ongoing computing power into the future, two 10G fiber backbone risers provide almost twice the capacity required at opening.

In order to ensure technological ubiquity, the project technology lead, Shawna Sadler, worked closely with the interior designer in the choice of diverse furnishings allowing the incorporation of electrical and network connections directly into student seating, tables, and carrels. "Smart building" sustainability features include sensors controlling interior lighting and exterior blinds. Elevator information displays change with each floor, and media displays identify unoccupied workstations on multiple floors.

Success in the vital partnership with students throughout the construction and after the opening of the TFDL is indicated by Library and Cultural Resources being honored twice as the recipient of the University of Calgary Students' Union Presidential Distinctive Service to Students Award.

Continuing Transformation

Critically important is the ability to continually redesign interior spaces in response to programmatic changes or campus partnerships. Initial partnerships included the Cuthbertson Student Success Centre, a program of the Office of the Vice Provost for the Student Experience, the Canadian Music Centre, and an office and meeting room for the Alumni Association. Repurposing of space has included the creation of a graduate student research commons and allocation of space enabling the move into the TFDL of the Prairie Regional Research Data Centre, a part of the national Research Data Centre Network that provides researchers access to a wide array of Statistics Canada confidential microdata files in a secure computer facility, including social, economic, and health surveys, along with census and administrative files. This relocation from a nearby building to a space immediately adjacent to LCR Spatial and Numeric Data Services enables new research synergies.

Significant spatial redesign has been conducted to establish Lab NEXT and the Glenbow Western History Research Centre. Lab NEXT is a spatial hub for a constellation of library services, infrastructure, and expertise critical to today's academic research enterprise. This digital scholarship center, including a makerspace, was created in response to research conducted at the University of Calgary beginning in 2015. This research, supported by The Andrew W. Mellon Foundation, identified principal researcher needs, and Lab NEXT serves as a point of connection and collaboration for scholars and students and community partners.[13]

The establishment of the Glenbow Western History Research Centre followed the transfer of stewardship of the substantive archival holdings of the Glenbow Museum in downtown Calgary to the University of Calgary.[14] In order to give prominence to this major enhancement of the university's historical collections, an entirely new public space was created on the second floor of the TFDL, and LCR's Archives and Special Collections reading room and research services were also moved to this new location from their previous location on the fifth floor.

These significant spatial and programmatic alterations provide dramatic evidence of the effectiveness of permeable design and construction.

Changes Yet to Come

This is a challenging and inspiring time when new thinking about the mission of higher education is evolving in response to societal needs and expectations. New roles are developing, and new means of realizing educational and research goals are being created. In this environment, the academy will be expected to realign internally and reposition publicly, and at an increasingly rapid pace. It is a time to reenvision through a new prism.

The future profile of the library will be transformed both by changes in library mission and practice and by new alliances and partnerships on campus and beyond. Adaptability must be a forethought. In renovating or building libraries, permeable thinking will be essential.

This is an exciting time when library professionals will have the opportunity and responsibility to decide what they will be next. In this new ecosystem, we must design for the library that we have not yet imagined.

Notes

1. Paul Ginsparg, "ArXiv at 20," *Nature* 476 (August 2011): 145–47, https://doi.org/10.1038/476145a.
2. Scott Carlson, "The Deserted Library," *Chronicle of Higher Education* 48 (November 16, 2001), https://www.chronicle.com/article/the-deserted-library/.
3. Scott Bennett, *Libraries Designed for Learning* (Washington, DC: Council on Library and Information Resources, November 2003).
4. Ray Kurzweil is an award-winning technologist, inventor, writer, and futurist. His best-selling books include *The Age of Spiritual Machines* (1999) and *The Singularity Is Near: When Humans Transcend Biology* (2005).
5. Jim A. Gibson, *Tip of the Spear: Our Species and Technology at a Crossroads* (Calgary, AB, Canada: self-published, 2018): 4–5, 24–25.
6. Gibson, *Tip of the Spear*, 153–57.
7. Jeanne L. Narum, Thomas Hickerson, Barbara J. Speziale, and Jorge A. Vanegas, "Permeability by Design: Fostering Flow, Creating Connectivity, Promoting Creative Solutions," *Learning by Design*, Spring 2019: 12–16, https://pubs.royle.com/publication/?i=575655#.
8. Narum et al., "Permeability by Design."
9. Narum et al., "Permeability by Design."
10. *Award*, (February 11, 2011), http://kasian.com/news/taylor-family-digital-library-preparing-for-a-digital-future/ (page discontinued).
11. Loraine Fowlow, "Inaccessible Access: A Paradox of Design," *Canadian Architect*, June 1, 2015, https://www.canadianarchitect.com/inaccessible-access-a-paradox-of-design/.
12. Adriana Voegeli, "Human-Centered Architectural Design: What Is It and How It Makes a Difference," *Dormakaba* (blog), September 24, 2020, https://blog.dormakaba.com/human-centered-architecture-what-is-it-and-how-it-makes-a-difference/.
13. Christie Hurrell, "Aligning the Stars: Understanding Digital Scholarship Needs to Support the Evolving Nature of Academic Research," *Partnership: The Canadian Journal of Library and Information Practice and Research* 14, no. 2 (2019), https://doi.org/10.21083/partnership.v14i2.4623.
14. Laura Beauline-Stuebing, "U of Calgary Offers a New State-of-the-Art Home for a Massive Collection of Western Canadian History," University Affairs, University of Calgary, October 26, 2020, https://www.universityaffairs.ca/news/news-article/u-of-calgary-offers-a-new-state-of-the-art-home-for-a-massive-collection-of-western-canadian-history.

2

C H A P T E R T W O

LIBRARY AS PLATFORM

The Transformed Library's Impact on Teaching, Learning, and Research

GREGORY K. RASCHKE

In the summer of 1998, I was home visiting my parents fresh off obtaining my undergraduate degree and preparing to enter the School of Information and Library Science at the University of Illinois at Urbana-Champaign. I was telling some of my parents' friends about my plans, and a friend of my Dad's said, "That is a terrible idea, everything is going to be on the web and we will not need libraries." Then he walked off, proud as could be about his honesty, wisdom, and foresight. Many librarians have been faced with some form of that declaration during the course of a career, particularly those who were active in the initial decade or so of growth of the World Wide Web. My Dad's friend was, of course, wrong. Thankfully even then I had enough resilience to be only mildly shaken while still committed to my graduate enrollment and future career. Even more thankfully, I stumbled into a career's worth of projects—spanning everything from student assistant at the Grainger Engineering Library at the University of Illinois, to a new librarian at Georgia Tech watching the earliest seeds of the learning commons, to library administrator at North Carolina State University—redesigning libraries at the end of the 20th century and first two decades of the 21st century, experiences that stand as examples of just how wrong that statement was and is.

Declarations of the death of the library have become cliché. We are well past that. What my Dad's friend failed to recognize is one of the tenets of evolutionary biology, that organisms or organizations faced with changing environments do themselves evolve and change.[1] Libraries have never been fixed entities. They have steadily evolved, adapted, and grown. In the last decade of the 20th and first decade of the 21st century, the evolution of libraries was most obviously seen in the growth and incorporation of digital collections and the accompanying changes that occurred. In the second decade of the 21st century, the evolution of libraries is most prominently seen in the redesign of their spaces and the related transformation of the organizations and staff that support those spaces and associated services. There is no more *prominent* example of the transformation of libraries than the new buildings and many major renovations that have occurred in the past 20 years. There is no more *enduring* example of the transformation of libraries than the array of creative work coming out of those new and renovated buildings. New spaces provide the platform from which libraries can launch a thousand ships and reposition themselves at the center of the academic and research enterprise.

The Library as Platform

The Libraries at NC State have leveraged the transformation of physical environments to explore the potential of the library as platform. Those explorations have taken several forms, including the expected user-focused developments around research, teaching, and learning, but also the evolution of the suite of skills and expertise library staff can provide. The story of the efforts to renovate and build spaces at NC State has demonstrated realities for libraries more generally—realities around the necessary ingredients to activate new spaces. There are a myriad of lessons we have learned from building and renovating new spaces, but five major themes emerge and help encapsulate our experience.

1. Renovating existing spaces builds momentum that manifests in several forms, including the likelihood of further experimentation with and renovation of additional library spaces. Once the benefits of transformed spaces, however small, are demonstrated, momentum builds for further efforts.
2. With the aid of new spaces, libraries can thrive firmly at the center of both experiential, active learning and boundary-spanning interdisciplinary teaching and curriculum development.
3. The integration of emerging technologies is fundamental to the transformed library. It signals the availability of resources for multidisciplinary collaborations and a shared set of advanced tools for the user community. New spaces must be built with the adaptability to change technology as formerly emergent tools become commonplace and new technologies come forward to the market.
4. The true transformational potential of spaces as platforms is driven by the combination of programming, events, workshops, design, and the staffing expertise that evolves as the spaces evolve.
5. New spaces open doors to reimagined and new partnerships, partnerships that need to be strategically nurtured and developed for the benefit of both the library and its parent organization.

New spaces open new doors, literally and figuratively. Those new horizons are fraught with challenges, but provide an almost unending landscape of opportunities. Those opportunities provide a gravitational pull to the library and a momentum that must be leveraged for further experimentation. In sharing the story of transformation at NC State, this chapter will explore those major elements that form the recipes for success, the lessons learned for future adaptation, the growing energy an organization can build for further experimentation, and what those efforts signal for the future of libraries—a present and future where libraries can go from being a provider of collections and services to, as associate professor of English at NC State Paul Fyfe puts it, "The Libraries have been more than a service provider, even more than a collaborator and partner, they have expanded my idea of the possible."

First Steps: The 2007 Hill Renovation

At NC State, we began with the premise that the transformation of library spaces and associated technologies provides significant opportunities to fundamentally engage and foster creative models of research, teaching, and learning. That premise was first tested with the first renovation of the D. H. Hill Jr. Library (Hill Library). Planning began in 2004, and the renovated East Wing of the Hill Library opened in 2007. The 2007 renovation introduced several hallmarks of projects at NC State that have reflected and driven trends in redesigning libraries: for example, the importance of offering a variety of spaces within a single project that can meet the needs of distinct learning styles and the different needs of individual users throughout a day, week, month, or year. While the 14,000-square foot learning commons was the signature vehicle for testing emerging concepts in library design, the 2007 Hill renovation included well-appointed traditionally styled reading rooms and getaways for individual work and quiet contemplation as well. The importance of bringing in and engaging communities through programs, events, and workshops was reflected in the design of a museum-quality exhibition gallery, adjacent event space, and flexible classrooms for workshops and curriculum-integrated teaching.

The ambitious learning commons reflected our vision to create a campus center for creativity, research, and collaboration. The integration of cutting-edge technology, learning space design principles to promote energy and communal connection, and improved access to emerging library services drove development of a space designed for both individual and group work, inspiration and socializing, research, and relaxation. It was a project that students played an integral role in shaping and continued to help by envisioning the future of vibrant learning and community spaces. The Libraries' emphasis on utilizing color, whimsy, expansive natural light, and bringing in outside architects and designers to reflect the latest and best practices was all born from this project and continued to evolve as future efforts unfolded. Concepts around single points of access, in-person and online, were cemented. Finally, the idea of having core production, consumer, and emerging technologies was realized in the 2007 renovation. Production PCs and laptops coexisted with iPods, iPads, and digital cameras, while digital making and GIS-based data services, technologies, and expertise were highlighted in dedicated spaces. Reorienting portions of existing staff and vacant positions around emerging technologies and services also became a fundamental strategy in maximizing the impact of new spaces, while also pushing the organization forward in service of students and faculty. From the 2007 renovation, the major pillars of integrating premium design, advanced technical capabilities, and organizational evolution—all with a healthy dose of risk and ambition included—would carry forward to future efforts. The foundations were laid, and the success of the Hill renovation gave the NC State community an appetite for much more. All of this combined to generate the support, energy, and funding necessary to build the James B. Hunt Jr. Library.

Major Leap: James B. Hunt Jr. Library

Opening in January 2013, the James B. Hunt Jr. Library (figure 2.1) started with a bold vision: to provide nothing less than the best learning and collaborative space in the country. "In the country" was the only hedge incorporated into that vision when Susan Nutter created it during the planning phase in 2009,[2] as the Taylor Family Digital

Library was on the way to opening at the University of Calgary in 2011. Calgary's new library, along with a host of learning commons–oriented renovations, changes in public libraries across the United States, and experimental library space design in Europe and Australia all combined with what we learned in the 2007 Hill Library renovation to drive the Hunt Library project to new heights.[3] In aiming to capture the innovative, forward-looking spirit of NC State University, the Libraries staff searched extensively for inspiration and ideas outside of the world of libraries. Building from the momentum and lessons gained in 2007 and beyond, we knew that to reach the bar Susan had set we needed to engage the best designers, consultants, and technology advisors we could find. We incorporated an intense and sustained focus on how students learn and how faculty create and share knowledge in an age of digital technology and collaboration.

fig 2.1

The James B. Hunt Library Jr. Library shortly after opening in February 2013.

(Credit. North Carolina State University.)

The Hunt Library was a nearly $100 million project made possible with a mix of state funds, donor support, and corporate gifts and in-kind furniture and technology. Its over 200,000 in gross square footage established a second main library for NC State University while housing several university centers and institutes. The building includes almost 100 group study rooms and technology-equipped spaces to support learning, research, and collaboration. The automated storage and retrieval system (aka "bookBot") holds up to two million volumes in one-ninth the space of conventional shelving, enabling the building program's emphasis on collaboration, dedicated research space, and technology-enabled learning spaces. The design team that brought the vision for Hunt to life included lead designer Snøhetta, one of the premier firms on the globe, responsible for the new Library of Alexandria, Egypt, and the National September 11 Memorial Museum Pavilion in New York. North Carolina executive architects, ClarkNexsen, provided day-to-day oversight of the project, managed the coordination between the design and construction teams, and added its own award-winning experience to the overall concept. Designed to be a major competitive advantage for the university, the Hunt Library is a signature building that both enables and reflects NC State's vision as a preeminent technological research university recognized for its innovative education and research addressing the grand challenges of society.[4] Its bold design is a visual statement of its bold purpose: to be a place not of the past but of the future, a place where our students, faculty, and partners can gather to research, learn, experiment, collaborate, and strengthen NC State's long tradition of leading transformational change.

This book is a testament to what we all now take for granted as accepted wisdom. A great research library is more than collections, technologies, and comfortable work spaces—a great library inspires. Its architecture and technology create spaces that encourage collaboration, reflection, ideation, and awe. At the core of the vision for the Hunt Library is the ability for students, faculty, and partners to immerse themselves in interactive computing, multimedia creation, and large-scale visualization—tools that are enabling revolutionary ways of seeing and using information. In the digital age, libraries have become the creative space where students spend enormous amounts of their time—working, studying, and interacting with peers. Faculty members and researchers, as well, need specialized spaces that support their research and teaching and build a sense of scholarly community. These spaces need to be comfortable; they need to make it easy to collaborate; they need to be inspiring. Every corner of the Hunt Library is designed to be memorable and stunning—an environment where people are encouraged to embody the aspirations of an outstanding university (figure 2.2).

fig 2.2

Coffee and "Viz" Program in the Hunt Library Teaching and Visualization Lab.

(Credit: North Carolina State University.)

The Hunt Library expands the traditional concept of the library as the heart of a university or community. It proposes that the library can be both a heart and a circulation system, a place where people, ideas, creativity, and productivity flow into the library and out to its parent organization. Hunt proposes, and largely delivers, the concept that the library can be a major draw for attracting the very best students and faculty and that it can be a primary driver of their success once they arrive.

Momentum and Learning: From 2013 to the 2020 Hill Library Renovation

This more dynamic vision for library spaces and organizations enables libraries to become experiential in nature. The experiential library is a place and organization where the full suite of a college's or university's active learning offerings are available for the entire community and the next generation of experiential learning is pioneered for faculty and students. As the delivery of core academic curricula and foundational learning increasingly move online and into asynchronous modalities, the library becomes a platform for deeper learning and emergent research, as well as a lead distinguishing element of the educational experience for the university. It becomes a difference maker in why students come to build their futures and how they actively learn while they are there. It becomes a creative engine for reengaging faculty in the library and for the library in reconnecting to the full life cycle of research. Platform and experience connect in transformed spaces.

The reconnection with certain faculty in the life cycle of research via library spaces was facilitated through the introduction of immersive and large-scale digital technologies in Hunt. The Libraries were fortunate to have several faculty members from disciplines as diverse as computer science, English, transportation engineering, and design (to name a sample) willing to help make the sausage of imagining their research through the lens of visual and immersive scholarship. These faculty members rightly saw the opportunity not only to change the mode of communication, but also to expand the audiences with which they could connect. Visual narrative enabled faculty to reach interdisciplinary and public audiences at a broad scale. The Paul's Cross project recreated John Donne's 1622 Gunpowder Day Sermon at Saint Paul's Cathedral in London through immersive visual and audio technology in Hunt's Teaching and Visualization Lab. A similar approach enabled scholars to create the Virtual MLK Project (figure 2.3) as an immersive digital experience of Dr. Martin Luther King, Jr.'s "A Creative Protest (Fill Up the Jails)" speech, which was delivered at White Rock Baptist Church in Durham, North Carolina, in February 1960. The project is displayed in virtual reality, large-scale video walls, immersive audio, and a simulation experience. Transportation engineers used immersive technologies to explore cutting-edge design solutions for traffic problems in cities across the United States and demonstrate those potential solutions to clients and the general public. Computer scientists used real-time inputs to visualize social media responses to news and current events. Each of these projects partnered with the Libraries to host public programming that enabled campus and public audiences to connect with the visual scholarship and incorporate that engagement into further exploration, critical analysis, and research. Further, they adapted elements of the produced research into experiential pedagogy while making the content available in other immersive environments across academia, including emerging commercial virtual reality.[5]

fig 2.3

Introduction to the Virtual MLK Experience at NC State University.

(Credit: North Carolina State University.)

As we continued collaborating with faculty to enable scholarship created within high-definition environments, we realized that spaces combining collaborative capabilities, advanced technologies, and librarian expertise were creating new modes of scholarly communication and immersive pedagogy. These emergent models could be experienced within spaces, or via digital surrogates on the networked web or through virtual reality. Viewing the library as a research platform for these emergent forms of digital scholarship presented several opportunities and challenges. Opportunities have included reengaging faculty in the use of library space, integrating across the full life cycle of the research enterprise, supporting open and publicly engaged communicated scholarship, and connecting broad, interdisciplinary communities in the changing nature of digitally driven scholarship. Issues such as identifying and selecting collaborations, strategically managing staff resources, creating surrogates for immersive scholarship, certifying and evaluating the scholarly products, and preserving content for the future are ongoing challenges. The

Libraries and a cohort of partner institutions explored these issues and more through a Mellon-funded initiative centered on immersive scholarship.[6]

The most illustrative and expansive effort to utilize Hunt for new modes of research came in the form of "The Black Mountain College Story: A Hunt Library Happening" with visiting scholar David Silver. With the entire Hunt Library as a storytelling platform, Silver used the library's dramatic visualization spaces to chronicle the rise and fall of Black Mountain College, founded in 1933 near Asheville, North Carolina. Most importantly, the Libraries were fortunate to work with Silver twice, once in 2014 and then again in 2015. Within the context of those explorations, Silver illustrated in almost perfect form the single most important lesson the NC State University Libraries can share for designing libraries. Speaking to Susan Nutter at the second public performance/happening in 2015, Silver said, "Remember the first time I wanted to come work here at NC State? Do you remember what I said? I said, can I come to work with your video walls?" After a moment of recollection by Nutter, Silver goes on, "The second time, I said can I come to work with your staff. It is the staff that I am after now...." That is the major takeaway from all of our efforts to redesign the Libraries at NC State. Renovations and new projects rise and fall on many factors—the quality of the design, the consultants and designers brought in to help, the engagement with students and faculty in the process, the creativity and determination of the leadership, the resources, the integration of technology, the programming, and more. But the staff, their expertise, their creativity and energy, and their skill sets are the most important ingredients in making library-centered capital projects a success. Nothing matters more in the long run than the skills, abilities, and engagement level of the staff.

After opening the Hunt Library in 2013, we learned a number of additional lessons one might expect. Lessons such as more power outlets in this spot, these chairs are not being used, this table needs to be moved were all quite manageable and common realizations. Where possible, adjustments were made and we moved forward. More fundamental realizations, such as the importance of programming and staffing in optimizing the potential of spaces, were and are ongoing lessons previously described. Two additional strategic directions emerged in the years after opening the Hunt Library and as we began to envision a second renovation of the Hill Library in 2017 that are now fundamental in redesigning library space. Concepts of student recruitment and success were woven into the fabric of the Hunt Library program from the beginning. However, the idea of the library being a centerpiece in preparing those students for a lifetime of success in competitive job markets after they leave NC State was a growing realization after opening Hunt. Experiential learning, cocurricular engagements, and hands-on access to emerging technologies were not part of just a successful higher education experience, but a successful lifetime of learning and application in the marketplace. By reconceptualizing our spaces, the library can become an engine for economic and labor prosperity, as well as an engine for intellectual and cultural prosperity.

And that prosperity can be influenced by the library for a lifetime, not only in creating curious, open-minded learners, but also in developing skills that could help distinguish NC State graduates. Most directly, that lesson was applied in 2017 by creation of a dataspace in the Hunt Library. Funded by a foundation grant, the Hunt Dataspace contains 12 computer workstations with the storage, RAM, GPUs, processing power, displays, and specialized software needed for data analysis and visualization work. During the 2018–19 academic year, Dataspace computers had 8,311 logins and 1,580 unique student users—over half of them undergraduates. High undergraduate utilization of the Dataspace indicates that offering a physical space, rather than just an online request or presence, helps library staff connect with students who might not otherwise reach out for support and increases awareness of emerging services. The Dataspace has also helped the Libraries to pilot a peer-to-peer consulting model with graduate student data science consultants (DSCs). The DSCs' knowledge of cutting-edge data science skills and digital research methods helps the Libraries to expand our offerings, and the consultants gain valuable experience designing workshops and applying data science methods to a variety of research problems. The result is that thousands of students are engaged, via the library, in emerging skills and modes of thinking that are in high demand across academia and nonprofit and for-profit enterprises. In addition, dozens of students gain experience mastering and teaching those skills to their peers. This example focuses on data science, but similar stories can be told for other emergent areas in libraries, such as digital media, making, design thinking, and immersive technologies.

The second lesson that is now another fundamental element of redesigned library spaces is the deep collaboration with and provision of space to campus partners. Earlier digital scholarship spaces, writing centers embedded in libraries, and learning commons broadly introduced concepts of providing space to campus partners within a broader capital program, but more recent efforts have expanded those early experiments into holistic visions that center renovation and building around the idea of partners. Efforts at the University of Washington, Georgia Tech, the University of Arizona, and others have brought to the forefront concepts of putting partners such as researcher enterprise services, student services such as academic support and wellness, and centers for teaching and learning at the heart of capital projects. The library as platform extended fully to strategic campus partners where users' holistic needs around learning and student success, teaching, and research services can be addressed. The second Hill Library renovation at NC State—a $15 million project that opened in August 2020 (figure 2.4)—reflects this approach. The centerpiece of the renovation is an academic success center that includes library services and support along with tutoring, writing, career counseling, undergraduate research, non-curricular skill-based workshops, a data experience lab, and an innovation studio all in one central location.

fig 2.4

The renovated Hill Library and Academic Success Center at NC State University.

(Credit: North Carolina State University.)

Heavily trafficked and easy to locate, newly built and renovated library spaces are ideal locations for one-stop offerings. The introduction of dynamic partnerships through spaces puts the library at the center of boundary-spanning interdisciplinary teaching, learning, and research efforts while driving even more traffic, resources, and visibility to the library.

Library as Competitive Advantage

NC State's competitive advantage: that vision statement has been at the heart of the Libraries' efforts to redesign its spaces since the early years of the 21st century through the latest renovation that opened in 2020. Capital projects are the lighthouse that signals to the community that the library is different, that the library can offer something to surprise, delight, and benefit their educational experience, advance their research, and provide lifelong benefits. The opening of any capital project is but the midpoint of the journey. The exciting, surprising, and sometimes exhausting realization is that there is still so much more to come in terms of the transformational impact newly opened spaces will have on the library and the larger organization in which it resides. That journey is still very much in front of an organization as new spaces open.

The true potential of spaces as platforms is driven by the combination of design, technology, programming, events, and the staffing expertise that evolves as the spaces evolve. If you build it, they will indeed come. But it is the staffing expertise of the library, the workshops, the programming and events, and the way the community engages the library that drive its impact in the long term. The design and technology can help bring in students, faculty, staff, and the community and help them reconnect with and reimagine libraries—but it is the expertise and infrastructure around it that drive cultural change, deep utilization, and reputational increases. The library at NC State University has been fortunate to pioneer efforts to redesign and reimagine libraries through a series of capital projects. The results have been several strong declarations, led by the opening of the James B. Hunt Jr. Library in 2013 about the presence, importance, and potential of spaces in 21st-century libraries. Above all we have learned that once started, no matter how small the project, the momentum for redesigning libraries builds and never really stops. Like a spark, new spaces light the creativity of users, library staff, and university decision makers. The sustained fire can help a parent organization reimagine and expand its idea of the possible.

Notes

1. Andrew P. Hendry, Michael T. Kinnison, Mikko Heino, Troy Day, Thomas B. Smith, Gary Fitt, Carl T. Bergstrom et al. "Evolutionary Principles and Their Practical Application," *Evolutionary Applications* 4, no. 2 (March 2011): 159–83, https://doi.org/10.1111/j.1752-4571.2010.00165.x.
2. "Remembering Susan Nutter," NC State University Libraries, August 28, 2019, https://www.lib.ncsu.edu/news/focus/remembering-susan-nutter.
3. Learning Space Toolkit home page, accessed March 12, 2021, https://learningspacetoolkit.org/; Rick Meghiddo, "Cerritos Library: 'Cooler Than the Mall,'" Cultural Daily, December 6, 2012, https://cultural-daily.com/cooler-than-the-mall/.
4. The Hunt Library has been recognized with several awards and honors, including the 2014 Stanford Prize for Innovation in Research Libraries and the 2013 AIA/ALA Building Award. For a full listing, see "Honors and Awards," NC State University Libraries, https://www.lib.ncsu.edu/honors-and-awards.
5. For fuller explorations of example projects and their ongoing work, see "About the vMLK Project," Virtual Martin Luther King, Jr. Project, NC State University, https://vmlk.chass.ncsu.edu/about; Virtual Paul's Cross Project website, NC State University, https://vpcp.chass.ncsu.edu/; and Christopher G. Healey and Mohan Ramaswamy, "Visualizing Twitter Sentiment," NC State University, last modified October 16, 2019, https://www.csc2.ncsu.edu/faculty/healey/tweet_viz.
6. Abigail E. Mann and Micah Vandergrift, *Immersive Scholar: A Guidebook for Documenting and Publishing Experiential Scholarship Works* (Raleigh: NC State University Libraries, 2021).

3

CHAPTER THREE

LIBRARY AS LABORATORY

Transforming Scholarly Services and Spaces

HARRIETTE HEMMASI

From their early days, academic libraries have been invaluable laboratories for research and learning, where the products of scholarship have been housed, scholarly processes practiced, and scholars formed. As practices and products of scholarship continue to evolve and the formation of scholars is redefined, the design and function of libraries reverberate with change.

The roles and responsibilities of academic research libraries reveal a history shaped by external forces as much as by internal choices. Subject to shifting social, political, and economic pressures, as well as massive technological developments, libraries have been vigilant and creative in their adaptations, regardless of the circumstances. Inextricably tied to the cultures, priorities, and contexts of their home institutions, academic libraries have both mirrored and influenced the identity and reputation of their universities. Through their revitalized services and spaces, libraries have supported and also effectuated advances in research and educational practices across their campuses and have contributed to the academic success of students and faculty throughout the decades.

The establishment of the new model university and the modern academic library, circa 1876, marked a transformation of scholarship. The new American university brought synthesis and coherence to the disjointed elements comprising the intellectual world of the late 19th century.[1] Building and gathering its own capacities, the university sought to employ and support faculty who were engaged in both teaching and research. Graduate education programs expanded, and more diverse undergraduate curricula emerged. The new model university invested in critical infrastructure needed to support its overarching goals of advancing knowledge and creating areas of specialized knowledge. Key elements in the university's burgeoning scholarly infrastructure included the establishment of university presses and editorial offices for journals, well-equipped scientific laboratories, enhanced museums, and increased support for libraries.

The library's centrality to academic life was acknowledged and also enabled by the new university. Expected to support a growing body of scholars and students engaged in a wide array of research and curricular interests, research libraries refocused their efforts from primarily preserving collections to actively building and promoting their use. This was a period in which both students and faculty made frequent use of the library. Scott Bennett refers to late 19th-century libraries as reader-centered designs that provided space for sustained scholarship, with close physical proximity between readers and books.[2] Reader-centered libraries were laboratories where scholars relied on books—their primary tools—as surely as scientists depended on microscopes and other specialized instruments to conduct rigorous intellectual investigation and discovery.

Transferring the production of knowledge from the domain of independent amateur intellectuals to educationally trained professionals affiliated with the modern university had major implications for the transformation of scholarship and the growing prominence of the library. As the modern university and its faculties became the locus for organizing, institutionalizing, and advancing intellectual pursuits, pressure to invest in a more robust range of library collections came from all directions. Established faculty, new PhDs, and graduate students were especially eager for the library to acquire scholarly publications available in their particular areas of teaching and research. With growing demands, availability, and support, libraries responded by multiplying their collections and building larger facilities that were often more accommodating to books than readers. The mid-20th-century design of book-centered libraries reflected an environment in which collections and their maintenance monopolized not only library space, but also the time and attention of library staff.[3]

Libraries old and new—all overflowing with print collections—welcomed the emergence of online journal publishing and the distribution of electronic back files in the late 20th century. Many academic libraries began investing in these new formats and transferring print journals and other less-used analog collections to off-site shelving facilities. At the same time, libraries were envisioning new uses for the reclaimed space.

Reimagined Library Spaces

From previously static spaces built to house immutable collections surrounded by silent learners, there erupted fresh, highly flexible spaces that encouraged not just the rearrangement of furniture but also the redefinition of learning (and research) in the library. Bennett describes the process of designing late 20th-century learning-centered libraries as putting the learner at the center of space planning.[4] Initially defined as information commons and later as learning commons, the re-envisioned spaces offered library users a choice about where, when, and how to learn. No longer restricted to reading alone in the stacks or in overcrowded, stuffy reading rooms, users could come together in informal, inviting, and functional spaces that were designed to support the blending of social, interactive, and experimental learning experiences. Configured to empower individuals as well as groups to take control of the space, manipulate the technology for their own creative objectives, and learn with and from one another, the lab-like environments of learning-centered libraries have helped students transition from passive consumers to become masters of purposeful inquiry and innovation.

These reimagined library spaces have become catalysts for the formation of scholars, connecting students and faculty with each other and with the content and tools they need. The updated areas engender collaborative learning as well as quiet, sustained study; they encourage experimental methods of teaching and research using the latest technologies and enable the hosting of exhibitions and academic symposia, as well as community and social gatherings. Through the various collaborations between and among students, faculty, librarians, and other campus partners, today's libraries help open students' minds, release their creativity, promote their self-confidence, contribute to their ability to make connections and contributions to the world, and instill in them the value of lifelong learning.

This reconceptualization of space set the stage for dramatic changes in and for the 21st-century library—contributing to evolutions in its use and function, as well as its partnerships and impact across the university campus and beyond. Expanding its conventional role as a place for the distribution and consumption of knowledge, the library as laboratory—both physical and virtual—has been reanimated as a place for experimentation, production, and processing of new knowledge.

Over the past 20 years, the introduction of digital scholarship labs and maker labs within academic libraries has done much to advance research and learning practices. Digital scholarship practices grew out of the pioneering work of humanities computing, circa 1950, and the digital humanities community, circa 1970, both of which focused on the application of information technology to humanistic research. While early humanities computing prioritized the application of computational methods, digital humanities emphasized the relationship between theory and practice, employing humanistic interpretative strategies along with digital tools and methodologies to enhance the understanding of texts, artifacts, and culture.

Even though some academic departments and centers within the university offer their own students and faculty specialized, subject-based training in traditional and digital research methods (e.g., humanities, public humanities, spatial studies, archaeology, art, and new media), library-based labs present a neutral, welcoming environment with extended hours of operation, hosting a diverse array of tools, services, and training opportunities designed to address discipline-specific needs as well as cross-disciplinary concerns. Digital scholarship labs, typically staffed by an interdisciplinary, multifunctional team of experts, may offer services and training in data management, textual and quantitative data analysis, visualization, two- and three-dimensional digitization, design and interface development, digital mapping, metadata, archiving, and publishing, as well as project management. Providing a designated gathering space and robust infrastructure for the development, production, dissemination, and preservation of digital work, today's digital scholarship labs invite and support scholars at all levels and from all disciplines to explore new ways of conducting and communicating their research.

Opened in 2012, Brown University Library's Patrick Ma Digital Scholarship Lab (figure 3.1) features a large-scale visualization video wall comprised of twelve 55-inch high-resolution LED screens. Offering high-quality viewing and analytical space not publicly available elsewhere on campus, the lab has been used widely as a research tool, from visualizing tiny molecules, to studying and comparing shards of ancient pottery, to examining massive lunar images. It also has proven to be a valuable teaching tool in both traditional and experimental style courses and is used by students for ad hoc project development and by librarians for presentations, internal workshops, and the development of their own digital skills and research. The adjoining Sidney E. Frank Digital Studio, created in 2016, offers a range of high-end collaborative environments with the latest interactive technologies, oversize high-definition touch screens, advanced software, and a large-scale plotter and 3D printer, along with a seminar room, private consultation rooms, and small group collaborative areas. Complementing the visualization capabilities available in the lab, this suite of spaces, tools, and services gives scholars opportunities to realize both material and digital results of their ideas and supports individuals as well as groups who need additional time and space as they engage in sustained digital work.

fig 3.1

Art history class taught by Brown University Professor Itohan Osayimwese in the library's Patrick Ma Digital Scholarship Lab, using both digital and physical archival evidence to perform in-class research. With its large-scale display wall and reconfigurable furniture, the lab serves as both a traditional and an experimental teaching and research space..

(Credit: Brown University Library.)

In the last few years, many academic libraries have invested in maker labs, promoting the making of physical and digital objects as pathways to innovative learning, creative problem-solving, and entrepreneurship. Growing out of hackerspaces, circa 1990, and the fabrication labs and DIY culture of the early 2000s, maker labs are informal spaces for creative production, community building, and knowledge sharing. Akin to discipline-specific makerspaces in engineering, applied sciences, and the arts, library-based maker labs offer access to a variety of manual and computer-controlled tools, often including 3D printers, laser cutters, electronics, sewing machines, arts-and-crafts supplies, bookbinding and printmaking, and woodworking tools. Intended to provide makers across the disciplines with opportunities for self-directed tinkering, experimentation, and diversion, as well as more structured curriculum-based research and learning experiences, library maker labs facilitate project and product development and encourage process-oriented practices that have the potential to extend and deepen knowledge. Many labs introduce makers (and non-makers) to the theoretical framework of design thinking. This iterative, not necessarily sequential, set of steps, bearing similarity to those of the research life cycle, includes *empathizing*, or exploring questions or problems; *defining*, or analyzing and synthesizing core problems; *ideating*, or brainstorming, exploring, and developing ideas; *prototyping*, or modeling possible solutions; and *testing*, or sharing, evaluating, and validating solutions.[5] The maker culture, often thought of as "research in action," reflects the connection not only between traditional research and design thinking, but also between thinking and doing, between writing and making, between theory and practice.

On some campuses, there is either a makerspace or a design thinking lab; sometimes both are available. Such is the case for the University of Rochester, where both exist but are managed separately. Campus fabrication facilities are housed in and overseen by the School of Arts, Sciences and Engineering, whereas the Barbara J. Burger iZone (figure 3.2), a creative problem-solving and idea exploration space, is managed by the library. At Georgetown University, the library hosts both the Maker Hub (figure 3.3) and the IdeaLab (the only instance of either entity on campus). Launched in 2016, the Maker Hub is a compact 1,500-square-foot space equipped with high- and low-tech fabrication equipment, offering a variety of open workshops for basic maker skill building and thematic or course-based workshops, developed in partnership with faculty and other campus groups, such as the Feminist Wearables Workshop with the GU Women Coders group. The adjacent IdeaLab is used to facilitate communication, collaboration, and design. With movable whiteboard tables and screens and multiple design games, the IdeaLab is frequently reserved for classes and other groups seeking guidance and space for design thinking workshops or communication sessions, often including hands-on making as part of the process of ideation, design, prototyping, communication, and iteration.

fig 3.2

University of Rochester Libraries Barbara Burger iZone, showing Kessler Forum in foreground and the Norris Piazza in the background.

(Credit: HOLT Architects. Photo credit: Revette Studio.)

fig 3.3

Georgetown University Library Maker Hub with students engaged in self-directed individual and group projects making use of craft supplies, electronics, vinyl cutters, and a printing press.

(Credit: Georgetown University Library.)

From conceptual making to material and digital making, teaching and learning activities in today's library laboratories have taken on new dimensions and new meanings. Students are provided with opportunities to participate in research on a collaborative basis, not just with each other, but also with faculty—and not just as assistants, but also by doing original work as scholars in their own right. The Theatre That Was Rome is an exemplary collaborative project between a Brown University faculty member, students, and library staff that has been sponsored for several years by the library's Center for Digital Scholarship. Reuniting text and images from specialized books on Roman architecture, decorative art, and maps from the 16th through 18th centuries, student team members are taught to document and index individual artists, engravers, and publishers found within the collection and enrich primary sources by adding metadata to the scanned images. Students contribute to the scholarly record by enabling the reconnection of these lost and often unrecognizable treasures. In addition, students write and publish short essays about the authors, artists, and books, providing valuable historical background and insight that will benefit future students and scholars.[6]

Faculty and librarians frequently work together to help students develop critical thinking skills and refine their ability to interpret, discern, and evaluate information. They help students make informed decisions about their research goals as well as their choice of resources and tools to conduct their scholarship. At Georgetown, faculty and librarians recently designed library-based practicums for several undergraduate courses. "Lau Labs," hosted in the main campus Lauinger (Lau) Library, are structured to encourage students to engage more deeply with course content, learn new skills, and develop research projects under the collaborative guidance of the faculty member and librarian. Adding a course credit for each Lau Lab, by increasing the previous three-credit course to four credits, conveys the value placed on students' learning and knowledge making in the library laboratory.[7]

In addition to advancing important academic goals, these library-based research and learning experiences can also become a source of insight and inspiration for students, opening up new directions in their personal and professional lives. Involving students in research engenders a sense of ownership and partnership in the learning process that not only helps students in today's classes but also prepares them for their future. A stellar example is Amani Morrison, assistant professor of African American literature and culture in Georgetown University's English department. Professor Morrison recounts her experience as an undergraduate research assistant on the Visualizing Emancipation project in the Digital Scholarship Lab at the University of Richmond and her work as a research associate for the Louisiana Slave Conspiracies project at the University of California, Berkeley, as precursors to her CLIR Postdoctoral Fellowship in African American data curation at the University of Delaware, where she worked with the award-winning Colored Conventions Project. In addition to her interdisciplinary training, these lab-based digital learning experiences have influenced Professor Morrison's research and teaching activities at Georgetown and continue to shape her scholarly identity overall. She defines her academic expertise and interests as encompassing 20th-century African American literature, race and space studies, performance studies, cultural studies, and the urban and digital humanities.[8]

Learning in library labs is not limited to just students. Scholars who are experts in their own fields increasingly seek opportunities to explore digital skills that will enable them to test and incorporate innovative approaches in their research. In many cases, they may not be aware of which methods or tools would achieve the best results. Senior faculty often learn from their students, junior colleagues, or librarians about software applications or other technical methods that will help them find new ways to articulate scholarly ideas, build and shape arguments, and provide synthesis or interpretation to advance their scholarship. What might begin as informal conversations and casual collaborations outside the library often develops into a more formal team-based approach inside the library laboratory, with scholars welcoming the skills, knowledge, and imagination of students, librarians, and technologists and the valuable contributions that each partner brings to the design, definition, and development of the research product. One such example is the Georgetown Slavery Archive, which thrives from its growing and diverse set of input from multiple partners within the library, as well as those across and beyond the Georgetown campus.[9]

Generative Scholarly Practices

Scholars throughout the ages have used whatever devices and methods were available to them to conduct their research, to document their findings and reflections, to ask questions, and to entice the engagement of readers. While the modes of scholarly practice are changing for many researchers, the concept of "scholarly primitives," expressed traditionally or digitally, has remained central to the process of scholarship and to the function, services, and design of libraries.[10] From roles limited to discovery and retrieval during the early days of the American university library, today's reimagined and redesigned academic libraries engage in and promote the use of a wide range of research tools and methods associated with both traditional and digital practices. *Discovery* in an analog environment involves physically browsing printed texts or catalogs, often requiring months or even years to single-handedly locate, survey, and digest large disparate bodies of literature. Today, online discovery has the potential to encompass search and retrieval of all forms of data, from all regions of the world, without regard to file size or format, time requested, or type of device used. While discoverability does not always lead to access, libraries continue to seek and advocate for avenues that advance open access to scholarly research and educational resources around the globe.

The practice of discovery also refers to conducting and creating statistical models, mathematical calculations, lab-based experiments, prototypes, or designs to solve a problem or prove a theorem. Discovery in STEM, as well as in the humanities and social sciences, is aided by computational methods, by the power of high-performance computing, and also by maker labs and the integration of design thinking. Products resulting from these scholarly activities may be archived in the library's digital repository or exhibited by the library's maker community. In addition, students in the sciences are trained to track and potentially share their own data, discoveries, and methodologies through the use of electronic lab notebooks and electronic portfolios, both of which are frequently supported by academic libraries.

Annotation has long been the practice by which scholars note their comments, interpretations, or additions to the original source document. Today, valuable historical annotations that have been lost or forgotten in the scholarly record can be recovered and, along with newly created annotations, can be preserved and linked to the original sources. This ongoing work is being developed by members of the annotation community, which includes librarians. Traditionally, scholars across the disciplines have made *comparisons* of texts, objects, formulas, or data to establish relationships or document differences. Today, such comparisons are facilitated by computational modeling and analysis and often are explicated through captivating visualizations displayed on library lab video walls (figure 3.4).

fig 3.4

RISD Professor Shawn Greenlee in the Patrick Ma Digital Scholarship Lab at Brown University Library, demonstrating innovative methods for generating, interpreting, and visualizing digital audio in graphic patterns.

(Credit: Brown University Library.)

Referring to other works through footnotes has been the means by which scholars have left intellectual trails signaling what they found useful or what helped shape the conclusions of their research. Today, referencing is no longer limited to footnotes or snippets from original source material. Instead, readers can link directly to the primary source (whatever its format) so that they can examine and reflect on the original data or test the reproducibility and validity of the researcher's findings.

Sampling is the method by which scholars have embedded small or large bits of evidence that may come from a variety of scholarly or popular sources—evidence (or data) that scholars deem relevant to their own arguments or conclusions. Today, researchers are using digital tools that enable readers to modify or test diverse layers of evidence. A convincing example of sampling is Erik Steiner's map that depicts the concentration of Jewish populations and restrictions on their movement, thus bringing to life the spatial context of the social, economic, and political behaviors in Budapest, circa 1944.[11] Scholars have sought to prove or strengthen their point of view through *illustrations*, using images that they or others created to pull readers into the narrative, to demonstrate and convince them of the author's theory, share an interpretation, or convey a state of mind. From the very early days of publishing, there have been scholars who have pushed the boundaries of the printed text by including *representations* or recreations of activities or experiences as a means of engaging the reader and at times allowing the reader to minimally interact with movable diagrams or images as a means of gaining greater understanding. Today, readers are able to control the elements, manipulate research results, and immerse themselves in virtual environments and simulations that can both convey and exceed reality. Promoted and enabled in large part by library laboratories, this plethora of modalities and interactivities has reignited the intellectual imagination of readers, researchers, and students alike and has generated new possibilities for the conceptualization, articulation, and reception of scholarship.

Not only have scholarly practices changed, the profiles of many scholars and the patterns in which they envision, conduct, and communicate their research also have changed. Grounded in the past as well as the future, new generations of scholars increasingly are trained in discipline- and tool-based knowledge, with the library as their laboratory for both. Elements considered essential to contemporary literacy and the formation of scholars include not only familiarity with domain-related research, but also learning about and using different tools, applying new methodologies, and understanding how and when to integrate these devices in the processes and products of scholarship. Today's scholars are not just undertaking research projects that may include innovative methods and tools, they are also grappling with how best to present and explicate evidence that is increasingly multimedia, multidimensional, and multilayered—all the while wondering whether such work will count as scholarship. These are serious, career-determining questions for scholars across the disciplines. Due to the university's largely conservative value and reward system, many digitally enhanced forms of scholarship have remained secondary members in the formal knowledge chain. Multimedia objects have been routinely confined to citations in journal articles and monographs or cast onto accompanying websites. A notable exception to this practice is in the sciences, where research methodologies and evidentiary data are becoming recognized as first-order elements of scholarship, valued for their use and reuse both before and after publication.[12]

While most scholars continue to write for their peers and otherwise adhere to the established structures of the academy, the gradual incorporation of digital methods and tools by researchers entice and empower a broader swath of readers to interact with and relate to scholarly text, media, and data. Researchers also increasingly pursue topics that have relevance and implications for public audiences, especially those works written in the language and locale of the public. Through the use of social networking services (such as blogging, Twitter, LinkedIn, and ResearchGate), scholars are constructing local and global identities as a means of gaining recognition of their work and establishing valuable connections with research communities. This globally distributed network not only serves as a dominant forum in which scholars can interact with their peers, but it also has the potential to become a platform for meaningful engagement and exchange with audiences and collaborators beyond the academic arena. The definition of *scholarly communication* has taken on new proportions through social media and other communication outlets—allowing scholars to build personas and partnerships among peers while also establishing visibility and engagement with the public. This dynamic and diverse ecosystem has involved and will continue to involve changing roles for all of the key stakeholders in the cycle of scholarly communications, including scholars, universities, publishers, funders, and libraries.

The Future of Scholarship | The Future of Libraries

The future of scholarship is the future of universities and the future of libraries. With our commonly held missions to discover, communicate, and preserve knowledge for the advancement of society, universities and libraries are called anew to transform scholarship. We are called on to revitalize the ways in which we stimulate, support, steward, and disseminate the scholarship of our students and faculty. We are called on, individually and collectively, to take actions that will open and democratize access to scholarship and education. Because the production and dissemination of new knowledge lie at the heart of the university mission and at the center of the library's evolving role, it is critical that in addressing today's research and learning we ensure that the forms and methods we use both reflect and shape the emerging capacities and realities of our times. We are thus called on to allow and enable the fullness of scholars and the breadth of their scholarly practices, products, and values to be transformed.

For scholarship to be transformed, students and faculty need their libraries to grow and flourish as laboratories and communal workshops where they can learn and share tools, skills, and ideas. Libraries need their university's support to invest more deeply and deliberately in their services and spaces that enable exploration, experimentation, and iteration of all forms and methods of making scholarship. Faculty and students need the freedom to express their ideas and openly share their research within and beyond the traditional forms and boundaries of scholarly communication. Faculty and students need their university's incentivization and endorsement for such work, as well as its commitment to change the criteria for tenure and promotion and the evaluation of multimodal dissertations in ways that will encourage and embrace new forms of scholarship. The same holds true for the willingness and capacity of university presses to accept and publish born-digital works, rather than mere PDFs of print-based manuscripts.

Institutions that will prosper in this period of transition will be those that do not merely tack a technological facade onto existing modes of research and learning, give lip service to open access, "innovate" long enough to attract internal incentives or external funding, or temporarily reshape themselves during a pandemic. Those that will prosper will not back away from the precipice of change on which we currently stand. Instead, they will redouble their commitment to the difficult task of jointly building and maintaining an equitable and effective scholarly infrastructure. Like the new American university and library of 1876, we have the opportunity and responsibility to assemble and synthetize the component parts of our intellectual life—a life that will reshape the university and its engagement with the public, as well as redefine its contributions to the common good. To expand the impact of academic scholarship, we need a more outward-facing, inclusive, and collaborative approach that not only draws on the strengths of the academy but also cultivates connections with the economic, cultural, and political institutions at home and around the world. With its unique configuration of spaces and services, the library as laboratory increasingly provides a bridge between theory and practice, between evolving scholarly practices and institutional missions, between scholarly communications and public discourse.

Through our transformation of scholarship, we will be transformed. And our transformation will lead us to embrace a broader, more substantive, more sustainable vision and version of what it means to educate and do research, what it means to be a learner and a scholar, what it means to be a university—and indeed, what it means to be a library.

Notes

1. Arthur E. Bestor, "The Transformation of American Scholarship, 1875–1917," *Library Quarterly* 23, no. 3 (July 1953): 169.
2. Scott Bennett, "Libraries and Learning: A History of Paradigm Change," *portal: Libraries and the Academy* 9, no. 2 (2009): 182–83.
3. Bennett, "Libraries and Learning," 184–85.
4. Bennett, "Libraries and Learning," 187–89.
5. "Design Thinking," Interaction Design Foundation, accessed April 1, 2021, https://www.interaction-design.org/literature/topics/design-thinking.
6. "The Theater That Was Rome: A Virtual Roman Library," Brown University Library, accessed April 1, 2021, https://library.brown.edu/projects/rome/.
7. "Working with Lau Lab," Georgetown University Writing Program, accessed April 1, 2021, https://writing.georgetown.edu/announcements/working-with-lau-lab/.
8. "Working with Lau Lab"; see also Amani C. Morrison, Ph.D., personal website, accessed April 1, 2021, https://amanimorrison.com/digital-humanities/.
9. "The Georgetown Slavery Archive," Georgetown University, accessed April 1, 2021, https://slaveryarchive.georgetown.edu/.
10. John Unsworth, "Scholarly Primitives: What Methods Do Humanities Researchers Have in Common, and How Might Our Tools Reflect This?" (part of symposium on Humanities Computing: Formal Methods, Experimental Practice, sponsored by King's College, London, May 13, 2000), https://scholar.google.com/citations?user=tfYqTx8AAAAJ.

11. "Mapping Mobility in Budapest Ghetto," Spatial History Project, Stanford University, accessed April 1, 2021, http://web.stanford.edu/group/spatialhistory/cgi-bin/site/viz.php%3Fid=411.
12. Brian Lavoie, Eric Childress, Ricky Erway, Ixchel Faniel, Constance Malpas, Jennifer Schaffner, and Titia van der Werf, *The Evolving Scholarly Record* (Dublin, OH: OCLC Research, 2014), https://doi.org/10.25333/C3763V.

4

CHAPTER FOUR

21ST-CENTURY LIBRARIES FOR STUDENTS

Learning and Belonging

JOAN K. LIPPINCOTT

Introduction

A beautifully designed library is bound to please students and attract them into the facility in droves. Architecturally striking buildings can be a source of pride for students, faculty, administrators, and alumni. However, new or renovated libraries may fail to fulfill their full potential to contribute to key aspects of their institution's mission. When academic library spaces are conceived of as generic places for studying, they miss opportunities for more direct connections to current and future directions of academic programs. In contrast, libraries that provide spaces and programs that support active learning and student content creation build stronger connections to emerging needs of students and faculty.

For decades, students came to the library to read print materials, many of which, such as journals and reserve materials, could not leave the building, and to browse the bookstacks for sources for their papers. Changes in pedagogy, new thinking about student learning, and assignments that require students to create many types of outputs, such as timelines, maps, videos, podcasts, blogs, and web exhibits, require libraries to rethink how they provide resources, including content, expertise, technologies, and physical spaces to support student learning. Spaces such as learning commons, digital scholarship labs, visualization labs, GIS labs, multimedia production studios, makerspaces, and virtual reality labs are the means by which libraries support new types of learning and, in particular, student content creation.

We are also beginning to understand the affective factors that have a bearing on students' sense of belonging on a campus, which in turn has an impact on their academic success and their persistence to degree. The library can play a direct role in student success by facilitating students' ability to complete academic work in many modes and by supporting students' sense of belonging on a campus.

Moving from Lecture to Active, Social Learning

In the 1980s, the writings of some educational researchers who were publishing their findings concerning the positive impact that active learning techniques had on adult learners were becoming more popular.[1] Such techniques included what are seen as learner-centered approaches: helping students understand how what they are learning relates to their work, the need for students to participate in activities like problem-solving exercises rather than merely reading about a concept or listening to an explanation in a lecture, and the use of peer-to-peer collaborative learning. Soon many educators realized that these principles applied more broadly, not just to students above the age of the traditional higher education cohort of 18-to-22-year-olds. More and more faculty transformed their pedagogy from lecture mode to inclusion of mechanisms that promote active, social learning. Employing problem-based pedagogy, which encourages students to collaborate as they tackle assignments and minimizes the passive, lecture mode during class time, yields deeper learning in courses. This emphasis on students working together on exercises, taking active part in discussions, and critiquing each other's work meant that classrooms morphed from the "sage on the stage" model to one in which faculty and students were partners in learning. This thinking had an impact on how academic libraries perceived their mission to support student learning. While libraries traditionally had been dedicated to quiet and even silent study throughout their facilities, in the early 1990s they began to develop physical spaces that encouraged active, collaborative learning. Such spaces were generally described as information commons or learning commons.[2] In addition, the burgeoning use of technology in education resulted in libraries introducing computers as public workstations, making technology an integral part of learning commons.

The "flipped classroom" approach, one type of problem-based active learning pedagogy, has emerged in the past few decades. In this model, the physical spaces of classrooms are remodeled to allow for students to cluster in groups around tables, which frequently connect with laptops and screens, allowing the instructor to roam around the room to interact with each group of students working on problems and also to call all of the class to attention to view an example on screens. In the flipped classroom model, students are assigned video lectures to watch in preparation for class, and the class time is devoted to hands-on problem-solving activities, involving peer-to-peer communication. Some new or renovated academic libraries incorporate these types of active learning classrooms, such as in the Odegaard Library at the University of Washington, the Wilmeth Active Learning Center at Purdue University, the College Library at the University of Wisconsin-Madison, and the Taylor Family Digital Library at the University of Calgary. These classrooms are usually used by academic courses or for information literacy sessions during the day and are open for general use during evening and weekend hours. While gains in student learning have been documented as a result of this approach, they are sometimes attributed to the classroom itself, while in actuality, the combination of the physical space, the pedagogy of the instructor, and the technology working in synergy is what yields the results. Similarly in libraries, it would be difficult to assess the difference that space in and of itself makes in students' academic lives without also taking into account the technologies available in that space, the expertise of staff providing formal and informal instruction in the space, and the inspiration and availability of library content and cultural heritage.

Learning Commons

Typically, learning commons feature spaces where students are encouraged to work together, whether in pairs or larger groups, and have technologies in place or for checkout, ensuring equitable access to hardware and software by all students. Many but not all commons also incorporate units administered by other campus offices into the space. The ideal configuration of a learning commons would provide a means for students involved in active learning classes, and any other students, to find spaces conducive for continuing collaborative, peer-supported work along with any technologies needed for course assignments. In addition to seating for groups, learning commons include surfaces for writing, such as whiteboards on wheels and group study rooms with writable glass and whiteboard paint walls. Providing collaborative, technology-rich spaces is often a stated goal of learning commons, but some design choices in these facilities run counter to their avowed purpose. For example, in many commons, most arrangements of work spaces allow for only one chair per station. To facilitate collaboration, a generous work surface needs to be available for students' devices and print materials along with enough seats, whether chairs or stools that can be easily moved into place, for students to work together comfortably. Collaborative spaces can be developed in open areas and in enclosed group study rooms in many configurations, and ideally a library will provide a number of different arrangements that will suit different groups of students working on various types of assignments. Furniture on wheels allows students to configure spaces in ways that are most appropriate for their group and tasks.

Another frequent concern in learning commons or any area of the library that is intended for collaboration is adequate separation from designated quiet spaces. In some newly renovated libraries, collaborative and quiet spaces are located mere feet from each other, setting up a situation ripe for conflict. In other cases, inadequate thought has been given to how the noise from the commons, often on the main floor, will affect higher, quieter floors when an atrium allows noise to drift up into the higher spaces. This can result in students in the quiet areas vociferously complaining about noise in the library, which runs counter to their preconceptions that a library must be entirely quiet and also genuinely disrupts their work. Architects and designers must make careful decisions about separating collaborative and quiet areas, and librarians must be vigilant in reviewing plans to ensure adequate separation. In some libraries, glass walls are used to minimize noise between quiet and collaborative spaces while maintaining an open design.

The learning commons or other area of the library often contains an assistive or adaptive technology lab or designated rooms that house specialized equipment and software to enhance accessibility for students with various needs, such as technology to enhance reading text for individuals who are visually impaired. Some of these facilities are managed in partnership with the campus unit with primary responsibility for disability or academic support services. Many libraries have invested in adjustable furniture and have created oversized work areas for students who may need additional space.

Very few learning commons attempt to connect their spaces to information resources and collections, which is a missed opportunity.[3] Often those spaces seem no different from any computer lab on campus. There are ways for a library to distinguish its unique value in commons spaces. This can be accomplished by displays, digital or analog, of library collections; marketing of services, such as workshops and online programs; and exhibiting products of classes that have benefited from use of library resources.

Integrating Other Campus Units into the Library

Many commons include in their vision the notion that the library will be a hub for one-stop shopping for student services. Often situated on the main floor of the library, some space in a new or renovated learning commons is given over to university units that do not report to the library. The rationale for this model is that students will be able to more easily access a wide variety of services and that the units could collaborate to develop programs that would enhance student success. Often such colocation of the units into the library is encouraged or mandated by the chief academic officer or the administrator who has responsibility for overall institutional space planning. The campus's writing center is most frequently the unit that moves whole or in part into the library. Other units that have moved into the library include the student success center, the math tutoring service, and academic advising. Early on, such plans are usually described as *collaborations*, but in actuality the units that move into the library are merely tenants in the space, not partners with the library.[4] There are exceptions to this, including programs at Dartmouth, the University of Washington, and Brigham Young University, where the library works closely with the writing center to develop joint programs.

Student Content Creation

During much of the 20th century, college courses used quizzes, tests, and papers as the primary assessment mechanisms to establish course mastery and to calculate grades. As hardware and software became more readily available to students, some faculty began assigning or offering an option to students to create new types of projects as outputs of course assignments. This enabled faculty to make assignments that utilized the tools of the discipline and that communicated knowledge in new ways that were developing in the field. These outputs included student creation of videos, podcasts, websites, representations employing GIS, and visual representations of time lines. These types of assignments were not new in such programs as film studies or geography; what was new was the integration of new modes of research and display of results in a wide variety of fields, including history, archaeology, political science, music, public health, and more. Digital literacies have been incorporated into the curriculum in some disciplines in some colleges and not in others; equipping students with digital literacy skills is usually very uneven in a given institution. Libraries can provide an equalizing function here by democratizing access to technologies and developing literacies through partnerships with faculty in the classroom and by offering workshops and classes both in person and online.

Academic libraries have had multimedia collections for decades and had listening or viewing stations in their facilities. Some innovative libraries realized that if they also developed facilities in which students and faculty could *create* multimedia content, they would enhance the potential for all disciplines in the institution to have access to the equipment, software, and expertise to guide them in these new modes, facilitating a move from passive to active learning. As libraries renovated their spaces, they transformed viewing and listening stations into audiovisual studios, created spaces for easy creation of lecture recordings with the introduction of concepts like the one-button studio, and provided rooms where students could practice giving multimedia presentations.

In the first decade of the 2000s, spaces that supported working with high-end technologies emerged more broadly in academic libraries, including data visualization labs, digital scholarship centers or labs, and makerspaces. More recently, some libraries are incorporating virtual reality areas where individuals can experiment with software and hardware that enables them to move around spaces to explore a historical site or an ecosystem. A small number of institutions, such as the library at the University of Rhode Island, are designating spaces in which they are working with faculty to develop artificial intelligence programs and services. While some individuals both within libraries and in the broader university community criticized such developments as being outside of the library's mission, in actuality they are clear extensions of the library's role in supporting research, teaching, and learning utilizing new methodologies and yielding new forms of content. Some of these technology-rich spaces have become very important components of education of upper-level undergraduate students and graduate students. Visualization labs and digital scholarship labs have hardware and software that is unavailable in many departmental facilities. Such labs in libraries give students in all disciplines the opportunity to apply new technologies in their major discipline and the chance to participate in library workshops and classes that provide students with the foundational knowledge they need to effectively use new tools. In addition, these spaces have brought faculty back into the library to work with the high-tech equipment themselves and in partnership with students. As data science programs emerge in academic institutions, these facilities are the site of new offerings in the form of workshops, courses, certification programs, and consultations. They also provide an environment that encourages peer learning and development of a community of learners.

Makerspaces provide the equipment for individuals and groups to create physical objects through the use of 3D printers and laser cutters and create wearables and other items using sewing machines and other equipment. Libraries provide staff in these facilities to consult and train users and to work with faculty on assignments whereby students will produce something in the makerspace lab. Many libraries are sensitive to the perception that makerspaces can be male-dominated and create programs and workshops that target female makers. They may also strive to hire a diverse staff to ensure that participation by all is encouraged.

As plans are developed for these new spaces, it is imperative to develop new programs, including classes, workshops, and one-on-one consultations. Staff who have the requisite skills in new technologies are critical to the success of such programs. Using qualitative and quantitative methods, libraries can document the impact these programs and spaces have on the curriculum and on preparing students for graduate education and professional roles. In designing spaces that incorporate new and high-end technologies, flexibility is key. No one knows what new technologies will be prevalent in even five years, and which will be obsolete. Designing spaces where walls can be easily moved or eliminated, where power is accessible through floor outlets or a grid mounted in the ceiling, and with furniture that is modular and easily moved helps to ensure that changes that are responsive to new technologies will be made efficiently and in a cost-effective manner.

Special Collections

Another area in which thinking about student projects has evolved is in special collections. In the past, some large universities had little focus on undergraduate use of special collections, unlike in many liberal arts colleges, where use was encouraged and integrated into the curriculum. When special collections public areas are being renovated, many include more classroom space (equipped with document cameras, etc.) and more visible exhibit space to promote wider use of their collections. As libraries digitize parts of their special collections, some are working with faculty to develop projects that involve students taking part in digitization activities or where students use digitized parts of the collection to create their own new representations of content, such as time lines, exhibits, or websites. Libraries can incorporate screens into their special collections room designs to feature digitized archival collections, signaling to students that they can enter the rooms to explore; Georgetown University's Lauinger and Princeton University's Firestone libraries feature such displays. Those screens can also display the products of student and faculty work with the library's digital or digitized collections.

Graduate Student Spaces

Graduate students are heavy users of special collections and technology-rich spaces such as digital scholarship labs. In addition, they often seek a designated space to work quietly on their projects. In recent years, there are significant changes in spaces designated for graduate students. In the past, the most common spaces allocated for graduate students were banks of individual locked carrels that were generally reserved for a semester or a year. Often graduate students at the dissertation-writing stage received priority for these spaces, and many libraries had waiting lists for those carrels. However, a number of libraries found that many of these carrels were actually seldom used or used only a small number of hours per week. As libraries began to address the needs of graduate students in renovated spaces, they usually moved away from the single, assignable carrel model and opted for enclosed spaces with workstations and storage areas for multiple graduate students. The University of Colorado, Boulder, and the University of Calgary are examples of libraries that renovated spaces for graduate students. One issue in such spaces is whether to accommodate conversations and collaborations or whether to designate these areas as quiet spaces. Some libraries such as Brown University's have developed adjacent, but closed-off spaces to accommodate both types of needs as well as a kitchen area.

Spaces for Reading and Analysis

As academic libraries develop plans to reinvigorate their facilities to include learning commons and multimedia production areas, there can be pushback from some traditional faculty and also from some librarians on staff. They believe that libraries taking such steps are minimizing the value of contemplative, quiet study and that libraries might become more like a student union than a place for academic work. However, provision of collaborative spaces and quiet spaces need not be in conflict. Contemporary libraries should provide both types of spaces, as students need different environments for different types of assignments, for different courses, at different times of day, and for different points in the academic year. Many libraries have created or refurbished large reading rooms intended for quiet study, and they are often very popular with students. Examples are the reading rooms in the Mansueto Library at the University of Chicago, the Mullins Reading Room in the Wilmeth Active Learning Center at Purdue University, and the Grand Reading Room in the Thompson Library at the Ohio State University.

Cafés

While it may seem out of place to include the topic of cafés in a chapter on student learning, it is actually very relevant. Many libraries report that their café has become a regular meeting place for students and their course professors or advisors. Interacting with faculty is one of the high-impact practices identified in the work of George Kuh and others focused on student engagement.[5] In addition, some of the data libraries have collected from students documents the long hours they spend in the library. Having a café on-site enables students to take a quick break without finding another spot on campus that is open when they need to refuel. This can be particularly important in geographic areas with harsh climates.

Outdoor Spaces

Outdoor spaces have become more important in light of the COVID pandemic, especially those that include access to a robust Wi-Fi signal. Screened porches may become a more common feature in academic libraries; the University of California, Santa Cruz, library has included screened reading porches for some time. The new Austin Public Library has a beautifully designed screened porch with comfortable seating areas. Many libraries have well-landscaped outdoor areas and patios.

The Affective Impact of Library Spaces

As a library renovation or new building is being planned, attention should be given to what students and any other library users will see as they enter the building, usually at a main floor entrance. Will they see a massive service desk, signaling that the primary function of this library remains managing and protecting a print collection? Will security guard stations make some students uncomfortable to enter, or conversely will they reassure some students, especially at night, that they can study safely in the library? Replacing security staff with student peers is a strategy used in some institutions to make students less wary.

Some libraries have made choices to signal that they are oriented to new technologies as individuals enter their space, such as the presence of the technology showcase in the Hunt Library at North Carolina State University. Others such as the Thompson Library at the Ohio State University have a prominent special collections exhibit on the main floor, inviting users to explore those resources. Some feature soft furniture and browsing collections of faculty publications or leisure reading or a specialized collection tailored to the interests of many students, such as the science fiction collection at the Georgia Tech library. In all of these cases, the library is sending a message to its user community about some of its priorities, its strengths, and its values. In the case of featuring a leisure reading or new books collection, they are reassuring the community that even though there is a lot of technology in the library, they still value a good read.

Creating Environments That Enhance a Sense of Belonging

Libraries have the potential to play an important role in enhancing students' sense of belonging on a campus, exemplifying the role of what Ray Oldenburg refers to as "the Third Place."[6] Physical spaces, staff presence, and a variety of programs, cultural representations, and displays can all play a part in making the library a particularly welcoming place on campus for students. As a longtime researcher of learning environments writes,

> Inclusive environments have surroundings, furniture, and tools that help learners understand how the space will support their activities and behaviors.... What learners see in the environment around them, such as physical artifacts and messaging, tells them whether they belong or not.[7]

When students have a sense that they belong in their educational institution, it can assist with their psychological and emotional well-being and can also encourage persistence at the university. The library has the potential to create welcoming, inclusive spaces for students who might otherwise feel out of place at an institution, whether they are first-generation students who don't understand the norms and traditions of their university, international students from other cultures, students who have been marginalized in their hometown high schools because of their sexual identity, or students who are from a racial or ethnic group that is in the minority on their campus.

More research is being conducted to assist in understanding what factors contribute to a sense of belonging and may yield instruments that campuses can use in their own locales. In a study examining what is needed for postsecondary education, the state of California recommends that its institutions "develop research-based metrics for evaluating campus climate and its impact on student success and retention." The data should include measures of students' sense of belonging and perceptions of to what degree the campus promotes diversity.[8]

Other efforts signal increased emphasis on understanding what promotes a sense of belonging to an institution. A fellow of the Society of College and University Planners (SCUP) is studying the physical expression of diversity, equity, and inclusion on three campuses.[9] The Learning Space Rating System added new components to its 2021 release, including elements related to physiological, cognitive, and cultural inclusion.[10]

On many campuses, students have embraced the Black Lives Matter movement and have an increased sense that universities need to be proactive in demonstrating their commitment to Black students. More and more libraries are seeking to understand what factors contribute to making their presence more welcoming and inclusive. The factors that matter may not be the same for all students. The Duke University Library focused a study on Black students' experiences in the library and on campus in order to better understand how to improve those students' interactions with services, facilities, and materials. While the Duke students generally feel that the library spaces are inclusive, they "do not see enough visible actions and signs supporting diversity and inclusion, efforts to limit White western European cultural dominance, or attempts to educate White students about minority experiences."[11] It is likely that students would feel similarly on many other campuses, and libraries can take steps both to understand the perspectives of Black students and to develop initiatives that make libraries more inclusive.

Libraries have included specifications in their buildings that signal inclusivity and belonging in different ways. For example, Mount Royal University in Calgary, which opened a new library in fall of 2017, recognized that the library is located on the traditional lands of the Blackfoot People; the library is "the first building on campus to include Blackfoot language signage in its destination and wayfinding."[12] The X̲wi7x̲wa Library, a center for academic and community Indigenous scholarship at the University of British Columbia, incorporates design elements representing Indigenous people, but even more importantly has the aim of serving as a home away from home for Indigenous students at the university.[13]

It is important not to assume that all students, or all students of a type, will have the same reaction to particular physical spaces or design styles. For example, some may think that first-generation students might feel out of place in older, more formal buildings, but first-generation students at the Oklahoma State University generally felt both comfortable and inspired by the library's historic building.[14]

The doctoral work of two individuals emphasizes the links between a sense of belonging and student success, particularly for first-generation and minority students. In her dissertation examining students' sense of belonging in informal learning spaces, Broughton suggests that in libraries, "exhibits and programming can expose students to study spaces at the same time as educating and demonstrating value and respect for differences."[15] In his doctoral work, Choddock found that, like many other students, first-generation students find motivation in doing their academic work in the library because they are surrounded by others doing the same thing, and they may also model the studying behavior of other students.[16]

FAMILY SPACES

Some universities have high percentages of students, whether graduate or undergraduate, who are parents of young children. Often such students are challenged to find places on campus where they can bring their children and complete their academic work, and their home environment may not have an adequate Wi-Fi signal or other resources that they need. They may feel uncomfortable and unwelcome in most library spaces if their children are noisy or physically active, provoking critical looks from other students. Brigham Young University and the University of Toronto are two examples of libraries that created enclosed rooms where students may bring young children. It would be interesting to study whether the use of such facilities affected the ability of students to complete their degrees.

SPIRITUAL AND EMOTIONAL WELL-BEING AND WELLNESS

Libraries are taking an interest in providing facilities and programs that address students' spiritual, emotional, and health needs, including a space for prayer. This may be a particular emphasis for Muslim students. A 2017 study reported that 50 percent of respondents stated that their library has or had a prayer space.[17] Some libraries have a space where students can meditate, practice yoga, or rest. When the Moffitt Library at the University of California,

Berkeley, was renovated, it created a wellness room that includes reservable spaces for short rests. The renovated Smith College library includes a "Reflections" room for meditation, prayer, and rest. Campuses across the US recognize that an increasing percentage of students report that they are suffering with mental health issues, often due to stress and anxiety. Some libraries sponsor food banks for students who are experiencing food insecurity. During exam study week and exam periods, many libraries schedule visits by therapy dogs, offer midnight snacks, or provide other services that send the message "We care about you; we understand you; you are part of this community."

REPRESENTATIONS: ART AND CULTURE

Many academic libraries include displays of art, some with formal gallery space. However, in some older libraries, the primary works on display are portraits of administrators and board members from eras past, often dominated by faces of older White men. There are so many possibilities for art to add vitality to a library. Artwork may be on loan from a university or community museum, permanently installed, or in a space meant for rotating exhibits. It can be in tangible formats such as paintings and sculpture or in digital form on screens. North Carolina State University's Hunt Library features a large, colorful abstract painting in the lobby along with a large digital display that includes artwork. Oklahoma State University Library features a painting of a cowboy, reflecting the roots of its state, and the Central Washington University library has a totem pole made by the Chief of the Wiummasgum Clan in its lobby. Exhibits can feature artwork by faculty and students, inspiring pride in the institution and signaling what can be accomplished at that university.

Books and language can feature prominently as themes in artwork in libraries. Their representations are signifiers of the nature and even the soul of libraries: words, language, thought. Brigham Young University features some whimsical metal sculptures that include books in its lobby area. The renovated Firestone Library at Princeton University includes an installation of old catalog card drawers, and the University of Colorado, Boulder, has an imaginative sculpture composed of parts of catalog card drawers in its library. These are all signifiers of the library brand, incorporating library heritage but making it new.

Modes of communication can also be represented through art. The floor of the Buckeye Reading Room at the Ohio State University's Thompson Library is a public art project featuring raised letters that represent a concordance. In other areas of the library, 49 metal plates in the floor document a variety of written communication from around the world (https://library.osu.edu/thompson/art). Binary code etched into glass in windows at the Mount Royal University Library or into glass walls of the Cube in the digital humanities laboratory at Yale represent our digital world of information.

GLOWING AND SAFE PRESENCE

The feature of an oculus enabling light to pour into the library during daytime hours has become a signature of many new or renovated libraries; examples include the Calgary Public Library and the libraries of Temple University and Smith College. The Taylor Family Digital Library at the University of Calgary, the Hunt Library at North Carolina State University, and the library at Virginia Commonwealth University literally glow when all lit up at night. The buildings serve as a beacon to students arriving from their classes, dorms, or jobs at night and signal that the library is a safe space where students will find others committed to academic pursuits. Library deans making the case for library renovations can emphasize the importance of the library in serving as a secure environment at night, particularly for female students.

While it is true that there are other places on campus that can enhance students' sense of belonging, such as student unions and dormitory lounges, the library is important in this regard because students need to feel comfortable, secure, and encouraged as they pursue their academic work.

Into the Future

Libraries can be so much more for students than places to study. They can be places to create content, to exchange ideas with peers, and to feel a sense of belonging. It is essential to plan for new programs and services while making practical decisions about new or renovated physical space. Those processes need to work in tandem, and they must be iterative and flexible. Libraries that have renovated spaces that feature collaborative spaces for learners and that incorporate a variety of technologies available to all students, along with the expertise and programs to guide them, can greatly contribute to the teaching and learning mission of their institution. The best of them "present people with options, facilitate, and inspire: This is the heart and soul of promoting knowledge accessibility."[18]

Many colleges and universities will be in a tight budgetary situation as they emerge from the COVID pandemic. There will be much competition on each campus for funds for renovations, expansions, and capital expenditures on new buildings. The library can make a strong case for priority for its physical spaces for many reasons: serving the entire campus community, providing a venue that promotes both learning and research, offering a natural place for interdisciplinary work, giving access to expensive technologies along with expertise and programs to enrich the skills of many parts of the community, and extending a welcoming and inclusive environment. All of these attributes contribute to students' academic success, retention, and persistence to degree.

Communicating the value of the library as a place to integrate access to and creation of content in a wide variety of formats can be a key argument for the value of the library. To reach that ideal, planning for new physical spaces must also give equal attention to planning for new programs, new types of staff expertise, and new technologies to support the emerging trends in learning.

Thanks to my valued colleagues Malcolm Brown of EDUCAUSE and Jeanne Narum of the Learning Spaces Collaboratory for their role in deepening my understanding of the connections between learning, spaces, and technologies.

Notes

1. Malcolm S. Knowles, *The Modern Practice of Adult Education: From Pedagogy to Andragogy* (Englewood Cliffs, NJ: Prentice Hall, 1980), and K. Patricia Cross, *Adults as Learners: Increasing Participation and Facilitating Learning* (San Francisco: Jossey-Bass, 1981).
2. Liz Milewicz, "Origin and Evolution of the Commons in Academic Libraries," in *Beyond the Information Commons: A Field Guide to Evolving Library Services, Technologies, and Spaces*, 2d ed., ed. Charles Forrest and Martin Halbert (Lanham, MD: Rowman & Littlefield, 2020), 3–22; Joan Lippincott, "Surveying the Landscape," in *Beyond the Information Commons: A Field Guide to Evolving Library Services, Technologies, and Spaces*, 2d edition, ed. Charles Forrest and Martin Halbert (Lanham, MD: Rowman & Littlefield, 2020), 23–31.
3. Joan Lippincott, "The Link to Content in 21st-Century Libraries," *EDUCAUSE Review*, January 29, 2018, https://er.educause.edu/articles/2018/1/the-link-to-content-in-21st-century-libraries.
4. Lippincott, "Link to Content."
5. George D. Kuh, *High-Impact Educational Practices: What They Are, Who Has Access to Them, and Why They Matter* (Washington, DC: AAC&U, 2008).
6. Ray Oldenburg, *The Great Good Place: Cafes, Coffee Shops, Community Centers, Beauty Parlors, General Stores, Bars, Hangouts and How They Get You through the Day* (New York: Paragon House, 1989).
7. Susan Whitmer, "Inclusive Campus Environments: An Untapped Resource for Fostering Learner Success," *Current Issues in Education* 22, no.1 (2021): 6, https://cie.asu.edu/ojs/index.php/cieatasu/article/view/1902.
8. California Governor's Council for Post-secondary Education, *Recovery with Equity: A Roadmap for Higher Education after the Pandemic*, February 2021, p. 42, https://www.capostsecondaryforall.org/initiatives/recovery-with-equity/.
9. Shannon Dowling, *The Planning and Design of Diverse, Equitable and Inclusive Campus Environments*, May 19, 2022, Society for College and University Planning (SCUP), https://www.scup.org/resource/fellows-report-the-planning-and-design-of-diverse-equitable-and-inclusive-campus-environments/.

10. Richard Holeton, "Toward Inclusive Learning Spaces: Physiological, Cognitive, and Cultural Inclusion and the Learning Space Rating System," *EDUCAUSE Review*, February 28, 2020, https://er.educause.edu/articles/2020/2/toward-inclusive-learning-spaces.
11. Joyce Chapman, Emily Daly, Anastasia Forte, Ira King, Brenda W. Yang, and Pamela Zabala, "Understanding the Experiences and Needs of Black Students at Duke," April 2020, p. 2, https://dukespace.lib.duke.edu/dspace/handle/10161/20753.
12. "Forgive Us for Not Being Quiet: MRU Opens Riddell Library and Learning Centre," Media Stories, Mount Royal University, September 7, 2017, https://www.mtroyal.ca/AboutMountRoyal/MediaRoom/Newsroom/mru-opens-rllc.htm.
13. Sarah Dupont, "Does DEI Need Another 'D' and 'I'? Situating Decolonization and Indigenization Work in Academic Libraries" (virtual presentation, Coalition for Networked Information Digital Scholarship Planning 2020 Webinar Series, October 1, 2020), in Coalition for Networked Information, "Diversity, Equity, and Inclusion," October 2, 2020, YouTube video, 1:00:43, https://www.youtube.com/watch?v=Oi9XJmazRaA.
14. Karen A. Neurohr and Lucy E. Bailey, "First-Generation Undergraduate Students and Library Space: A Case Study," in *Assessing Library Space for Learning*, ed. Susan E. Montgomery (Lanham, MD: Rowman & Littlefield, 2017), 167–82.
15. Kelly M. Broughton, "Students' Sense of Belonging in Study Space" (PhD diss., Patton College of Education of Ohio University, December 2019), 151–52, Electronic Theses and Dissertations Center, Ohio University, https://etd.ohiolink.edu/.
16. Ted Chodock, "Mapping Sense of Belonging in Library Spaces" (presentation, Library Assessment Conference, held virtually, December 16, 2020), YouTube video, 2:36:18–3:32:57, https://www.libraryassessment.org/program/2020-schedule/#dec16.
17. Emily Mross and Christina Riehman-Murphy, "A Place to Study, A Place to Pray: Supporting Student Spiritual Needs in Academic Libraries," *College and Research Libraries News* 79, no. 6 (June 2018). https://crln.acrl.org/index.php/crlnews/article/view/17010/18758.
18. Brian Mathews and Leigh Ann Soistmann, *Encoding Space: Shaping Learning Environments that Unlock Human Potential* (Chicago: Association of College and Research Libraries, 2016), p. 107.

II

SECTION II

ALIGNING WITH THE INSTITUTIONAL VISION

5

CHAPTER FIVE

"A POSITIVE DISRUPTION WITHIN THE URBAN FABRIC"

The Charles Library* and Institutional Mission at Temple University

JOSEPH P. LUCIA

* The new main campus library at Temple University is named for donor, university trustee, and Temple alumnus Stephen G. Charles, who made a major naming gift during the building's construction.

More Than a Building

A library is more than a building. As a designed structure it often expresses important aspects of institutional identity and aspiration as a central feature in the built environment on many college and university campuses. In this context, it can be seen as the emblematic site of a unique academic purpose. In many cases, the library becomes the carrier of memes that connote an ideal vision of the higher education enterprise: libraries in the collegiate gothic style, for instance, signal the sacredness of learning, implying an almost ecclesiastical function, with perhaps no more dramatic exemplar than the Suzallo Library at the University of Washington, inside and out (figure 5.1).

fig 5.1

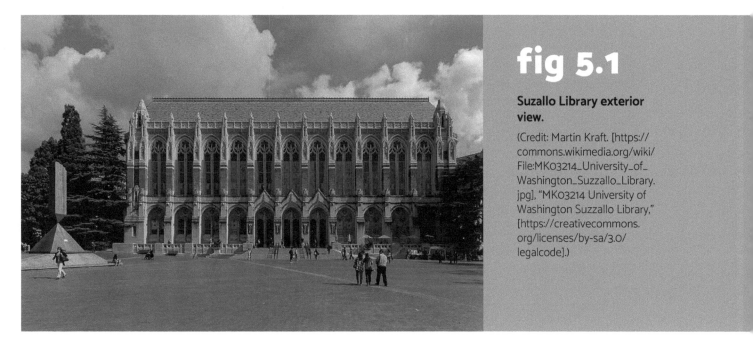

Suzallo Library exterior view.

(Credit: Martin Kraft. [https://commons.wikimedia.org/wiki/File:MK03214_University_of_Washington_Suzzallo_Library.jpg], "MK03214 University of Washington Suzzallo Library," [https://creativecommons.org/licenses/by-sa/3.0/legalcode].)

Any initiative to design and build a new academic library brings to the foreground questions of institutional mission and identity, even in exploratory conversations about such a project. In the early 21st century, lack of a shared view of what a library can or should be in a networked, digital, and mobile technology world amplifies the intensity of such deliberations. This fraught context inevitably requires a careful vision-setting and programming process to unearth the bedrock assumptions about what institutional values, expectations, and characteristics need to be embedded in the vision for the library and expressed in some manner in its ultimately realized form. The vision-setting, planning, and design process for the Charles Library at Temple University in Philadelphia, Pennsylvania, is a paradigmatic case of embracing these complex and contested elements and working through them to achieve a result that embodies the best of the institution's historical identity and that also expresses a dynamic vision for its future.

Temple University Background

Founded in 1884 as a night school for members of Philadelphia's working class by Baptist minister Russell Conwell, Temple University is distinctive for its long-standing commitment to serving as an engine of social and economic advancement for students who seek higher education but do not come from privileged or wealthy circumstances.[1] That, however, is only part of the story. Throughout its history, Temple has sustained a deep sense of connection to the city of Philadelphia and its shifting fortunes, its phases of decline and renaissance, its struggles with deindustrialization and urban poverty, its resilience and reinvigoration through the last several decades into the early 21st century.

In the early 1960s, Temple affiliated with the commonwealth of Pennsylvania, and in the intervening decades it has become increasingly identified as the public university of the city of Philadelphia. In addition, over the past 60 years, Temple has grown dramatically and is now among the 30 largest universities in the United States by enrollment. Temple currently enrolls approximately 40,000 students, 25,000 of them undergraduates. The student body is demographically among the most diverse in the country. The university offers programs and degrees through 17 schools and colleges, making for an intellectual and creative environment that is as varied and wide-ranging as the student body is diverse.

Not only has Temple grown in size, but it has also grown in stature, becoming one of the country's leading research universities (achieving R1 status in 2015) and also one of the most productive of graduates with professional degrees. The main campus has transitioned over the past three decades from being largely a commuter environment to one that is now predominantly residential. Temple students—and the institution itself—are often characterized by their grit, persistence, and entrepreneurial spirit, which is captured in the tagline "Temple made." These aspects of institutional character informed the program development and design work that shaped the Charles Library.

In recent years, Temple's institutional trajectory has become increasingly ambitious, yet those ambitions are rooted in a close embrace of the university's legacy, which is well articulated in the recently refreshed university mission statement, as follows:

> **Opportunity. Engagement. Discovery.**
>
> Temple University educates a vibrant student body and creates new knowledge through innovative teaching, research and other creative endeavors. Our urban setting provides transformative opportunities for engaged scholarship, experiential learning, and discovery of self, others and the world. We open our doors to a diverse community of learners and scholars who strive to make the possible real.
>
> We are committed to the ideals upon which Temple was founded:
>
> - providing access to an excellent, affordable higher education that prepares students for careers, further learning and active citizenship.
> - creating a collaborative community of outstanding faculty and staff who foster inclusion and encourage the aspirations of Temple students.
> - promoting service and engagement throughout Philadelphia, the Commonwealth of Pennsylvania, the nation and the world.[2]

Key elements of this mission statement richly inform the community deliberations that ultimately yielded the plans for the Charles Library.

Project Origin and Evolving Context

A major capital project such as a new library for a university, with its implications for institutional identity and mission, is necessarily a long-term undertaking, often requiring over a decade from earliest inklings through serious leadership commitment to fundraising, programming and design, and construction and occupancy. At a time in higher education when change cycles are compressed, often lasting less than five years, and when top-level leadership transitions are far more frequent than they had been in prior eras (Temple's most recent three presidents have occupied their positions for six, three, and five years respectively), shepherding a library project through phases that will most likely involve several major administrative changes (and the accompanying shifts in strategic focus) can be a dynamic process, sometimes turbulent, always at best a balancing act. It requires both a commitment to a deeply rooted long-term view of the library role at the institution and a flexibility of perspective that can frame that role in a range of potential contexts. The Temple experience with the Charles Library exemplifies the challenges of changing visions, evolving contexts, and the re-weighting of priorities.

Improving and expanding library facilities for Temple's main campus emerged as a prospect late in the presidency of David Adamany (2000–2006), who originally proposed a series of additions to the Paley Library, which opened in 1966 and was never substantially renovated, expanded, or updated over its four decades of use. Discussion of Paley expansion (or the possibility of an entirely new building) was taken up more seriously under the leadership of president Ann Weaver Hart (2006–2012), during whose tenure funding for the project was earmarked by the commonwealth of Pennsylvania. Dr. Hart presided over an era of significant growth and new construction at Temple that also coincided with a construction boom in the city and an economic renaissance that slowly marched northward up Broad Street toward Temple. It was a moment of great civic renewal for the city and also a moment of significant enhancement for the Temple campus. An initial library programming study was prepared during Hart's presidency, under the leadership of then university librarian Larry Alford. That study envisioned the library as a grand civic presence for the university on North Broad Street—a 350,000+-square-foot structure that would visibly welcome the urban community to Temple and that would also house the university's substantial research collections on miles of browsable bookstacks. Two factors resulted in the rethinking of this proposal—one was a change in university leadership, the other was the development of a campus master plan that examined carefully the layout of the Temple built environment. The plan looked toward achieving a greater sense of coherence and organic connection between facilities, reflecting the university's rising national profile and increasingly residential student body, replacing aging buildings and adding new ones to support ambitious and rapidly evolving academic priorities.

Leadership Change and a Project in Transition

In 2013, the change in Temple leadership (the beginning of Neil Theobald's presidency) brought with it an intensified focus on the student learning experience at Temple, with a parallel commitment to establishing a more supportive environment for student success and timely degree completion. While under Theobald's leadership the university continued to embrace its civic role in the city and to recognize the importance of engagement with the surrounding North Philadelphia community, there was a shift to a more inward-looking approach to those aspects of the institution along with a strong sense that the physical core of the campus would benefit from a more unified academic identity. These perspectives clearly reshaped the final stages of campus master planning and led to some new thinking about the library project. Locating the building on Broad Street was reconsidered, and a promising site near the geographical center of campus was identified. The university was just completing the construction of a new Science Education and Research Center, and the old physics building, Barton Hall, an undistinguished modernist structure dating from the early 1960s, was about to be vacated.

That this site was located at the intersection of the two busiest pedestrian thoroughfares on campus—the east-west axis of Polett Walk and the north-south axis of Liacouras Walk—was fortuitous. The site was also adjacent to the Temple Founder's Garden (now known as O'Connor Plaza) on the southern end and on its east side across the street from the Paley Library and its associated Bell Tower that had been seen as the center of campus for almost 50 years. Once this site selection was confirmed, other elements of the campus master plan came together in a manner that affirmed the potential of the new library to serve as the anchor facility for a rejuvenated campus core and as a signature building embodying a vision of Temple's future.

One element of all the recent planning efforts at Temple is the creation of more green space on campus (an initiative named Verdant Temple) and the hope of establishing a central quadrangle at its heart. The Barton Hall site afforded the possibility that the square block bounded by the library on 13th Street at the west end, 12th Street to the east, Norris Street to the north, and Polett Walk to the south could become that quad. While realization of that possibility will require the removal of a number of actively used academic buildings, those buildings are themselves at or near end of life and will most likely over the next decade be replaced by new facilities at other locations. The potential of campus green space to the east of the new library was carefully incorporated in the final design.

Site selection for the Charles Library occurred just as a building program development was being completed and as conceptual design was about to begin. While site selection and a shift to a more institutionally inward-looking approach to planning the new library reflected altered emphasis on behalf of university leadership, the detailed programming process is where the deeper alignment between library vision and university priorities was articulated.

Program Development

Program development was facilitated by brightspot strategy over a period lasting roughly six months, from June through December 2013, and involved broad and deep engagement with a cross section of university constituents including top administrators, many members of the provost's staff, facilities staff (including the university architect, who was a major participant and creative voice in all planning activities), college deans, undergraduate and graduate students, faculty, library staff, academic support staff from across the university, IT and educational technology staff, and community members. The programming process is the crucible in which the general university mission, requirements, and expectations for a library project combine and interact with library mission and vision as articulated by library leadership, ideally yielding a unique set of directives, in effect a special recipe for a distinctive and often signature university building. One of the implicit challenges in this process is that over the past several decades, academic libraries have taken on what often seems to be a collective and continuous revisioning project through successive waves of technological and social transformation. The pressures and strategic priorities reshaping library work are significant in their own right, yet often separable at least in some degree from the broader mission and strategy questions facing the university on the whole. While it is not an impassable obstacle to alignment of library planning with university needs and priorities, it is at present an obdurate reality. A further challenge in programming is that asking library constituents what they want or need can be self-limiting, especially with respect to ways in which an imaginative view of the library's role on the campus—a vision that will support central university ambitions and strategies—is not always immediately grasped by top administrators. Elliot Felix, brightspot strategy's founder, stated this extremely well in a symposium on the planning process for the Charles Library:

> Community input as a starting point in the design of a library is of primary importance, but asking people what they want in a library will yield answers based on a pre-existing idea of a library. Ask people about their activities and to describe the services they need and they can be very clear—not only about what their needs are and how they're changing, but also about precisely what could meet those needs.
>
> This is the fundamental tension in project planning. When we ask people about needs, in smaller conversations we hear lots of new things, but then on surveys we hear about the typical concerns in a library: "We need more books;" "We need more quiet space" because people can only imagine a slightly improved version of today as opposed to something entirely new. New ideas about space use must balance with understanding traditional needs, and a productive process allows for new uses while recognizing the integrity of what still works.[3]

The pertinence of these insights is reflected in a remark made to the Charles Library planning team by the university president during an interview. While the president recognized that there would probably be some new and unexpected elements in the building, his most critical (and legitimate) concern was that we increase substantially the campus study seat count for a student body starved for adequate study space. He'd seen students sitting on the floor to study in the Paley Library and did not want that to happen in the new facility.

The programming process yielded a 157-page design brief that described in exhaustive detail the requirements for the building, down to square footage assignments for all key functions and spaces, from the most traditional and expected to the most innovative and unexpected, in a manner that was at once visionary and practical and that, the planning team believed, meshed institutional priorities and mandates with a compelling vision that embodied state-of-the-art thinking about the present and future of the research library enterprise. These are the ways in which programming supported the design of a library that serves many practical purposes for Temple while also envisioning a bold and ambitious future trajectory for the institution that embraces creativity, innovation, interdisciplinary learning and research, collaboration, and deep community engagement. Key aspects of the building program that aligned with university-level mandates and expectations include

- creation of a facility that serves as a signature feature of the university's built environment, reflecting the urbanism of the campus and communicating welcome to the community surrounding the campus,
- integration of a monumental 21st-century building design into the existing campus context in a manner that is both bold and respectful,
- creation of diverse spaces for learning and collaboration while increasing overall campus study seating in a service environment that supports student success,
- creation of an environment that inspires creativity and intellectual engagement for the academic and local community,
- affirmation of the value of physical collections while reducing storage footprint to support other functions,
- provision of enhanced public access for events and programs and Temple's Philadelphia-focused special collections, and
- creation of new library environments that support exploration and use of digital tools and emerging technologies for scholarship and creative expression.

Library Vision and University Context

The planning team envisioned the new library facility as a catalyst for learning, inquiry, research, and the creation of new knowledge. That vision embraced the urban vibrancy of the campus setting, identified inspiration and innovation as hallmarks of the library's purpose, talked directly about creativity as an element of the Temple learning experience, identified community engagement and collaborative learning as core activities the library would be designed to support, discussed the library as a transformational new environment for the campus, and embraced the notion—to use language from the university mission statement—of "mak[ing] the possible real." The building was conceived as an emblem of the most ambitious aspirations of the university and expressed the conviction that in the context of an urban public university like Temple, the highest level of excellence in design and function was also compatible with affordability—that the students who come to Temple from diverse and often not very privileged circumstances (many of them first-generation university students) are in fact world-class and deserve world-class facilities. If you look back at the Temple University mission statement cited earlier, it becomes clear that the vision for the building rhymes in many ways with Temple's core institutional commitments and aspirations. The Charles Library building as delivered to the campus lives up to this vision. In the remainder of this discussion we will look at some specific features that realize the vision.

Let's take a look at the big moves first. During conceptual design, the planning team discussed some key terms for the ways in which the new library should function on the Temple campus, both as a physical structure and as an emblem of the institutional learning experience. Central to those discussions was the idea of the library as a gateway—both as a physical gateway to campus and as a figurative gateway to knowledge. Touchstone elements of the final design included the large transparent arched entryway on 13th Street (figure 5.2) and the smaller entry at the intersection of Polett and Liacouras Walks that echoes the larger entry and that also creates a transparent view through the building into the heart of campus as one approaches from Broad Street on the west side (again, a literal gateway).

fig 5.2

13th Street entry.

(Credit: Michael Grimm.)

Another immediately notable feature of the building is the dramatic curvilinear form of the central dome and the use of wood cladding as a softening element in the main lobby and its adjacent spaces. A second touchstone term employed during conceptual design was *courtyard*, signifying a protected space that calls you to the interior of the structure and that communicates a feeling of shelter and welcome. These design elements (the upward spiraling form, the wood surfaces) realize an explicit goal for the design—that it would invite people in, signaling welcome and communicating a feeling of human scale and comfort in an otherwise rather monumental space (figures 5.3 and 5.4). Visitors who enter the library for the first time often comment on feeling the warmth and welcome the major lobby spaces evoke, using some of the very terms the designers employed in describing their hope for these spaces. Moreover, the wood structure of the lobby, up-lit at night, glows visibly through the large glass archway in the dark, hearth-like and enticing.

fig 5.3

Main lobby view.

(Credit: Michael Grimm.)

fig 5.4

24-7 interior view.

(Credit: Michael Grimm.)

Integration of the unique Charles Library structure into campus surroundings relies on a number of elements. First, maximum building height was limited to four stories to echo the scale of all immediately adjacent structures. Second, to keep the pedestrian thoroughfare along the west side of the building open and uncongested by a block-long exterior wall, the western edge of the building was oriented along two axes that angle in from the widest points at the north and south ends, intersecting at a mid-block entrance (figure 5.5) and yielding a dramatic cut into the building's mass where a large window reaches down from the fourth floor, lightening the facade and letting in daylight. Another element that aids in connecting the structure comfortably with its surroundings is the use of ribbed granite panels for the facade material (figure 5.6), which, while modern and unique, also picks up the materiality (actually mostly limestone) of the nearby collegiate gothic structures of Sullivan Hall (the main administration building), Mitten Hall, and the Baptist Temple (now a performing arts facility) that flank the campus entrance from Broad Street.

fig 5.5

Mid-block entrance.

(Credit: Michael Grimm.)

fig 5.6

Exterior stone.
(Credit: Michael Grimm.)

Functional Spaces

While the building's formal characteristics in the campus landscape are striking and distinctive, it's the building's interior features that most directly support the academic mission. Conceived as a diverse ecosystem of different types of spaces to enable a great variety of activities, for increased study seating (a build goal mentioned earlier) the interior includes large open areas adjacent to expansive glass walls that might be considered semi-active spaces; designated quiet study areas and a dedicated space for graduate students; roughly 40 study rooms of various sizes, all equipped with collaborative display systems for team and group work; a 24-7 study area with an embedded café; and a set of flexible multipurpose rooms that can be used for events, instruction, or student study access depending on needs and priorities. The more distinctive aspects of the building are those that most directly reflect the Temple mission and context.

STUDENT LEARNING AND RESEARCH SUPPORT

One goal for the library is to simplify access to academic support services for students—to give them a single place where they can study, read, do research, write, and get subject-specific tutoring. In addition to a one-stop referral desk in the main lobby area (figure 5.7) and library consulting and instructional rooms where librarians interact

fig 5.7

One-stop desk.
(Credit: Michael Grimm.)

with students to address information needs, the building incorporates an administratively separate Student Success Center, with services delivered at several locations by peer and professional tutors and writing instructors on drop-in and appointment bases.

GENERAL COLLECTIONS

Temple's diverse academic community includes students and researchers for whom direct access to print collections still matters greatly. This was expressed passionately to the programming team by art, architecture, and art history students and faculty, by music and theater students and faculty, and by students and faculty in some humanities and social science disciplines. Cost constraints and complex programmatic requirements meant that we could not hold the roughly 1.5 million-volume general collection from the Paley Library on open browsing shelves in the Charles while adequately supporting other functions. This dilemma resulted in a lengthy study process regarding collection storage and access alternatives and ultimately yielded a decision to put approximately 180,000 books on open browsing shelves and to situate the remainder in a high-density robotic storage and retrieval system within the building, enabling retrieval and access to most items in the collection within 10 minutes for library users. Access to materials requested from the automated storage system is at a location adjacent to the one-stop help desk. This arrangement allowed us to preserve an open stacks serendipitous discovery experience for those most frequently consulted portions of the physical book collection and avoided the latency and inconvenience of putting the remainder of the collection in a remote location. Browsing stacks are located on the building's top (fourth) floor (figure 5.8), which is a unique setting in the building, entirely clad in glass, and where the dome that spirals up from the main lobby opens into an oculus (figure 5.9). This daylight-flooded space where knowledge is stored and accessed in physical form connotes a metaphorical place of enlightenment and is the destination point for many building users—it is also where a great percentage of the building's study seating is found.

fig 5.8

Fourth floor browsing stacks.

(Credit: Michael Grimm.)

fig 5.9

Fourth floor oculus seating area.

(Credit: Michael Grimm.)

SPECIAL COLLECTIONS

Temple's Special Collections reflect the university's unique civic, social, and cultural role in Philadelphia. The library is internationally recognized for its Urban Archives, which documents the social, economic, political, and physical development of the greater Philadelphia region throughout the 19th, 20th, and 21st centuries. These resources and many others that are adjacent to them in focus are heavily consulted by community members, researchers, documentary filmmakers, and Temple students and faculty. Prior to the construction of the Charles Library, they were dispersed among several storage locations and difficult to access for the public because of the obscure location of a very modest Special Collections Reading Room in Paley Library. In Charles, these collections are fully accessible by request from the automated storage system. Perhaps more significantly, the Special Collections Reading Room (figure 5.10) is highly visible, directly accessible from the 13th Street entrance on the first floor and with street level

fig 5.10

Special Collections Reading Room.

(Credit: Michael Grimm.)

views. It is welcoming to all and is a conspicuous public feature of the new building, with an adjacent exhibit space for showcasing materials and a secured instruction room for teaching with rare and unique items.

EVENTS AND PROGRAMS

Another distinctive element of the Charles Library is its commitment to public events and programs (lectures, readings, panel discussions, musical performances, workshops, etc.) that bring the intellectual and cultural life of the campus to diverse audiences, including residents of the neighborhoods surrounding the campus. The first floor of the building, easily accessible from the 13th Street entrance, features an events space (figure 5.11) with uniquely crafted acoustic qualities and capable of event streaming and AV capture. The space can be flexibly set up in a variety of seating and table configurations, is designed to host dining events, and features a large glass wall on its west side to bring the street in and to make program activities visible to passersby, though when necessary those same windows can be concealed via room-darkening shades. The event space is a prime set of community engagement for the Temple campus.

fig 5.11

Events space.
(Credit: Michael Grimm.)

COMMUNITY COMPUTING

Another way the Charles Library serves its surrounding community is by provision of a community computing lab in the main lobby. These are computers with network access that are restricted to use by members of the surrounding community, which is one of the most economically disadvantaged in the city while also being underserved by the public library system. This resource represents a significant contribution to the local community by Temple.

DIGITAL SCHOLARSHIP

One of the signature features of the Charles Library is the Loretta C. Duckworth Scholars Studio (figure 5.12), which occupies the entire south end of the building's third floor. This is a location with state-of-the-art technology, a large and variously equipped makerspace (figure 5.13), media production and presentation capture facilities, a virtual reality and gaming lab, a tech sandbox, and a cluster of collaboration spaces. It is a prime locale of digital scholarship exploration and research at Temple and features technical experts, faculty fellows, grad student interns, a faculty academic director, and a number of funded research initiatives. It represents one of the growing tips of interdisciplinary academic enterprise at the university.

fig 5.12

Scholars Studio.

(Credit: Michael Grimm.)

fig 5.13

Makerspace.

(Credit: Michael Grimm.)

SUSTAINABILITY ASPECTS

While the fact is not stated explicitly in Temple's mission statement, the university has formally embraced environmental sustainability as a core value and has invested substantially in the overall greening of the campus. In this connection, Temple is a signatory to the American College and University Presidents' Climate Commitment. The Charles Library manifests this commitment in several ways. The first and most obvious is its dramatic green roof (figure 5.14), which at over 51,000 square feet is one of the largest in Pennsylvania. More holistically, because of its many energy-efficient and environment-friendly characteristics, the building has recently been certified at LEED Gold.[4]

fig 5.14

Green roof.

(Credit: Michael Grimm.)

In the University and Urban Fabrics

The Charles Library has garnered much attention and recognition for design excellence since it opened its doors in late August 2019. It has clearly emerged as an iconic presence on the Temple campus—but it is also seen in Philadelphia and beyond as an indicator of an institution with big ambitions, bold vision, and a deep community legacy. Writing of its immediate success upon opening, Phillip Crosby said,

> The new library has given an immediate sense of gravitas to the center of Temple's campus. The adjacent public spaces, like O'Connor Plaza, have never felt so filled with activity as they have in recent months. The building's corduroy-like granite façade provides a backdrop to the surrounding life of the campus—creating a plethora of places to meet friends on the way to lunch or simply to take a short break between classes. Such is its impact that it is already difficult to remember what the campus was like without the library standing there at the intersection of Polett and Liacouras Walks, welcoming visitors into the embrace of its rolling cedar archways and light-filled gathering spaces (figure 5.15).[5]

fig 5.15

Main lobby from stairway.

(Credit: Michael Grimm.)

In closing, let me offer one more quote, this one from Dozie Ibeh, associate vice president for the project delivery group at Temple, a Temple-trained architect, and one of the key individuals who saw the building through its complex construction process:

> The Charles Library's extroverted form opens the building to its surroundings, encouraging collaboration, creativity and innovation. It is a community building—the Temple community is a base that defines a core of the Temple campus and includes the larger community of the neighborhood and city in concentric circles. From a campus perspective, the building provides a positive disruption within the urban fabric and has been a positive force in shifting the campus architecture and social spaces. Its purpose in the campus landscape is to serve as a connector—between buildings and open spaces, between faculty and students, between the university and the neighborhood, between Philadelphia and the world (figure 5.16).[6]

fig 5.16

View from O'Connor Plaza.

(Credit: Michael Grimm.)

Notes

1. The story of Temple's founding and evolution can be found in James W. Hilty's *Temple University: 125 Years of Service to Philadelphia, the Nation, and the World* (Philadelphia, PA: Temple University Press, 2010). Much of the historical background information about Temple in this chapter is sourced from Hilty's book.
2. This statement can be found on the Temple University website: "About Temple University," Bulletin 2021–2022, Temple University, https://bulletin.temple.edu/undergraduate/about-temple-university/.
3. Temple University, Kate Wingert-Playdon, with Philip Cosby, *Library as Stoa; Snøhetta, Public Space and Academic Mission in the Charles Library* (Novato, CA: ORO Editions, 2020), 86.
4. Information on the Leadership in Energy and Environmental Design (LEED) rating system can be found on the US Green Building Council website: "LEED Rating System," USGBC, https://www.usgbc.org/leed.
5. Temple University et al., *Library as Stoa*, 234–35.
6. Temple University et al., *Library as Stoa*, 219.

6

CHAPTER SIX

THE UNIVERSITY OF ARIZONA STUDENT SUCCESS DISTRICT

Vital Signs of Library Alignment with the Institutional Vision at Scale

SHAN C. SUTTON

Leave out conditions
Courageous convictions
Will drag the dream into existence

(Neil Peart, "Vital Signs")[1]

Dawn of the Dream

Across academic libraries, there is a growing trend of colocating various kinds of student support units, such as writing programs and tutoring centers, in library buildings. The University of Arizona (UA) recently took this concept to a new level of scale in creating the Student Success District.[2] This project involves colocating an array of student support services and library services across four buildings in the heart of campus to create a seamless student experience among the buildings and their connecting outdoor spaces.

The district concept emerged as a collaborative dream in 2015 through conversations between UA Libraries (UAL) leadership and colleagues overseeing UA's student support services. At that point in time, several student services were recently relocated to historic Bear Down Gym (BDG), which is immediately between the Main Library and the Albert B. Weaver Science-Engineering Library (WSEL). UAL leadership mentioned to colleagues in neighboring BDG their plans for partial renovations of these two libraries to create floors dedicated to collaborative, hands-on learning with various technologies in support of UA curricular strategies and student learning priorities. This news prompted a response that full renovation of BDG as a student learning and services center was also under consideration. It was quickly recognized that with three side-by-side buildings set to undergo renovations to elevate how their services impact the student experience, there was a unique opportunity to approach the renovations with a comprehensive design process across the buildings.

The concept quickly gained momentum and was expanded to encompass a proposed new five-story building, the Bartlett Academic Success Center (BASC), immediately behind, and connected to, BDG. The integrated renovations of Main Library, WSEL, and BDG, combined with the new BASC building, became the Student Success District, covering 8.5 acres in its entirety. The courage to dream at this scale introduced additional complexities in terms of budget, planning and construction logistics and balancing the interests of a large number of stakeholders, but the project leaders resisted being constrained by those challenges and the status quo of existing conditions.

While Main Library, WSEL, and BDG had stood next to each other for decades, they were completely siloed from each other, with each building having a single entrance that faced away from the others. The outdoor areas between these three buildings were a veritable no-man's-land with minimal landscaping and no seating areas, in spite of being located in the center of campus with thousands of students passing through daily. Leveraging the Tucson climate, a fundamental element of the District vision was to transform these outdoor areas into "outdoor buildings" with shaded seating areas, Wi-Fi, and electrical power, connecting the four buildings in conjunction with new entries that face each other to enable easy transit within seconds from one to the others.

As a key part of this model, the District would consolidate many student support services scattered across campus into BDG and BASC. This consolidation enables an "integration through adjacency" approach (figure 6.1) in which library users can quickly and easily access a broad range of nonlibrary student support services, without the administrative complexity of UAL dedicating space within the library buildings to various campus tenants. The adjacencies also present numerous future collaboration opportunities among the campus units in the District. The District vision liberated UAL from limiting its aspirations to just library renovations, embracing instead a reimagining of how this entire area of campus could be shaped to advance student learning and success on a bold scale.

fig 6.1

Bird's-eye view of the Student Success District.

(Credit: Poster Frost Mirto architectural firm, Miller Hull architectural firm, and Sundt construction company.)

Alignment with the Institutional Vision

The Student Success District concept was developed with several key university priorities in mind, ensuring alignment with the institutional vision for transformative student experiences. This was instrumental in demonstrating that investment in creating the District would pay dividends on multiple fronts to advance the UA's commitment to student success.

These university priorities include

- student recruitment and retention
- collaborative learning
- experiential learning
- technological skill building

STUDENT RECRUITMENT AND RETENTION

Naturally, these are priorities for every university, and the District concept seeks to create a competitive UA advantage in student recruitment, serving as a centerpiece for campus tours by prospective students and their families. They will experience the District as an integrated model on a scale not found at other universities. In this manner, the District can serve as a compelling student recruitment tool, illustrating the UA's institutional commitment to student success writ large. The District will also be a focal point of new student orientation to establish engagement with its services and facilities from the start of a student's college career.

The UA has placed a special emphasis on undergraduate retention. In describing the potential impacts of the District to senior administrators, the project team emphasized how bringing student support services together in one centralized location would lead to greater awareness and utilization of them, including among students who are at risk of dropping out but could see their prospects greatly improved by using these offerings as well as the adjacent library services and spaces. This holistic strategy to integrating support for various aspects of the student experience is a hallmark of the District vision to attract students to the UA and then equip them to flourish at the UA and beyond.

COLLABORATIVE LEARNING

In 2014, the UA launched the Collaborative Learning Spaces initiative to create collaborative classrooms across the university through redesigning existing lecture-style classrooms and other campus spaces to serve in this role. Collaborative classrooms feature students sitting in small groups at tables, with the instructor moving about the entire classroom, and pedagogical techniques focused on small groups working together on case studies, creative problem-solving, and other forms of active learning instead of rote memorization.

This shift from the traditional "sage on the stage" modality to a "guide on the side" approach has grown exponentially, with UA-based studies demonstrating that students in these classroom settings generally outperform their peers in traditional lecture hall modalities on exam scores and course grades.[3] Regents Professor and Provost Emeritus George Davis observes,

> The collaborative setting creates the opportunity for more hands-on, practical activities, and I think most of us have had experiences in which we would say it's one thing to listen, but if you really want to learn you have to do some things, you have to try it out.[4]

The first collaborative classroom, with a capacity of 270 students, was established at WSEL, in what previously served as the current periodicals room. The District concept promised to leverage this classroom, which draws over 1,500 students per day into WSEL, by providing these students with additional collaborative learning spaces, especially in the renovations of both library buildings. This strategy will further strengthen the UA's commitment to collaborative learning by creating extensive nonclassroom spaces designed to facilitate this mode of teaching and learning.

EXPERIENTIAL LEARNING

There is a strong commitment to students engaging in experiential learning activities at the UA. This university priority is manifested in the 100% Engagement program that facilitates experiential learning experiences to build on curricular instruction and develop professional and personal skills.[5] Students who participate in approved research projects, creative endeavors, and other forms of hands-on learning can earn an Engaged Learning Experience notation on their transcripts.

Many services across the Student Success District can serve as hosts for 100% Engagement experiences, with the Main Library's new CATalyst Studios created specifically for experiential learning through technologies such as virtual and augmented reality, data visualization, and fabrication equipment.[6] These services, along with experiential learning opportunities among the District's student support units such as the Strategic Alternative Learning Techniques (SALT) Center, Health Promotion and Preventative Services, and Student Engagement and Career Development, position the District to become a central location for 100% Engagement activities as an essential part of the UA educational experience.

TECHNOLOGICAL SKILL BUILDING

In a similar vein, integration of technological skill building into student learning is a university priority, as illustrated in its strategic plan, which "is inspired by the Fourth Industrial Revolution—a time of augmented intelligence and the fusion of digital, physical and biological worlds."[7] Pillar 1 of the strategic plan, the "Wildcat Journey," is dedicated to preparing "our students with the skills and mindsets to lead the Fourth Industrial Revolution," including an initiative to "dramatically scale innovative learning spaces."[8] In addition to aligning with these university-level commitments, UAL's evolution as a campus center of technological engagement and experimentation informed the library renovation designs to further strengthen and expand this role.

The libraries' impact in developing students' digital literacy and technological skills is viewed as a university asset for advancing both academic success and career preparation across professional fields. Combined with a commitment to facilitating student learning through collaborative creative processes utilizing technologies, this strategy advances career preparation as summarized by UA Vice President for Strategic Initiatives Jane Hunter: "Students today are different from those of 20, 10 or even five years ago. They are digital natives and the job environment they will graduate into is focused on collaboration and creativity."[9]

Funding Model and Project Timeline

An essential phase in developing the District concept was engagement with architectural firms to establish the parameters of the project, as well as the associated cost estimates. UA Planning, Design, and Construction became a critical campus partner at this juncture, determining that this would be a design-build project in which the architectural firms and the construction company work as a team from initial concept through completion under one contract.[10]

After several iterations of comprehensive designs for the District's buildings and outdoor spaces, the final version resulted in a total project cost of $81 million. The project leaders from UAL and student services units considered various budget models and eventually chose a framework based on three funding sources:

- reserve funds from UAL and UA student services units
- philanthropic donations
- increases to existing student fees to fund the payment of construction bonds (impacted fees: Student Services Fee, Library Fee, and Recreation Center Program Fee)

Fundraising efforts focused largely on named spaces within the District. Examples include the Bartlett Academic Success Center, Albert B. Weaver Science-Engineering Library (in conjunction with a gift from the Frederick Gardner Cottrell Foundation), Terry Seligman Virtual Reality Studio, and the Rhonda G. Tubbs Tech Toolshed. Support from undergraduate and graduate student governance leaders was an important component in securing the required planning and budget approvals from the Arizona Board of Regents and the Arizona Legislature's Joint Committee on Capital Review. UA senior leadership's strong support for the District vision was reflected not only in its advocacy throughout these approval processes, but also when UA President Robert C. Robbins highlighted the District in his formal presentation of the university's new strategic plan to the Arizona Board of Regents in 2018.

STUDENT SUCCESS DISTRICT TIMELINE

- 2015: Student Success District concept is first discussed.
- 2015–2018: District design and budget model development.
- 2018: Final design and budget model approved.
- 2019–2020: Renovation of Main Library and WSEL and new construction of BASC. Renovation of landscape architecture in selected areas.
- 2020–2022: Renovation of Bear Down Gym. Renovation of landscape architecture in selected areas continues.
- 2022: Completion of landscape architecture renovations in remaining areas.

District Layout and Design

The Student Success District encompasses an 8.5-acre rectangular area on the south side of the UA Mall, a grassy pedestrian thoroughfare that bisects the campus from east to west. This area is also adjacent to the primary dormitory complex on campus, further enhancing District access for thousands of students. A brief review of the four buildings' individual qualities illustrates their varied origins and evolutions over time, as well as their complementary roles established through the District design.

- Main Library
  - Completed in 1973.
  - Five stories, including basement.
  - Mid-to-late-century Brutalist style, concrete.
  - The largest library on campus, where the vast majority of UAL faculty and staff are located.
  - Renovation of 57,000 square feet focused on spaces and services designed to facilitate collaborative, hands-on learning with various technologies.
- WSEL
  - Completed in 1963.
  - Five stories, including basement.
  - Mid-century modern style, red brick.
  - Classic book repository design, with windows only on the north and south sides of the building.
  - Renovation of 19,000 square feet focused on spaces designed to facilitate collaborative, hands-on learning.
- BDG (figure 6.2)
  - Completed in 1926.
  - Two stories, including basement.
  - Classical revival style, red brick.
  - Listed on the National Register of Historic Places, BDG served as the home to varsity sports such as basketball and volleyball until 1973. It functioned as a gym for intermural and general use until 2012, when it became home to various student services, including tutoring and advising. Its complete renovation of 51,000 square feet creates a three-level student learning and services center that includes
    - Think Tank tutoring
    - Wayfinders new student advising services
    - College of Social and Behavioral Sciences advising
    - Arizona Science, Engineering, and Math Scholars program serving STEM students from under-represented groups
    - Health Promotion and Preventative Services
    - Campus recreation satellite exercise facility
    - "Grab and go" food service
- BASC (figure 6.3)
  - Completed in 2020.
  - Five stories, including basement.
  - Contemporary style, concrete.
  - BASC is 56,000 square feet and connects to BDG both physically through two bridges and the ground level, as well as programmatically through hosting services that include
    - Think Tank tutoring
    - "A" Center general advising services
    - College of Social and Behavioral Sciences advising
    - College of Humanities advising
    - College of Science advising
    - Support-Outreach-Success (SOS) student support services
    - Strategic Alternative Learning Techniques (SALT) Center satellite serving students with learning and attention challenges
    - Student Engagement and Career Development
    - Thrive Center services focusing on underrepresented students

fig 6.2

Bear Down Gym interior.

(Credit: Poster Frost Mirto architectural firm, Miller Hull architectural firm, and Sundt construction company.)

fig 6.3

Bartlett Academic Success Center exterior.

(Credit: Poster Frost Mirto architectural firm, Miller Hull architectural firm, and Sundt construction company.)

The spatial relationships among the four buildings are essential in establishing a new level of cohesion among them. New entries in all four buildings face adjacent entries in the other buildings, enabling people to shift from one building to another in a matter of steps. This positions BDG as the District hub in the center of the other three buildings, with entries on all four sides that allow for transit to occur through BDG as well as around it in navigating the District.

The new entries spill out onto newly landscaped "paseos," or walkways, between the buildings. The paseos include large shade canopies above sections of them that provide a visual indicator of where the building doors connect. In addition to this wayfinding purpose, the shade canopies also provide protection from the Arizona sun when traversing from building to building. The new landscape architecture provides various types of seating areas, from patios designed for collaboration to secluded spaces for quiet contemplation, with extensive use of native plants and trees. The paseos serve as the arteries of the District, running through the outdoor spaces and seating areas that form the connective tissue between the four buildings. Together, the paseos, landscape architecture, and new entries provide students with easy access to various destinations within the District when exiting any of the buildings (figure 6.4).

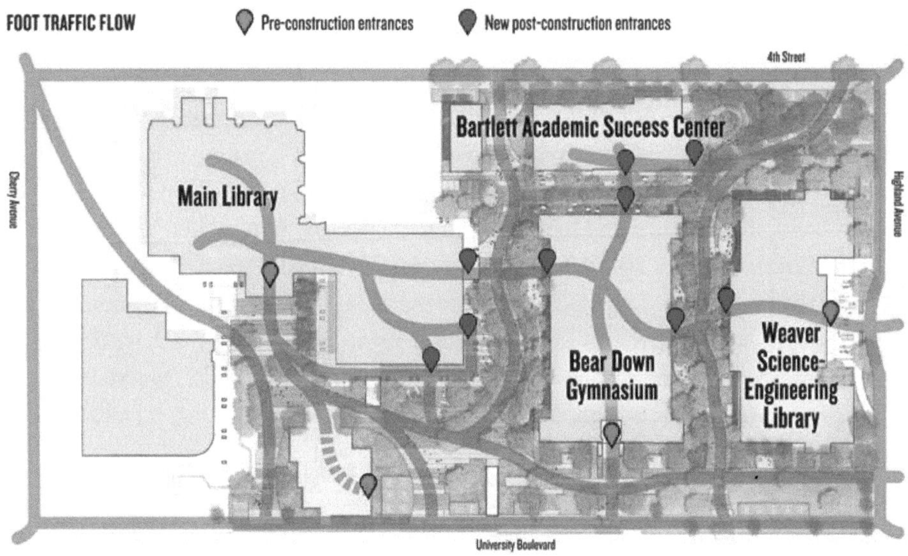

fig 6.4

Student Success District foot traffic flow map.

(Credit: Poster Frost Mirto architectural firm, Miller Hull architectural firm, Ten Eyck landscape architectural firm, and Sundt construction company. Traffic flow design by Marty Taylor, University of Arizona Libraries. Landscape image by Ten Eyck Landscape Architects.)

This design establishes spatial relationships among the structures that were completely lacking prior to the District construction. The overarching objective of enabling horizontal connectivity across the entire District is complemented by another overarching objective of enabling vertical connectivity between floors inside of each of the District buildings. The design of both library renovations illustrates this approach to traffic flow and the spatial relationships of services and areas across the renovated floors.

Libraries Design

The renovations at Main Library and WSEL focused on redesigning two floors in each building to become dedicated to collaborative, hands-on learning with deep technological engagement. There was a related objective of implementing new levels of vertical connectivity between the two floors by introducing high-profile staircases in strategic locations. This design reinforces the identity of these floors as one ecosystem that is active and noisy with lots of group work and access to technology tools. As a result, students have a clearer sense of which floors are appropriate for this kind of research and which floors are more conducive to quiet individual study with print collections at hand, allowing the students to choose a library ecosystem that meets their specific needs at the time.

UAL's vision for reimagining portions of Main Library and WSEL was informed by surveys and focus groups with students and faculty conducted at the beginning of the District planning process. The results generally showed students want choices between quiet individual study areas and more collaborative spaces. In addition to typical requests for more comfortable furniture and natural light, one unexpected trend in the feedback was an interest in outdoor study areas to enjoy the Tucson climate, which is very moderate during the academic year. This "indoor/outdoor experience" input inspired the multiple outdoor seating areas around Main Library and throughout the District, as well as the extensive use of glass walls to create a sense of porousness between outdoor and indoor spaces.

Input was also sought during the planning process from the UA Disabilities Resources Center in embracing a universal design approach to make spaces, furniture, and services accessible to all people, to the greatest extent possible, without the need for adaptation. Its staff's input on the custom design of the libraries' new bi-level Information Desks ensured they not only meet ADA standards but also embrace universal design principles by not requiring adjustments for clients in wheelchairs. In another example, the Main Library's new "monumental staircase," which features terraced seating platforms as well as stairs, was designed to allow the seating areas at the top and bottom to be accessible to people who cannot use the stairs due to physical disabilities.

MAIN LIBRARY DESIGN

Located on the ground floor, the centerpiece of the Main Library renovation is CATalyst Studios, a 9,700-square-foot interdisciplinary facility dedicated to hands-on learning through the utilization of various technologies in research processes and creative endeavors. CATalyst Studios is made up of the Maker Studio (featuring a range of 3D printers, laser cutters, vinyl cutters, CNC routers, sewing machines, and other fabrication equipment; see figure 6.5), the Terry Seligman VR Studio (featuring various virtual and augmented reality devices for sitting and standing experiences as well as a green-screen room with cyclorama and lighting rigs to create VR/AR programs), the Data Studio (featuring a 20-by-7-foot visualization wall with associated server for image and data processing), three Learning Studios (collaborative classrooms designed for classes also using the technology studios), and a common area with various seating options between the studios. Most of the studios have retractable glass walls that allow them to open up onto the common area or be closed off, as appropriate for the activities taking place. The Maker Studio also has a retractable glass wall that can open onto a patio that was refurbished with new lighting, furniture, and power outlets to enable outdoor fabrication activities.

fig 6.5

Maker Studio within CATalyst Studios at Main Library.

(Credit: Poster Frost Mirto architectural firm, Miller Hull architectural firm, and Sundt construction company.)

CATalyst Studios is founded on a commitment to formal and informal learning as essential parts of the UA student experience. In addition to working with faculty across disciplines to integrate the use of the studios into the curriculum, informal workshops in areas such as GIS, software carpentry, and user experience (UX) design are offered, as well as extensive drop-in hours for impromptu learning from student staff experts distinguished by their CATalyst lab coats. CATalyst Studios programming also reflects the recognition that computational forms of research are increasing across all disciplines at the UA. Two examples involve the recent launches of the Center for Digital Humanities and the Data Science Institute, both with strong ties to UAL faculty expertise and programs that are further advanced by CATalyst Studios.

Values of diversity, equity, and inclusion are strong elements in how CATalyst Studios operates. Conscious that makerspaces and technology facilities often have a homogenous user demographic that trends heavily toward male and White, CATalyst Studios was conceived as an interdisciplinary space with an overarching goal of utilizing proactive outreach and programming to welcome and cultivate a broad and diverse community of users. For example, it is the new home to the Women's Hackathon that UAL has hosted for several years, drawing hundreds of participants. Other events and programs designed to attract and support a diversity of users are also being developed.

While CATalyst Studios occupies the east wing of the Main Library ground floor, the entire west wing was renovated to create a variety of collaborative study areas, with floor-to-ceiling, 14 feet tall windows on three sides to bring natural light pouring in while also providing views onto the District's outdoor areas. The monumental staircase is the architectural feature around which this wing's design revolves. Its installation required removing a 30-by-30-foot square in the 24-inch-deep concrete slab floor, providing a new, highly visible vertical connection to the spaces and services of the basement level that were also renovated.

Just as the renovated ground floor includes three adjacent technology-focused facilities within CATalyst Studios, the Main Library's basement floor features three other technology service areas. The Rhonda G. Tubbs Tech Toolshed builds on UAL's decade of success in technology lending that encompasses various laptops, tablets, cameras, scanners, Wi-Fi hot spots, and other devices. The Toolshed's renovated home includes a new sandbox area where devices can be explored to better understand their potential applications before being borrowed. Across from the Toolshed is the Zone, a software lab focused on video, audio, and computer-aided design software that is staffed by University Information and Technology Services (UITS). One example of cross-pollination among different Main Library tech services involves students who design prototypes in the Zone and 3D print them in CATalyst Studios as their creations evolve.

The third tech service on the basement floor, 24/7 IT Lounge also managed by UITS, moved into Main Library as a result of the renovations that created a space for its operations adjacent to the Tech Toolshed and the Zone. It provides support to UA students and employees on any IT issue, including those on personally owned devices. This shift to Main Library provides 24/7 IT Support with a high visibility location for providing on-site services as well as online and via phone.

Together, the CATalyst Studios, the Rhonda G. Tubbs Tech Toolshed, the Zone, and 24/7 IT Support create technology-focused synergies across their two floors in Main Library, with extensive collaborative study environments mixed in to create a two-floor library ecosystem dedicated to these kinds of learning and research experiences.

WSEL DESIGN

In the same spirit, but with a greater focus on collaborative learning, the WSEL renovation also encompasses two floors, the ground floor and the third floor above it. WSEL's 270-seat collaborative classroom is located on the ground floor, and the renovation's primary focus was to redesign the ground floor and third floor as extensions of this classroom, providing spaces and furnishings that facilitate group work and study.

Prior to the renovations, UAL staff observed that groups of students from courses taught in this library's collaborative classroom were using these floors extensively to work together before and after class. Reinforcing these observations, a chemical engineering professor began holding some of his office hours on the third floor of WSEL after realizing this was a gathering spot for groups from his courses in the collaborative classroom. The dedication of this floor to collaborative teaching and learning is also reinforced by the presence of a training room for collaborative classroom instructors to share guidance and best practices on a peer-to-peer basis.

The planning assumption was if groups of students were already using these areas in spite of the limitations of the building's original design and outdated furniture, they would be significantly more successful if the areas were fully renovated with a design, furniture, and furnishings intended for collaboration, with movable, modular furniture, various types of whiteboards, and an open floor plan. Due to the building's original layout, there was a major bottleneck at the one public door into the collaborative classroom as hundreds of students moved in and out when classes change throughout the day. The renovation transformed the "T" shape of both floors into an "8" shape with circular traffic flows. This shape on the ground floor also created greater physical connectivity between the collaborative classroom and a commons area with extensive computer access at the opposite end of the building.

Two other design priorities, the introduction of natural light and greater vertical connectivity between the ground floor and third floor, were accomplished through a new two-story, atrium-like entry on the east side of the building, facing BDG (figure 6.6). This two-story glass entry was built onto a side of the building that completely lacked windows, now bringing plentiful natural light onto both floors. It also includes a new staircase within its lobby to the third floor that greatly improves traffic flow and conveys the sense that the floors have a common identity and purpose. This reinforces the research ecosystem concept also present in Main Library, clearly signaling to students which floors are for noisy group work and which floors are for quiet individual study.

fig 6.6

Albert B. Weaver Science-Engineering Library exterior.

(Credit: Poster Frost Mirto architectural firm, Miller Hull architectural firm, and Sundt construction company.)

Programmatic Synergies across the District

Since the District won't be completed until 2022, at the time of this writing it's too early to know precisely how the adjacencies of the various services across the District will lead to new collaborations. In a broad sense, there will be referrals among the services that would have been previously difficult for students to navigate when service points were scattered across campus. Some current collaborations, such as the UAL UX unit's work with Think Tank tutoring services, will likely expand, while other new potential partnerships are already being explored.

A prime example involves the SALT Center in BASC and the Terry Seligman VR Studio in Main Library. The SALT Center is a national leader in its field, and its staff is constantly researching and developing new strategies to support UA students with learning and attention challenges. Its staff have expressed strong interest in working with UAL faculty and staff in the VR Studio to study how augmented and virtual reality programs can be designed to present information in ways that address learning and attention challenges. Other possibilities include partnerships between UAL and services in BDG and BASC, such as career services, tutoring, advising, and especially the multiple programs focused on facilitating success for students from underrepresented groups, a purpose that is closely aligned with the strategic objectives of the UAL service portfolio.

Realizing the Dream

The University of Arizona Student Success District reflects a collective dream that was realized largely through alignment with the UA's institutional vision. The dream was driven by convictions that collaborative, hands-on learning with technological skill development are core elements in the UA educational process, positioning students for both academic and career success. It was also based on the recognition that the impact of multifaceted student support and library services can be amplified by strategically colocating them.

The concept of integration through adjacency on a large scale was integral to bringing library spaces and services in close proximity to an array of other student support spaces and services. The power of this model is perhaps best illustrated by an example of a day in the life of an undergraduate student in the District:

> Julieta begins her day by attending a geosciences class in WSEL's collaborative classroom. After class, Julieta heads to the library's third floor, where she will continue working on a group project with peers from this class. A little later, Julieta goes next door to BDG for an appointment with her advisor in the Arizona Science, Engineering, and Math Scholars program. Afterward, Julieta picks up lunch in the BDG food service area and eats with friends on the large patio connected to Main Library. Then Julieta goes inside to CATalyst Studios to work on a circuit board prototype she is building for an electrical engineering class and also attends a drop-in workshop on programming with Python. Before leaving Main Library, Julieta checks out a 3D scanner to use tomorrow with rock samples for the geosciences class and proceeds to the Think Tank area of BASC, where she works as a tutor. Feeling the need to reenergize in the late afternoon, Julieta spends some time on an elliptical machine in the BDG exercise facility. Her last stop for the day in the District is back in WSEL, where she checks out a laptop and a study room to attend an online class.

Different versions of this journey across the District will occur on a daily basis for thousands of UA students in the coming decades. The convergence of the District concept with core elements of the UA institutional vision provided the foundation for success. As a result, what started as a plan to renovate library buildings was transformed into the centerpiece of a student experience that is distinctive to the UA, while also serving as a model for other academic libraries to consider how they might scale up their own dreams of redesigning libraries.

Notes

1. Neil Peart, "Vital Signs," by Rush on Moving Pictures (Mercury Records), 1981, track 7.
2. The Student Success District website is at https://successdistrict.arizona.edu.
3. Alexis Blue, "Evidence Suggests Improved Student Outcomes in Collaborative Learning Spaces," October 4, 2018, UA@Work, University of Arizona, https://uaatwork.arizona.edu/lqp/evidence-suggests-improved-student-outcomes-collaborative-learning-spaces.
4. Blue, "Evidence Suggests."
5. "100% Engagement Faculty and Staff," Student Engagement and Career Development, University of Arizona, accessed December 30, 2020, https://career.arizona.edu/faculty-staff/100-engagement.
6. The capitalized "CAT" in CATalyst Studios is a nod to the Wildcat mascot of the University of Arizona.
7. "Strategic Plan," University of Arizona, accessed December 30, 2020, https://strategicplan.arizona.edu.
8. "Strategic Plan."
9. Jane Hunter, "What Do Collaborative Classrooms Really Look Like on Campus?" eCampus News, December 5, 2017, https://www.ecampusnews.com/2017/12/05/collaborative-classrooms-campus/.
10. The District design-build team was Poster Frost Mirto (now Poster Mirto McDonald) architectural firm, Miller Hull architectural firm, Ten Eyck landscape architectural firm, and Sundt construction company.

7

CHAPTER SEVEN

VISION, ADVOCACY, NARRATIVE, OUTREACH

Strategic Communication for New Library Buildings

JOHN E. ULMSCHNEIDER

The scholarly and practice literature on communication strategies reveals the importance of both strategically crafted message content and a multilevel messaging process that reaches all stakeholders and potential supporters. This chapter will describe how Virginia Commonwealth University Libraries developed and implemented a visioning, advocacy, and communications strategy in support of a major library construction initiative. The successful effort led VCU Libraries' disparate communities to embrace and support a distinctive, award-winning library design that departed both from architectural practice at the university and from initial expectations for library buildings among stakeholder communities.

The Setting: VCU and VCU Libraries

Virginia Commonwealth University is a major public urban research university designated by the Carnegie Classification of Institutions of Higher Education as R1, a doctoral university with very high research activity and $335 million in sponsored research awards for 2019–20. It enrolls approximately 31,000 students, with particular distinction for programs in medical sciences, life sciences, education, social work, and the fine arts.

VCU Libraries consists of James Branch Cabell Library on the main campus, the Health Sciences Library on the health sciences campus, the Health and Wellness Library in VCU's main hospital, and the VCU Qatar Arts Library at VCU's School of the Arts on the Education City campus in Qatar (a campus shared by Texas A&M, Cornell, Northwestern, Georgetown, and Carnegie-Mellon). VCU Libraries became a member of the Association of Research Libraries in January 2018, becoming the first US academic library to join ARL in over 15 years.

VCU's library facilities experienced a steady consolidation between 1990 and 2005 with the elimination of branch libraries. A series of renovations at both library facilities on the Richmond campus from 2000 to 2010 improved the buildings significantly, but the building footprints, and consequently available space, had not changed since construction on them finished in 1975. The Health and Wellness Library opened in 2002 with space dedicated to patient education and support in the main university hospital. The VCU Qatar Arts Library opened in 2001, moved to a greatly expanded location in 2010, and added additional square footage for a makerspace and a materials library in 2020.

Two deeply impactful changes at the university accelerated the need for greater library space beginning about 1995. First, enrollment grew significantly, from total head count of 21,349 in fall 1995 to 32,300 in fall 2010. Second, although always classified as an R1 institution, VCU's research enterprise expanded as well, from $63.5 million in 1995 to $255.4 million in 2010. These expanded numbers greatly increased pressure on library space. The changes led to severe challenges for James Branch Cabell Library, and it emerged as the overwhelming focus for capital improvement in the library system.

Beyond these quantitative realities, during this period the university undertook long-term efforts to promote its academic and research distinction in an increasingly competitive market for both students and research dollars. Although long one of the three major research universities in Virginia, VCU now sought broader recognition of its stature and accomplishments.

The university's expansion, together with its campaign toward greater recognition and distinction, set the stage for a focused campaign to both renovate and expand library facilities to advance both goals. The campaign required VCU Libraries to devise and carry out a visioning, communications, and advocacy strategy that illuminated library space needs and inspired stakeholders to invest in VCU's libraries at all levels.

Communication and Advocacy for New Library Buildings

Academic library buildings and major renovations commonly require a decade or longer to move from the first crystallization of need to the final opening of a new building. Of that long need-to-reality arc, less than half the time (four to five years) involves actual design and construction. The majority of time in the building development cycle is devoted to advocacy and communications that create community support and establish new library facilities as an institutional priority.

Effective communication and marketing strategies build upon well-understood keystone elements for communications plans articulated by communications professionals. Guidance for such plans generally include some variation of

- a clear strategic plan
- style and branding guidelines
- identification of target audiences
- key messages (derived from strategic plans and institutional needs)
- clear messaging priorities
- communications tools and venues (digital, print, in-person)
- responsible parties for implementing the strategies
- assessment of effectiveness[1]

Helpful library and university communications plans are easily obtainable and can act as templates for constructing a local plan.[2] They provide a rich resource for designing communications plans that meet many different library needs.

Communications plans generally focus on marketing services or collections to constituencies; they only occasionally incorporate advocacy for major new initiatives such as library funding or library buildings. Instead, advocacy for libraries exists as a practice largely separate from communications planning.

Library advocacy plans develop and promote tool kits both to influence policy affecting libraries and to strengthen funding for libraries, often in political arenas, and increasingly embrace efforts to demonstrate the benefits libraries deliver to their communities and the return on investment for library funding.[3] Advocacy employs many tools from accepted communications plans and practice, but it generally pursues a better-defined outcome (such as policy changes or funding support) and extends its efforts to constituencies beyond those directly served by libraries.

Both communications and advocacy practice provide building blocks for a strategic framework and the full range of tactics needed for a sustained, years-long effort to promote and build a new library. Chief among these building blocks are

- a clear and compelling vision for a new library that inspires campus leaders and partners and excites admiration and support among stakeholders and constituencies,
- a powerful, data-informed case for a new library that addresses key questions around need, library use, return on investment, and best use of available funds,
- creation of broad awareness and support for vision and need across parent institution communities and, where appropriate, regional and state-level stakeholder and funder communities, and
- enlistment of allies to advance goals for institutional funding and philanthropic support, almost always in environments characterized by highly competitive funding demands and priorities.

Renovate, Create Anew,... or Both?

A crucial decision preceding all else will be whether to renovate an existing building, create a new building, or pursue a combination of renovation and new expansion. What considerations drive the decision?

- *Cost:* New construction is almost always more expensive per square foot than renovations. That means potentially available funds often emerge as a major factor in deciding to renovate a library space rather than construct new space. Other factors about existing facilities may mandate new construction despite costs.

- *Location:* Location is key to library viability. Existing academic libraries not uncommonly are among the first buildings constructed on a campus and so occupy precious, high-value real estate at the center of academic building complexes. Consideration of a new library building starts with available real estate in a location suitable for the library's role in meeting diverse academic community needs. That usually requires a sufficient footprint near or at a vibrant campus hub. Renovation as a strategy gains favor absent available real estate in such a location.
- *Adequacy of existing space:* The starting point for renovations is space that meets minimum standards and provides adaptable spaces suitable for upgrading. Irredeemably compromised existing facilities—buildings without fire suppression, with massive asbestos contamination, with dangerously deteriorated structural or foundation elements, or other safety issues—or poorly planned or inflexible spaces (structural stacks, for instance) can motivate replacement rather than renovation. And renovations cannot of course address urgent space needs: the existing footprint of a renovated building is a hard limit on available space unless the building is extended upward, connected to other buildings, or the footprint otherwise adapted to add space.
- *Legacy:* Existing library buildings sometimes possess irreplaceable architectural and community legacy. Legacies can complicate renovations but also motivate academic communities to a higher level of investment than might otherwise be considered. In addition, renovated legacy buildings can sometimes rival new buildings for architectural distinction and the utility of the renovated spaces.
- *Possible incremental changes:* Renovations can provide some relief to space pressure by reconfiguring existing space to accommodate more users. For example, renovation projects might relocate internal library operations to smaller, more efficient spaces or move them to other buildings, opening floor space for users. Smaller, incremental space renovations also can demonstrate in tangible ways the promise a new library building offers to stakeholders and communities served by a library. VCU Libraries used this strategy as part of its communications and advocacy plan.
- *Advantages of a new facility:* New building projects provide design flexibility far beyond a renovation plan to meet contemporary needs and anticipate needs into the foreseeable future. Instead of allocating funds to fix inadequate spaces, new design and construction can use those funds to create far more useful space with an architectural vision that aligns with broader institutional culture. Importantly, a new facility opens the door to distinctive, even inspiring architectural expression that is not constrained by an existing design or footprint.

Rather than either renovation or new construction, many celebrated academic library buildings over the past two decades have instead combined renovations with new construction. Renovating an existing facility that meets basic qualifications—good location, flexible spaces, no serious compromising conditions—combined with new construction to expand the facility can take advantage of both approaches. Total project costs that are divided between renovations and new construction can deliver many of the advantages of newly designed spaces at a cost less than all-new construction. Combination projects also can capture most of the advantages of new spaces, sometimes in a footprint comparable to that of an entirely new building. Crucially, a combination project can provide a compelling opportunity for a distinctive architectural expression while retaining a highly visible and highly trafficked location.

VCU Libraries chose to pursue a combination project from its very first visioning exercises. James Branch Cabell Library possessed an ideal location for academic life at a key campus nexus, along with adjacent real estate sufficient for a sizable expansion. Although it had a Brutalist design without particular architectural distinction, its highly visible central location, flexible interior spaces (typical of Brutalist 1970s design), and relatively uncompromised physical infrastructure (improved by asbestos abatement and fire suppression projects from 2000 onward), made a well-supported case for renovations. Adding a large new addition offered the promise of an architecturally distinctive expression at the center of the most active pedestrian corridors of the university. Ultimately, VCU added approximately 93,000 square feet of new construction paired with 63,000 square feet of extensive renovations.

Long-Term Visioning and Advocacy for Library Facilities

New library buildings begin with the library and institutional strategic vision and mission, along with foundational discoveries and decisions about a library's needs. Years before an architectural firm meets with library staff for the first time, library leaders must lay the groundwork for future library facilities with a vision for libraries and library spaces that aligns with overall library and institutional vision, mission, and goals, along with data-informed profiling and benchmarking that illustrate library needs.

The vision for a library building and its use likely will not closely resemble expectations for library facilities among many stakeholder and supporter communities, whose vision for such facilities generally relies (at least initially) on their narrow personal experience of libraries. Changing the narrative about libraries and their use is a key element to articulating a clear, compelling, and expansive vision for the role of a new building.

At VCU, institutional ambitions for growth and change provided a powerful starting point for a new library vision: the university's strategic quest for broader recognition and distinction. VCU Libraries promoted three themes to advance that strategic goal.

CREATE A RESEARCH LIBRARY COMMENSURATE WITH R1 RANKING

First, beginning in the early 2000s, VCU Libraries laid out investment plans that would bring VCU's library expenditures to a level commensurate with its R1 peers, culminating with membership in the Association of Research Libraries (ARL) as recognition of achieving that goal. The university's 2011 strategic plan embraced that goal, leading to ARL membership in 2018, joining the other two R1 universities in Virginia (University of Virginia and Virginia Tech). The overall goal of research library status was crucial to developing a vision of distinction for VCU's libraries that supported both library expansion and the university's efforts in elevating recognition of the institution as a whole. With a library system becoming increasingly sized and recognized in a way similar to peers, distinctive library facilities became the final linchpin for completing the process of transforming VCU's libraries.

VCU Libraries' improved staffing and budgets also were essential to providing the capacity to operate larger spaces with ambitious programming goals. Operating capacity is a consideration often overlooked by university planners concerned chiefly with just the costs of facilities and furnishings, although all early exercises associated with planning any academic building should recognize increased operating costs.

MAKE A COMPELLING CASE STATEMENT

Second, VCU Libraries developed and promoted a compelling case statement for library space that elevated a new library in the university's capital construction plans. That effort began in 2001 by compiling data on three crucial benchmarks.

- *Space per student:* VCU Libraries assembled data on library space per student for universities in Virginia, using figures from regular inventories conducted by the State Council of Higher Education for Virginia, the state's coordinating (but not governing) body for higher education in Virginia.[4] Simple but powerful presentation of the data made a compelling statement about library space at VCU and across the state (figure 7.1). The data clearly showed VCU near the very bottom in library space per student.
- *Use of library facilities:* VCU Libraries presented data on the use of library facilities to the VCU community on an ongoing basis. The data showed relentless and even alarming growth in library use (figure 7.2), creating immense pressure on limited space. At VCU, the numbers became so large that alternatives, such

as showing library visits per head count, became necessary (figure 7.3). Using door count data provided by other academic libraries in Virginia, VCU Libraries demonstrated that growth in library use was part of a larger expansion at every academic institution in the state (although the data showed that Cabell Library had the highest use of any academic library facility in Virginia; see figure 7.4).

- *Collections growth:* Data on collections growth demonstrated that library collections were consuming a larger and larger portion of library floor space. This data led VCU to create on-site storage for print volumes in 2010, later expanded with a modest off-site storage facility in 2014. These facilities freed up an entire floor for student use and stabilized collections encroachment on library space, but door count growth continued unabated, and pressure on library space remained intense.

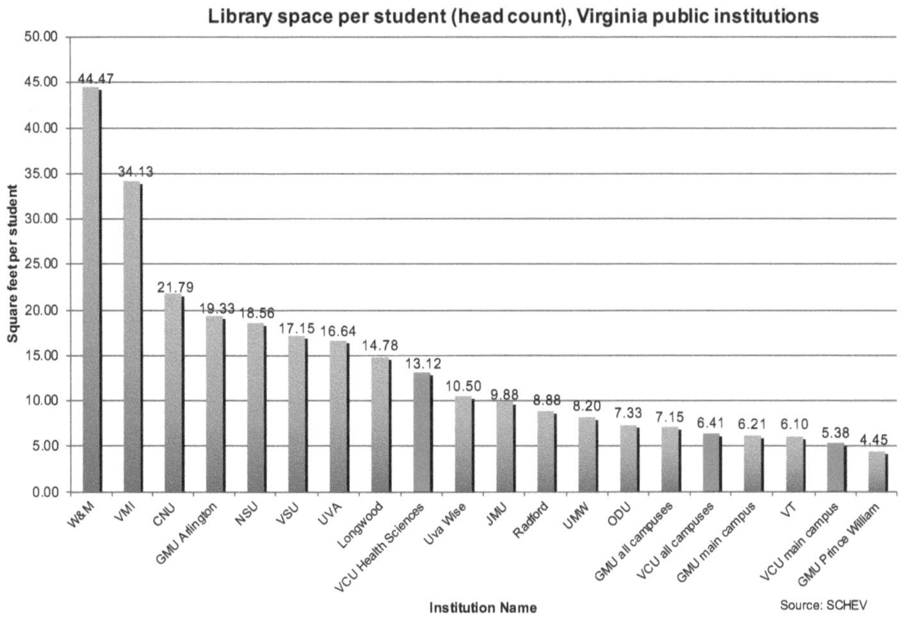

fig 7.1

Virginia academic library space per student in 2006.

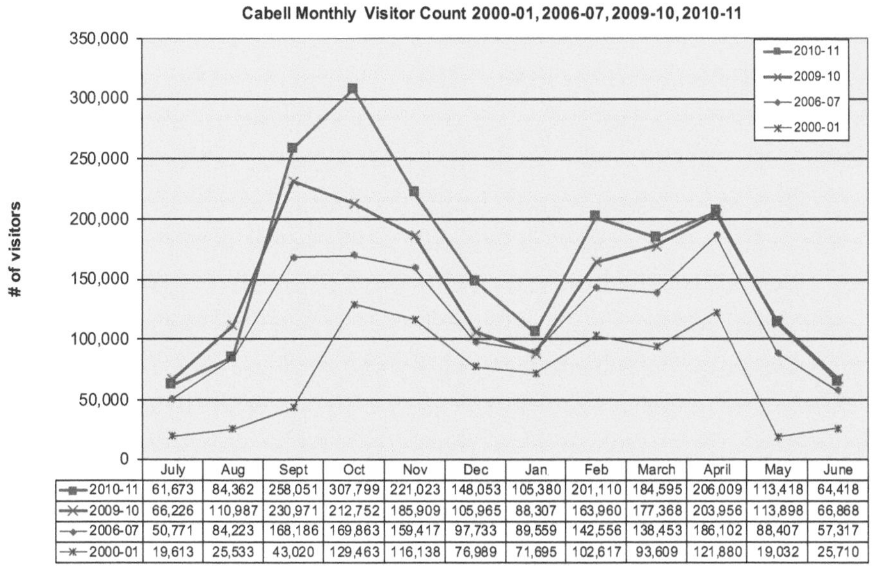

	July	Aug	Sept	Oct	Nov	Dec	Jan	Feb	March	April	May	June
2010-11	61,673	84,362	258,051	307,799	221,023	148,053	105,380	201,110	184,595	206,009	113,418	64,418
2009-10	66,226	110,987	230,971	212,752	185,909	105,965	88,307	163,960	177,368	203,956	113,898	66,868
2006-07	50,771	84,223	168,186	169,863	159,417	97,733	89,559	142,556	138,453	186,102	88,407	57,317
2000-01	19,613	25,533	43,020	129,463	116,138	76,989	71,695	102,617	93,609	121,880	19,032	25,710

fig 7.2

Cabell Library visitor counts through 2011.

fig 7.3

Cabell Library visitor counts per enrollment head count. (Note decline during new building construction 2014–2016; increase after new building opening 2016.)

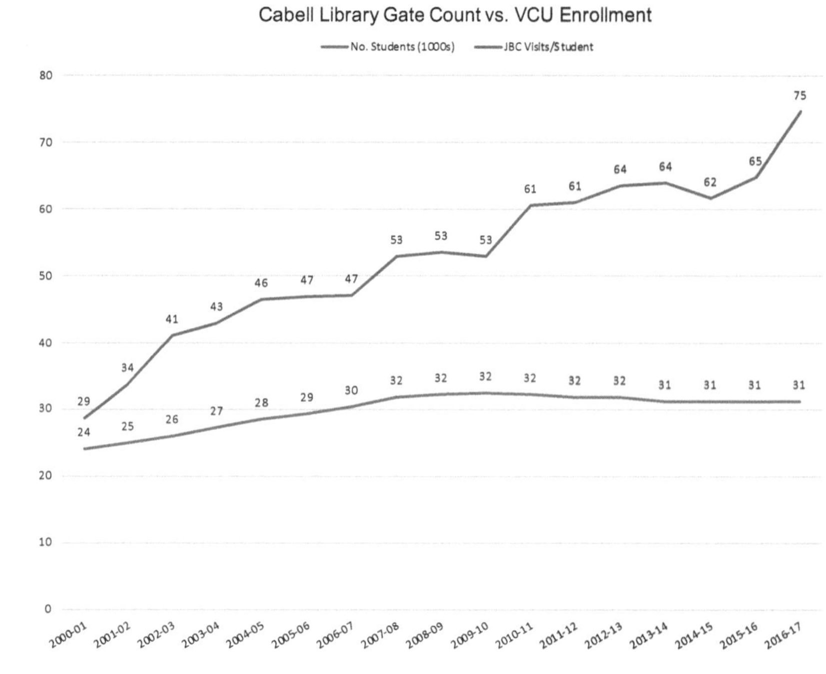

fig 7.4

Visits to Virginia academic library, 2006–2015.

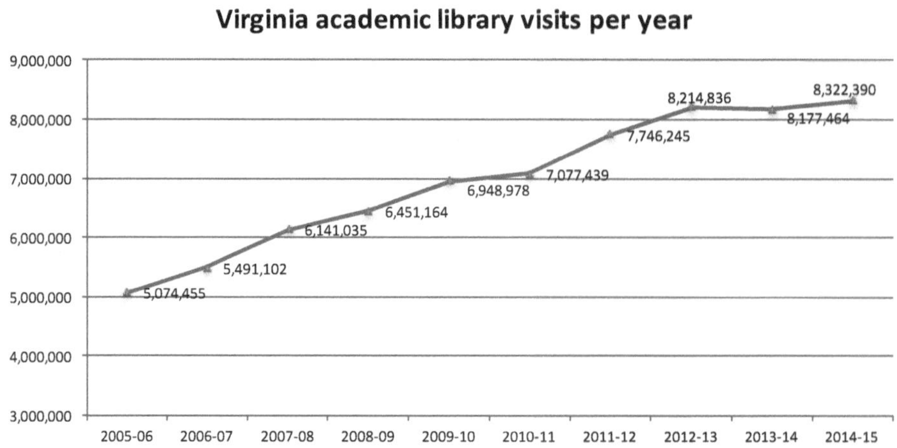

VCU Libraries presented this data in every possible forum at every available opportunity for over 12 years, from VCU's governing board of visitors to talks before alumni groups. By 2009, every constituency or stakeholder at VCU was aware of an acute, near crisis-level shortage of library space.

ESTABLISH A NEW NARRATIVE ABOUT THE LIBRARY

Third, despite decades of changes in libraries and library buildings, many faculty members and institutional leaders of academic institutions retain antiquated perceptions of libraries as underused storage facilities for print materials. Further, significant stakeholder communities seldom enter library facilities. They enjoy library benefits through online services and collections, but have no direct experience with library facilities and do not witness their heavy use by students.

In 2014, OCLC's report *At a Tipping Point* showed that the library brand was overwhelmingly books.[5] It has been a remarkably stubborn perception of libraries by their constituencies; since OCLC began its survey of library perceptions in 2005, books came to mind first for 69 to 75 percent of respondents (figure 7.5).[6] No matter how vibrant library spaces appear to librarians, and even in the face of data showing steadily growing use of library facilities in the digital age, a significant segment of academic library communities still perceive library buildings primarily as repositories of physical materials.

AT A TIPPING POINT

LIBRARIES = BOOKS, INFORMATION, BUILDING, READING

What is the first thing you think of when you think of a library?

	TOTAL RESPONDENTS	AGE 16–24	AGE 25–35	AGE 36–50	AGE 51–59	AGE 60+
BOOKS	75%	70%	80%	79%	74%	75%
INFORMATION	12%	18%	9%	8%	11%	8%
BUILDING (ENVIRONMENT)	6%	8%	5%	5%	4%	6%
READING	3%	2%	2%	3%	4%	4%

OCLC

At A Tipping Point: Education, Learning and Libraries. | P51

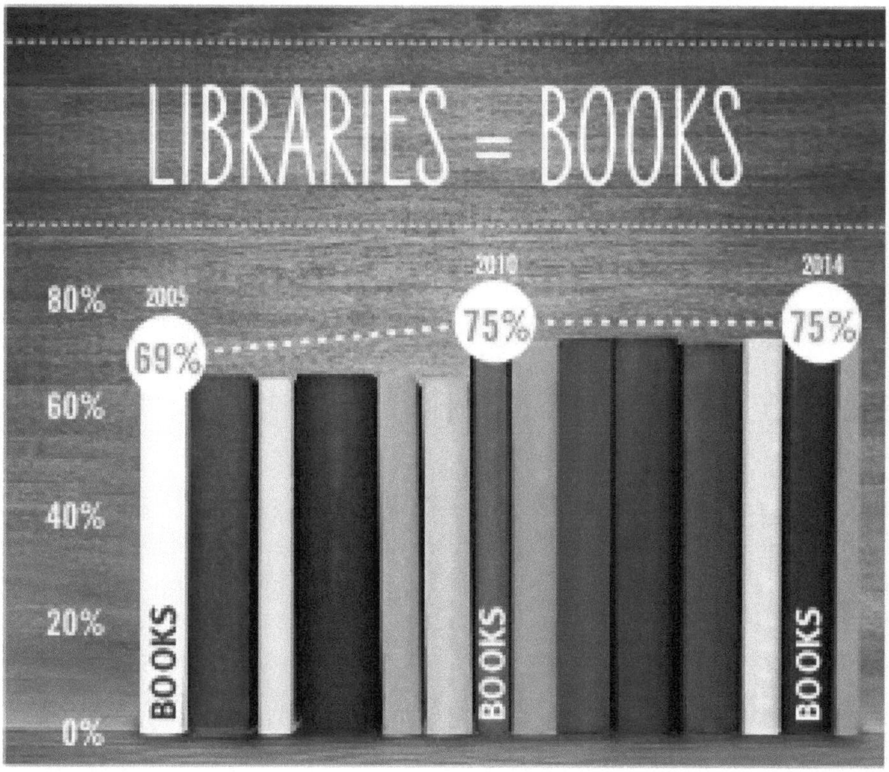

fig 7.5

Library brand as perceived by users.

Clearly, space statements are not sufficient in the face of such persistent perceptions. Academic libraries must change perceptions and create a sense of excitement around new buildings if they wish to pursue contemporary architectural expressions and assemble sufficient financial assets for design and construction. VCU Libraries built upon its work in making a compelling case statement by promoting a distinctive, distinguished, and contemporary library facility as the best solution to its challenges.

Creating the New Library Story

To create a new narrative about its libraries, VCU Libraries adopted a strategy focused on pursuing a renovation/new construction project that could address needs; achieve national recognition and distinction for new library construction, for VCU Libraries, and for the university as a whole; and substantially upgrade and beautify the existing, ideally located James Branch Cabell Library. The framework called for communications and advocacy that focused on

- incremental upgrades and preparatory work that tangibly displayed exciting possibilities for new library space,
- articulating a vision of libraries as "more than books,"
- educating stakeholders about inspiring and distinctive contemporary architecture for libraries, and
- highlighting capabilities, potentials, and benefits unimaginable to stakeholders and the community, including the distinction brought to the university by a new library building and its potential as a competitive advantage in recruiting students.

Incremental upgrades: At the start of the new century, VCU's library facilities had remained largely unchanged since their completion in 1975. Even furnishings and carpeting in the two major facilities dated to that time or earlier. VCU Libraries leadership devised a renovation plan for library facilities that highlighted acute needs but also aimed to showcase functionality and new capabilities that contemporary libraries could offer the university's academic communities.

Figure 7.6 summarizes the renovation strategy. First, with no hope for major investment in the long term, VCU Libraries redirected a small, $1.3 million renovation fund intended to spruce up both facilities through significant alterations of portions of the entrance and first floors of both buildings only. A new coffee bar within the library, an innovative feature at the time that resulted in a nationally broadcast NPR program segment, immediately emerged as a powerful demonstration of the dynamism library spaces promised to their academic communities.[7]

Following the first renovation, a series of four succeeding renovations eliminated branch libraries and reshaped both main library facilities in ways that further demonstrated the capabilities provided to academic communities by contemporary library space. Further, these renovations established off-site print storage as an acceptable option for library materials and demonstrated how library space could publicize and elevate VCU's academic distinction in fine arts and health sciences. Finally, library use grew enormously as a result of attractive, useful renovated spaces. The growth accelerated a sense of urgency among stakeholders around a new library facility to meet needs and also fulfill the exciting promise for VCU's academic environment that renovations demonstrated.

Exposing stakeholders to inspiring library architecture: Along with renovations as examples, VCU Libraries set out to educate VCU's diverse communities and stakeholders about the capabilities of new library facilities and the inspiring architecture shaping many of them. Beginning in 2006, numerous presentations to disparate VCU communities focused on examples of how other libraries, particularly but not exclusively libraries at aspirational peer institutions, addressed library needs in inspiring ways. Plans and illustrations from the Seattle Public Library; Emory University; University of Nevada, Las Vegas; Goucher College; Ohio State University; and others seeded VCU's communities with exciting architectural designs that built on and extended features in VCU's renovated facilities with which they already were familiar.

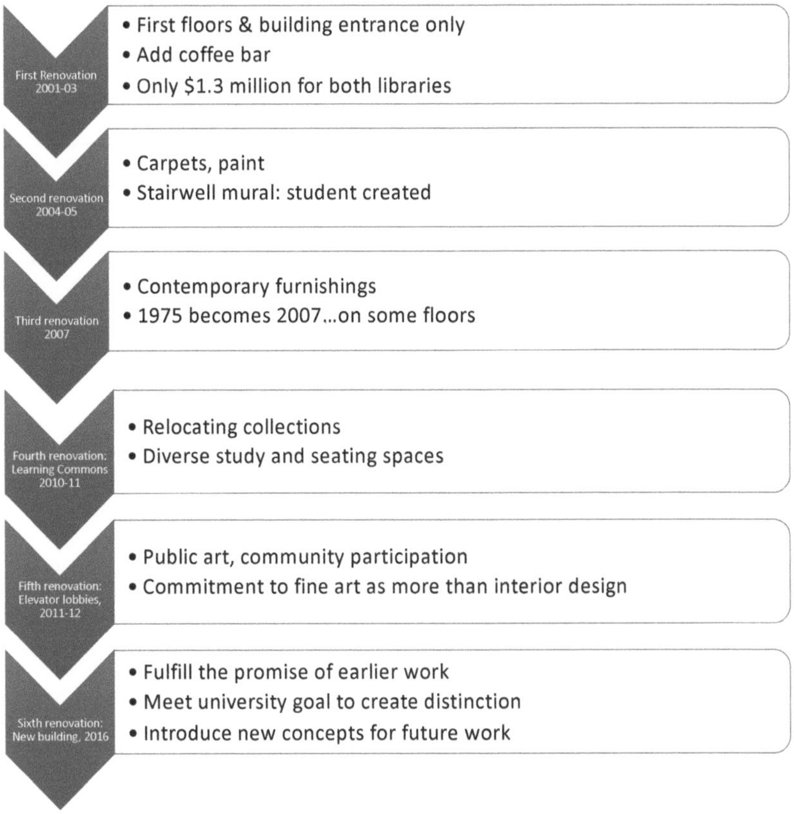

fig 7.6

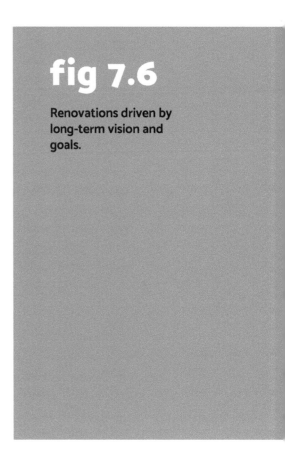

Renovations driven by long-term vision and goals.

VCU Libraries amplified the appeal of new architectures by highlighting the way in which a new library building could advance the university's own ambitions. Combining a 2006 study that showed the impact on prospective students of library facilities with OCLC *Tipping Point* data proved particularly powerful in showing the way new library facilities affected decisions by students and alumni (figure 7.7).[8] Both showed that library facilities were second only to facilities for academic disciplines in their importance to prospective students and, crucially, the university's philanthropic community.

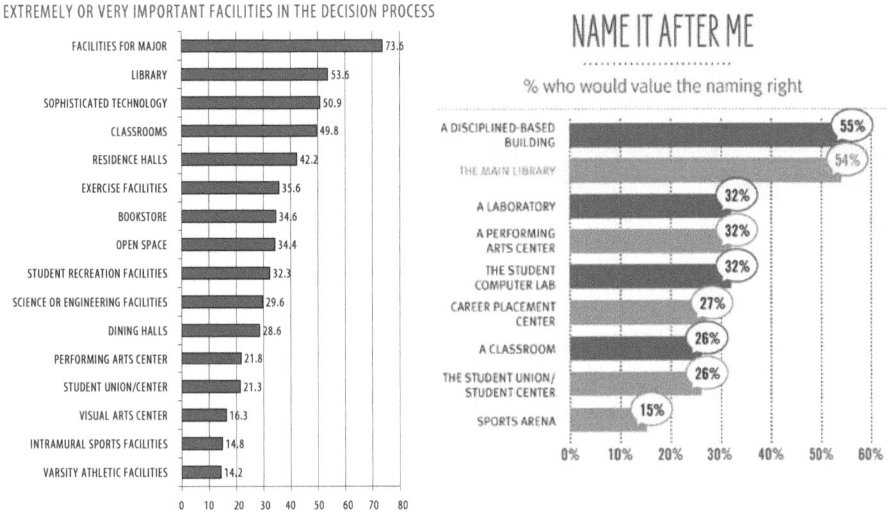

fig 7.7

Impact of library facilities on prospective students (left) and donors (right).

Unimagined possibilities for a new library building: Promoting the promise and functionality of new library facilities plays a central role in assembling the financial investment needed for a new building. Keeping in mind that for most stakeholder communities the library brand still brings to mind books, VCU Libraries developed a vision for its new library building that addressed urgent needs identified in the case statements, but also included innovative and highly distinctive features important to goals set forth in VCU's strategic plan. Vision elements included

- Visually stunning appearance: The architecture of VCU is dominated by brick facades and Brutalist architecture. The vision for a new library departed from prevailing architecture: VCU Libraries sought a bright, transparent, glass-and-stone design that could act as a beacon at the intersection of campus life, illuminating the campus around it and creating an architectural presentation unique among Virginia academic institutions.
- State-of-the-art academic work spaces for students: VCU's renovated library spaces, combined with presentations about new library facilities at other institutions, developed momentum around replacing inadequate 1975 study space with space designed for 21st-century academic work. The building proposal included a media laboratory and makerspace, a feature emerging nationally as indispensable for student work.
- Diversity of seating: Student input and testimonials (gathered via surveys) opened eyes among university leaders regarding student hopes for a diversity of seating—group study, individual study, lounge seating, and especially small group study rooms—of the sort their peers at other institutions enjoyed.
- Dedicated space for faculty and graduate students: VCU Libraries highlighted plans to dedicate significant space to graduate students and faculty, a feature prominent at other academic libraries. At VCU, this space would have the best furnishings and best natural light in the entire new building.
- At 5,863 square feet, one of the largest Starbucks on the East Coast, extending the first café established in 2001, fully integrated into Cabell Library with seating open during all library hours.
- A 400-square-foot exterior LED display (figure 7.8) used to display artwork from VCU's vibrant fine arts community.
- A 5,000+-square-foot lecture hall on the third floor of the new library equipped with a full catering kitchen, flexible seating and lighting, and the largest single video display at VCU, opening via a fully retractable glass curtain wall to a 400-square-foot outdoor terrace for event receptions (open to students outside of event hours).
- A reading porch on the third floor overlooking the main campus pedestrian thoroughfare with windows that opened, wicker furniture, and ceiling fans that emulated a screened porch.

fig 7.8

Exterior display.

(Credit: VCU Libraries.)

Carrying the Message

Capital projects for libraries rely on multiple funding streams. For public institutions like VCU, those consist principally of institutional funds, philanthropic support, and government funding. Each funding stream comprises multiple sources. Institutional funds may draw from capital monies, reserves for safety and security, or even student fees; philanthropic support includes foundation grants, major capital gifts, and small donations; and government funding may include bond-supported allocations or capital funds, as well as permanent operating monies required for utilities and maintenance.

Securing these funding sources requires cultivating a broad array of institutional decision makers and key institutional staff; potential corporate, foundation, and individual funding sources and influencers; and government leaders in both executive and legislative branches. VCU Libraries engaged in a decade-long strategy of outreach to these funding key holders to build awareness of its needs and goals. Four strategies proved effective.

- *Empowering staff as ambassadors:* As part of regular operations, VCU Libraries held meetings of the entire staff three times a year throughout the 12 years leading up to the start of construction. The dean of libraries also met with the staff of each department once a year, with the library faculty once a month, and with department managers once a month. Nearly every meeting included updates and solicited input on plans for renovations, off-site storage, space needs, and design considerations for a new building. Though immensely time-consuming, the effort prepared every staff member to act as an ambassador to promote a new library facility, vastly increasing the settings in which other university communities could learn about new library space.
- *Engaging all campus communities and allies:* All academic institutions experience intense competition for capital investment among many different units. Academic libraries must constantly enlighten a broad assortment of institutional communities about the benefits of new library buildings to them and the university as a whole in order to become a leading priority for funding.
  - As in all research universities, VCU's academic communities are immensely diverse in discipline richness, program offerings, and physical location. Although the university's health science campus is over a mile removed from the main campus, where the investment need was greatest, VCU Libraries invested significant effort to keep leadership and faculty on that campus apprised. Staff of the health sciences libraries participated in all internal meetings and took every opportunity to educate health sciences campus community members about a new library on the main campus.
  - VCU Libraries used regular monthly meetings with its faculty advisory committee (comprising faculty from every school and college on both campuses), school and college committees, and the student governing associations on both Richmond campuses to present the case statement and describe the future.
  - Philanthropic and community supporters were engaged early in the process, both to raise funds for a new facility and also to empower those communities to share the library's goals with university, regional, and state leaders and funders through their own contacts with them.
- *Persevering in making the case to institutional leadership:* Beginning in 2001, VCU Libraries began using every possible opportunity to present the case for significant library expansion to senior university leadership, including deans, vice presidents, the provost, the university president, and the university's board of visitors. In large part because university leadership had already absorbed the message, VCU's current president publicly declared upon his arrival in 2009 that a new library was one of his key short-term strategic goals. By 2013, funding had been assembled for the project.
- *Leveraging opportunities to educate executive and legislative branch staff at the state level:* The dean's work in state-level advocacy for the Virtual Library of Virginia (VIVA) and the Virginia Library Association (VLA) opened opportunities to present library space issues, with VCU Libraries as a chief example, to executive branch staff (budget directors, secretarial staff and the secretary in the Education Secretariat, and others) and legislative branch staff for House and Senate finance committees, along with, on occasion, House and Senate members themselves. Elements of the case statement for VCU had particular

appeal, especially the need for student space suitable for 21st-century academic work demands. Inspiring academic library buildings as exemplars of economic momentum, demonstrations of the state's forward-looking culture, and expressions of regional and state pride engaged executive and legislative leaders with unanticipated returns on investment for capital funds allocated to academic library buildings.

Bringing It All Together

VCU Libraries' deliberate, long-term cultivation of university, regional and state government, and philanthropic communities to support a new library building holds three key lessons for institutions contemplating new library space or space expansion.

First, VCU Libraries built its work upon a foundation of persuasively crafted case statements, incremental upgrades to demonstrate the potential for library space, and changing the narrative about libraries to establish a new vision of libraries as valuable assets that advance university goals and vision. Importantly, VCU Libraries tied its vision for a new library to the university's changing sense of itself, its academic vision, its pride, and its ambitions for itself and its region.

Second, incremental renovations and expanded awareness of offerings at other library facilities reinforced the appeal of benefits offered by new library facilities. Contemporary study and work space for students proved particularly powerful for that community, whose voice lent support for prioritizing a new library. The architectural and functional distinction that underlay the vision for a new library—illustrated by renovated spaces and new buildings at other institutions—directly and substantively advanced the university's overall goals for visibility and recognition.

Finally, comprehensive, persevering outreach to many communities led to broad embrace of a new library building as a key goal for the university. Presentations to staff and library supporters created an advocacy community with expanded opportunities beyond those open to just library leadership. Engagement with students and leadership throughout the entire university, including individuals and units at a far remove from a library expansion project, persuaded the university community of the benefits for every university affiliate of a revitalized library. Opportunities with regional and state leaders to make the case created instant familiarity when funding requests for the new building came under consideration.

Creating new library facilities cannot rely simply on need. By combining case statements, vision, a new library narrative, and outreach, librarians can elevate library facilities from a less-than-urgent consideration to a lead priority for their institutions.

Notes

1. For examples, see Doralyn Rossman, "Creating an Organizationally Embedded Strategic Communication Plan for Libraries," *Library Leadership and Management* 33, no. 2 (2019), https://journals.tdl.org/llm/index.php/llm/article/view/7322; Rick Schell, "Successful Communication Strategy: Five Elements," *Glasscock Blog and News*, March 21, 2017, https://glasscock.rice.edu/blog/successful-communication-strategy-five-elements; Carolyn Dowd, "Build, Brand, Boost! Marketing and Communication Planning 101" (presentation, Academic Library Advancement and Development Network [ALADN] 2019 Conference, Louisville, KY), https://digitalcommons.murraystate.edu/aladn2019/2019/Presentations/17.
2. For example, see "Strategic Communications Plan 2016–2020," University of Louisville Libraries, https://library.louisville.edu/ld.php?content_id=28182897; "2019–2021 Marketing and Communications Plan," Hartford Public Library, https://www.hartfordlibrary.org/Marketing%20and%20Communications%20Planb.pdf; "University Communications Plan 2019–2024," University of Virginia, https://communications.virginia.edu/sites/communications/files/UC-StrategicPlan-1924.pdf; "Strategic Plan Update: Creating a Communications Plan," Washington University in St. Louis University Libraries, https://library.wustl.edu/strategic-plan-update-creating-a-communications-plan/.

3. “Advocacy and Issues,” Association of College and Research Libraries, accessed December 20, 2020, https://www.ala.org/acrl/issues; “Marketing the Academic Library,” Association of College and Research Libraries, accessed December 20, 2020, https://www.ala.org/acrl/issues/marketing; “Frontline Advocacy for Academic Libraries,” American Library Association, accessed December 20, 2020, https://www.ala.org/advocacy/frontline-advocacy-academic-libraries; Indiana Library Federation, *Advocacy Planning Guide: Advancing Library Services for the Benefit of Indiana Residents* (Indianapolis: Indiana Library Federation, 2018), https://cdn.ymaws.com/www.ilfonline.org/resource/resmgr/legislative/advocacy_plan_2018.pdf.
4. “Higher Education Facilities (Guidelines, Forms, and Reports),” State Council of Higher Education for Virginia, accessed December 20, 2020, https://www.schev.edu/index/institutional/guidance-policies/finance-and-facilities/higher-education-facilities.
5. OCLC, *At a Tipping Point: Education, Learning, and Libraries* (Dublin, OH: OCLC, 2014), report and supporting materials at https://www.oclc.org/research/publications/2014/tipping-point.html.
6. OCLC, *At a Tipping Point*, chapter 3 slide deck, slides 2 and 3, https://www.oclc.org/content/dam/oclc/reports/tipping-point/slidedecks/215133-bookppt-OPT-Chapter3.pptx.
7. Susan Stone, “Latte Library,” *All Things Considered*, NPR, August 22, 2003, https://www.npr.org/templates/story/story.php?storyId=1405486.
8. David Cain and Gary Reynolds, “Impact of Facilities on Recruitment and Retention of Students,” *Facilities Manager* 54 (March/April 2006): 58; OCLC, *At a Tipping Point*, chapter 4 slide deck, slide 19.

III

SECTION III

WORKING WITH ARCHITECTS, DESIGNERS, AND PLANNERS

8

CHAPTER EIGHT

TRANSLATIONS

Optimizing Collaborations between Librarians and Their Designers

ANDREW FRONTINI

If you are a librarian and you are planning on working with an architect, there are some things that I think you should know. Architects are very peculiar as a species, full of contradictory impulses. They can be mercurial in their creativity, poetic even, and then turn around and be obsessed with some crippling technicality that, for you, may defy comprehension. It is my experience, however, that the professions of the architect and the librarian share many common values and an altruism that comes from serving the broadest goals of society. Drawing from my own reflections and experiences working as an architect with librarians over 20-odd years, I will, in this chapter, try to help you (as a librarian) prepare for your interactions with architects in order to capitalize on the unique chemistry that leads to great library spaces. But first, some general observations as to the potential of this partnership between librarian and architect.

Through much of recorded history the library, as a building typology, has received special attention as an almost sacred space where knowledge is kept, organized, and protected. The role of its architecture was both practical and symbolic, communicating the significance of knowledge as well as facilitating its ordering. Then and today, the architecture of the library acted in tandem with the librarians, serving and supporting them in their role as knowledge keepers, gatherers, and disseminators. When I work with librarians today, I feel that the essence of this relationship between architecture and librarian is very much intact. Librarians tend to be very interested in architecture and, not surprisingly, have very astute observations as to how the architecture of a library helps or hinders them in their mission. Architects, on the other hand, are mad about libraries. Many of us view the design of libraries as one of the most desirable commissions, both for the spatial explorations it may support and for its communicative potential. Many of the most revolutionary architectural designs of the 20th century have been libraries. The Viipuri Library by Alvar Allto (1927), the Beinecke Rare Book Library at Yale by Gordon Bunshaft of SOM (1960), and the Seattle Public Library by Rem Koolhaas of OMA (2004), in their respective times, presented bold new visions of what a library could be, but also an intriguing reflection of the values that their society aspired to. For this architect, one of the most seductive aspects of designing a library is engaging with the idea of knowledge—how we value it, organize it, and share it. Another attractive aspect of the library as a design challenge lies in its openness as a spatial and cultural system. Libraries literally have a lot of open, fluid space, and they are, as a building typology, very open to interpretation. This would suggest that the librarian and architect together can invent something entirely new. When librarians engage with architects, they may sense this enthusiasm and perhaps be wary of it. After all, the purpose of the endeavor from your perspective is to address the needs of your institution, not to build a concrete poem to the meaning of knowledge in the 21st century. Don't be afraid. It is wonderful to work with passionate people. Instead, learn how to direct that enthusiasm toward your task at hand. This is where communication comes in. Architects use a particular kind of language that can, for many outside the profession, be somewhat mystifying, and they have a particular set of priorities that may go beyond their client's explicit needs. In this chapter I will start by defining some of these terms and priorities. I will also go into some specifics about how you, as a librarian and a client, can best define and communicate your needs so that they can be realized through an architectural solution.

Architectural Language

Architecture, like any profession, is replete with technical jargon, most of which a sensitive architect will translate into common language to convey ideas. However, there is no getting around architectural language, which refers not to this jargon but to the techniques that architecture (and architects) uses to communicate ideas, shape space, and support human activity. There are innumerable volumes dedicated to this lexicon, ranging from Vitruvius's *Ten Books of Architecture* of the first century BC, to Gaston Bachelard's *The Poetics of Space* from 1958, plus many before, in between, and after. A comprehensive summary of the language of architecture being impossible and unnecessary in this context, I will focus on a few key explanations that I have found to be useful when it comes to bridging potential communication gaps between librarians and architects.

CONCEPTUAL

Conceptual includes all things related to the concept or central driving idea for the architectural approach. This central idea will be the DNA of the design, and it is critical that it resonate with you and that it be capable of supporting your goals and aspirations. Architects will refer to the conceptual framework that indicates the combined overlay of building elements that will support the big idea through every aspect of the design—structure, lights, furniture, finishes, all working toward one goal. When you want to add something and they think it doesn't fit, they will invoke the need for conceptual clarity. Conceptual clarity and integrity may seem abstract notions at best, and at worst unnecessary restrictions. To shine some light on the importance of this fixation with conceptual clarity, I would say that conceptual clarity is the basic condition for beauty, harmony, and a sense of things being just right. On the other hand, one must be wary of architectural concepts that are seemingly at odds with the stated requirements and objectives of the project. If this is the case, ask your architect to come up with a better fit. If your architect doesn't seem to have a concept, tell them to try harder.

PLANIMETRIC

Planimetric is an adjective that relates systems and qualities to the floor plan of the architectural proposition. We are all familiar with the idea of a floor plan as a two-dimensional drawing that represents the scale and locations of spaces as well as the adjacencies and relationships between them. Architects worship floor plans and see them as not only a critical tool but also an abstraction of spatial poetry. For the architect, a plan tells a story of how to occupy the building as well as how to build it. From the plan, the essence of the architecture should be evident. Architects see the plan as a composition in its own right. Proportion, symmetry, balance, line weight, hierarchy, and a host of other aesthetic considerations are brought to bear on the creation of the plan diagram with the earned conviction that if the plan is not beautiful, then finished architecture can never be. Your architect may talk to you about planimetric flow, planimetric qualities, planimetric order, planimetric overlays, or planimetric anything. Please indulge them, as they are searching for a graceful solution through the agency of the floor plan. The floor plan can contain spatial poetry, but it is obliged to carry a massive amount of technical information. Get your architect to help you read the plan so that you can find both.

SECTIONAL

Like the term *planimetric*, *sectional* refers to all things related to a two-dimensional drawing that is used to imagine, represent, and build a three-dimensional space. The section is a slice through the building or part of the building showing horizontal and vertical relationships in that vertical plain. It describes the relationships between spaces, but in a way that clients are often not as concerned with, as the drawing tends to contain less user-oriented technical information than a plan. The section, however, is a critical drawing in the design of any library of two or more floors. A building's sectional properties will determine how spaces and programs relate vertically and create opportunities to shape a great diversity for learning and research environments. If the plan establishes relationships, then the section describes experiences. Imagine being up high in a building, overlooking the forest, away from the noise of the main entry. It sounds nice, but how did you get there? Imagine the section as a vertical journey through the library. What helped you find your way? What did you see on your way? Did it inspire you or draw you forward? When your architect shows you a section, she could be asking you all of these questions and more.

INTEGRATION

Some architects aspire to the ideal of the *Gesamtkunstwerk*, or complete work of art, where every part is thoroughly integrated into the whole. Most will be happy to make a nice tidy job of it. The contemporary library contains a great number of, and often competing, architectural, structural, mechanical, electrical, and information technology systems. Add to this furniture (often procured from various sources), shelving, equipment, and signage, and you have the potential for a visual and spatial cacophony. When architects speak about integration, they are referencing the ability of the design concept and process to bring all of these systems together into an aesthetically pleasing, coordinated, and highly functional whole. In a library, with its swaths of open fluid space, two principal surfaces are the fields upon which the battle for integration will play out—the ceiling and the floor. In the context of a public institution, the procurement of all these systems is often complex, and a good portion of it may not be under the influence of the architect. This is an unfortunate reality that should be considered by clients before the design process begins. Libraries must offer a supportive environment for focused work, contemplation, and intentional collaboration. Think of a space exuding calm, harmony, and balance where all of the tools and technologies are at your disposal—that would be a product of integrated design. Work with your architect and your administrative body to find a way to an integrated solution. Your patrons will thank you.

HIERARCHY

Architects use the word *hierarchy* in several different ways. A spatial hierarchy may refer to the relative scale of spaces, but it can also refer to the relative prominence or importance of the spaces in the way that they are presented within the architectural framework. They will also use *hierarchy* to describe the relative qualities of spaces or the relative behaviors that are supported by different types of spaces (e.g., bright, hushed, silent or social, collaborative, focused). The contemporary academic library must support a wide range of activities carried out by a great diversity of users. A library is not a collection of soundproof cells where all of these different uses can sit side by side in harmony. The relatively fluid nature of space in a library means that cleverly arranged spatial hierarchies are critical. The modern library user must be able to navigate between a variety of scales of space, with a variety of light conditions, available technologies, acoustic properties, furniture solutions, and relationships to the outside world. The library becomes a menu of spatial, technical, and behavioral choices that are understood relative to one another through an architectural hierarchy.

Architecture Today

In working with an architect, you will hopefully be confronted with the issues of our time that are of greatest concern to architects and to which they rightly feel obliged to respond. The library is your project, but it is also part of a greater built framework that houses humanity and its various endeavors. One could say that, as the Librarian is the custodian of knowledge, the Architect is the custodian of society, with an obligation to order, express, and protect it. Below, I have listed some of the forces that are having a strong impact on the architecture of our day and that you will invariably have to address in any responsible building project.

SUSTAINABILITY

At this point in human history, we have broadly acknowledged that human activity is now the dominant force shaping biological and climatic systems. According to the United Nations Environment Program, building operations and construction account for 36 percent of global energy use and 39 percent of energy-related carbon dioxide emissions annually.[1] These rather grim statistics place a heavy mantle of responsibility on anyone involved in a building project to look well beyond their immediate needs and to address as best they can the imminent threat posed by environmental degradation and climate change. For you as a client, this will have an immediate impact, placing some additional burdens on your project budget and a whole roster of decisions as you evaluate the implications of incorporating renewable energy systems, more sophisticated heating and cooling strategies, an enhanced building envelope, more efficient lighting and plumbing fixtures, and a more sustainable landscaping and site development strategy. Your architect will inform you as to which of these approaches is mandated in your jurisdiction, and your university administration will also have a set of mandated requirements aimed at greening the campus. There is, however, always the ability to go further, and you will need to be both open-minded and critical as you evaluate how sustainability integrates into your vision for the library project. Your architect should provide you with a comprehensive analysis of the up-front costs, immediate benefits, long-term benefits, and eventual payback period for any proposed systems or sustainability strategies.

WELLNESS

One aspect of sustainability that resonates with librarians is the concept of wellness, which speaks to how buildings impact our mental and physical health. For librarians and their patrons working long hours indoors, there are many aspects of the design that will affect their overall state of mind, physical well-being, productivity, and general happiness. The spatial characteristics that support wellness correlate closely to more universal descriptions of good design, and architects are generally advocates for the notion that great space feels great.

Humans are diurnal and thrive in the light of day. Our cognitive functions, mood, and energy levels are all positively affected by exposure to sunlight. The library, where long hours are spent researching, writing, and studying, needs to support our mind and bodies through access to daylight and views to the outside world. In large institutional buildings, especially when we are renovating an existing library whose vast floor plate was designed principally as a book storage facility, daylight is often a scarce commodity. Your designer will want to share this precious resource with the greatest number of people. We call this "democratizing the light." This will mean organizing open spaces for the greatest number of people at the perimeter where the windows are and bringing enclosed offices, meeting rooms, and workshops inboard, where they will "borrow the daylight" through glass-fronted partitions. This approach requires an adjustment away from the office with a window and a closed door that prioritizes individual privacy and access to daylight over the communal benefit of a daylit floor plate for the greatest number of people. Don't be shy or selfish—share the light. With a good design there will be enough to go around.

Poor air quality makes us lethargic and unproductive at best. At worst, it makes us sick. Air quality is affected by two key factors, the air that comes into the building and what the building does to that air. Resources like the American Institute of Architects' (AIA) red list and Perkins and Will's own Precautionary list represent exhaustive research into the effects that commonly used building materials, including paints, solvents, sealants, flooring, and upholstery, can have on human health. Over time, these effects can range from skin irritations and respiratory ailments to neurological disorders.[2] Conscientious architects and designers will make you and your team aware of potentially hazardous materials and steer the design and specification process toward healthy materials. There is also an increased focus on improving indoor air quality in new and renovated buildings. Many of our library clients express the desire for operable windows to allow fresh air into the work environment. While there is nothing like cracking a window and feeling a breeze, the scale and complexity of large institutional buildings can make this operationally and economically unfeasible. Mechanical systems that make use of direct outside air (DOAS) and heat recovery rather than recirculating stale air with a small percentage of fresh makeup air provide an optimal solution. The air is fresh with high oxygen levels, any impurities are constantly flushed out of the buildings, and the energy used to condition the air is recaptured through a heat recovery system.

Libraries are dependent upon a wide variety of furniture solutions to support the broad range of tasks and behaviors that both librarians and their patrons engage in. Furnishings not only support tasks but are also signifiers of how a space should be used. For instance, a set of high stools at a window ledge suggests a quick touchdown for one or two people; a large round table with light movable chairs suggests a collaborative conversation for an hour or two; an ergonomic task chair at a high-sided carrel suggests solitary focused work. Furniture must work in concert with the scale of spaces and the nature of their finishes to communicate the intended use and support the human body in that use. Ergonomics, the study of how the human body interacts with its environment at rest or in the performance of any task, has evolved to consider new ways of working and the full range of human proportion and ability. The proper selection of furniture with an eye to ergonomic performance, the full range of tasks, and the broadest range of users will go a long way to shaping a culture of inclusion, workplace well-being, and student success.

A critical factor in the comfort level and functionality of a library is the acoustic design. Good acoustics promote focus, calm, and peace of mind, while bad acoustics are simply maddening. Good acoustic design looks at dampening reverberation within spaces as well as mitigating the transmission of sound between spaces. The desired levels of reverberation and separation can be achieved through materials and detailing, but there are also organizational and cultural factors. You may ask your architect a series of questions to this end. Does the plan correctly locate loud spaces relative to spaces requiring quiet? Does the section promote the migration of noise? Do the spatial characteristics and finishes promote lively and therefore noisy behavior? How does the architecture promote a scholarly atmosphere? Acoustics must be considered from the foundations of the building concept up to finest details.

ACCESSIBILITY, EQUITY, AND INCLUSION

The library in the 19th and 20th centuries evolved into a democratic ideal where knowledge could be made equally accessible to all citizens. It is unfortunate that through the late modern period, when so much of the built fabric of our campuses came to be, architectural strategies often revolved around a series of level changes that make these buildings largely inaccessible. Accessibility is often a primary consideration in the retrofitting of late modern libraries from the 1960s and 70s, but the conversation has moved well beyond physical access. Today, architects are committed to the ideal of universal access and view accessibility in a holistic fashion to include all disabilities (physical, visual, auditory, and cognitive) as well as cultural factors that could make an architectural environment more or less inviting to a particular demographic. Recent mass movements such as Me Too and Black Lives Matter have highlighted the degree to which our societal structures can exclude or deprive one demographic while favoring another. Architecture has the power to reflect our society in concrete terms, including our negative and cultural biases. In our recent work on Canadian campuses, we have enjoyed robust consultation with Indigenous stakeholders and, through them, been made aware of the colonial impulses that still drive our architectural strategies. For Indigenous peoples to feel welcome in our designs, we have had to consider new relationships to the natural world, new planning strategies, and new approaches to materiality. This is only one example of the effect that architectural language can have on a particular group. Architects today are confronted with the challenge of creating spaces that offer an equal opportunity and experience to all. This challenge is also extended to you, the client, and is particularly important when planning the programs and supporting spaces that will be offered in the library.

HERITAGE AND ARCHITECTURAL LEGACY

The opportunity to envision, fund, design, and build a new academic library is a rare one, and the vast majority of library systems consider themselves fortunate if they can sponsor a significant addition or renovation. For those of you facing the daunting task of renovating an existing library, you can take comfort in knowing that you are doing the right thing on several fronts. Seen through the lens of sustainability, the most sustainable building is the one you don't build. The embedded energy and capture carbon within an existing structure are significant and will be saved, less material will be disposed of, and less new resources and energy will be consumed. You also have the potential to do the right thing from a cultural perspective. The architecture of an existing library building will always have some form of cultural and historical value. Whether we can see that value or not depends on how much distance, and therefore objectivity, we have from the period in which it was built. The late modernist style referred to as Brutalism is seen on campuses throughout the world due to a global frenzy of campus building in the 1960s and 70s. This particular style of building features massive sculptural forms, extensive use of cast-in-place concrete, articled stair towers and structural frames, and, by today's standards, low levels of natural illumination. These structures are everywhere and, as they enter their sixth decade of hard use, are in need of serious renewal. With their brooding, massive character and inflexible concrete structure, they are often little loved by their owners and users. They are also challenging to rehabilitate. Nevertheless, within this massive crop of buildings (many of them libraries), there are some beautiful and significant pieces of architecture with real potential. Today, architects have come to appreciate the Brutalist legacy and are bringing a new sensitivity to the repositioning of these works. Two recent renovation projects led by our firm; the Wentworth Institute of Technology Schumann Library and Learning Commons and the renovation of the Weldon Library originally by John Andrews at the University of Western Ontario, point to the potential to bring accessibility, sustainability, and humanity to these massive structures. It is my experience that in any library renovation project, many of the shortcomings of the found condition have to do not as much with the original architectural vision as with the damage that has been done by successive generations of piecemeal renovation. I encourage my clients to see the "beauty in the bones" and imagine how the visual and spatial clutter could be removed to expose the positive attributes of the original structure. It is the exception that a library structure from any era has no redeeming qualities, and a thoughtful examination of the existing condition can usually reveal remarkable potential. Work with your architect to understand the real potential of your existing building. This may mean commissioning a master plan that imagines the complete renovation being carried out over time and through multiple projects. This allows client and architect to see the big picture where the existing asset is optimized and to make meaningful contributions to a larger vision one step at a time as funding permits.

Elements of a Partnership: The Role of the Architect and the Role of the Librarian

In this chapter, I have provided my observations regarding the way architects and designers think, the language that they use, and some of the driving preoccupations that they will likely bring to the design of your library space. At this point, I think it will be useful to reflect on roles that both the architect and the client play in the creation of a successful library project. Designers will design the project, and though they will bring their own prior knowledge, experience, and inspiration to the table, they are professionally bound to help you realize your project objectives and aspirations and need your effective participation in the process to succeed. In my profession, we often observe that there is no great design without a great client. What do we mean by this? Invariably it comes down to a productive and mutually inspiring relationship that assumes good communication and clear perspectives and priorities. The client must know what they want and know how to communicate it in terms that the architect can translate into a design. In both the ambition and the communication there must be specificity and commitment. Libraries are programmatically and culturally complex, as they draw on a broad range of users, and achieving clarity of purpose requires a good deal of reflection and hard work both with your architect and before you even meet them.

The Vision: Defining the Ever-Changing Library

What makes designing libraries so exciting for architects is the fact that the typology has evolved constantly through history to reflect different forms of knowledge storage, transfer, and dissemination. The pace of change in the past two decades has been rapidly accelerating to the point that librarians and architects are obliged to define the essence of the library on an almost constant basis. Before a library can be effectively programmed or designed, the definition of its essence needs to be in place. Architects like to call this the Project Vision and amplify its meaning with a set of guiding principles, which in turn are used to measure the success of the evolving design. You may develop a project vision prior to engaging an architect, or you may develop it with them. In either case, it is important to draw upon a broad range of stakeholders, one that represents the full demographic of both users and administrators.

The vision statement must be concise, inspiring, and specific enough to guide while being elastic enough to allow interpretation. Working with our clients at Ryerson University on the Daphne Cockwell Health Sciences Complex, we developed the project vision "Creating Connections for a Healthy City." This simple phrase can be unpacked to explain manifold objectives. "Creating" referred to the project's transformative potential and to the spirit of creativity that the users wanted the building to support. "Connections" spoke to the desire to integrate four previously siloed departments of the health sciences faculty into a shared space and culture, as well as a desire to connect the new facility to the campus population and the campus to the city. "Healthy" referred to the health sciences faculty but also the health of the planet, the surrounding community, and the building occupants, capturing aspirations for high levels of sustainability, wellness, and inclusion. "City" captures the urban character of the campus and a commitment to both integrating the building into the city and creating a supportive public realm. Each word in this simple phrase is important, and these words were derived from a series of inclusive engagement sessions involving the design team, faculty, students, university administration, subject matter experts, and community members. In these engagement sessions, we placed diverse users in groups and had them ideate using a combination of visual listening tools, writing, and reporting back. The common priorities from a diverse set of users quickly rose to the top and influenced the project vision as well as a series of guiding principles for the design on the subjects of sustainability, public realm, accessibility and inclusion, and design excellence. While the vision statement provides a quick overview of the project mission, the guiding principles offer a more detailed set of directions that help the design team and client make decisions and navigate the long road between concept and reality.

In this chapter, I have attempted to provide some insight into the way that architects think, the language that they use, the broad issues that are shaping architecture today, and the particular fascination that libraries hold for all designers. I have also touched on the need to craft a guiding vision for your library project before any meaningful design activities can commence. The success of your library project will be based on an enduring and highly productive relationship, fueled by mutual respect and good communication. The process of design and construction is one that is challenging, long, and complex and, as the details of preparing for and structuring this process are covered elsewhere in this book, I have focused on defining the language that the librarian and the architect can share.

One day, after years of planning and hard work, you and your architect will walk through the doors of a new or transformed library space. You will see thousands of users engage with your shared vision of what a library can be. The conversation that you have shared in shaping the vision and details of the library will be repeated again and again as it transforms into a culture of use. As an architect, I often reflect on what a great responsibility and honor it is to be entrusted with shaping the physical fabric of society. I am certain that most architects share this sentiment and look to their clients as partners in the shaping of a better world. The library is a noble and democratic institution whose spaces and technologies are constantly evolving, but whose mission to bring knowledge to every citizen remains constant. When you engage with an architect to design a new library space, you will be starting a conversation and, perhaps, co-writing a new chapter in the book of the Library.

Notes

1. UN Environment and International Energy Agency, *Towards a Zero-Emission, Efficient, and Resilient Buildings and Construction Sector*, Global Status Report 2017 (Paris: UN Environment and International Energy Agency, 2017).
2. Sumheda M Joshi, "The Sick Building Syndrome," *Indian Journal of Occupational and Environmental Medicine* 12, no. 2 (August 2008): 61–64, https://doi.org/10.4103/0019-5278.43262.

9

CHAPTER NINE

IT'S A TEAM EFFORT

Roles and Responsibilities of Project Team Members

STEPHEN DANTZER

Introduction

Many individuals from various units in the university, working in teams, provide the vision, develop the planning process, and oversee the implementation of a building or renovation project. Each team member in a building project, whether it's a significant renovation, an addition, or a new building, must understand his or her respective roles and obligations in the project and avoid crossing over into areas of other professionals. This chapter will discuss roles and responsibilities and describe key steps in a typical library building project, drawing on experience from the Taylor Family Digital Library project at the University of Calgary, a facility that opened in 2011 and hosted the first Designing Libraries for the 21st Century Conference. The chapter will highlight the relationship between the library and the university's planning, facilities, and project management offices, which are vital partners in any major project. In addition, some key observations on typical project pitfalls will be offered.

Establishing the Need

The concepts discussed within this book guide the library in the development of an overall library master plan for the future, much of which involves moving from a current operating model to a new one. To advance, a key requirement is the establishment of a process to determine, articulate, and then create all of the *physical resources* needed to see the library's plan to fruition. In essence, you will need to identify, clearly describe, and then ultimately seek help in creating the physical environments needed to support your master plan's objectives. In simplest terms, you need to initiate a building project and work with the myriad experts required to see it through. Some key questions are how does the library make this happen, where does the library fit into the building process, and how do we ensure the library's objectives are met?

Resources

Most institutions have resources to assist the library in developing and executing a building project. Universities typically have campus planning, facilities management, and project management professionals on staff who have responsibilities to plan, manage, and optimize use of the physical assets of the institution. These internal experts will play key roles in assisting the library in meeting its objectives. In addition to staff, each institution will have mechanisms to engage external expertise as needed to provide the full complement of professionals required to implement a building project.

For the purposes of our discussion, we will use the term *campus planning* (CP) to describe all those involved in determining the future of the campus. We will use the term *facilities management* (FM) to discuss those managing existing assets, and we will use the term *project management* (PM) to describe those involved in the process of turning plans and ideas into a physical reality.

Let us first discuss the roles that each of the three areas will generally play in the building process.

CAMPUS PLANNING

The university's campus planning teams are typically associated with the future direction of all of the physical resources of the institution. Every institution wants to have a very vibrant and inviting campus, and, to that end, CP at most institutions has created a campus master plan that, among other objectives, outlines what the physical nature of the university will be in the future. Most often, the campus master plan will set out principles and objectives that will shape the desired environment and then seek to describe conceptual aspects that would characterize it. The master plan typically addresses the envisioned feel of the campus, describes what the built form will generally look like, and determines open spaces, pedestrian pathways, transportation corridors, utility corridors, and the interface with any surrounding community. Any library project will likely be developed in the context of the university's master plan and will be significantly shaped by it. Campus master plans are typically conceptual in nature, however, and not often entirely prescriptive. In a building project, CP must therefore interpret the guidance of the master plan during the development of any building design. It is essential that the library develop close and effective relationships with the campus planners to ensure that the objectives of the library are very well understood. Ideally, this needs to occur at the very early stages of the development of the library master plan. Given that CP will likely be the arbiter of the master plan guidelines, it's critical that it be aware and fully onside with the library's objectives so as to ensure the library gains the most advantageous interpretation of the master plan guidelines.

Programming is the first element of a building project that seeks to move broad conceptual space and organizational ideas into a documented form, and this is usually a key resource (either internal or contracted) within CP. As the library establishes a vision and an implementation plan and the need for space to execute the plans becomes apparent, the programming function will begin to articulate the need as a prelude to design work. Programming will begin to describe the kinds of spaces required to house library functions, describe the objectives of the space, estimate the possible size, and seek to determine the optimum relationship between spaces. As programming develops, it will describe in some detail all of the requirements that a building project will have to fulfill to meet the library's master plan. This will also begin to include external matters such as utility services, code requirements, and siting issues (see "Facilities Management" below). Note that the program is not (and should not be) a design per se, inasmuch as it is not an architectural solution. Rather, it is a description of what the architectural design must accomplish and will be used in preliminary estimates of project scope, cost, and complexity.

Space allocation is often an important responsibility of campus planning. Campus buildings are often the largest of any institution's assets. Accordingly, prudent and optimized utilization of space is a key concern on any campus, and typically CP is involved in establishing space utilization standards, which tend to be restrictive and prescriptive. These space standards are often used as a measure of utilization efficiency as well.

Readers are encouraged to consult the website of the Society for College and University Planning: https://www.scup.org. This website has a wealth of information about a range of campus planning issues.

FACILITIES MANAGEMENT

The facilities team is most often seen as the steward of the university's physical assets. Fundamentally, it's the team's job to work in the background to keep everything operating as designed to ensure the orderly functioning of the university. It's relevant to keep in mind that its job has increased in difficulty over the past few decades, as funding pressures have led to an accumulated deferred maintenance liability that shows no signs of being adequately addressed. In addition, increases in public health and safety standards, building codes, and environmental aspirations have made its jobs increasingly complex. FM staff might therefore be forgiven for assuming a somewhat direct and pragmatic approach to making change, and one that has a focus on long-term value and the concept of total cost of ownership.

In its quest for prudent investment in future buildings, FM often develops design standards or guiding documents to shape projects from an infrastructure point of view. It is important for the library to understand what standards exist at its institution. For example, at some locations, there are no architectural standards whatsoever and basically anything goes. As a result, the look and feel of the campus can be very incoherent. On the other hand, at a campus with rigid architectural standards, one must follow them strictly, which imposes constraints on design. Other design standards, applied at a lower level, relate more to the quality and the functionality of the building. They may stipulate the kind of materials that will be used in public spaces, the electrical and mechanical strategy for the institution, and the type and size of maintenance facilities required in each building. While it may seem that librarians need not spend too much time thinking about these initially, they're in the background and will impact cost and may impact functional considerations.

In more recent years, FM has also engaged in addressing environmental and sustainability issues, including whether the institution will pursue LEED or other sanctioned status. Environmental requirements will have impact on material selection, mechanical and electrical strategies, and architectural decisions. Typically, these will drive an increased capital cost, which in the end will be rewarded by reduced operating costs. These are fundamental decisions in a project and should be thoroughly discussed by the project teams. Given that capital projects have finite budgets, investments in infrastructure impact dollars available for the program.

Readers are encouraged to consult the APPA website at https://www.appa.org. This website has a wealth of information about a range of facilities management issues facing institutions.

PROJECT MANAGEMENT

A building project is basically a process that moves something from its current existence to a new physical form. It has a beginning, and it has an end. The process itself has been well studied over the past decades, and an entire body of knowledge has developed around effective steps for ensuring success. Just as you have no doubt engaged a project manager to guide the development of the library plan, a building project must have an overall project manager responsible for establishing the processes that will lead to success, however the library defines it. Depending on the size of the institution, the PM may or may not be a staff person, as often consulting firms are hired on a project-by-project basis.

Generally, the PM will guide all those involved through defined stages of a building project, ideally from the very early discussions onward. It's important that the PM be positioned to ensure that all key elements of a project are properly identified, described, and completed in a transparent and effective manner. It is important to understand that a building project manager does not make project decisions. Rather, they develop a process wherein appropriate information is gathered and presented to appointed decision makers for direction.

Readers are encouraged to consult the website of the Project Management Institute: https://www.pmi.org. This website has a wealth of information about project management strategies.

Developing a Vision

An early and essential step in planning for a new building, a significant renovation, or an addition is for the library to articulate a vision for the physical environments required. It is essential that this vision address the very high-level principles and aspirations of the library. It can be somewhat ethereal in nature, as it should not address solutions in any fashion. Rather, it should attempt to describe the nature of the spaces to be created and how they will work to fulfill the mission statement.

It is critical for the library to create the vision statement in a documented form that can be used to establish buy-in from senior management and the campus community. If the campus community does not agree with the vision of the library at the outset, the project will be challenged continually by various stakeholders.

It is critically important throughout the project to return to the vision document at key decision-making points to assess whether the project is on track to achieve the vision or whether it is drifting off center. The vision document should include indicators of what success will look like at the conclusion of the project.

Defining Leadership

As you move forward from establishing a vision to planning a building project, the programming phase will be initiated to put form to a plan. This will start the assembly of a much broader team of experts, typically much beyond the staff of the library itself.

An important first concept in the project process is that of ownership—Who owns the project? Who will be in the ultimate leadership role, and ultimately who will be responsible for the outcome? While this question seems fundamental in nature, it's often a huge source of confusion, often more so in a collegial environment. If leadership is ambiguous, then the project will either flounder in frustration and indecision or be hijacked by whomever seizes control as a result of an assertive personality or a position of perceived authority. In such instances, leadership changes with the wind and chaos ensues.

To be successful, the leader of the project should be the person who led the development of the library master plan and who developed the vision statements. The head of the library would be the project leader in most instances, as it's critical in all phases of the project that all major decisions be mapped back against the library's vision; no one is better placed to do that than the head of the library. While most aspects of the project will involve teams, committees, external advisors, and solicited and unsolicited advice, one person must have authority to synthesize all of the competing and ofttimes contradictory information and be able to make a decision that will guide the project. It's a tough position, but a necessary one.

Assembling the Team

Of course, none of the above is to suggest the leader works alone. A team of key personnel must be assembled to support leadership and to deal with the thousands of detailed issues that must be addressed. In the past decade particularly, the term *integration* has been emphasized in all aspects of project work. In simplest terms, the idea is to identify early on all of the key players who will be involved in the project from planning to execution. Wherever possible, designated decision makers from each subject area (e.g., library, CP, FM, PM, architects, engineers, constructors, etc.) are identified and introduced to the project early. This allows their expertise to be utilized in developing solutions that are both creative and feasible. Many a project has gone miles down a path of design, only to find out later that there is an engineering obstacle or site constraint that will force everything back to square one. Integrated design seeks to bring all brainpower to the table early, enhancing the creativity of the solutions being brought to the project and increasing the opportunity to manage risks in the early stages.

The library is of course best positioned to assemble the expertise within the library itself. The internal departments of CP, FM, and PM will wish to designate their representatives to the project, and for the most part that may be satisfactory. A key concept to consider, however, is team member fit. While a thorough discussion of team building and team dynamics is beyond the scope of this chapter, suffice it to say that a successful project can be achieved only through a successful team. The project leader and team members must have complete trust in the expertise, commitment, authority, and character of the team players. If a conflict is determined in the early stages, it is imperative to resolve it early and effectively. This can be a most unpleasant exercise indeed, but failure to address the issue will inevitably cause failures in the project process somewhere along the line—well after it is possible to correct in many cases. It is also important to ensure that each departmental representative is empowered to speak and make decisions on behalf of the department they represent.

Assembling the external members of the team—architects, engineers, constructors, and so on—will most likely involve the procurement department of the university and be subject to the institution's procurement policies. The library must assert a key role in this process as well because the dynamic of working with consultants is also of prime importance. Fortunately, most campuses do not seek tenders for external professionals, but rather select consultants through some form of request for proposals (RFP) process. RFPs allow the selection to be based on a wide range of criteria beyond the lowest price. These criteria include experience of the firm, experience of the individual consultants, ability to staff the project in a timely fashion, and perhaps other project-specific issues. Given that the project will depend heavily both on the expertise of each consultant and, perhaps more importantly, on the character of the individuals, it is important that library leaders play a significant role in developing the evaluation criteria within the RFP and also play an integral and direct role in scoring the RFP candidates. Again, project leadership should not be shy in assessing the ability of every candidate to work with the team in an effective and trustworthy fashion.

Developing a Program Document

The vision will guide the development of a program document (see "Campus Planning" above). While many institutions have programming expertise on staff, often it is recognized that programming the library of the 21st century requires a particular kind of expertise and that an outside consultant is needed to create the program document. A consultant with expertise in both planning and working with libraries can be important for bridging the perspectives of the library and the planning and facilities units on campus.

As part of moving the project from a vision to a documented set of requirements, the PM will guide the development of a business case to outline the feasibility of the project. Very high-level cost estimates can be formed based on prior constructions of a similar nature, and the library can begin to assess funding sources available, such as endowments, government grants, and private or corporate donations. At the programming stage, there is an attempt to match the requirements of the library with the resources available to fund the project. As they converge, a project becomes feasible.

Determining what the actual cost of a project will be is sequentially developed over several stages and won't be known until construction documents are out to bid. It is important to understand that at this point, the calculated figures are not a budget; they are high-level estimates only. Many institutions will bring in cost-estimating consultants for this work, and the consultants will definitely want to emphasize that they're estimating a building or renovation project plan that doesn't yet exist.

Developing a Project Charter

A project charter is a rather formal document that articulates in clear and concise terms many key elements needed to ensure the success of the project. It's a critical step in the initiation process and one that is often overlooked or addressed in an incomplete fashion. Elements include (but are not limited to) a thorough outline of the intended project, the team players that have been chosen and their respective roles and authorities, an outline of stakeholders beyond the project team, an outline of probable risks, the budget estimates to date (and their estimated level of accuracy), the funding sources, the estimated schedule, and the project approval structure. The more the charter can list the guiding assumptions and constraints, the better. A professional project manager will be adroit at assisting the project team through the creation of the document, as the Project Management Institute offers excellent guidance.

Drafting the project charter can be a difficult exercise, as it tends to expose any and all ambiguities still existing at the time of creation. Therein lies the power of the document. Resolution of many uncertainties or outstanding controversial issues can and should be done at this early stage. The charter also becomes an excellent mechanism to achieve senior-level approval of the project at the initiation stage, as well as a communication document for stakeholders.

New Building or Renovation

For a large project, often institutions will face the question of whether to extensively renovate the existing library building, and possibly add an extension, or whether to construct an entirely new building. Some may perceive this as an environmental issue in terms of favoring the preservation of the old and reuse of existing materials. Accordingly, there may be some pressure in many institutions to renovate the old building if it can be preserved in some fashion. That said, most old buildings are very inefficient, and their deferred maintenance has accumulated to the point where designers must take the building back to structure to make it viable going forward. The project will then face all of the constraints of trying to create solutions to the vision within an existing structure that may not work (e.g., position of columns, bad spacing of window openings). Many institutions that have renovated existing buildings have found that it was a mistake because the elements that were saved weren't worth the constraints that were imposed upon them by the original building. The renovations end up costing the institution more, at least in terms of functionality, than what the institution has achieved from a preservation perspective.

Ideally the team should go into the project with an open mind in terms of whether renovation or a new building (or a combination) is the optimal solution. The question of whether or not to renovate should be seen as a solution to the demands of the vision and the program and not decided prior to adequate planning.

Design Process

After programming is completed, the project typically enters the schematic design phase, where the designers turn concepts into rudimentary building plans. This phase is conducted as an iterative process where options are explored. Librarians really need to be aware that the schematic design phase is where a lot of decisions are going to be made, guided by the vision and the program. It's at this point that issues like spatial relationships, flexibility of space, and even the distribution of data access around the building are determined.

As design development phases progress, the strategies for mechanical and electrical systems will be developed and many technical questions will be answered. At each iteration, the project progressively moves into a more specific level of detail. At the end of design development, the project will be fully described to the library team and all functional issues should be addressed.

Following approvals of the conceptual design, documents are prepared that allow the project to actually be constructed. This usually requires a great deal of time, and the library should not be surprised by anything that is going into the construction documents. The facilities people will watch the process from a design standards point of view, but the library must watch carefully to ensure that application of the standards is appropriate to the vision and program.

What has been described above is a very linear process, from programming to schematic design to design development to construction documents. In recent years that has sometimes fallen by the wayside, resulting in a more chaotic process whereby various elements of the building design are advanced, and even constructed, out of sequence. The PM should be able to manage the added complexities such that the library inputs and evaluation are not compromised.

Construction

Project management will most likely be responsible for determining the type of construction process that will be used to implement the plans. The library should remain integrated throughout the construction process, however, as there will inevitably be obstacles encountered and issues that arise, solutions to which require quick and effective decision-making. The library must be fully involved to contribute to the decision-making.

Communications Strategy

Classic project management theory describes the importance of identification of stakeholders early in a project's life. Accordingly, primary, secondary, and tertiary stakeholders will each need a different communications strategy. Each group has different needs in terms of what they want to know, different timelines as to how quickly they have to know it, and different methods for how they would like to provide feedback to the project.

Institutions are becoming more open in revealing what the building process is, articulating to stakeholders at each phase what the thinking is, and then inviting input. At an earlier point in time, that input might have been strictly from faculty, but now students, as well as people from surrounding neighborhoods, often are invited to make comments. If the project leaders don't communicate well, people will offer commentary far along in the process, criticizing decisions that were made months ago. It's a point of friction because you can't go back, and yet you have alienated a part of your community that you wish to have on your side.

Developing a communications strategy warrants bringing in communications expertise at the early stages to develop a communications plan. The plan should describe the project, how the teams are going to communicate, what opportunities there will be to provide input, and what will be done with that input. We can't be everything to everybody, but everyone will at least have an opportunity to express an opinion and understand how their input will be taken into account. One of the benefits of the communications plan is that it asserts the decision-making process as well as stipulates who's in charge and who's going to be making the decisions. It can be particularly important for the library staff to understand when the planning office makes decisions and when the library has the authority for making decisions. This will be helpful in a collegial environment and helps build trust between the planning and facilities offices and the library.

In addition to communicating about the planning process, it's also important for the library to communicate what to expect to the staff and to all constituencies who will use the new or renovated facility. When a library will be dramatically different from a traditional space that may have been what the campus was used to, it's important that the campus community understand what the vision of the new or renovated library is and what the advantages will be for them.

Typical Project Pitfalls

Senior management approval: It is important for the library to engage the appropriate senior administrators in the university, such as the provost or president, to endorse key documents and elements of the project as they are developed. This process should start with approval of the vision statement, continue at the end of programming, and happen at each subsequent stage thereafter. There are many examples of institutional projects that advanced way down an unapproved path, only to find they had to begin again or make significant changes.

Estimates versus budget: Where possible, hold off establishing and broadly communicating cost estimates until the project charter stage. Many projects broadcast an estimate of project cost far too early in the process and find out later that it was unrealistic and must be increased. The campus community then believes the project is over budget right from the start. If necessary, communicate cost estimates with a +/– percentage of accuracy attached.

Scope and budget control: In simplest terms, budget control is scope control. Once a project is approved and a budget established, a common pitfall is so-called scope creep. As design proceeds, it's often discovered that space requirements identified in the program may be slightly inadequate or that additional space is required for mechanical spaces or utility rooms. Both will place pressure on the design to expand a little bit by bit. Soon, without proper review, the project has expanded beyond approved scope and a budget overrun becomes inevitable. It is incumbent upon the project team to be vigilant in monitoring such creep. If real pressures are identified, then either scope must be reduced elsewhere or additional funding must be identified and approved immediately.

Market conditions: Construction projects are typically tendered or competitively bid in some fashion. While professional cost estimators may be involved in the project, the ultimate cost of the project will be determined by the construction market. Bids received will be influenced by many factors, including construction company capacity in the local area, material availability or shortages, current labor market, ongoing trade negotiations, and so on. Since approved budgets are often fixed, the library needs to be prepared to make cuts (sometimes significant) to address the budget pressure at this late stage.

Contingency budget: In any project, there can be myriad issues that were not anticipated regardless of the expertise assembled on the team. A generous contingency fund is always needed to address such situations. The need for such funds should not be seen as a failure on anybody's part, but rather a recognition of the dynamic of any project. The amount of the contingency budget required will vary by project. However, both cost estimators and project managers can assist with a recommendation.

Post-construction contingency: Regardless of whether a project is developed and implemented by expert professionals, there will always be issues identified at the completion of the project that were not foreseen. These may be oversights that occurred as early as the programming stage, or changes to a service delivery element that occurred during the many months or years of the project's gestation. Consider creating at the outset a post-construction contingency fund to allow changes to be made at the final stages of a project or even after commissioning.

Create a building service plan early: A new building on campus will bring with it a new set of servicing requirements that should be addressed early. These will include such things as loading dock staffing, mail and parcel delivery, telephone directories, security staffing, food service provision, and so on. Establishing early and effective connections with campus service providers will assist in a smooth opening.

Disruption during construction and renovation: It is a big challenge for a library to maintain services during a renovation. There are going to be many disruptions. Even at the early stages of a project, the library can begin to plan for handling how staff and the user community will be able to move around existing spaces, how services and collections might need to be moved and reorganized for access, and so on.

In addition, librarians need to think about the complexities of operations and moving into a new facility. Ideally, there will be effective facilities managers within the library as well as people at the leadership level who understand the need to put planning time and resources into these areas.

Space standards issues: This can become a point of conflict when standards are imposed in contexts that are different from the ones for which they were created. For example, they may stipulate the maximum size of a meeting room or an office, which might function very well for a building with faculty offices, meeting rooms, and classrooms, but may not be suited to the variety of functions needed in a library building. Those space standards might start to collide with the library's objectives because the space needs of the library are very different from those of the typical academic department. Complicating matters, there are few currently agreed-upon standards for library facilities, and if some antiquated standards exist, that can be worse than having no standards at all. Establishing close relationships with the CP office can be very important in ensuring that guidelines are applied where appropriate, but reinterpreted where necessary in the context of a new library vision.

Conclusion

Library deans and directors who are charged with overseeing a major building project often have a steep learning curve. It is critically important that they and the key library staff appointed to significant roles in the project understand the nature of the building process: which university and outside offices will have critical roles, how teams will be developed, and where decision-making authority lies for various phases of the project. Taking the time to understand the process and to build effective relationships should pay off in achieving the overall vision of the library project.

10

C H A P T E R T E N

THE ROLE OF THE LIBRARIAN ON THE PROJECT TEAM

PATRICK DEATON

Introduction

A major construction project at an academic library can last three to five years, from design through construction. These projects constitute a major investment of resources from the academic library and its home institution. Librarians assigned to the project will spend hundreds of hours in meetings, reviewing the design documents at key stages, and participating in the selection of finishes, furniture, and equipment. Understanding the roles and responsibilities of each team member and knowing when to raise questions and concerns are important tools for effective communication during the project.

This chapter will provide an overview of the typical project organization and schedule milestones, focusing on key opportunities for the library's leadership team to participate in critical decisions during design and construction. Examples from two projects at NC State University Libraries will be referenced. The James B. Hunt Jr. Library, a new building that opened in 2013 on the university's engineering-focused Centennial Campus, is known for its variety of high-tech and study spaces housed within an award-winning architectural design (figure 10.1). The D. H. Hill Jr. Library on the university's main campus consists of four connected buildings constructed between 1952 and 1990 (figure 10.2). A major renovation of two floors was completed in 2020.

fig 10.1

The James B. Hunt Jr. Library. View from the northwest.

(Credit: © Jeff Goldberg/Esto.)

fig 10.2

The D. H. Hill Jr. Library. View from the southwest.

(Credit: Chuck Samuels/NC State University Libraries.)

Project Organization

The typical project team consists of the academic institution (referred to as the owner, or client); the design team of architects, engineers, interior designers, and consultants; the construction team of the general contractor and subcontractors; and vendors for items such as furniture, audiovisual equipment, and signage.

The academic institution is represented by one or more campus departments concerned with design and construction, usually the campus architect's office, along with a second department related to construction or capital project management. During design, the campus architect's office will be concerned with several aspects of the project to ensure that it proceeds into construction while meeting campus guidelines. These aspects include keeping the project on schedule and within budget; ensuring that the project aligns with the campus master plan in terms of use, siting, sustainability, and external appearance; evaluating the appearance and durability of interior finishes and furniture; ensuring that the size of rooms (such as staff offices) comply with campus standards; and configuring formal learning spaces for maximum utilization.

At the beginning of the project, it is customary to form a building committee, whose members will participate in the selection of the design team and make key decisions during design and construction. The building committee usually has representatives from the campus leadership, faculty, staff, and sometimes students. The role of chairperson of the building committee is best filled by someone at the provost level, who can objectively represent the best interests of the university as the owner of the project.

Since many building projects on campus contain classroom and laboratory space that may be used by multiple departments with no clear owner, staff in the campus architect's office may be inclined to think of the library as a tenant rather than as a primary client. This may result in the library representatives being less involved in the project than they should be. To deal with this, library leadership must insist on strong representation on the building committee, including the library dean or director, along with one or more additional librarians. The library representatives should strive to position themselves as a valuable resource on the building committee who can respond quickly when information or decisions are required.

When the project moves into construction, a whole new set of campus staff may take over from the campus architect's office. Their primary concerns will include the safety of the construction site, keeping the project on schedule and within budget, limiting changes, ensuring construction quality, and coordinating the work of vendors who are not working under the general contractor. The general contractor is responsible for the construction of the building and uses both its own employees and the services of many other companies with which it has subcontracted for various aspects of the work. If the general contractor is selected early in the design phase, it can provide valuable insight into constructability issues and market conditions than could affect the project budget and schedule.

As construction begins, it will again be important to stress that the library representatives are key project team members who must be included in meetings, copied on e-mails, and involved in all decisions. There could be some skepticism from campus construction office staff, who are not accustomed to so much involvement, and they may not welcome it. As suggested above with the campus architect's office, presenting the library staff as useful resources who are familiar with the construction process can help to overcome any resistance.

As with any large project, it is vital to have clear communication channels (figure 10.3). Librarians may be surprised to learn that they should have no direct contact with the design team or the construction team outside of meetings; all such communication must first be directed to the project manager in the campus architect's office or construction office to ensure that all team members are in the loop and that no contradictory information is being provided. The library team working on the project should adopt this same model. There should be one person on the library staff who is the single point of contact for all questions during design and construction, and this person should be on the building committee.

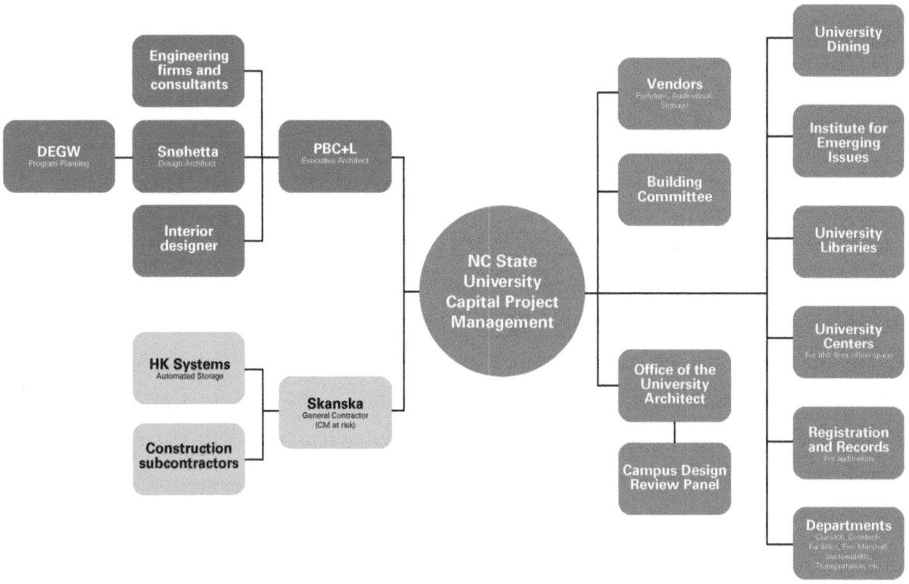

fig 10.3

The project organization chart for the James B. Hunt Jr. Library at NC State University. Although most of the space in the building is for library use, there are several other campus departments housed there. Note how all communication from the libraries to the design team goes through the office of capital project management.

(Credit: Chuck Samuels/NC State University Libraries.)

If no library representatives on the building committee have experience with major construction projects, the library should consider adding a design professional to the library staff, as described in the next section.

Project Expertise

Between the campus architect's office and the building committee, there are likely to be several people involved in the project with years of expertise in the design and construction of major projects on campus. However, none of these people may have recent experience with academic library projects. Some of them may have worked on a library project many years previously and expect that the new project will consist mostly of bookstacks and study carrels. Librarians should be prepared to educate fellow building committee members on the spaces, technologies, and services that make up a modern academic library. Tours of recent examples of similar projects may be helpful.

The building committee should select a lead architectural firm with a strong background in the design of academic libraries, but it can also be valuable to have someone on the library staff with those credentials. If none of the library representatives have had experience with similar projects, the library should consider adding a design professional to the staff.

A staff architect or designer on the staff of an academic library, and not working under the campus architect's office, remains rare. A few large academic and public libraries have embraced this strategy. The main benefit to this approach is that there is someone exclusively representing the library who is familiar with the design and construction process, who can speak the technical language of the design team, and most importantly, who can ensure that the design, construction, and furnishing of the new facility will meet the needs of the library.

The ideal candidate for a staff designer position is an architect or interior designer with extensive recent experience in academic libraries. Previous experience working with the campus architect's office may be beneficial. Depending on the size of the project, a part-time position may be sufficient initially, with the option to switch to a full-time position as the project workload increases or other projects are initiated.

The Project Budget

Before a project can proceed into design and construction, a budget must be established. The total budget for the project should include the costs for construction, furniture, and equipment; design fees; and a robust contingency to cover inflation and unforeseen conditions. The budget may include many other costs, such as moving the library's collection, campus infrastructure improvements to support the new facility, and even seemingly unrelated costs such as the environmental restoration of a stream adjacent to the site. For a renovation project, the budget might also include the abatement of harmful materials such as asbestos and the cost of temporary swing space.

In the early planning stages of the project, a design firm or the campus architect's office may be tasked with developing the initial project budget. One common method to calculate the construction cost is to look at similar recently completed projects, calculate a cost per square foot, and apply that to the estimated size of the new project (the size having already been determined in a building program document). If this method is used, the library staff must look carefully at the projects on which the budget is based to ensure that they are, in fact, equivalent and appropriate comparisons.

If the library's vision for the project includes unusual technology, finishes, or furniture, it is vital that these items be represented accurately in the project budget. During the planning of the James B. Hunt Jr. Library, the initial construction budget was based on a recently completed academic library elsewhere in the state. That building had none of the high-tech spaces planned for the Hunt Library, and as a result the initial budget was far too low to support the vision for the project. In this case, it may have been more useful to look at the cost of other project types that had more in common with the vision for Hunt Library, such as a retail space, museum, or corporate office building.

The Architect Selection Process

Of all the decisions that are made through the duration of the project, there is perhaps no more important decision than the selection of the lead architectural firm. If the most successful academic library projects are a collaboration between architect and client where each is challenged to think creatively, there are many more examples where the architecture firm did not deliver its best work. During the typical selection process, it can be difficult to cut through the marketing hype and get a sense of what it would be like to work with the firm over the next few years. It is essential that library representatives be involved in the selection process from the beginning, including providing input on the selection process itself.

The most common selection method starts with a request for qualifications from architecture firms. This request can be open to any firm or issued to a list of prequalified firms (if this is the case, library representatives should be included in the prequalification process). The qualifications are reviewed and references are checked in order to develop a short list of firms to be interviewed. The interviews are usually conducted by a subgroup of the building committee, and each firm may have no more than 45 minutes or an hour to present its qualifications.

During the interviews, you may see people representing the firm that you will never see again. This includes marketing personnel, employees of the firm who leave or who work on other projects, and consultants who are later switched out for someone else. Therefore, it can be dangerous to base your selection on the strengths or charisma of just one person on the team, even if they are presented as the principal-in-charge.

Given the shortcomings of the usual selection process, there are some alternatives for the effective evaluation of the finalists. For the Hunt Library at NC State, a charrette process (figure 10.4) was used to evaluate the six short-listed firms. Over the course of one weekend on campus, each firm's team began with an initial presentation of their qualifications, worked on a hypothetical design problem with assistance from students from the College of Design, and then presented their proposed solution. This process gave members of the building committee enough time to visit with each of the six firms and get a sense of what it would be like to collaborate with them and how each firm works with owner and student feedback during the design process.

fig 10.4

Members of one of the design teams during the architect selection charrette for the Hunt Library at NC State University, held on campus in November 2007.

(Credit: DSC03602, UA 012.001, Special Collections Research Center, North Carolina State University Libraries, Raleigh, North Carolina.)

Setting up a charrette does require an investment of time and money, as each participating firm is usually paid a fixed amount to compensate for its expenses. If a charrette is not a viable option, consider other creative ways to spend more time with each of the finalists. This might mean a visit to their main office or a tour of one of their recent projects with its lead designer.

Once the architect is selected, they will negotiate a design fee with the campus architect's office. You should ensure that the fee includes any renderings that may be needed for library fundraising or publicity purposes. The library may require several detailed interior renderings that are not in the usual scope of work for either the architect or the campus architect's office. These can be quite expensive if requested later in the design process, so they should be included in the initial contract.

The Design Phases

Once the architecture firm is selected, the project will proceed into the design phases. This may include a programming or predesign phase to develop the building program, select the site on campus, and confirm the budget. When that work is complete, there are three phases that follow: schematic design, design development, and construction documents.

PROGRAMMING OR PREDESIGN PHASE

If the project does include a programming or predesign phase, this is the best time to question even the most basic assumptions about the project. This includes the vision for the building, what will be contained within it, how big it will be, and where it will be located. During this phase of planning for the Hunt Library at NC State, two decisions were made that had an enormous impact on the remainder of the design process. First, a site analysis proposed shifting the building to one side of the monumentally scaled courtyard and changing the footprint of the building from a formal, symmetrical shape to a warped rectangle that reflected and responded to the site conditions (figures 10.5 and 10.6). Second, an analysis of the space requirements within the building proposed housing most of the print collection in an automated storage and retrieval system (nicknamed the bookBot; see figure 10.7) to create more space for other functions such as group study rooms and high-tech collaboration studios. Without these two decisions, the Hunt Library could have been a much less innovative building, and it might have seemed dated on its opening day.

fig 10.5

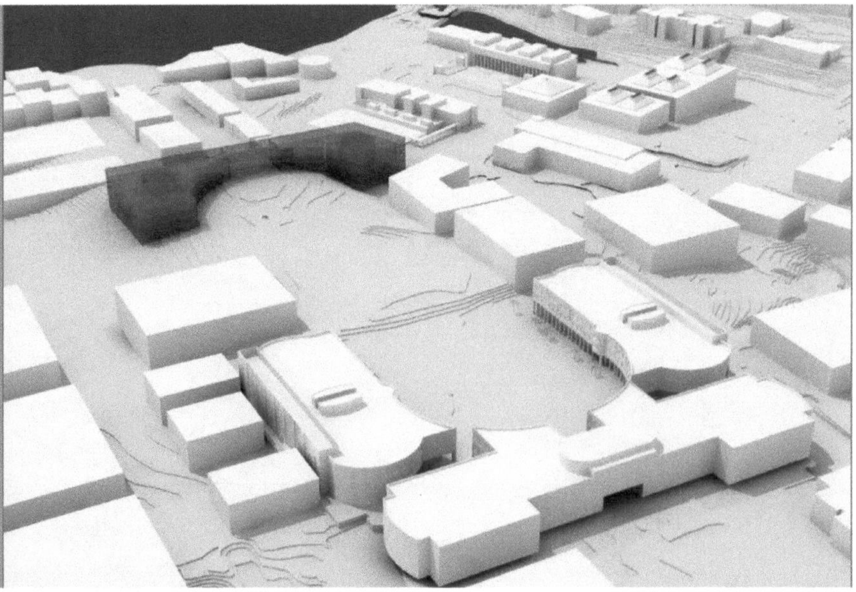

The proposed location and footprint of the Hunt Library provided to the design team at the beginning of the programming and predesign phase.

(Credit: Snøhetta.)

fig 10.6

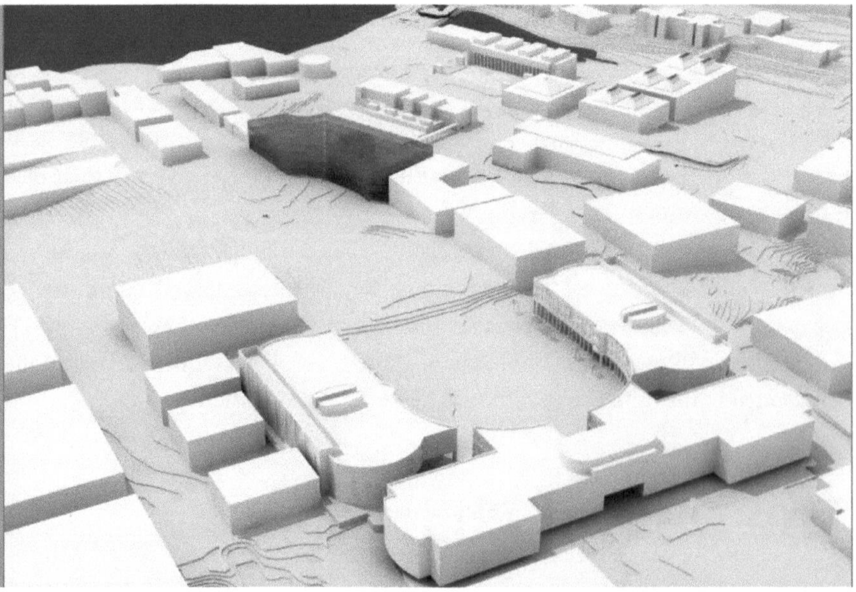

The recommended location and footprint of the Hunt Library from the design team, as shown in the programming and predesign report, October 2008.

(Credit: Snøhetta.)

fig 10.7

The automated storage and retrieval system (bookBot) at Hunt Library, seen from the first-floor lobby.

(Credit: Brent Brafford/NC State University Libraries.)

SCHEMATIC DESIGN PHASE

During the schematic design phase, the basic configuration of the building will be determined. Major components, such as the structural system, HVAC, and elevators, will be evaluated and selected. It is tempting to look at this phase, at the beginning of a much longer design schedule, and think that there will be plenty of time later to make key decisions or to revisit them. This is not the case, and this fact is not always made clear until it is too late.

It is never too early to remind the design team about any key features or components that the library staff have determined must be included in the building to support the overall vision for the project. Examples of this are a large column-free space, high-tech spaces with unusual electrical or HVAC requirements, or a required adjacency between two or more spaces. There should be thorough documentation of these requirements in the building program.

When key decisions are made during the schematic design phase, library staff should make a special effort to ask about potential implications that may not become apparent until later in the design process. During the planning of the Hunt Library, library staff requested raised access floors throughout the building to allow for easier future reconfiguration of electrical, data, and audiovisual wiring in the floor. A seemingly unrelated decision made during schematic design was to use a chilled beam system to cool the building. Only later in the design process was the library staff informed that the decision to use chilled beams meant that the access floor would be installed on only one floor of the new building. The explanation was that a raised access floor is usually paired with an underfloor air distribution system, but chilled beams must be installed in the ceiling. Having raised access floors throughout the building for wiring only (and not air distribution) was deemed unnecessary. Had the full implications of the decision to use chilled beams been discussed, library staff would have asked about other HVAC systems that could utilize underfloor air distribution.

Another example of a key decision during the schematic design phase has to do with access to the bookBot at Hunt Library. To reduce construction costs, none of the five elevators in the building extends down to the main level of the bookBot, excavated 20 feet below the first floor. As built, stairs at each end of the bookBot connect its basement level to the first floor above (figure 10.8), which is problematic when maintenance staff are replacing equipment. Had there been a full discussion of the implications of this cost-saving measure, the library staff would have insisted that the service elevator extend down to the basement level of the bookBot.

fig 10.8

View of the Hunt Library bookBot under construction. In the background at left is one of the two stairways that connects the basement level with the first floor. There is no elevator access.

(Credit: Skanska USA.)

At the end of the schematic design phase, there may be a formal review period for the collection of comments from campus representatives. Whether this happens with your project or not, this is an excellent time to go back to the building program document and compare it with the schematic design. Do not assume that the design team has addressed all the requirements listed in the building program; at this point it has likely spent just a few months working on the project. Does the design reflect what is described in the building program in terms of room sizes, capabilities, and required adjacencies? More importantly, does the design capture your vision for the project? If it does not, you should document your concerns and share them with the building committee before the project proceeds into the design development phase.

DESIGN DEVELOPMENT PHASE

During the design development phase, the schematic plans are refined in detail. Materials and finishes are selected. This phase is the last opportunity to make major changes to the design of the project, usually without the risk of incurring additional design fees or schedule delays. This reality can be difficult to understand when the project schedule shows several more months before construction begins.

The design development phase provides an opportunity to discuss how the building might change over time. The most common example is stack areas being converted to seating areas, but the issue is far more complex than that. Other examples might include a change in furniture layouts that requires additional infrastructure in the floor or walls, staff areas converted to study areas, and even knockout panels in exterior walls for future additions.

When infrastructure such as power, data, and audiovisual wiring is being located during the design development phase, it can be tempting to look at the configuration of rooms and furniture that is planned for the opening day and base all decisions on that layout. But what will the configuration be in five years, or 10 years? No one knows, but you can make some educated guesses and determine locations for additional infrastructure that might be needed in the future. You will likely encounter some resistance; you might even be asked why you need extra infrastructure in the floors, walls, and columns. Be prepared to provide some scenarios based on your own experience or from other libraries.

Two areas of library design that require careful attention during the design development phase are lighting and acoustics. For a large project, consultants in both specialties should be part of the design team. Both lighting and acoustics, if done well, may never be noticed by many occupants of the library. If they are done poorly, library staff will hear many complaints and requests for improvements.

A lighting designer must balance energy efficiency, functional requirements, and aesthetics to create a successful design. During the design development phase, there are many lighting details to address. If there is a lighting control system, discuss who will be able to access and modify the settings. Confirm that there are manual light switches that library staff can use to override the lighting control system, and that all the lamps (light bulbs) in the project will have the same color temperature. Sometimes the lighting designer will specify a fixture with an unusual lamp or a light fixture will be proposed in a location that is difficult to access, such as in a high ceiling or over a stairwell. Campus construction or facilities staff may raise objections to these fixtures and locations. All too often, these objections are overruled by the design team. Library staff should take these objections seriously and ask the design team for options to address the concerns.

Insufficient acoustic separation between rooms such as offices and group study rooms is an invisible problem until the complaints begin. Walls between these rooms must extend to the structure of the roof or floor above, not stop a few inches above the ceiling. For additional acoustic separation, consider the use of sound-masking equipment with individual volume controls for each room.

The design development phase is the appropriate time to engage the design team in discussions about scenario planning, which can be useful in evaluating whether there will be sufficient backup systems in place to protect the building and its contents. Library representatives may be the only members of the project team with the expertise necessary to construct various scenarios. For example, the bookBot at Hunt Library contains a basement floor level that is excavated 20 feet below the first floor. The walls around the bookBot create what contractors call a "bathtub"; if any water accumulated in this area, it would cause major damage to both the bookBot equipment and the collections it contains. During the design development phase, there were extensive library-initiated discussions about scenarios in which the building lost power and water began to accumulate on the floor of the bookBot. Based on these discussions, appropriate backup measures were added to the building. A similar exercise was conducted for the building's main server room, resulting in the addition of a second, independent HVAC system connected to the building's emergency generator.

Whether in design development or another phase, inevitably you will disagree with the architect at some point, and you should not hesitate to voice your concerns. At the Hunt Library, the architects specified a tinted concrete floor for the first and second floors of the building. Both the campus architect's office and facilities staff expressed concern about the long-term appearance and maintenance of the concrete. In addition, library representatives were concerned that the industrial appearance of the concrete did not correspond to their vision for the building. Against the recommendation of the architects, the decision was made to use a terrazzo floor instead of the concrete (figure 10.9). Although more expensive than concrete, the terrazzo is more durable and presents a more refined appearance.

fig 10.9

The terrazzo floor in the second-floor lobby at Hunt Library.

(Credit: © Jeff Goldberg / Esto.)

At the same time, library representatives should be willing to trust in the expertise of the design team. One common criticism an architect might hear from a librarian is that their proposed design has a lot of wasted space—usually when discussing a high-ceilinged space that rises through two or more floors of the building. To the librarian, the space could be reduced to a single-story height to create occupiable floors above. To the architect, there could be several reasons for the space to be taller: to signal its importance, to achieve a pleasing proportion, to serve as an orientation device, and to allow daylight into the center of the building. A successful library design will provide a carefully modulated sequence of spaces that flow together. Some spaces will be mostly functional, and others may have a grander scale, such as the stairway at Hill Library that was extended upward two floors as part of the recent renovation (figures 10.10 and 10.11).

fig 10.10

The stairway at D. H. Hill Jr. Library in 2019, before the renovation.

(Credit: Brent Brafford/NC State University Libraries.)

fig 10.11

The stairway after the renovation.

(Credit: Tzu Chen Photography ©.)

CONSTRUCTION DOCUMENTS PHASE

During the construction documents phase, the design team will generate detailed drawings and specifications that will be used during the bidding and negotiation phase. Although the construction documents phase is usually several months long, most key decisions should have already been made. Any substantial changes made during this phase will usually result in a request for additional fees from the design team and possible schedule implications.

Occasionally something arises during the construction documents phase that must be addressed with a substantial revision. At this point there are two choices: update the construction documents so that the revision is included in the bid documents before the project is bid, or wait and make the revision as part of a change order after the bids are opened. The construction cost for the revision will be greater if it is done as a change order after the bids are opened, as change orders provide an opportunity for the contractor to increase its profit. But if making the revision before the bids are opened would cause a delay in the overall project schedule, there may be no other choice. Either route can also involve negotiating additional fees with the design team.

During the construction documents phase of the Hunt Library, library leadership realized that the design of one area near the main entrance did not match their vision and required a redesign. This area had been described variously as a technology sandbox, genius bar, or gadget point before it was officially named the Technology Showcase (figures 10.12 and 10.13). Despite the best efforts of the architects, the initial version could be mistaken for a traditional service desk, and its technology-embedded casework would make the space difficult to reconfigure. Library representatives raised the issue a few months before the bid opening and expected that it would be addressed before the project went out to bid. Instead, the design team was instructed to address the issue after the bids were opened. This resulted in a substantial change order, along with additional design fees.

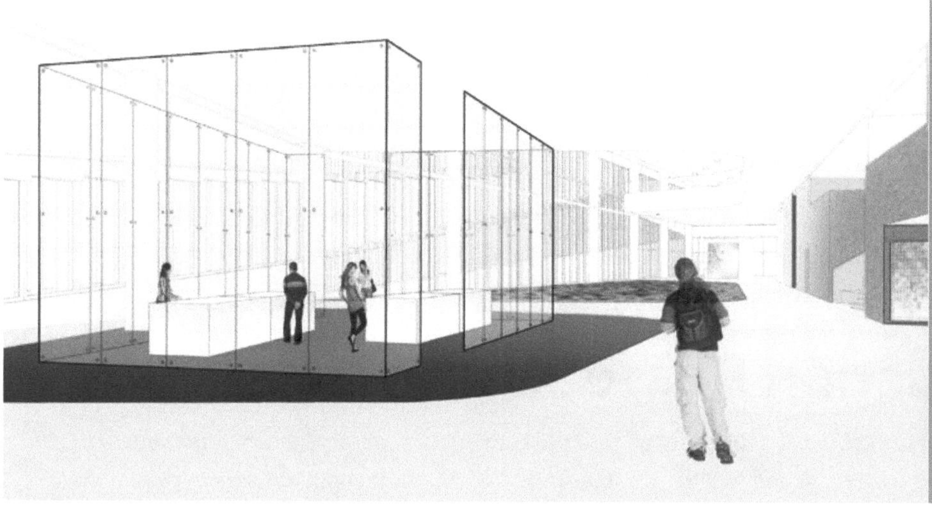

fig 10.12

The Technology Showcase at the Hunt Library. Sketch from the redesign process.

(Credit: Clark Nexsen.)

fig 10.13

The Technology Showcase as completed.

(Credit: © Jeff Goldberg/Esto.)

The Bidding and Negotiation Phase

The bidding and negotiation phase is comparatively short and consists of determining the final construction cost (whether through an open bid process or another project delivery method, such as construction management at risk), and then executing a construction contract. Because the price of construction materials can be volatile, it is common to use construction bid alternates to provide some budget flexibility. Bid alternates are documented and priced separately from the base bid so that the owner can include any or all of them in the contract, as their budget allows. Examples of common bid alternates include upgraded finishes, the upfit of an otherwise unfinished space, or a particular component or technology that can be easily priced. It is important to review the list of bid alternates before the project goes out to bid. If anything listed as a bid alternate is a must-have for the library, that item should be included in the base bid instead.

If the construction bids are higher than the construction budget, a process called value engineering (VE) may be used. The VE process involves asking the design team and general contractor to develop a list of suggestions that would lower the cost of the building. An approximate savings is assigned to each item, and then the list is reviewed. Depending on the amount of savings required, the VE process can include anything from lower-grade finishes to eliminating a wing or floor of the building. The VE process can seem rushed, and it can derail a project that has otherwise gone smoothly. Depending on which VE items are accepted, all the careful work done throughout the design phase can be obliterated. Some of the suggestions mentioned in the design phases listed above are applicable when reviewing the list of VE items: check the item against the building program, understand the implications of accepting the item, and ensure that the future reconfiguration of the building is not compromised.

The Construction Phase

After many months of meetings, the project will finally go into the construction phase. Library representatives should attend weekly construction meetings and visit the site frequently. You may hear about unforeseen conditions involving something discovered during excavation, or during demolition for a renovation project. The project's budget contingency is used to cover these items.

During your walkthroughs of the construction site, inevitably you will see something that you would like to change. Minor changes, such as adding power outlets, are to be expected and can be accommodated as part of a change order. More substantial changes, such as moving a wall, can involve additional design fees along with possible schedule delays; your request may be denied to keep the project on schedule and within budget.

For every major component in the building, the vendor submits "shop drawings" that detail the material or product and how it is to be installed. The shop drawings are reviewed by the design team, with input from the owner, typically using an online platform managed by the general contractor. Although it can be tedious, library representatives should review many of these submittals such as door hardware, floor and wall finishes, elevators, floorboxes, light fixtures, interior glass walls, signage, and any specialized equipment. The general contractor is responsible for tracking the shop drawing submittals and revisions to them; the final approved versions should be downloaded for the library's project archive.

Project Closeout and Commissioning

Between the completion of construction and opening to the public, many activities are underway. The general contractor is assembling record drawings, operations and maintenance manuals, and warranty information as part of the project closeout process. The delivery, installation, and inspection of furniture, audiovisual equipment, computing, and collections must be coordinated. The timeline for this phase of the project should allow for damaged or otherwise incorrect items to be replaced before opening day if they are critical to operations. Be prepared for 5 to 10 percent of furniture orders to arrive damaged or not as specified. If the project contains major audiovisual installations, the programming work for these might extend well beyond opening day.

Commissioning agents (usually engineers) may be working on site during this time to ensure that the building's HVAC and other systems are meeting performance specifications. Their work may continue beyond opening day as part of a post-occupancy evaluation of the building's energy use and occupant comfort.

Conclusion

While many of the suggestions and warnings in this chapter focus on what can go wrong during a library building project, they should not dissuade anyone from seizing the opportunity to participate in one. Serving as a member of the project team can be a once-in-a-lifetime experience in a librarian's career. Few work assignments are as rewarding as seeing the design, construction, and furnishing of an important building that includes your input and ideas.

11

CHAPTER ELEVEN

THE DESIGNER'S LENS

How Architects See Space

JANETTE BLACKBURN and CAROLE WEDGE

A library is a community's portal to knowledge and culture and is a means to exercise curiosity and exploration. Within this framework, the purpose and meaning of each library and its places are distinct.

Just as a city or campus tells the story of its history, so too does the library, as a compendium of experiences, collections, and buildings that each reflect a specific time and place. You could say that together these elements create a library of libraries. As a physical place, the library embraces a dual initiative. It must celebrate these stories of the past and yet project a contemporary and forward-looking identity that is relevant to its constituents.

What makes your library unique? What are the stories that your library should tell?

As library designers, we begin each project by exploring these two essential questions with our clients and their stakeholder communities.

Row Together

Time after time, we have witnessed the journey a library building project takes as it is buffeted by changes in leadership, priorities, finances, and social contexts. The statistics of the 2019 ALA Building Project Survey of 22 academic libraries that have recently been built or renovated paint a picture that matches our own experience:

The average and median library building project durations were 7.5 and 8.7 years, respectively. Remarkably, six years of the total project duration were spent on planning, funding, and design before the start of construction.

The project journey is a long paddle, and the librarian must be prepared to act as explorer, guide, and translator. The project river can run fast and then become still. There will be rapids to navigate. To tame the current and reach the destination, each member of the crew (librarian, architect, contractor, and a host of other project cohorts) must row together.

Through the course of a project, the design team must learn from the library how the spaces they create will be inhabited and experienced. In turn, the library will benefit from understanding how designers see space and marry it to the project goals.

Beginning Tenets

How do designers see space? Each designer is likely to have a slightly different approach. Shepley Bulfinch adheres to these foundational ideas as a framework for the environments we design and build.

LONG LIFE, LOOSE FIT

Shaping versatile space that can flex as needs evolve is a core tenet of designing enduring architecture. As we seek to position libraries for the future, each project presents unique considerations that must be analyzed and addressed. Designers can evaluate a proposed solution's ability to adapt to change by working with the library to model multiple use scenarios. These can be tested through design studies and through physical prototypes that are mocked up in existing spaces.

Architects and designers view the attributes of flexibility and versatility along a continuum and apply the library's specific needs and operations to the development of the design (figure 11.1). The flexibility of a design becomes tangible and achievable when time, resources, and needs are more specifically defined.

fig 11.1

The contemporary library, unlike its predecessors, must accommodate an increasingly diverse range of resources and programs. This calls for a dynamic spatial model planned to accommodate emerging, blending, and evolving modes of use throughout the life of the building.

(Credit: Shepley Bulfinch.)

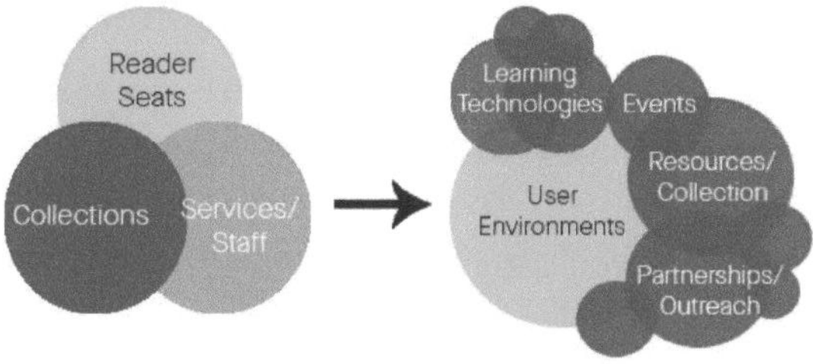

Flexibility Terminology

Fixed
Who implements: Construction team
Time: Significant, requires time and funding of renovation to change
Mobility: Not mobile
Funding: Significant

Adaptable
Who implements: Campus staff or furniture construction team
Time: Planned, but potentially with short turnaround (new furniture, remove static shelfing, etc.)
Mobility: Not a factor
Funding: Likely required

Evolving
Who implements: Library staff
Time: Quick, could be change in protocol, actual space does not change
Mobility: Things may move or change but by staff, not users
Funding: Likely limited or no funding required

Flexible
Who implements: Users
Time: Instantaneous
Mobility: Very mobile—casters especially important
Funding: No funding required for change

INCLUSIVE AND WELCOMING TO ALL

The library—and its positioning within a campus or civic realm—offers the opportunity to bring people together across all disciplines, providing a common resource for both scholarship and social interaction that is an inviting meeting place, welcoming to all.

Universal accessibility, including easy-to-navigate entrances, vertical movement systems, and signage that is ADA compliant are essential, as are inclusive program components such as mother's rooms, family restrooms, and all-gender facilities. These design components are essential, but they are not enough.

In library design, inclusivity is an intrinsic part of the design parti *(in architectural parlance, a parti is the designer's overall guiding idea for a design).*

The project designers must understand the inherent diversity of library communities and the necessity for the library to provide a broad range of spaces—from public and active to private and contemplative—so that the collective and the individual can each find their place to explore and discover.

To promote inclusivity, libraries must be easy to access and use. Strong features of orientation, such as a central stair and sight lines between floors, help users navigate from place to place and read the building without help from guides or signs (figure 11.2). Visual cues can distinguish quiet study from active collaborative space. Creating zones within the library—microenvironments or neighborhoods—for varying types of activities will help make the library more understandable.

fig 11.2

At Salem State University's Berry Library, the central stair provides a clear pathway and visual connections to major areas of the library providing ease of orientation and intuitive navigation.

(Credit: Photo by Chuck Choi.)

HEALTHY PEOPLE I HEALTHY PLANET

People and environment are linked. In our design process, we introduce sustainable design strategies by beginning with four themes that integrate sustainable thinking about the environment with concerns for human health and well-being: energy, culture, comfort, and nourishment. Today's designers are placing sustainable strategies—such as switching to alternative energy sources, minimizing embodied carbon, and realizing a net zero or climate positive building systems—at the forefront of design conversations. To implement these strategies, projects require a design that closely integrates site and building systems early in the process.

A library is an ideal platform to make visible a community's sustainable values and to deploy them as educational tools. To develop sustainable and healthy design approaches, architects and designers must work with the library community to develop a deep understanding of place, climate, history, and culture. With this understanding established, the designer can identify opportunities to incorporate human-scale environments, protect and restore local habitat, and develop climate and site appropriate approaches that maximize access to daylight and nature and use local materials and building methods.

fig 11.3

Shaded outdoor reading porches (left) and diffuse daylight (right) contribute to healthy and sustainable environments in the LEED Platinum-certified Austin Central Library.

(Credit. Photos by Nic Lehoux.)

INSIDE OUT I OUTSIDE IN

Where the image of a library building may seduce the eye, it is how the space is fully experienced—from the inside to the outside—that defines its continuing worth. With this in mind, we approach the library as a network of interconnected destinations that are meaningful places cherished by their users. Designers make a library intelligible and navigable through the way they shape form, bring in light, and frame views.

Library buildings are rooted in a place. They belong to a culture and community. They must both react to and contribute to their context—from the outside to the inside. In our library work, we map the flow of campus and neighborhood movement so that our design responds to established view corridors and pathways. We shape library entrances to naturally capture interest and lead to welcoming, active spaces that provide points of orientation. We then extend that flow through the interior of the building, creating organizational structure and clarity.

Through this approach, designers can position the library to reinforce larger campus or urban planning strategies and enliven adjacent exterior space with sustainable site solutions that will contribute to responsible development.

Shaping Library Architecture

To design a library is one of the richest creative endeavors that an architect can undertake. Aspirations are high. Influencers are many. A framework is needed to harness a wide range of built responses. Shepley Bulfinch uses themes such as Lanterns and Soldiers, Earth and Sky, and Clarity to shape the design exploration process and arrive at a lasting spatial experience that is fitting for the library's purpose and story.

LANTERNS AND SOLDIERS

Building in a city or campus milieu can be approached by defining the role of each structure as a *soldier* or a *lantern*. A *soldier* is a background building. It provides a simple canvas as a backdrop to other activities or places. Its physical form is quiet and simple. Its materials are equally quiet and often match or complement the surrounding buildings.

A *lantern* is a building that establishes identity and meaning. It acts as a beacon that draws people in. Dynamic forms, evocative views from exterior to interior, and striking material palettes distinguish the library as a memorable destination that is in lively and suitable conversation with its surrounding context.

We see libraries as lanterns. They act as welcoming portals that create a sense of belonging and a place to exercise curiosity and exploration.

EARTH AND SKY

The architectural construct of Earth and Sky refers to how a building makes connections to its surroundings, both immediate and more distant. How do people engage with the library building as it meets the ground? Designers are concerned with how the library sits on its site because this is where its collections and programs meet the world. Through plazas, porches, and picture windows, the library can mediate with its surroundings to create multiple moments for entry and gathering.

Today's library is positioned as permeable—often with multiple entrances and ways of engaging with the campus or neighborhood outside its doors. Planning for multiple ways in, out, and through a library involves rethinking service models, library use zones, and security. Entrances and interior spaces may be designed to be adaptable—changing use and levels of access depending on time of day, season, or events. The benefit of these endeavors is a building that is welcoming and embraced rather than strict and authoritative.

How the library meets the sky can set the stage for broader connections across the city or campus. The library is a place to gain perspective. Destinations such as penthouse reading rooms and roof gardens that gracefully top the library provide its inhabitants with opportunities to orient themselves to their surroundings. These far and near places offer both prospect and refuge and provide the library with settings for inspiration and reflection that are removed from the daily buzz of the working library.

CLARITY

The primary design objective of clarity can find its way into a library project in a myriad of ways. Clarity in navigation and movement will render the facility legible to visitors. Clarity of access and entry will improve the library's relationship to the city or campus.

If the library has been built over time, how can it clarify the conversation among its pieces? Will clarity of aesthetic expression allow each architectural era to shine? What type of Gordian knots have developed from an organic accretion of library spaces through the years?

Consider the spatial experience of the library as a journey of discovery, with a sequence of destinations and special places, nooks and crannies, and other surprises along the way (figure 11.4). The journey is as important as the destination because it is in this movement that visitors to the library will explore, discover new resources and opportunities, be inspired, make connections with others, and uncover spaces that feed the soul.

fig 11.4

A series of destinations, both grand and intimate, are linked together to provide clarity and a diverse spatial experience in Firestone Library, Princeton University.

(Credits: Photos by Robert Benson [left], Jeremy Bittermann [right].)

The Spatial Experience

Well-designed spaces enhance life experiences. They provide people with energy, they support their need to communicate with others, and they supply inspiration and comfort. Our design approach is rooted in an understanding of the physical and psychological impacts of elements of scale, lighting, color, views, and spatial organization, as well as indoor air quality and healthy materials. These elements can positively impact one's behavior, mood, and ability to collaborate or concentrate.

A successful interior environment represents its community. Scale is an important characteristic. For instance, in the design of a grand reading room, the inclusion of human-scale components creates a welcoming place that is inspiring yet not intimidating. In our designs, we focus on a few key qualities that evoke the desired experience of inhabiting the space: for instance, approachable, energetic, and transformable. We use these qualities to guide interior design decisions such as bold use of color, material palette, and lighting.

All successful spaces, and especially libraries, possess a sense of place, that ephemeral feeling you get when a place just feels good to be in, a place people will love and take care of for generations to come. There is no one way to create a sense of place. It will be born from distinctive cultural values, history, and the library's context, and it will reflect where a civilization has been and the vision of where it will want to go. Embrace a project process that reexamines cultural values and accepted institutional history to create an inclusive and progressive library that is truly welcoming to all.

Defining Design

Designers are skilled, and often most adept, at communicating their ideas through visual imagery. In our work, we seek to define aesthetic approaches through text as well as visual imagery to communicate intent to a diverse audience and enhance the dialogue with our clients and their project stakeholders. Here, we have illustrated a few terms that may be used to define a design strategy with narrative and examples from our work. Which of these terms will resonate with you and your cohorts?

RESPONSIVE

Responsive design is first and foremost based on the idea that a building be responsive to, and in a dialogue with, its context. Materials, climate, light, orientation, and views are considered as the design is developed so that the resulting architecture celebrates the richness and character of its context and by doing so reinforces a unique sense of place (figure 11.5).

fig 11.5

The Goldstein Library at Ringling College exemplifies how the outward expression of a building is a response to the multiple external influences acting on it. Located in Sarasota, Florida, the building has a design that responds to its environment with a building form and exterior spaces that open to and engage with the adjacent bayou. Deeply recessed windows, architectural shading systems, and light-colored cladding help mitigate solar gain in Sarasota's subtropical climate.

(Credit: Photo by Jeremy Bittermann.)

LAYERED

In a layered building composition or organization, the designer suspends revealing everything about the building at once, but rather creates layers, transitions, and thresholds through which its contents gradually unfold (figure 11.6).

fig 11.6

Here again at Ringling College, the building is organized around sight lines that draw you in from the street, pull you through its interior spaces, and then release you out onto the reading terrace, located on the rooftop to the left in this image.

(Credit. Photo by Jeremy Bittermann.)

LEGIBLE

A legible building reveals its spatial organization and relationship to its surroundings through a composition that conveys visual hierarchy, purpose, order, and legibility. New is differentiated from existing, entrances and destinations within the building are articulated in building form and facades, and climatic responses are revealed in the building design (figure 11.7).

fig 11.7

At Virginia Commonwealth University's Cabell Library, the expansion presents a contrasting conversation with the existing building. The new vertically patterned glass facade echoes the precast fins of the 1970s era library. A giant portico draws you in, its columns supporting the grand reading room destination on the top floor,

(Credits: Photo by Robert Benson [top]. Graphic courtesy of Shepley Bulfinch [bottom].)

TRANSPARENT

Transparency as a design element makes the library more welcoming and engaged with the surrounding community. Transparent components of the library's facade provide moments when one can see into the depth of the building. From dusk onward, libraries can become community beacons (figure 11.8). Windows designed to frame views to the interior communicate the library's vibrancy. During the day, active spaces carefully positioned at the library's perimeter foster engagement with exterior surroundings.

fig 11.8

With this example of the Brody Learning Commons at John Hopkins University, you can see deep into an interior landscape. Lit up at night, it is a beacon. During the day, the transparent facade lets daylight penetrate deep into the space.

(Credit: Photo by Anton Grassl.)

The Librarian's Role: What to Pack for the Building Design Journey

BALANCE

The library design process relies on equal parts of vision and nuance. Both the librarian and the library designer must balance these two attributes in their project roles. The architect strives to balance a grand vision with details that make it uniquely meaningful and technically and operationally suitable. The librarian brings a vision responsive to strategic goals, as well as a discerning lens that provides context that will meet today's needs as it frames future growth.

DATA

Although data plays an essential role in defining library space needs, the past is not a prologue for the newly envisioned library. We are mindful that all the usage data you have is about the building today. It must be evaluated in the context of your new vision and its likely impact on building use. Both the library and the design team play a role in defining space and use metrics for your new library space. As a starting point, the library needs to provide the design team with an accurate collections inventory, metrics on library use, and capacity targets for staff work space and for library, event, and instructional spaces. Architects and designers provide guidance based on experience and on contemporary library-use benchmarks. They then work in close consultation with librarians to jointly interpret the meaning of current use metrics and the institution's vision for growth and change.

VOICE AND GLUE

The library team is not only the clear voice of the institution's vision, context, and data. It must also serve the essential and at times unglamorous role of being the project "glue." The project is best served when the library team members are active leaders in bringing stakeholders together, raising questions that nobody else is asking, and testing the design's adaptability to future scenarios.

Aligning Vision and Funding

MAKING THE CASE

To fund a library project, close collaboration between institutional leadership, the library, and the design team is needed. Each entity has a vital role. As institutions set capital priorities and identify potential funding sources, the library's voice is essential to demonstrating the value of its collections and services to the intellectual and social health of its community. To complete the picture, the design team will express the potential for transformation with evocative language and imagery that defines the physical space and the experiences it embodies. We frequently participate with libraries and their communities to demonstrate need and to raise excitement about potential.

In many instances, the project vision in the voice of the library is the focal point of the fundraising campaign. The library needs to communicate its needs and funding requests in language that supports the community's capital priorities. Although rehabilitation of worn-out spaces and updates to staff work areas are essential to maintaining a vibrant library, these themes by themselves are infrequently cited as fundraising goals. In the results of the ALA Building Project survey, the most successful capital campaign themes were improvement of patron services and the patron experience.

MANAGING BUDGET UNCERTAINTY

No matter how well funded, every library project must balance priorities and trade-offs to remain on budget. Budget uncertainties are an inevitable part of the process and must be professionally and proactively managed to ultimately arrive at a project scope and budget that are aligned.

Construction cost estimating for a complex project such as a library is an inexact science. Contractors, construction managers, owners, and the design team work together to identify areas of scope uncertainty and carry allowances until the parameters can be clarified. Based on data from similar projects, the design team will also recommend appropriate design contingencies to be carried in the cost estimate during each design phase. These best practices apply to all complex building projects. For libraries, there are additional cost considerations to be considered, including

- planning for continuing library operations during construction
- impact of construction phasing on cost and library operations
- costs of library shelving systems
- costs of collections moving, storage, and reshelving
- higher furniture and technology costs as a percentage of the total budget than for simpler building types.

Estimating should begin early in the process, with rough order-of-magnitude cost modeling based on building size and applicable benchmark projects to verify the program scope and vision with the agreed budget. Once the project is underway, each project phase should proceed only after a documented set of budget and scope alignment strategies has been agreed upon by the cost estimator, the owner, the library, and the design team.

VALUE FOR INVESTMENT

A library is built to last for generations, so the design approach should prioritize building investments that will afford future flexibility and enduring quality and avoid the elimination of a potentially necessary element. These investments have consistently risen to the top:

- scale and proportions that are pleasing and versatile
- adequate ceiling heights and space for services above the ceiling
- flexible structural system
- adaptable technology approach
- clear spatial organization and paths of movement
- sustainable, healthy, energy-efficient building systems and material choices
- ample access to daylight
- high-quality artificial lighting

Ultimately, every project will require prioritization of expenditures. By focusing on value for investment and attending to these essential components, architects and designers create library buildings that will remain relevant and adaptable far into the future.

Open Minds

The most successful library design projects are fueled by intellectual rigor and curiosity. At Shepley Bulfinch, we do not bring a predetermined architectural aesthetic, but rather a process of exploration and dialogue to arrive at the greatest and most beautiful solution. We create contemporary buildings, with the belief that architecture should represent the era in which it is created with flexibility for future growth.

In an open-minded design process, architects and designers begin their process by asking questions, such as

- *How does the library relate to its surroundings—the larger campus, neighborhood, or city?*
- *Where should we place the main entrance, or how can the building be legible if there are several points of entry?*
- *How can we resolve the functional knots of the building and simultaneously project a clear expression?*

How do architects and designers see libraries, and how do they define the success of a library building? We see libraries as records of a society's evolution through time, with their success shown through the vibrant use by their community. Libraries are places where both the historical and the contemporary coexist.

For us, a library building project presents the opportunity to reflect on an institution's known history and forgotten stories. We explore in a way that gracefully and respectfully adds to the architectural conversation, all the while developing a contemporary design language that expresses the library's vision for a forward-looking facility.

Design inquiry begins with an open mind. Let there be nuance.

Acknowledgment

We would like to thank our design colleagues at Shepley Bulfinch, whose creative insights on the nature and power of design are woven throughout this chapter and made real in our built projects.

Reference

Blackburn, Janette S. "Techniques to Imagine, Fund, and Build the Academic Library of Your Dreams." *Johns Hopkins University Press, Libraries and the Academy* 20, no. 1 (2020): 7–14.

IV

SECTION IV

KEY ISSUES IN PLANNING

12

CHAPTER TWELVE

FROM COLLECTIONS TO CONNECTIONS

Rethinking the Print Presence and Use of Space on Campus

LEONORA CREMA

If there is a single trend underlying the evolution of library design in recent years, it is the move from collection-centered to more active, people-centered space. Library space plans that at one time simply had to demonstrate collection growth to gain support must now address new questions, some of which have been articulated in library design thinking, some of which are newly emerging.

Today with online resources predominating, most use of library collections has "left the building"; access is no longer tied to a physical place. Decades of weeding and storing print collections have allowed libraries to redeploy bookstack spaces to other purposes. Storage approaches, even for the largest research libraries, are now being planned in the context of state and provincial, regional, or national arrangements. Purchased print collections shared commonly by many libraries are giving way to more specialization, stronger focus on unique and archival collections, and growing investments in open access resources.[1]

With print no longer at the center of what libraries do, it is time squarely to address print's value in space planning. What is the continuing case for print, and what are the new opportunities to consider? What new configurations and delivery means are possible? In what ways, beyond support for research and learning, can print advance the institutional mission?

To ask such questions is emphatically not to diminish the importance of print in library space. Rather, it is to demonstrate that where libraries continue dedicating space to print, they are making nuanced choices tied to their digital strategy, aligned with disciplinary and institutional interests, and ensuring sustainable stewardship of the scholarly record. Further, it is to reconceive the notion of print from a static presence to one that is more mobile and social, consciously curated to enliven new opportunities for community connection.

Below, drawing on examples from the University of British Columbia Library (at the UBC Vancouver campus) and libraries more broadly, we will consider these issues and their implications for the next stages of academic library design.

Let's Talk Numbers: Yours, Mine, and Ours

Launched by an inspiring vision of what it can become, at some point every library building project comes down to a set of choices based on numbers. One of these inevitably is "How much print do we need?" Decades of professional practice have equipped librarians for discussions about the quality and use of print collections on their campus. Where libraries sometimes fall short is in addressing the fuller range of planning factors and data employed by their colleges and universities in capital decision-making. Librarians who are unprepared for this may find unexpected factors coming to bear on their plans or fail to communicate in ways that effectively advance their case.

Academic libraries today find themselves with more collection data and analytics than ever before. Strategy in many has shifted from offsetting growth through sporadic storage moves, to managing the collection footprint at a steady state, to ongoing rightsizing based on multiple factors. Current assessment methods tend to look more holistically at the collection in its context, considering local teaching and research strengths, the holdings of partner libraries, the full-text offerings of vendors, and a growing range of buy-on-demand services.[2]

Libraries also now have decades of circulation data at their disposal, leading many to store or downsize print collections. Here the work of Sustainable Collection Services, now part of the global library cooperative OCLC, has been especially valuable, showing through analysis of hundreds of academic libraries that in most, 50 percent of stack space is occupied by books that are rarely or never used.[3] Architectural firms specializing in libraries have seen dramatic reductions in the percentage of central library space allocated to collections.[4] In its triennial faculty surveys, Ithaka S+R tracks researchers' growing comfort with journal e-versions and their waning belief that their local library must retain print versions, provided they have been preserved elsewhere.[5]

> One question that the wary or reluctant sometimes ask is, "What will our physical library collection look like if most of our new material is digitized and most of the older material is only accessible in collaborative storage facilities located miles away?"
>
> **Suzanne M. Ward**
> *Rightsizing the Academic Library Collection*

Organizations including OCLC and the Council on Library and Information Resources (CLIR), along with many regional consortia, have taken insightful approaches to questions of collection overlap among institutions, building collaborative management capacity, and assessing collection strength at the network level. In a landmark study, Courant and Nielsen demonstrate the lower life cycle costs of housing print in high-density storage versus open stacks,[6] from which Malpas extrapolates what a large research library spends to locally retain collections that have already been preserved in digital form.[7] These and similar studies, along with increasingly robust delivery methods and the added storage benefits of security and preservation, have brought new professional considerations to bear on managing print collections.

But in practice, most librarians know that these findings go only so far in working with faculty and student stakeholders at the center of this transition. As one astute librarian observes, "Aggregate data are interesting, but for any individual library, what matters most is the trend at that particular institution."[8] There will always be a desire to understand the local context, particularly disciplinary differences, and here more qualitative approaches are needed.

TO STORE OR NOT TO STORE: STILL THE QUESTION

In 2005, as part of a major new building project, the UBC Library had implemented an automated storage and retrieval system (ASRS) in response to crowded stacks, the need to upgrade environmental conditions for its collections, and the need to make new uses of its public space. Any move to storage removes an in-person browsing experience and, though concerns were expressed across disciplines, the assurance of on-site, rapid delivery from the ASRS in the new building satisfied most constituents. Nearly a decade later, in 2014, the library embarked on a next wave of storage planning, targeting the lowest-use collections and those with stable digital versions, where the contemplated solution was a Harvard-style facility away from the campus core (figure 12.1). The success of the ASRS and growth of online content in the intervening years had established a trajectory to more storage, and borrowing had continued to decline across disciplines. Born-digital media and virtual browsing had emerged, and with them forms of research inquiry impossible to replicate in print. Still, questions persisted whether scholars had embraced these trends, and a more finely calibrated approach was needed.

fig 12.1

High-density storage two ways: UBC's automated storage retrieval system (top) and Library PARC, its Harvard-style storage facility.

(Photo Credits: UBC Library Communications [top]; Brandon Crema [bottom].)

The library accomplished this through a survey, notifying academic departments about its new plans for storage, and inviting them to take part in consultations that would assist in developing a collections location strategy. The library e-mailed all 102 departments about these issues, with the offer to hold in-person interviews. Of these, 35 agreed to an interview, 27 responded but declined an interview, and 40 did not respond after three separate contacts over four months. Their lack of response was taken to signify no major concern. Of those interviewed, 21 expressed no great concern about moving more collections to storage, and 11 expressed some concern, though supporting the initiative overall. Only three of the departments expressed major issues, with a marked difference between arts-based faculties, and science faculties who had little trouble allowing older materials to be stored. The most common questions concerned delivery timelines, access to the new facility, and criteria for selecting items for storage. Browsability remained a pronounced concern, but substantially less than when the ASRS facility was being planned. Another concern was the quality of digital copies being delivered from storage: for example, the loss of fine details or textures in scanned art books or the readability of scanned music scores. Catalog findability of some formats, records lacking metadata, and ability of storage retrieval staff to read non-Roman scripts were also among the issues mentioned.

The survey report addressed these in its recommendations, ensuring the ability to customize storage criteria according to discipline-specific concerns. Delivery standards were established and ongoing avenues for faculty input were identified, including the ability to request the return of stored items to branch libraries based on anticipated use. Collections management standards for discoverability of items in storage, including enhanced catalog records for some formats, and exploration of virtual alternatives to browsing were also among the recommendations.

Through this deeper dialogue, the library was able to fine-tune approaches for those disciplines where print remains the essential medium.[9] But critically, based on the same local evidence, it was also able to advance in its storage planning, having established that "most departments were satisfied with a service model that has stored materials electronically delivered to the user, or physically delivered to a central campus library location by next business day."[10]

CAMPUS METRICS

Another area where libraries must be active interlocutors is with those who are developing campus plans and metrics to inform capital decisions. Campus planning offices typically keep comparative data on enrollments, Net Assignable Square Feet-Metres (NASF-M) space allocations by faculty and function, age and condition of facilities, maintenance overheads, student seating, and standards for space utilization. The library collection often appears as a separate line item in these schemata, subject to special consideration. But as libraries take a more programmatic approach to space, like other academic departments, this will decreasingly be the case. A related issue is the growing amount of study space being built elsewhere on campus. Revitalized student spaces are often cornerstones of faculties' capital plans, and libraries that were formerly the primary providers of study space may start seeing new lines in the planning matrix tracking this growth.[11] Though libraries can rightly make the case for their long hours and central, secure, and technology-infused space, in fact similar student spaces are proliferating across campus. This development may lessen the library's own case for expanding or retaining physical space.

Provosts are perhaps the most influential stakeholders for space use on campus. In this they may be responding to a range of internal factors: student needs, institutional strategies, growth in faculties and service departments, donor interests, and more. But they will also be responding to external imperatives for space utilization, including their standing relative to peer comparators. In publicly funded institutions particularly, leadership must be attuned to these comparators. Some may find government funding for future building projects jeopardized if utilization benchmarks are not met. In urban-adjacent campuses, a variety of land use and density standards may also come to bear.

Librarians who are not conversant with how these standards apply will be missing key information driving decision-making. They must be knowledgeable about how their institutions use such metrics, and ideally be members of any campus-wide committees with capital oversight. Ultimately it will be in these terms and these venues where the library's building plan can falter, or where it can instead seize opportunities aligned with the institutional mission.

SHARED PRINT

Another important area for libraries to engage in conversations on campus is shared print—that is, libraries collaborating to manage their print holdings and reenvision them as part of a broader "collective collection."[12] Considering how long the shared print movement has existed, and despite some resounding successes in recent years, many libraries have been slow to adopt this as a fully articulated or resourced strategy.[13] Nor have they always conveyed the issues and costs to campus leadership. The considerations here can be complex. For research libraries, serving local clientele but also acting as keepers of record, the questions extend to who are our trusted partners in retention, what are the resource commitments, and what prospectively to acquire. For their institutions, shared print funding agreements can raise questions about transferring funds to peer competitors (not always understood) rather than paying content vendors (established model). Questions of ownership must be addressed when collections are relocated and not stored in place. And though libraries themselves may be moving beyond collection size as a quality determinant, the perception that size matters persists in faculty and student recruitment, accreditation, and institutional ranking systems.

> The future of print collections is shared. Embedding shared print within the lifecycle of library collections promotes equity of access, enriches the scholarly record, and increases opportunity for research and teaching.
>
> **California Digital Library,**
> *Center for Research Libraries, and HathiTrust Collaborative Vision*

As part of its case-making for UBC's newest storage facility, the library ensured it was engaging leadership with these issues. It outlined the space optimization and preservation benefits of shared print, pointing to a partnership it had recently joined through the Council of Prairie and Pacific University Libraries, to an emerging Canada-wide shared print movement, and to established models in the US.[14] It confirmed the stable nature of these agreements, spanning decades and within networks of long-standing partners. It described growing synergies among shared print programs to expand and diversify holdings and preserve digital surrogates. Today, as these programs have matured, libraries can point to many success stories showing that distributed stewardship is viable, durable, and cost-effective. The recent COVID experience, in which the collaboratively created collection of digitized books, HathiTrust, allowed libraries to rapidly redirect from locally held to networked holdings, has been a shining example of payoff from these sustained, multi-institutional investments.

Print Unbound, Redux

Assuming print continues to be a significant part of the library's offerings, a next question becomes how and where to situate it in public space. Unlike earlier days, the collection as a monolith occupying some central space has broken down in favor of active zones, usually near the entry, with the bulk of collections on other floors signaling a transition to quieter, contemplative space. Even many bookless libraries have retained some print presence as a visual cue. But with print no longer the core organizing factor, many new design possibilities arise.

One helpful concept of recent years is collection as service. Among other things, this suggests the collection is not a stand-alone entity, but something more amenable to the convenience and location of the user. For the print circulating collection, this raises new questions about physical access and delivery with implications for library design. Like most libraries, UBC has introduced self-serve circulation functions, motivated by the ability to free staff for more complex inquiries and allow users to manage items at their convenience. At some libraries, the coupling of book RFIDs with self-checkout has enabled more flexible foyer design and decreased the impression of service desk staff as a security presence. Other approaches have included book dispensers or retrievals placed in stand-alone book lockers, pre-signed out to users and accessible 24-7.

These changes enable a fulfillment delivery model, rather than direct stack access. A recent variation on the fulfillment model is curbside pickup, an amenity that in some libraries will persist beyond the pandemic as a walk-up or drive-by service.[15] Delivery physically or to the desktop has become commonplace as more collections are sourced from off-site or from adjacent ASRS-type systems. Drawing on other lessons from the pandemic, libraries should move toward decommissioning the course reserve collection, traditionally housed next to a service desk so readings can be supervised. Considering students' frustration vying for limited copies and the convenience of online access, librarians should work with faculty "to imagine higher education with fully digital e-reserves and a commitment to born-digital, zero- or low-cost learning materials" that have no continuing claim on space.[16]

Cumulatively the effect has been library entries being less control points for the circulating collection and enabling more free-form interaction of staff, users, and technology within space. Many libraries today have moved away from the imposing service desk and the controls it implies, in favor of more guide-on-the-side kiosks, or casual expert bars. Perhaps the most important new design possibility enabled by this is more permeability between indoor and outdoor space. As circulating collections occupy less space, are monitored through sophisticated sensor systems, or delivered to users, every outdoor egress does not need to be fenced off for security purposes.[17] Programming that can seamlessly move between indoor and outdoor space is particularly appealing, combining for example the outdoor performance of a play with an indoor discussion group. Biophilic design benefits can be realized by adjoining gardens, porches, and patios.[18] Even in extreme climates, prospects for libraries to incorporate exterior spaces increasingly in their design await.

Staff space, too, once decoupled physically from the collection, is likely to take on new aspects. Like most libraries, UBC has experimented with distributed staffing, whether this be librarians embedded in faculty and departmental spaces, roving among sites, or in storefronts designed to reach new audiences such as the downtown community. Pop-up presences have become common as ways for libraries to act as rapid responders, trialing and delivering new services. Though the topic is beyond the scope of this chapter, we are clearly at a moment of discovering the fuller possibilities of a distributed library presence, with library staff engaging in powerful new ways.

SHOWCASING NEW ROLES

Another role for print is signposting the library as enabler of print-to-digital workflows. We know that more and more, as content is mediated through code and computation, "library collections and services must be positioned as infrastructure that is no longer defined by physical, intellectual, or even directly human-oriented pursuits but, rather, extends into virtual, digital, and even machine learning and AI research modes."[19] Even so, physical texts, images, and other artifacts will persist, and students and scholars will need to incorporate them into their work. In their native form these materials are not machine-actionable. But today libraries, along with museums, offer sophisticated reproduction equipment with the ability to convert material objects to digital, and, through services such as 3D printing and makerspaces, render digital back to material.

Among the strategies in a thoughtful 2017 white paper on the future of print collections, Arizona State University librarians suggest taking an "open kitchen" approach to showing users work done behind the scenes to make information accessible, such as putting conservation, book repair, or technology innovation on display.[20] Several building

> [T]he time for favoring one medium over another has passed; for the foreseeable future, digital and print materials will co-exist in academic library spaces. Libraries have the opportunity, then, to adapt spaces and collections to remove obstacles to access and enable the interplay of the physical and digital, leveraging print volumes so that our users can build literacy skills with confidence.
>
> **McAllister and Adams**
> *Designing a Bright Future for Print Collections*

projects of the past decade have achieved this: the Joe and Rika Mansueto Library, opened in 2011 at the University of Chicago, is a striking example of an openly viewable preservation lab housed in stunning architecture. A further evolution of ASU's open stacks program involves redesigning stacks to serve as showcases and enlisting students and scholars in curation of print collections around thematic interests, featured texts, or other programming designed to create an engaging, interactive experience.[21] One can further envision multimedia collections animating historic reading rooms, or infused throughout stack space via touch screens and spot-directed sound, activated through beacon technology.[22] Digital browsing walls, such as those increasingly used in museums (figure 12.2), take these technologies to the next level, allowing groups of users to browse and capture digital objects on mobile devices in a shared experience. All signal to users that they have entered a space where the physical and digital seamlessly interact, the library being the venue that reveals these possibilities.

fig 12.2

Browsing the interactive ArtLens Wall at the Cleveland Museum of Art.

(Photo Credit: Flickr Museums and the Web CC BY-SA 2.0 Museums and Digital Strategy Today–American Alliance of Museums [https://www.aam-us.org/2017/07/10/museums-and-digital-strategy-today/].)

At UBC, exposing the library's emergent expertise in these areas has been a conscious design goal. It led to locating offices for a new institutional repository in a high-traffic space to showcase the library's role curating and disseminating digital works. When the time came to establish its research commons, the library ensured this new space was located prominently in an open, glass-walled site immediately below offices of the president and other senior officers of the university. One feature was an informal presentation area fronting the space, designed with potential to showcase and celebrate launches of new faculty works. This reflects the notion of the book as a "final exhibition"[23] object, leading a predominantly digital life before and after publication, but for which the tangible item retains important social significance. This kind of space can also potentially support the new, community-involved processes by which authors are creating works, ranging from book sprints to edit-a-thons. One could extend this to the roles libraries now play in publishing, including launching open textbooks being produced on campus. Open educational works are not by their nature bound to the institution, but their displayed existence is a powerful statement to the local ethos and investment that has made them possible.

Enter the Social Collection

One of the important trends currently in the academy is the move to new forms of public engagement. Today many research institutions are seeking to connect the work of scholars with the wider public and promote community knowledge exchange. Teaching institutions, too, are seeking ever-wider reach with programs geared toward economic and social impact. Libraries are often natural partners in these efforts.

For many libraries, opportunities for societal connection lie in their unique collections and archives, valued not just for artifactual, learning, or research uses, but also as venues for engaging new audiences. More and more, libraries are dedicating spaces to their unique holdings, supporting them with curation platforms, online programming, community documentarians, research internships, and other means. At one of the world's oldest libraries, Bodley's librarian, Richard Ovenden, has powerfully described an evolving vision of collections as primarily serving scholarship to "collections as community conduits."[24] The Bodleian Libraries' spaces speak to this. Any visitor will be immediately struck by the contrast between the Old Schools Quadrangle, where doors to the scholarly societies face inward in cloistered contemplation, and the Weston Library, a bustling exhibition site across the high street. Programming takes this to new levels. Ovenden describes how the libraries' expanded program of exhibits, events, and curation inviting community participants has diversified its relationships and celebrated achievements from Oxford's civic past. He stresses that at a time when public institutions are coming under question, universities and libraries must push their boundaries to engage communities in more meaningful ways. Few libraries may possess such majestic collections and spaces. But the power of this approach is that every community—old or new, large or small—has its own unique history and character. And so every library has its opportunities for partnership and cocreation with its community.

COMMUNITY ENGAGED SPACE: THE IRVING K. BARBER LEARNING CENTRE

Opened in 2008, the Irving K. Barber Learning Centre at UBC (figure 12.3) was a catalyzing force for the library and the university to renew their focus on community. Though the Learning Centre was rich with new spaces for students and campus partners, the strength of its vision was its reach beyond campus and the recognition that learning is a lifelong endeavor, mutually engaged in with the university's communities. Signature to the building were newly prominent archival and special collections, a showcase for the region's heritage and creative culture. The building itself sits at a campus crossroads and has several front doors—one leading to a new student center and alumni center, one to the historic core of campus, and one to a transit hub linking with the city. The rooms within are named for British Columbia communities, featuring creative and cultural works commissioned by local artists, signifying what Amy Brunvand has described as "a re-localized information space that curates, preserves, and tells a story about a specific place."[25] Furnishings are comfortable, flexible, and social. From the outset, programming included public lectures, events, and webcasting. Event spaces, visual displays, and exhibit cases abound, not just

fig 12.3

The Irving K. Barber Learning Centre: a facility dedicated to the intellectual, social, cultural, and economic development of the people of British Columbia.

(Photo Credit: Leonora Crema.)

for library offerings, but for a range of student-, faculty-, and community-created works. From its first days the Learning Centre has offered BC History Digitization grants, a program that helps local archives and historical societies throughout the province digitize their collections either in situ, or with support from the library's digitization center. The program was recently expanded in partnership with the BC Electronic Library Network (BC ELN) to support digitizing of unique collections throughout the provincial GLAM sector.[26]

The Learning Centre spurred new thinking across the library about how collections could be curated with community in mind. This was not limited to special collections but included the general collection itself. It was recognized that academic library collections serve many purposes in the life of the individual: the same core text for a first-year literature class can also be a source of recreation and personal enrichment. In 2010, this led the library to extend outreach to a growing on-campus residential community in market housing, for whom the university wanted to ensure the appropriate range of civic services. The relatively small size of this population at the time, under 10,000 residents, made investing in a new branch of the local public library unlikely, and the university library did not itself have sufficient funds to create a popular reading collection. A related question was the extent to which students and faculty members could benefit from such a collection. After the library surveyed the academic and community-based populations, both were found to have significant leisure reading needs.

These were fulfilled not by new acquisitions, but rather by drawing upon the existing collection to curate a new popular reading collection, branded as Great Reads (figure 12.4). At the main humanities and social sciences library, this was spatially instantiated with a grand new fireplace (figure 12.5) and lounge seating signaling welcome and relaxation, flanked by display shelving. Great Reads proved to be wildly popular with students and drew in new community users, driving up circulation on what were thought to be retired collections. In perhaps the most surprising survey finding, when respondents were asked to recommend titles for the Great Reads program, 81 percent of their recommendations were already held by UBC.[27] The program has since been distributed to other branches in the system, a successful example of how collections reconceived through the lens of community engagement, enabled by space, can take on new life.

fig 12.4

The Great Reads collection at the Walter C. Koerner Library.

(Credits: UBC Library [left]; Martin Dee [right].)

fig 12.5

The Walter C. Koerner Library foyer features a welcoming hearth flanked by the Great Reads collection.

(Photo credit: Martin Dee.)

REFLECTING UPON KNOWLEDGE SYSTEMS

Another way academic libraries can use legacy collections toward new ends is by examining assumptions about systems of knowledge themselves. There is today growing awareness of how lacking in diversity many library collections are, including their methods of description and discovery.[28] Moreover, any approach to organizing them based on past circulation tends to enshrine

> traditional perspectives and risks losing more diverse cultural perspectives. Sensitivity to emerging voices means considering how our holdings are displayed. It is not enough to merely include historically marginalized voices and perspectives in our collections: We need to display them within the open stacks alongside traditionally privileged voices.[29]

Among Canada's universities, there has been recognition of the decades-long history of exclusion of Indigenous peoples and their perspectives from higher education. At UBC, several spatial efforts have been made to address this. Among these, opened in 1993, was the First Nations Longhouse, a magnificent intellectual, social, spiritual, and cultural hub for Indigenous students attending UBC. Opened more recently, in 2018, the Indian Residential School History and Dialogue Centre (IRSHDC) is designed as a place of respite and support for residential school Survivors and their families, where legacies of this devastating part of Canada's history can be critically examined and understood.

Also among these is the X̱wi7x̱wa Library, allied with the First Nations Longhouse and a branch of the library system reflecting Indigenous approaches to teaching, learning, and research. All too often, biases based on settler systems of knowledge appear within academic libraries' collections, not just in the textual matter, but also in the naming and classification systems that to this day are colonial characterizations of Indigenous cultures. In recent years, one of X̱wi7x̱wa Library's signature initiatives has been reclassifying its collections, using the Brian Deer system in place of the Library of Congress system (figure 12.6). Kahnawake Mohawk librarian Brian Deer was one of Canada's first Indigenous librarians and in the 1970s created this system to describe Indigenous materials and "arrange items together on the shelves in a way that better reflects relationships from an Indigenous worldview."[30] X̱wi7x̱wa Library has reclassified its holdings using this system, distinguishing them from the library's other holdings, and has supported other libraries that are also seeking ways of decolonizing their collections.

In this way, we can see how the collection can in a sense stand alongside itself, in an act of reckoning, as both evidence of an exclusionary past and testament to a more inclusive future. One can imagine many such opportunities to consider legacy collections in this self-reflective light, at once questioning the systems that have created them, while illuminating the way to more insightful, respectful approaches.

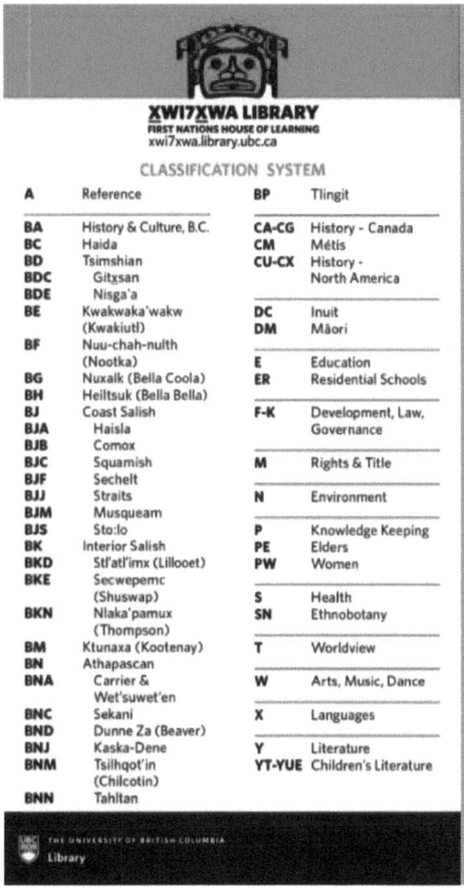

X̱WI7X̱WA LIBRARY
FIRST NATIONS HOUSE OF LEARNING
xwi7xwa.library.ubc.ca

CLASSIFICATION SYSTEM

A	Reference
BA	History & Culture, B.C.
BC	Haida
BD	Tsimshian
BDC	Gitxsan
BDE	Nisga'a
BE	Kwakwaka'wakw (Kwakiutl)
BF	Nuu-chah-nulth (Nootka)
BG	Nuxalk (Bella Coola)
BH	Heiltsuk (Bella Bella)
BJ	Coast Salish
BJA	Haisla
BJB	Comox
BJC	Squamish
BJF	Sechelt
BJJ	Straits
BJM	Musqueam
BJS	Sto:lo
BK	Interior Salish
BKD	Stl'atl'imx (Lillooet)
BKE	Secwepemc (Shuswap)
BKN	Nlaka'pamux (Thompson)
BM	Ktunaxa (Kootenay)
BN	Athapascan
BNA	Carrier & Wet'suwet'en
BNC	Sekani
BND	Dunne Za (Beaver)
BNJ	Kaska-Dene
BNM	Tsilhqot'in (Chilcotin)
BNN	Tahltan

BP	Tlingit
CA-CG	History - Canada
CM	Métis
CU-CX	History - North America
DC	Inuit
DM	Māori
E	Education
ER	Residential Schools
F-K	Development, Law, Governance
M	Rights & Title
N	Environment
P	Knowledge Keeping
PE	Elders
PW	Women
S	Health
SN	Ethnobotany
T	Worldview
W	Arts, Music, Dance
X	Languages
Y	Literature
YT-YUE	Children's Literature

THE UNIVERSITY OF BRITISH COLUMBIA
Library

fig 12.6

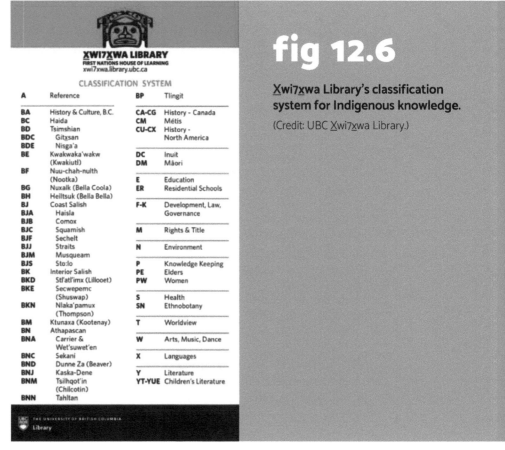

X̱wi7x̱wa Library's classification system for Indigenous knowledge.
(Credit: UBC X̱wi7x̱wa Library.)

Every Book Its Community

The great collection and its grand reading room are icons of academic culture. For many of us they remain sources of pride and monuments to human inquiry. That the grand reading room still resonates in modern library design is remarkable, even as the rest of the building shape-shifts, showing the wondrous adaptability of libraries and their uses. But more and more, for many reasons, space for vast and growing book collections on campus can no longer be assured. We can no longer keep building wider walls around them or equate expanse with impact. We can now entrust more of these legacies to a networked space and manage them within a collective collection where they can have maximum visibility and value.

The engagement-centered library has come into being, and with it we can reconceive print collections in their fuller potential. By asking "Who is the community?" for a work, we open new prospects for connectedness and cocreation with diverse audiences, learning from them the deeper lessons the past has to tell us. And by our doing so, the library space becomes a more expansive one, measured not only by its collections but by the connections they bring.

References

Sources for quotations featured in this chapter: Suzanne M. Ward, *Rightsizing the Academic Library Collection* (Chicago: ALA Editions, 2015), 32; Greg Eow, Mike Furlough, and Günter Waibel, "CDL, CRL, & HathiTrust Collaboration for Shared Print Infrastructure," June 2020, quoted in Alison Wohlers, "CDL, CRL, & HathiTrust Collaboration for Shared Print Infrastructure," announcement, July 1, 2020, California Digital Library, https://cdlib.org/cdlinfo/2020/07/01/cdl-crl-hathitrust-collaboration-for-shared-print-infrastructure; Lorrie McAllister and John Henry Adams, "Designing a Bright Future for Print Collections," *Against the Grain* 30, no. 3 (June 2018): article 13, p. 2, https://doi.org/10.7771/2380-176X.8242.

Notes

1. Specialization of both collections and services will grow as academic libraries evolve "on different vectors, influenced by the increasingly different needs of the types of universities or colleges they support." (Constance Malpas, Roger Schonfeld, Rona Stein, Lorcan Dempsey, and Deanna Marcum, *University Futures, Library Futures: Aligning Library Strategies with Institutional Directions* [Dublin, OH: OCLC Research, 2018], 10, https://doi.org/10.25333/WS5K-DD86.)
2. Madeline M. Kelly offers an excellent framework in *The Complete Collections Assessment Manual: A Holistic Approach* (Chicago: ALA-Neal Schuman, 2021).
3. Rick Lugg notes that "in most of our libraries 50% of the shelves are occupied by books that have not circulated in more than 10 years." (Rick Lugg, J. Cory Tucker, and Chris Sugnet, "Library Collaboration and the Changing Environment: An Interview with Rick Lugg, R2 Consulting," *Collaborative Librarianship* 2, no. 1 (2010): article 4, https://digitalcommons.du.edu/collaborativelibrarianship/vol2/iss1/4.) A further SCS Monographs Index study of 179 US academic libraries comprising over 70 million volumes found that on average, 41 percent of books had never circulated. (Rick Lugg, "Benchmarking Print Book Collections: A Beginning," *Next* [blog], May 10, 2016, OCLC, https://blog.oclc.org/next/benchmarking-print/.)
4. Architects at Shepley Bulfinch cite reductions from about 50 percent of space allocated to collections in mid-20th-century libraries, down to 10 to 15 percent in more contemporary buildings. (Janette Blackburn and Kelly Brubaker, "Collaborating for a Successful Master Plan—Art or Science?" in *Library Design for the 21st Century: Collaborative Strategies to Ensure Success*, ed. Diane Koen and Traci Engle Lesneski [Berlin/Munich: DeGruyter Saur, 2019], 10.)
5. Ross Housewright, Roger C. Schonfeld, and Kate Wulfson, *Ithaka S+R US Faculty Survey 2012* (New York: Ithaka S+R, April 8, 2013), 30, https://doi.org/10.18665/sr.22502. In figures 11 and 12, scholars across disciplines express decreasing agreement with the statement "Regardless of how reliable and safe electronic collections of journals may be, it will always be crucial for my college or university library to maintain

hard-copy collections of journals," but higher percentages agree that "some libraries" should maintain hard-copy equivalents, suggesting their support for shared stewardship.

6. The authors cite annual costs of keeping a book as $4.26 for open stack versus $0.86 for high-density storage, calculated in 2009 US dollars. (Paul N. Courant and Matthew "Buzzy" Nielsen, "On the Cost of Keeping a Book," in *The Idea of Order: Transforming Research Collections for 21st Century Scholarship*, CLIR Publication no. 147 [Washington, DC: Council on Library and Information Resources, June 2010], 91.)
7. Constance Malpas uses the University of Minnesota example, with the library annually spending from $1 million to $5 million to retain local copies of content preserved digitally in HathiTrust ("Reconfiguring Academic Library Collections: Stewardship, Sustainability, and Shared Infrastructure" [presentation, University of Minnesota, February 24, 2011], https://www.oclc.org/content/dam/research/presentations/malpas/umtc2011.pdf.)
8. Rick Anderson, "Less Than Meets the Eye: Print Book Use Is Falling Faster in Research Libraries," *Scholarly Kitchen* (blog), August 21, 2017, https://scholarlykitchen.sspnet.org/2017/08/21/less-meets-eye-print-book-use-falling-faster-research-libraries/.
9. Many studies of format preferences by discipline are available, tracking the evolution of digital use in both research and teaching. See, for example, Joe C. Clark, Jonathan Sauceda, and Sheridan Stormes, "Faculty Format Preferences in the Performing Arts: A Multi-institutional Study," *College and Research Libraries* 80, no. 4 (2019), https://crl.acrl.org/index.php/crl/article/view/17394/19173.
10. Jo Anne Newyear-Ramirez, *Library PARC, Collections Location Strategy and Campus Consultation: Report and Recommendations for Movement of Collections* (Vancouver: University of British Columbia Library, December 2014), 7, https://about.library.ubc.ca/files/2013/02/PARC_ConsultationReport_Summary.pdf.
11. As an example, in 2016, Ontario's universities began tracking study space in faculties distinct from study space provided by libraries. (Committee on Space Standards and Reporting, *2016–17 Inventory of Physical Facilities of Ontario Universities* [Toronto: Council of Ontario Universities, June 2018], 6, https://cou.ca/reports/2016-17-inventory-of-physical-facilities-of-ontario-universities/.)
12. Though the concept has long existed, the term *collective collection* was popularized in Lorcan Dempsey, Brian Lavoie, and Constance Malpas with Lynn Silipigni Connaway, Roger C. Schonfeld, J. D. Shipengrover, and Günter Waibel, "The Emergence of the Collective Collection: Analyzing Aggregate Print Library Holdings," in *Understanding the Collective Collection: Towards a System-wide Perspective on Library Print Collections* (Dublin, OH: OCLC Research, 2013), 1–5.
13. In a recent survey, library respondents who do not take part in shared print cited ongoing costs, one-time costs, and insufficient staff resources as top barriers to participation, suggesting many still have not incorporated this into their organizational priorities. (Reported in Susan Stearns, Heather Weltin, Allison Wohlers and Amy Wood, "Inclusive Models to Sustain Shared Print and the Future of Print Collections" [presentation, ACRL 2021, virtual conference, April 13–16, 2021].)
14. For more on Canada's shared print strategy, see Canadian Association of Research Libraries and Libraries and Archives Canada/Bibliothèque et Archives Canada Working Group, *Final Report of the Canadian Collective Print Strategy Working Group* (Canadian Association of Research Libraries and Libraries and Archives Canada/Bibliothèque et Archives Canada, September 2020), https://www.carl-abrc.ca/wp-content/uploads/2020/09/CCPSWG_final_report_EN.pdf.
15. Architect Peter Bolek notes how some libraries that introduced curbside pickup during the pandemic are now, due to its popularity, seeking ways to incorporate it in future building plans. ("Boundless Libraries: Future-Forward Design and Uses," Designing for a Flexible Future, webinar, LJ & SLJ Professional Development, May 19, 2021, libraryjournal.com/event/designing-for-the-flexible-future#program.)
16. Steven Bell, "Farewell Print Textbook Reserves: A COVID-19 Change to Embrace," *EDUCAUSE Review*, January 14, 2021, https://er.educause.edu/articles/2021/1/farewell-print-textbook-reserves-a-covid-19-change-to-embrace.
17. A library's rare and special collections are, of course, materials for which stringent high-security measures must continue to be made.
18. With their strong programming emphasis, public libraries have long recognized the possibilities of outdoor space. A compelling recent example is the Carol Stream Public Library's use of adjacent parking lots and parks, along with conversion of unused grounds into a welcoming 2,400-square-foot patio at grade, complete with gazebo stage, flexible seating, and Wi-Fi. (Susan Westgate and Mary Clemens, "Boundless Libraries: Maximizing Outdoor Spaces," Designing for a Flexible Future, webinar, LJ & SLJ Professional Development, May 12, 2021, libraryjournal.com/event/designing-for-the-flexible-future#program.)

19. Darby Orcutt, Hilary Davis, and Greg Raschke, "Collections as Platform: Synthesizing Content, Computation, and Capacity," in *EDUCAUSE Review*, August 10, 2020: 60, https://er.educause.edu/articles/2020/8/collections-as-platform-synthesizing-content-computation-and-capacity.
20. Jim O'Donnell, Lorrie McAllister, and John Henry Adams, *The Future of the Academic Library Print Collection: A Space for Engagement* (Arizona State University Library, 2017), 27.
21. Described by Shari Laster, Emily Pattni, and Tammy Dang in "An Engaged Future for Open Stack Print Collections" (presentation, ACRL 2021, virtual conference, April 2021).
22. Sarah Lippincott cites beacon technologies as one prospect for integrating smart systems into space: "While many libraries have now built technology-rich makerspaces, VR/AR spaces, and digital media labs, transforming libraries into smart buildings can also mean infusing technology into the entire building and user experience, from sensors that anonymously monitor space usage to networked devices that allow users to customize their own study environments. Rather than drawing an artificial distinction between 'hi-tech' and 'traditional' library spaces, librarians are considering how emerging technologies can inform all aspects of space planning and design." (*Mapping the Current Landscape of Research Library Engagement with Emerging Technologies in Research and Learning.* Edited by Mary Lee Kennedy, Clifford Lynch, and Scout Calvert [Washington, DC: Association of Research Libraries, Born-Digital, Coalition for Networked Information, and EDUCAUSE, April 2021]: 166.)
23. Lorcan Dempsey, "The Library in the Life of the User: Two Collection Directions" (lecture at Transformation of Library Collecting: A Symposium Inspired by Dan B. Hazen, Harvard University, Cambridge, MA, October 2016), online video, 1:03:13, https://projects.iq.harvard.edu/hazen/welcome-transformation-academic-library-collecting-symposium-inspired-dan-c-hazen.
24. Richard Ovenden, "Outside In: Research Libraries and Research Collections as Community Conduits" (keynote presentation, JISC and CNI Leaders Conference, Oxford, UK, July 2018).
25. Amy Brunvand, "Re-localizing the Library: Considerations for the Anthropocene," in "Libraries and Archives in the Anthropocene," ed. Eira Tansey and Rob Montoya, special issue, *Journal of Critical Library and Information Studies* 2, no. 3 (2019): 4, https://core.ac.uk/download/pdf/234708091.pdf.
26. See Irving K. Barber Learning Centre and British Columbia Electronic Library Network, "BC ELN & IKBLC Partnership Connects Small GLAM Organizations with Essential Digitization Support," news release, July 6, 2021, https://bceln.ca/sites/default/files/news/2021_BCELN-BCHDP_Support_Service_News_Release.pdf.
27. Bailey Diers and Shannon Simpson, "At Your Leisure: Establishing a Popular Reading Collection at UBC Library," *Evidence Based Library and Information Practice* 7, no. 2 (2012): 75, https://doi.org/10.18438/B84W4G.
28. In OCLC's 2017 study of how libraries were planning to change practice informed by principles of equity, diversity, and inclusion (EDI), the four top areas identified were search and discovery (77%), metadata descriptions in catalogs (70%) and digital collections (58%), and terminologies/vocabularies (52%). ("Equity, Diversity, and Inclusion in the OCLC Research Partnership Survey," OCLC Research, https://www.oclc.org/research/areas/community-catalysts/rlp-edi.html.)
29. O'Donnell, McAllister, and Adams, *Future of the Academic Library Print Collection*, 8.
30. Sarah Dupont, quoted in Jessica Woolman, "Sharing Knowledge: How UBC's Xwi7xwa Library Is Helping Community Aboriginal Libraries Better Serve Their Communities," *About Us* (blog), UBC Library, June 23, 2017, https://about.library.ubc.ca/2017/06/23/sharing-knowledge/.

13

CHAPTER THIRTEEN

TECHNOLOGY AND INTERACTIVE EXPERIENCES

KRISTIN ANTELMAN
and DAVID WOODBURY

Leading through a Forward-Thinking Technology Vision

> *If we are successful, we will see that it was because we were able to release the energy inherent in the intersection of cutting edge technology, brilliantly designed spaces and the library users of the future.*[1]

Successful 21st-century library spaces are both welcoming and useful to library users. Just as creative design and natural light enhance the user experience, so should the technologies employed in the library. Good libraries tap a library user's instinct to explore and create. They enable people to gather and interact—with others, present or remote; with images and data; and with tools to create things. Technology-rich spaces enable this kind of library.

Each university has its own distinct culture and at any given moment is on a trajectory from somewhere to somewhere else. This may be reflected in a campus strategic plan, but it also may not be; a campus that does not have an explicit plan has its own culture and trajectory just as much as the one that does. As the library stretches itself in new directions, and as it asserts its role in evolving new ways to support learning and research, its technology spaces will advance those goals by reflecting and reinforcing the campus culture and direction.

The library technology vision will make visible how the library is a driver of innovation across the academic enterprise. The technology vision should reflect the overall aspirations for a renovation or space project. Technology-rich spaces reveal the library's personality. They reveal its ambition to stake out an active role in enabling knowledge creation and learning. Technology spaces revitalize the idea of a library for students and researchers.

Articulating a vision is the first step in designing successful technology-rich spaces (see figure 13.1 for an overview of the technology space design process). A vision developed and proposed by the library, and grounded in the services those spaces will enable, will generate excitement, a sense of potential. Envisioning innovative spaces is a process that builds on what others have done and extends it. A compelling vision is one that does not have all the answers to important questions in advance—Who will use the spaces and how? How much will they really cost? How will library staff support them? A compelling vision stakes out a destination and then figures out how to get there. It will launch the library on an adventure, a road trip full of detours, dead ends, and unexpected vistas. Seeing the library itself as a platform for experimentation and learning will lead to a "sandbox" and iterative sensibility across the organization.

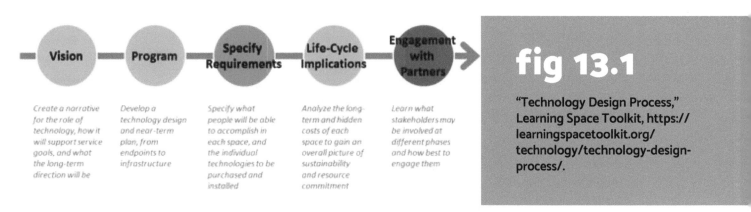

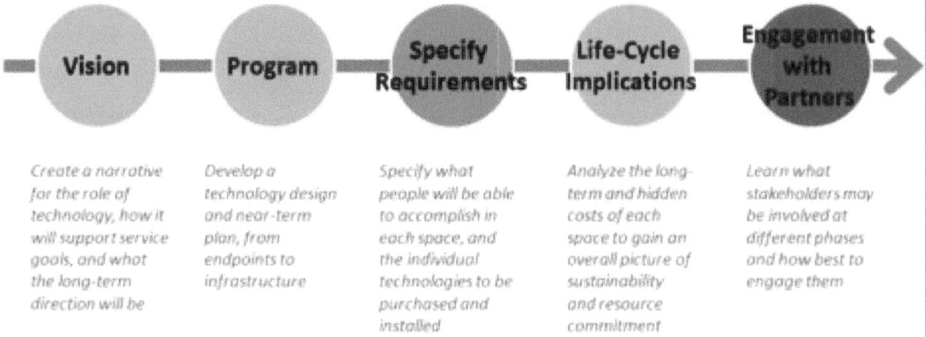

Vision
Program
Specify Requirements
Life-Cycle Implications
Engagement with Partners
Create a narrative for the role of technology, how it will support service goals, and what the long-term direction will be
Develop a technology design and near-term plan, from endpoints to infrastructure
Specify what people will be able to accomplish in each space, and the individual technologies to be purchased and installed
Analyze the long-term and hidden costs of each space to gain an overall picture of sustainability and resource commitment
Learn what stakeholders may be involved at different phases and how best to engage them

fig 13.1

"Technology Design Process," Learning Space Toolkit, https://learningspacetoolkit.org/technology/technology-design-process/.

One challenge in developing a forward-thinking vision is that it can be hard to find applicable, engaging examples from the library world. It is useful to look across libraries, of course, but also to seek out examples from other sectors that are meeting similar needs in industries such as museums, tech companies, and corporate public spaces.[2] These examples can also help inspire your stakeholders and design partners and lead them into understanding the library's vision. It is hard to overstate the power of compelling images. During the design phase for North Carolina State University's James B. Hunt Jr. Library, a single image from the University of Sussex, a site never visited by anyone on the team, served as the blueprint for an innovative visualization and collaboration space, the Creativity Studio.[3]

A Conceptual Framework

It can be useful to adopt a conceptual framework for the vision. For example, the research life cycle is a framework that has the advantage of encompassing many library services beyond spaces. It is also a good model for technology-rich library spaces that are focused on using and teaching, and for research objects of value beyond the formal published product.

For Hunt Library, the conceptual framework for the technology program was drawn from the work of the design team partner, DEGW, during the planning phase. DEGW's program plan divided technology into four tiers: basic, enhanced, advanced, and experimental. This work was complemented by identifying high-level goals. The technology spaces would empower users and leverage their own stuff; be ubiquitous and integrated; be visible and "exude their functionality"; and support functions and services not readily available elsewhere on campus.[4]

Trends in both technologies and how students and researchers work can serve as a trail of breadcrumbs that leads to ideas for what you want to support and how. For instance, seeing that scholarship and learning increasingly engage teams and that distributed teamwork is made easy now by ubiquitous access to the internet and commodity web platforms, creating spaces that support working that way is certain to be useful for both researchers and students. Following the trail of the growth of data- and compute-intensive inquiry while desktop displays remain small leads to large-scale visualization as a logical opportunity for a library. Another type of breadcrumb trail is finding what people want to do that leads to a dead end on campus: for example, limited availability or high-barrier access to useful tools such as those available in fabrication shops. Building a creator lab in the library removes those barriers.

Using the Technology Vision

As a practical tool, the vision prepares the library and design teams for the program planning stage where the spaces and uses will be designed. It serves to cohere the library leadership team around the goals of the technology-rich spaces and how those align with the library's broader service goals. A high-level technology vision will also jump-start conversations with academic departments, individual researchers, and campus IT leaders. Their feedback will then help the identification of focus areas and specific candidate technologies.

Like a soccer player passing the ball to where her teammate will be, an ideal vision will leave you heading in a direction that puts the right infrastructure and staffing expertise in place to support both the present and the future.

The Technology Program

A technology program translates the technology vision into how the spaces will be used and defines how those will be met through space design and implementation of specific technologies. The process of creating the program will be augmented by deep use cases cultivated with campus partners to understand and refine the functionality of the technology spaces.

As the vision moves toward a program plan, when requirements will be defined for how specific functionalities will be supported, it can be helpful to look at the space as existing along a continuum from how that function has been supported in the past to how it will be supported going forward. For example, image and data visualization has evolved from printed books and maps to projection and computer monitors, to large-scale displays (LCD, LED, plasma, OLED), to virtual and augmented reality. Some of these are clearly evolutionary jumps while others are paradigm shifts. Where the data that supports visualizations is located has evolved from lab notebooks to magnetic tapes accessed by mainframe computers, to local servers or CDs on local area networks, to powerful desktops or on-site data centers, to commercial cloud platforms. As these examples illustrate, it is natural that at every given point in time library users will be using different generations of technology at the same time. For this reason tech spaces in the library should plan on supporting more than one generation of technology concurrently.

TEAMS AND ROLES

Library Stakeholders

The visioning process coalesces the library's project leadership team around their high-level space goals and what functions the spaces should enable for library users. The program planning and requirements definition stages will engage more deeply the library's technology, facilities, and public services staff. Technology and facilities staff will work closely with the design team at the earlier stages of project planning to ensure that the infrastructure can support the desired technologies and uses and also that those technologies are realistic to support with existing (or planned) library and campus staffing and skill sets.

Technologist

The technologist is the subject matter expert on the library team who is responsible for leading the implementation of the library's program, which the technologist may have played a meaningful role in developing. The technologist role should be defined and assigned early in the project so that all technology-related questions have a clear point person. The technologist is knowledgeable about broad trends, specific technologies, and how to apply those to advance specific library goals. As they collaborate with the design and library leadership teams, the technologist can help create a sustained and consistent narrative for the technology program over the course of the project. The technologist keeps all stakeholders informed and engaged around how technology is advancing the goals for the spaces and serves as a technical translator between IT and audiovisual (AV) experts and the library and design teams.

Campus Partners in Teaching and Learning and Research

It is important to have a program planning process that takes into account the general technology needs across campus. The library can be a place where pockets of expertise and innovation within campus departments can be expanded within the context of a collaborative space in the library. Spaces in the library are ideal for emerging technologies that need hands-on or early experimentation to better understand how they might be applied more broadly at scale. An example from NC State is virtual reality (VR). As VR adoption accelerated on campus, the NC State Libraries helped bring faculty, technical staff, and students together to share and better understand where and how these technologies were being used. This process revealed that while the technology was affordable and accessible, everyone struggled to find dedicated space to host room-scale virtual reality experiences. These ad hoc meetings helped inform the process to build out a mixed reality studio in the library that could be used by researchers, instructors, and students.

The library can also be an accessible showcase for technologies that are dispersed across campus. For example, the Be a Maker (BeAM) program at the University of North Carolina at Chapel Hill brings together a network of makerspaces on campus, including a small makerspace in the Keenan Science Library, which enables students to access equipment such as 3D printers, sewing machines, VR equipment, and soldering tools, while nearby nonlibrary spaces offer other equipment, including a wood shop and metal shop. In this model, the library also serves as an on-ramp for students that can lead them to other spaces on campus.

Even when the library is adopting technologies broadly applicable across many use cases, the technology program will be well served by being grounded in several actual and specific use cases. Those lead use cases will inform technology prototyping and testing. Campus partners will later serve as your first users of those spaces, so in addition to seeking lead use cases with breadth across disciplines and functions, you are also looking for good collaborators.

In the planning for the NC State's Hunt Library, over three dozen potential use cases were refined to a representative set of four lead use cases.[5] The lead use case engagements informed the definition of areas of focus for the four broad categories of research and learning spaces: large-scale visualization and display; gaming, interactive computing, and programming; communications and collaboration; and prototyping and creation.

Campus IT Leaders

Campus IT landscapes vary significantly but have certain commonalities relevant to planning library technology services and spaces. One is that central IT units typically focus on core infrastructure (computing, networking, help desk) and administrative applications rather than research IT infrastructure, which is often supported within the colleges or divisions and academic departments. Within that context, there are opportunities for central campus entities, such as the library, that straddle the boundary between centralized and distributed IT. There typically exists a university-wide IT governance group that supports coordination between central and distributed IT units. It is critical that the library have a seat at that table where the technologist or administrator can make the case for the library's role in contributing to leveraged investment in spaces that support research and learning. This collaboration can also lead to service partnerships and additional funding streams to maintain and enhance library technology services and spaces over time.

Design Team

The design team will be comprised of a variety of players and roles, depending on the size of the project. There will be an architect, local facilities project manager, and contractors. For larger projects, there will be program planning consultants and an interior designer. If there are spaces with technology more advanced than desktop computers, an AV design professional should be part of the team.

In working with the library leadership team and architect on the functional program plan, the uses of spaces that will be enriched with technology should be well conceptualized at a high level so that they are properly accommodated in the final architectural plans. Technology-rich library spaces are not empty rooms with technology layered in after design and construction are finished. All technology spaces are purpose-built to a greater or lesser degree. They will typically require widespread power outlets (in the floor or ceiling), lighting control, and in some cases customized HVAC. Raised floors can assist with the power and data infrastructure to support technology-rich spaces. The library should advocate for versatility and adaptability for technology-rich spaces while recognizing that flexibility can be costly and, in fact, can reduce the effectiveness of a space for its primary and current use. (As one architect reminded a library team, a space that is infinitely configurable is a space that will never exist.)

Projects often go through a value engineering phase where small changes are made to reduce project costs. Be alert to what happens in this phase. Value engineering electrical outlets out of a library project *cannot* be allowed to happen; it will certainly inhibit a space's usability from day one and can be expensive to fix later. The library technologist will want to engage with all the building plans throughout the project, including electrical and network plans, to ensure that the infrastructure will support the technology program. Once the space project enters the final design phase, the project will be on a strict timeline with significant financial consequences for changes.

Audiovisual Designer

Depending on the nature of the project, an AV design professional may play a key role, both as a consultant to the library technologist and as a solution designer. A written technology vision will help to establish the library as the AV designer firm's customer, particularly if an entity other than the library is contracting for its services. The AV design professional will work with the library technologist to translate the vision into a specific technology program, identifying specific solutions and highlighting decision points that have functionality, support, or cost implications. Because building projects are often planned years in advance, for technology-rich spaces, you'll want to wait as long as possible to settle on specific products.

It is important to understand that AV design is its own domain of expertise, and the set of technologies employed, as well as pricing models, are distinct from information technologies with which libraries are more familiar. Consumer technologies are generally not appropriate for deployment in an institutional setting like a library. It is helpful for library stakeholders, especially the technologist, to visit an AV trade show to get to know the industry and its language, as well as to be inspired by what's possible.

The idea of a technology space that is designed to enable users to be hands-on, where technology is meant to be tinkered with, turns out to be an unusual concept in the AV technology industry. Institutional AV customers typically have a defined purpose for a space and want a solution put in place that will do its designated job until it is replaced. That approach may be appropriate for some library spaces (e.g., a conference room), but it is not suitable for the types of spaces profiled here.

The AV designer can also consult on total cost of ownership, including up-front and ongoing costs. An AV integrator will acquire and install the equipment,[6] with installation often priced as a percentage of equipment cost. Custom programming for complicated spaces will cost more, can be expected to take a significant amount of time, and will require detailed specification and oversight by the library technologist. A fixed-cost contract with final payment upon project completion is important for complex projects.

BUDGETING AND DESIGNING FOR SUSTAINABILITY

Assessing costs for technology-intensive library spaces involves costing considerations not typical of other library spaces. The total cost of ownership will include up-front costs (construction upfit, equipment, installation) plus ongoing costs (maintenance contracts, refresh) plus staffing costs (hiring and training). There will always be a tension between implementing emergent technologies—which can be expensive or high-risk from a performance perspective yet provide unique functionality to users—and selecting well-established technologies that may replicate what users already have access to or will be soon outdated. Financial and performance risks can be mitigated by balancing emergent with established technologies, higher versus lower support and refresh costs, and variant refresh cycles. By taking a life cycle approach and aligning the technology design, equipment choices, support model, and refresh schedules, cost and risk can be better understood during the planning phase.[7]

Diversifying funding sources also enhances sustainability, as it does for any aspect of a library's program. Tech-rich spaces do open up opportunities to be written into research grants and may be eligible for campus student fee or competitive grant support. Special spaces are also attractive to donors for naming opportunities.

Refresh planning is quite a bit more complicated than for desktop computing. Different components within a single space will have very different refresh cycles, and in many cases a fix-on-failure strategy, with or without having a backup on hand, is a more cost-effective solution than a planned replacement schedule. Prices of many of these components, especially displays, decrease over time, so a refresh of that component may cost significantly less than the initial upfit or even supporting the older model. Further complicating the refresh and space life cycle question is the reality that, because capabilities and needs evolve so rapidly, the first refresh of a space may very well reenvision its functionality substantially. Some space types, such as creation spaces, will be in a continuous state of refresh and are best served by having an annual budget for that purpose.

It is important to be aware that technology spaces run on software as much as they do on hardware. Back-end software controls content pipelines between storage and displays and user-controlled functions such as source selection or sound. This software will be provided by the equipment vendors or be developed by or contracted for through the AV integrator. Front-end software, such as to support scheduling or e-board content management, can also be outsourced but may be more amenable to local development, especially since standard web development platforms and tools can be leveraged to customize for local needs. One advantage of this approach is enhancing in-house expertise, which will improve the sustainability of the spaces and their ability to evolve to meet a range of user needs over time.

PROTOTYPING AND ITERATION

Technology-rich library spaces can be expensive and adopt technologies library staff aren't used to supporting. Prototyping and iteration can reduce the risk by training IT staff and cultivating a culture of iterative learning within the library staff. Prototyping can occur at any time, including while the project is in the design phase. Since technology generations are short, building prototyping into the space's life cycle is a preferable path, from the perspective of both service and cost, to gradual obsolescence, decommissioning, and redesign.

Technology Space Profiles

Profiled below are three types of technology-rich spaces that have broad applicability for academic libraries: large-scale visualization, creation spaces, and technology-enabled classrooms. These spaces represent a variety of user interactions and technologies, and each includes elements of research, instruction, and student engagement. They are also representative of the use of evolving technologies that create particular demands on the space design and technology infrastructure.

For each of these three space types, a range of possible *uses* are discussed, as well as *components* (hardware, software, facilities requirements) that directly support how the space enables its desired uses.

LARGE-SCALE VISUALIZATION

Teaching and Visualization Lab, NC State University Hunt Library. (Credit: NC State University Libraries.)

USES

- Presentation
- Exploring data or images
- Exhibit
- Gaming

LARGE-SCALE VISUALIZATION

Uses

Large-scale visualization spaces support many library programs because of their utility across many disciplines. They support viewing of media across a large canvas to present, share, collaborate, and interact with image-intensive research and data. They can be used to look at large quantities of data at once or to examine information of different types alongside each other, such as viewing data in tables and spreadsheets next to graphs and charts from that data. They offer high-definition and extremely accurate color reproduction capabilities that may not be easily accessible elsewhere on campus. These spaces are also great for dissemination of scholarship by providing a unique, immersive approach to presenting or exhibiting projects. Large-scale visualization may be deployed in enclosed, black-box theater or collaboration environments, or they may be placed in public contexts such as exhibit spaces.[8]

Components

In addition to visualization technology, these spaces may also include high-quality audio reproduction using multichannel sound systems; video capture to enable broadcast and remote collaboration; three-dimensional video; and user tracking for interactive video content. The display hardware for large-scale visualization can be tough to plan one or two years out. In particular, computing power and capabilities, and available content, can lag behind display capabilities. Quality standards and underlying technologies are constantly improving (e.g., HD to 4K to UHD), and equipment pricing can change rapidly.

How visualization spaces are intended to be used will have a big impact not only on the size of the room but also on the types of technologies that are appropriate and how to manage them in the space. For example, using a technology like digital light processing (DLP) projectors is a good way to get a lot of pixels across a wall. However, if you intend to have users very close to the wall, because of shadows, a short-throw projector or display might be a better option.

Facilities requirements, including HVAC design, can be particularly challenging because most display technologies and computing give off a lot of heat, and component-specific requirements are not likely to be known early enough in the planning process. Taking equipment cooling needs into account as early as possible can help prevent unpleasant surprises later. Considerations should be made for how racked equipment will be housed, secured, accessed, and cooled if it has to be located in the space. Likewise, it is good to consider equipment noise, for example from projector fans or racked equipment, as part of the facilities design process.

Display systems may use off-the-shelf software tools but may also need additional software to be developed for customized solutions. NC State, for instance, uses a custom content management system for much of the media displayed on the visualization walls and spaces in Hunt Library. These systems can also make good use of off-the-shelf technologies such as game engines (e.g., Unity and Unreal), presentation software (e.g., PowerPoint and Google Slides), and photo viewers (e.g., Adobe Lightroom) for efficiently bringing user- or library-provided content to the display walls.

TYPES

- Large-scale presentation
- Immersive, exploration, research
- Immersive, simulation
- Teaching and learning

EXAMPLES

- CURVE (https://library.gsu.edu/services-and-spaces/spaces-and-technology/curve/), Georgia State University
- PSC Visualization Lab (https://library.uoregon.edu/psc-visualization-lab), University of Oregon
- Teaching and Visualization Lab (https://www.lib.ncsu.edu/spaces/teaching-and-visualization-lab) and Creativity Studio (https://www.lib.ncsu.edu/spaces/creativity-studio), NC State's Hunt Library
- Digital Scholarship Lab (https://library.brown.edu/dsl/), Brown University
- Rumsey Map Center (https://library.stanford.edu/rumsey), Stanford

TYPICAL TECHNOLOGIES

- High-resolution LCD/OLED panel wall
- DLP projection/blended projection
- Direct view LCD/MicroTiles
- Computing with extensive GPU
- Room-scale mixed reality (AR/VR)

TRENDS

- Movement to mixed reality (VR/AR) and new ways to do large-scale visualization virtually (e.g., University of Oklahoma).
- Display technologies such as large UHD OLED monitors and video walls using direct view LED continue to become less expensive
- Use of video walls for higher-end film production (e.g., *The Mandalorian*)

CREATION SPACES

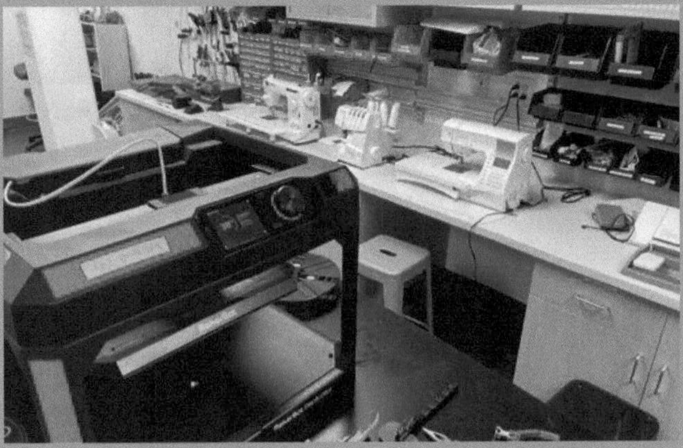

The Workshop, Virginia Commonwealth University Libraries. (Credit: Eric D. M. Johnson and VCU Libraries.)

USES

- Prototyping, experimentation
- Arts and crafts
- Cocurricular programming, course-based instruction
- Support of cross-campus initiatives such as design thinking, entrepreneurship, or citizen science

TYPES

- Simple dedicated "messy" space for project work (bring your own materials and tools)
- Lo-fi prototyping space with simple tools and materials
- 3D printing lab with multiple types of machines (laser cutter, sewing machines, etc.) and materials
- Entrepreneurship space oriented around prototyping products

EXAMPLES

- Makerspace (https://www.lib.ncsu.edu/services/makerspace), NC State University, D. H. Hill Library
- The Workshop (https://www.library.vcu.edu/spaces-tech/the-workshop/), VCU
- DeArmond MakerSpace (https://library.uoregon.edu/scilib/psc-dearmond-makerspace), University of Oregon
- Digital Media Commons (https://library.northeastern.edu/services/digital-media-commons), Northeastern University
- Knowledge Commons (https://mediacommons.psu.edu/locations/university-park/knowledge-commons/), Penn State University

CREATION SPACES

Uses

Creation spaces, also called makerspaces, fab labs, or prototyping spaces, are brought into the library to enable students to build and collaborate to produce physical or virtual objects using machines and tools that are not otherwise available to them. In that way, library creation spaces help democratize access to tools and expertise. They may offer instruction on cross-disciplinary topics such as design thinking and critical making.[9] They may also support multimodal course instruction and cocurricular workshops, serve as a resource for student and faculty research, aid citizen science initiatives, promote the development of new literacies, or simply enable individual exploration.

Components

Creation spaces offer a selection of tools, devices such as sewing machines and 3D printers, computing, VR equipment, and materials that can be used to make things. Creation spaces are typically enclosed spaces but are often adjacent to other types of digital creation spaces such as video and audio production studios. There may be a designated space for instruction. They will have flexible furniture and typically have work surfaces of varying heights to support seated and standing work. The spaces may also incorporate areas for showcasing completed projects.

The principal focus of these spaces is on creation devices and tools. 3D printing can be supported with consumer-level machines that offer fused deposition modeling (extruding plastic filament layer by layer) and occasionally stereolithography (using liquid resin that is cured by light). Spaces that support textile production include sewing machines, sergers, and digital embroidery machines. Laser cutters that can cut paper products, wood, and plastic can be found in a variety of sizes from desktop models to floor standing units. Other potential equipment includes power tools such as drills and saws, hand tools such as screwdrivers and hammers, electronics benches with soldering stations and multimeters, and blade tools from X-Acto knives to vinyl cutters.

Creation spaces include computing to support activities such as 3D design building, VR exploration, or laser cutting. These computers should support digital creation tools (Adobe Creative Cloud) and CAD software (AutoCAD or SolidWorks) as well as software specific to devices such as 3D printers or digital embroidery machines. Equipment to support instruction, such as large displays or projection screens, sound enhancement for the instructor, and wireless or wired computing connections, should be included. 3D printing software to support online submissions will improve the user experience and decrease manual processes in the space. Spaces that require training or are designed to be available when unstaffed may require an access control system using the campus ID with NFC or card swipe. If materials are sold in the space, then provisions should be made for point-of-sale equipment.

Special attention should be paid to the exhaust requirements to support equipment that produces fumes or particulate matter. The campus environmental, health, and safety department will use Material Safety Data Sheet (MSDS) information from the equipment selected to ensure users avoid potential hazards from these materials. Larger machines such as laser cutters and wood saws require their own additional dust mitigation. In addition, power supply is key in these spaces and may be provided overhead to allow for additional flexibility and to reduce trip hazards. A sink or other water supply access is ideal to allow for handwashing and an emergency eyewash station. Lockable storage is helpful for users to store in-process projects as well as storage for pickup of completed 3D prints.

TYPICAL TECHNOLOGIES

- 3D printers
- Sewing machines, including sergers and digital embroidery machines
- Laser cutters
- Cutting machines and tools
- Hand and power tools
- Button makers
- Electronics benches with soldering irons, multimeters, components, etc.
- Arduino/Raspberry Pi microcontrollers
- 3D scanners
- Mixed reality equipment and computing
- Computer laptops/workstations
- Whiteboards
- Lego
- Raw materials (wood/cardboard/filament)

TRENDS

- Improvements in 3D printers that make them easier to use and maintain (e.g., less need for chemical baths to dissolve supports)
- Desktop versions of equipment that once required a lot more space, such as CNC routers, laser cutters, and vacuum formers
- Incorporation of design thinking, experiential learning, and other maker-related pedagogies in curricula in many disciplines

TECHNOLOGY-ENABLED CLASSROOMS

Uses

Technology-enabled classrooms are spaces that offer participatory active learning environments within the library. These spaces serve as a resource that can be shared with campus, and the policy around that arrangement is central to how they are used. These classrooms can also serve as prototype spaces that allow faculty to experiment with new or emerging teaching technologies. The classrooms may be designed to support hybrid teaching with remote participants. When not being used by a class, these spaces may also be designed to be open for general-purpose collaborative study with access to the room's displays and other collaboration technology.

TECHNOLOGY-ENABLED CLASSROOMS

Odegaard Active Learning Classroom, University of Washington. (Credit: University of Washington Libraries.)

USES

- Active learning
- Supporting curricular and cocurricular instruction
- Informal collaboration (at night, for example)

TYPES

- Rooms with flexible furniture and displays
- Scale-up classrooms with fixed round tables and no defined front of room
- Spaces incorporating emerging technologies including VR and AR tools

EXAMPLES

- Odegaard Library Active Learning Classrooms (https://www.lib.washington.edu/ougl/learning-spaces/active-learning-classrooms), University of Washington Odegaard Library
- Active Learning Classrooms (https://www.lib.purdue.edu/walc/), Purdue University Wilmeth Active Learning Center
- Active Learning Classroom (https://libraries.ou.edu/content/active-learning-classroom), University of Oklahoma Helmerich Collaborative Learning Center

TYPICAL TECHNOLOGIES

- Lecture computer
- Multiple large screen displays
- Lecture capture system
- Lecture and student microphones
- Classroom response system
- Document camera
- Assistive listening
- Wireless screen sharing
- Wired sources
- Interactive whiteboard
- Dynamic schedule display
- Dimmable lighting
- Fixed whiteboards
- Huddle boards/rolling whiteboards

TRENDS

- Spaces used for formal instruction that can be converted to comfortable informal study
- Movement from fixed technology to support of BYOD, mobile devices, wireless videocasting
- Support of hybrid classes including learners in person and remote

Components

These spaces are often located in areas that are convenient for students to exit and enter in large numbers. They are designed to promote collaboration and are oriented for pods, with furniture that can be moved around to facilitate flexible uses. If intended to be used by both classes and by individual group study, the design of the space should incorporate ways to be open to the general population. Movable or glass walls can help make the space not feel as closed off from the rest of the library. Screens can be used to promote collaborative study or to secure technology. External digital signage can provide information about the availability of the space for general use.

The technology in active learning classrooms is nontrivial. It should be possible to send content from individual student computers to in-room displays to support interactive engagement with content beyond that of the instructor. Integrating remote participants will require appropriate design as well. Well-designed sound and microphones, unless the space is small, are important.

Supporting these classrooms will entail extensive AV capabilities, including routing video from the instructor and students, video and audio capture, document cameras, and interactive whiteboards. These environments can support bring your own device (BYOD), may be equipped with laptop carts, or may have fixed computing technologies. The spaces should be supplied with appropriate wireless access points that can accommodate multiple devices per person and easily accessible racks and cabling channels to enable the addition of new equipment.

DEVELOPING A SERVICE BACKBONE

As a library creates spaces to support new technologies, there should be a parallel development of the staff and processes for both the front-end (public services) and back-end (IT/facilities) staff who will own, run, and promote the spaces. These staff will be developing and promoting new services and helping to fully realize the potential of the spaces, as well as supporting and maintaining the infrastructure. New technologies require new knowledge. The planning process is an appropriate time to work through not only what equipment will be installed but also how it will be used and what staff should be provided with training or what new expertise is needed in new positions.

Participants in building projects tend to be focused on the project deadline, so it's easy for the library leadership team to take a sequential approach to who is involved and when. Yet the moment the space is completed, it becomes a living entity that needs to be maintained to survive. Future service owners should be engaged during the planning and prototyping phases, where they can plan for the complex service models, dependent upon close coordination among staff across a range of library departments, that high-tech spaces require. Establishing early how technical staff will communicate and work alongside public services and facilities staff will create smoothly functioning spaces and a harmonious workplace culture.

An expanded technology program can also lead to entirely new departments or areas of expertise for the library. For instance, creating a visualization space implies increasing support and expertise within the library for data science and visualization. These spaces can serve as flagship technologies that can help bring faculty into the building who may not have used library spaces in the past. They and their students then have needs that lead to the development of new services. A successful makerspace may lead to more classes coming to the library, which will result in the need for more instructional staff with experience in teaching through experiential learning.

Concluding Thoughts

Technology-rich spaces can be deeply transformative for a library. They make visible the library's intent to invest in ongoing innovation. They show the parent institution that the library is well prepared to meet an uncertain future—that it will not only adapt to but will also embrace new technology to advance learning and research. They invite faculty and students into new ways to learn and build knowledge.

Creating these spaces requires much more than an exciting vision. They require motivated curiosity, a commitment to problem-solving, and hands-on engagement at all stages of a library building project. They require library domain experts willing and able to learn more than they ever expected to have to about architectural design, IT and AV hardware and software, HVAC and electrical, furniture, and fabrication technologies and materials.

Designing, implementing, and supporting technology spaces will instigate transformative change within a library organization. Creating these spaces will raise the library's collaboration and project management skills to new levels. They will open up opportunities for creative application of staff skills and interests, raising morale and engagement.

Every library has a mission to remain not just relevant but essential. Implicit in every successful college or university vision is that its library is indispensable, that it cannot imagine succeeding in its core mission without the library. The ambitious library makes this rhetorical view of the library real. The library with one foot in the future reframes the role of the library to one that is ready to be a first-order partner in advancing teaching, learning, and research.

Notes

1. Maurice York and Kristin Antelman, "A Technology Program for the Hunt Library," NC State University Repository, March 2009, 26, https://repository.lib.ncsu.edu/handle/1840.20/38550.
2. For example, "ARTLENS Gallery," Cleveland Museum of Art, May 27, 2021, https://www.clevelandart.org/artlens-gallery/about; Andreas Hassellöf, "Welcome to the Future of Retail: A Very Smart Window Display: Clas Ohlson Case Study," Ombori Grid, accessed June 4, 2021, https://ombori.com/case-study/clas-ohlson; Peter Hall, "Media Wall," *Metropolis*, June 1, 2007, https://www.metropolismag.com/uncategorized/media-wall/; Pat Knapp, "Comcast Center Digital Experience," SEGD, December 9, 2013, https://segd.org/comcast-center-digital-experience.
3. Jisc infoNet, "Courtroom, InQbate, CETL in Creativity, University of Sussex," Flickr, March 12, 2008, https://www.flickr.com/photos/jiscinfonet/2328312473/; NC State, "Unleashing the Power of Visualization and Collaboration at the Hunt Library," YouTube video, 3:54, March 3, 2015, https://www.youtube.com/watch?v=Whry7DNzgtQ.

4. York and Antelman, "Technology Program for Hunt Library."
5. Business analytics (College of Management); game design, game artificial intelligence, and human-computer interaction (Departments of Computer Science and Electrical and Computer Engineering, College of Engineering, and College of Design); thunderstorm simulations, GIS visualization (Department of Marine, Earth, and Atmospheric Sciences, College of Sciences); and interactive text visualization (College of Humanities and Social Sciences).
6. Per professional ethics, implementation (integration) is not performed by the same firm that designed the space.
7. "Life-Cycle Strategies," Learning Space Toolkit, January 1, 2012, https://learningspacetoolkit.org/technology/life-cycle-strategies/index.html; "Integrated Budgeting Tool," Learning Space Toolkit, January 1, 2012, https://learningspacetoolkit.org/integration/integrated-budgeting-tool/index.html.
8. For a more in-depth discussion of research uses of visualization spaces, see "The James B. Hunt Jr. Library at North Carolina State University: The Library Building as Research Platform," NCSU Libraries, submission for 2014 Stanford Prize for Innovation in Research Libraries, January 15, 2014, https://www.lib.ncsu.edu/resolver/1840.20/38868.
9. Matt Ratto, "Critical Making: Conceptual and Material Studies in Technology and Social Life," *Information Society* 27, no. 4 (2011): 252–60, https://doi.org/10.1080/01972243.2011.583819.

14

CHAPTER FOURTEEN

SERVICE INNOVATION FROM OUTSIDE IN AND INSIDE OUT

AMEET DOSHI and ELLIOT FELIX

Introduction

This chapter focuses on the Georgia Institute of Technology (Georgia Tech) library renovation encompassing the Crosland Tower and Price Gilbert Memorial Library buildings. The renovated Crosland Tower opened in January 2019, and the Price Gilbert building in January 2020. The total project cost was approximately $75.9 million, almost entirely funded by the state of Georgia. Given the tremendous amount of institutional and state support required, early and frequent engagement with key stakeholders was critical to the success of the project. Additionally, since construction was anticipated to last several years, coupled with an institutional desire to push the frontier of library services, a needs assessment required both quantitative baseline metrics and engagement with lead users across Georgia Tech's campus. The chapter will address *why* conducting a needs assessment is so vital, *how* to effectively engage stakeholders to cocreate new library services and spaces, and *what* the outcomes are that inform the redesign of library services, spaces, staffing, and systems.

Overview of Case Study

The Judge S. Price Gilbert Memorial Library (1953) and Dorothy Crosland Tower (1968) are prominent examples of mid-century modern library buildings designed by regionally significant design firms. Although the two buildings are different in style and function, when built both buildings represented cutting-edge thinking in both design and library services for the 1950s and 1960s, respectively. Following their rehabilitation (figure 14.1), they are once again emblematic of the modern philosophy for libraries as an integral part of a research university's core educational infrastructure.

fig 14.1

Rendering of renewed library.

(Credit: BNIM/Praxis3.)

Campus and Library Context

Combined with the attached G. Wayne Clough Undergraduate Learning Commons, Price Gilbert and Crosland serve the breadth of Georgia Tech's diverse community—undergraduate and graduate students, postdocs, faculty, and staff—with specialized spaces aligned with teaching, research, and learning needs while capitalizing on the original design. In Price Gilbert, named for a lawyer, judge, politician, and philanthropist committed to higher education in Georgia, the views of campus, mezzanines, use of light, impressively tiled stairwell, original 1953 clocks, and overall feel and association with the mid-century remain. Crosland Tower, named for longtime head librarian and a founder of the Georgia Tech College of Computing Dorothy Crosland, continues its legacy as the graduate addition that Ms. Crosland fought for in the 1960s. Highlights include a cutting-edge data visualization lab and teaching space colocated with a retro-technology space on the third floor, a dedicated graduate student space known as the Graduate Community on the sixth floor, and spectacular views of midtown Atlanta from the seventh-floor silent reading room. Originally designed as a storehouse for print materials, Crosland Tower was adaptively reconceived by the design team in a manner that respects the changing needs of students and faculty, while acknowledging the reality that the vast majority of information circulation of a modern research library now occurs in the digital realm.

A History of Expansions and Renovations

A main driver of the library's expansions over the years was its ability to store physical collections. The impetus for the latest renewal at Georgia Tech, however, is quite the opposite. The data speaks for itself. Print book checkouts have declined for more than a decade. Use of the electronic collection, on the other hand, has increased dramatically. In 2017, 99.1 percent of collections that were accessed were electronic in nature. At the same time, visits to the physical library continue to increase—gate counts are up 39 percent from 11 years ago (figure 14.2). Taken together, this data indicates that less space is needed for books, and more space is needed for people. The elegant solution to this quandary has been to house 97 percent of the physical collections off-site in climatic conditions suitable for the long-term preservation of paper materials, a core stewardship responsibility for research libraries. As a result of this move, almost all the 130,000-square-foot Crosland Tower building was made available for other uses.

fig 14.2

Gate count versus print book checkouts.

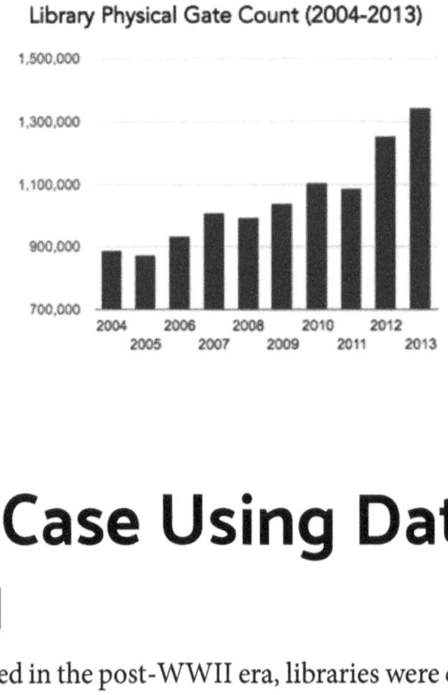

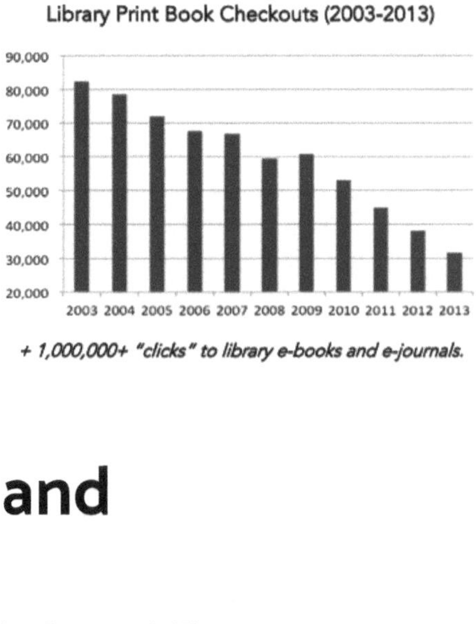

+ 1,000,000+ "clicks" to library e-books and e-journals.

Making the Case Using Data and Storytelling

As research universities expanded in the post-WWII era, libraries were central to this growth. There are many examples of mid-century library buildings across US universities in need of renovation. As is the case at most campuses, the list of Georgia Tech buildings requiring revitalization is lengthy and growing. There is fierce competition to gain priority among a large array of capital projects in need of attention and funding. Early in her tenure as dean of libraries at Georgia Tech, Catherine Murray-Rust recognized the problematic life safety issues in one of the most heavily trafficked buildings on campus and a need to collect granular data on building use. With the addition of the 24-7 Clough Undergraduate Learning Commons in 2011, the gate count rose even more. Life safety concerns included elevators too small to allow for medical stretchers, as well as large north-facing windows that were in danger of cracking or potentially falling. These safety concerns initially caught the attention of campus leadership and helped to elevate the project on the list of building renovations, but it was the "vision thing" that solidified institutional support for the Library Next project.

A first step involved gathering key metrics to help contextualize the current state of the library, much of which the library had long since been tracking and sharing on a publicly accessible dashboard. Perhaps the most important data point was the ratio of seats per student as compared to Georgia Tech's peer institutions (figure 14.3). Overcrowding had been a student complaint for several years, but we now had concrete data to illustrate just how dire the problem was. While we needed to gather this data individually in 2014, the Association of Research Libraries (ARL) and brightspot developed a space-forecasting methodology available to make this data collection more streamlined.[1] The data on rising gate counts, low seat counts, and declining circulation, when taken together, helped make clear the need to prioritize user space to key stakeholders.

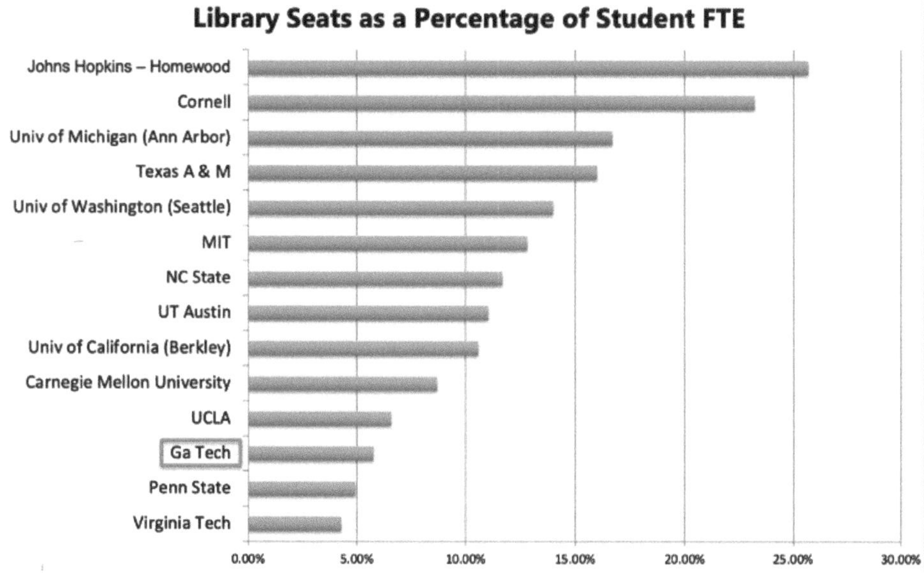

fig 14.3

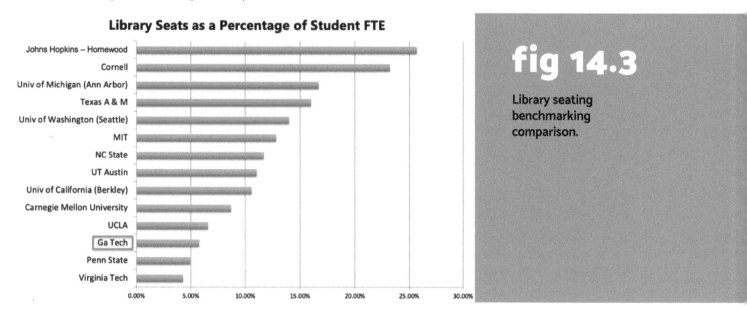

Library seating benchmarking comparison.

Moving Collections Offsite

The Library Next project was contingent on a public-private partnership between Georgia Tech and Emory University Libraries to collaboratively design and construct a Harvard-style off-site repository (Library Service Center of Emory and Georgia Tech), to house 97 percent of Georgia Tech's print collections. Any decision to relocate print collections away from campus is fraught with practical, logistical issues for continuity of access as well as eliciting a strong visceral response from the user community. It is important to acknowledge and address these issues head on. Given the transformational scope of the project, it became clear, early in the project, that we required a creative and multifaceted PR effort to be inclusive and successful. Faculty wanted to know—at a deep level—why this was being undertaken and how access to print collections would be maintained. Students were less concerned about access to the print collection—although strong feelings were noted by graduate students—but wanted to know what was to come.

Communicating Direction

To address this variety of questions and perspectives, we created a fun animation to highlight the benefits of the project (more space, more sun), while succinctly illustrating the trends regarding collection versus building use (figure 14.4). Additionally, a group of librarians wrote a philosophically centered white paper about the project. This document served as a high-level overview of the information science underpinnings and as a reasoned defense of the word *library*.[2] Finally, the communications and marketing team within the library developed a dynamic website to provide open access to all planning documents and a timeline so the campus would be aware of when the project was scheduled to begin and projected to end.

fig 14.4

Still from Library Next animated video.

Engaging Key Stakeholders

In very short order, the library and the consulting firm brightspot were able to develop an action plan for gathering user data, while simultaneously generating marketing and communications content to inform the Georgia Tech community about the project. Nonetheless, a cohesive vision still needed to be clearly defined for the Institute's executive leadership. At one point early in the project, the provost argued that the failing building systems were not enough to generate enthusiasm for state-funded investment in a library renovation. He directed us to clearly state "where you want to go." In order to appropriately and effectively develop this vision, we needed input from a variety of stakeholders.

The process of reimagining Georgia Tech Library's spaces, services, and staffing was guided by an institutional culture of experimentation on the one hand and brightspot's approach to adaptive innovation on the other. Georgia Tech had a long history of prototyping and piloting, such as the West and East Commons.[3] This was complemented by brightspot's experience in enabling practical innovation among university libraries and beyond. Brightspot's approach has been shaped by Edgar Schein's work on organizational culture[4], Everett Rogers's research on the diffusion of innovations[5], and brightspot's field observations from projects with over 100 institutions. These shaped both the theory and process of change for the project: that organizations must set innovative yet achievable goals; that people must have a hand in shaping their own future in order to buy-in and implement; that organizational learning, building momentum and scaling should be agile processes; and that organizations need to work from the outside in and the inside out simultaneously.

Designing the Process

Taken together, these principles mean that a strategy project is also a capacity-building project where brightspot's clients learn new mindsets, skills, and tools that they can use not only to renew the library but also in their day-to-day work going forward. For instance, through the project, Georgia Tech library staff learned new research tools and skills such as interviewing that they use on an ongoing basis. When we met with a newly assembled group, we also invested the time and energy to help them form a functioning team, whereas when we met with an existing group, we were careful to understand their culture and processes so that we were working with, not against, them.

Participation alone doesn't create change, though. You need the right people to be engaged in the right way. Here again, Rogers provides great insight: new ideas spread first to early adopters who want to do what's new, then to an early majority influenced by the early adopters, then to a late majority who jump on the bandwagon after the tipping point, and finally to laggards who change only when they are forced to. So we paid special attention to engaging the early adopters, who could champion the change, in the process.

Engaging Students, Faculty, and Staff

We applied these principles in a process that engaged students, faculty, and librarians in a variety of ways—surveys, focus groups, interviews, observations, and data mining. We engaged students through focus groups with existing undergraduate and graduate student advisory boards, meetings with student government representatives, interviews with lead users, and broader student surveys. Likewise, we met with an existing faculty library advisory board and the faculty senate library committee and conducted interviews with and observations of faculty lead users.

We engaged library faculty and staff broadly and deeply as well, with town hall meetings that had everyone from security guards to the library dean contributing. We also held regular workshops with the cross-functional project committee and with a staff task force for each key initiative. These task forces were perhaps the most innovative aspect of the engagement and governance structure because they allowed small groups of six to eight library professionals to each develop one of the big ideas of the library, such as becoming an event hub to showcase student and faculty work or reimagining the library service point to enable more proactive collaboration like you'd find in the best retail environments (figure 14.5).

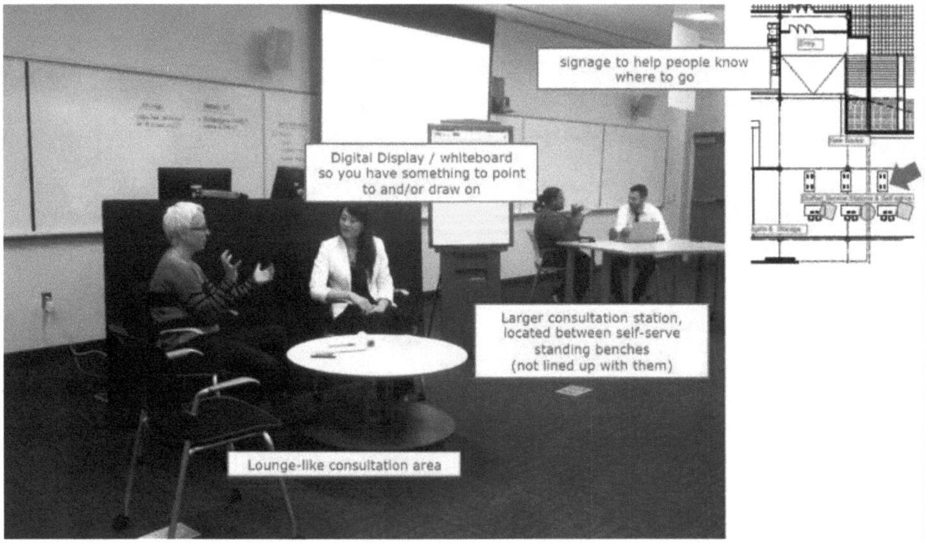

fig 14.5

Prototyping the library's new service point.

Working with Lead Users: Tools and Techniques

The underlying approach for our data-gathering process was rooted in Eric von Hippel's "lead user" theory. The concept, first outlined in his book *Democratizing Innovation*, provides compelling evidence that by interviewing and shadowing the most innovative members of an organization (i.e., lead users), it is possible to glean insight about where the remainder of that organization is heading.[6] In short, we are able to anticipate user needs and design library spaces and services for a building that may not be open for several years into the future. We began by identifying lead users from the faculty and student advisory boards. Other approaches included scanning Georgia Tech's newsletters for significant achievements such as grant and publication awards.

Learning from Lead Users

Several tools were applied to the user research effort, including journey mapping, shadowing, interviewing, and comparing observed behaviors with environmental trends (figure 14.6).[7] The foundation of our research effort involved conducting one-on-one 30-minute interviews with approximately 25 lead users. These interviews helped us to identify common themes across user contexts, as well as opportunities to recognize "personal innovations," a critical component of von Hippel's lead user theory. Another technique, journey mapping, is conceptually based on unpacking customer retail experiences along each stage of a purchase; however, this tool applies to library user experiences as well. A journey map consists of tracing a user's path with a service or space using the "5 E's": Enticing (*What aspects of the experience attract the user?*), Entering (*What happens when the user first enters the space or service?*), Engaging (*What is the nature of the service experience?*), Exit (*What, if anything, happens as the user ends the experience?*), and Extending (*Is there any follow-up from the service provider or institution afterward?*). Even post-occupancy, journey mapping has continued to be a very practical and easily applicable technique for tracing user experiences across contexts, whether physical or digital. We also engaged in shadowing lead users, a technique that involves spending a half-day or an entire day observing a single user as they conduct their work. This proved to be a heavier lift logistically, but paid greater dividends, as we were able to more deeply understand service constraints and lead user workarounds in the moment.

Finally, our user research effort did not occur within a vacuum. Although gathering lead user input from Georgia Tech students, staff, and faculty was the primary objective, we adopted an integrated approach by contextualizing that feedback with environmental trends from other academic institutions and industry. This helped us to validate the final array of new spaces and services.

fig 14.6

Faculty committee workshop photo.

Engaging the State

The Georgia Tech project was primarily funded by state appropriations and included in the governor's budget. This funding process is substantively distinct from nonpublic capital funding and deserves extra attention. Specifically, our campus engagement efforts needed to include the large and diverse array of governmental actors including the Board of Regents of the University System of Georgia, policy and budget staffers from the Higher Education Appropriations subcommittee, and the elected representatives chairing those key House and Senate committees. Fortunately, Georgia Tech, like all research-intensive universities, manages these complex relations via in-house experts within an office of government relations.

Our role primarily involved sharing the overall vision for the project with public officials at the state level, but only when specifically asked by the Office of Government and Community Relations. For publicly funded projects, close coordination with these experts is absolutely critical. In addition to sharing the vision with state officials, we were also challenged to discuss the motivations and proposed benefits for campus. Often, these meetings were abbreviated due to competing priorities, so flexibility and conciseness are key when developing the presentation.

Also important is recognizing that political developments can adversely impact projects of this scale and scope. We learned this lesson all too well when, at a critical point in the project, when the print collection had been relocated to the Library Service Center but construction had not yet begun, the project funding was delayed for a year due to political fallout from a completely unrelated Title IX issue.[8] The year delay, though no fault of the library, resulted in deleterious impact on the program: we got less bang for the buck due to price increases for raw materials. Throughout the complex and sometimes unnerving process of funding and executing a state-supported library project, it is vital to rely upon the expertise and guidance of your campus governmental liaisons.

Project Outcomes

Our engagement of lead users as well as students, faculty, staff, and leadership in a collaborative process resulted in an innovative, achievable vision for the future, a vision that's since been realized with inspiring and functional spaces, unique and responsive services, and aligned and effective library professionals.

From our user research, we learned that boundaries between research, teaching, and learning are blurring, but conversely, as people become more specialized, they are more likely to work in silos, and bringing them out requires effort. We also learned that mastering skills is just as important as mastering content and that there are many resources and library services that students and faculty are not aware of but could benefit from. We discovered that while collaboration is an important part of research, teaching, and learning, there is still a need for quiet, individual work and work spaces. Finally, to make this all happen, physical and digital tools and spaces must work together seamlessly.

Using Personas and Key Moments to Drive Service and Space Innovation

After identifying these themes, we developed user personas to inspire and evaluate new space and service concepts, focusing on their motivations, behaviors, and expectations rather than fixed demographic information. These included student personas such as the researcher, the entrepreneur, the novice seeker, the conductor, the designer, and the assistant. We also created faculty personas, including the futurist inventor, the expert connector, the junior juggler, the progressive traditionalist, the educator, the historian, and the sustainer. As part of our outside in/inside out approach, we also created library staff and faculty personas and a library staff and faculty experience model with their key moments to help understand the highlights and pain points as well as what shifts would be required.

After developing personas from our research, we created a user experience model (figure 14.7) that describes five key moments using the Georgia Tech Libraries spaces, services, technology, and collections that can be thought of as goals that users are trying to achieve within their research, teaching, and learning experiences. These were *discovering*—finding the right information, content, people, and tools; *focusing*—filtering information and identifying what's next; *growing*—mastering new skills and building relationships; *creating*—expressing and applying ideas; and *showcasing*—testing and sharing with the community. Perhaps more importantly, together we identified the library's relative strength in the discovering and focusing modes, but the need for improvement in helping users grow by building skills, creating everything from papers to prototypes to performances digitally and physically, and showcasing their work through publications, presentations, and other means.

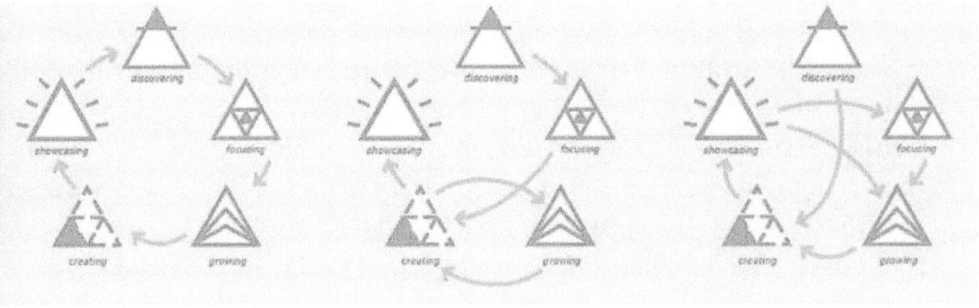

fig 14.7

Library user experience model with key moments for staff and faculty.

Collaboratively Crafting the Future Vision

Through an iterative process that pulled together inputs from a staff town hall, insights from lead users, observations about library trends, and an analysis of Georgia Tech's strengths, weaknesses, and differentiators, we created the library's vision, its description of the ideal future state of the library, inclusive of its spaces, services, people, technology, and collections: *Georgia Tech Library will define the technological research library of the 21st century. We will enable people to explore the past and design the future by bringing together inspirational spaces, curated content, expert guidance, and scholarly communities* (figure 14.8). Building on the research findings and working toward this vision, we set goals to guide the library renewal effort. These include supporting the whole scholar, embracing innovative teaching and learning methods, fostering interdisciplinary collaborations, forming campus communities, providing inspiration and serendipity, and enabling innovation and entrepreneurship.

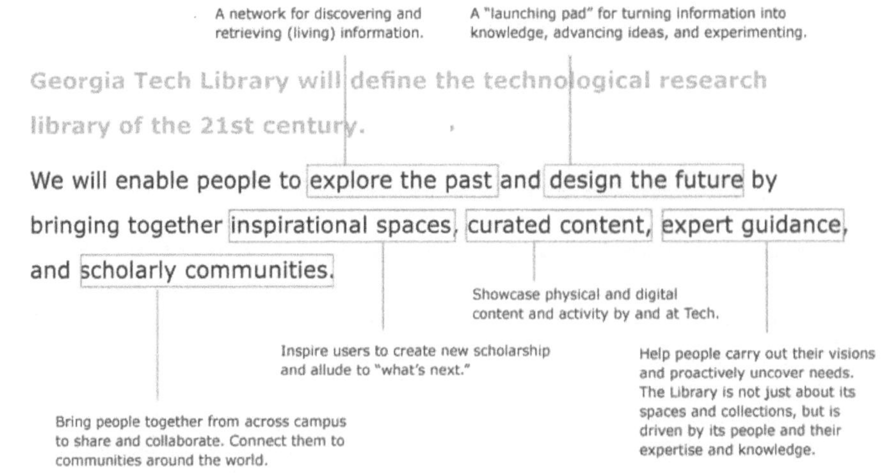

fig 14.8

Library vision statement, with annotation.

Developing a Playbook to Achieve the Vision

To achieve these goals, we developed a playbook of concepts to address the findings and then conducted a campus-wide survey of students and faculty to prioritize the most promising ideas. The eight priority concepts were to enable virtual browsing, a studio for innovation and ideation, a studio for innovative teaching and learning, project team rooms, pop-up showcases, research navigators, quiet spaces, and a network of event spaces to showcase and support scholars. Each of these concepts had a small task force as described above, with each charged with defining and developing the concept as a service—and each task force was chaired by a library faculty or staff member also on the cross-functional project team for coordination across groups.

A Methodical Approach to Service Innovation

Having done the research, established the goals and vision, and prioritized new service concepts, it was time to reimagine the Georgia Tech Library's services—and the spaces and staffing to support them. These efforts were grounded in an analysis of the library service transactions and user satisfaction data from a LibQUAL+ survey as well as the broader user research into changes in teaching, learning, research, and scholarship. Reimagining library services took each task force through brightspot's service design process (figure 14.9) encompassing the service philosophy (why), the service portfolio (what), the service points (where), the service delivery (how), and the service provider (who).

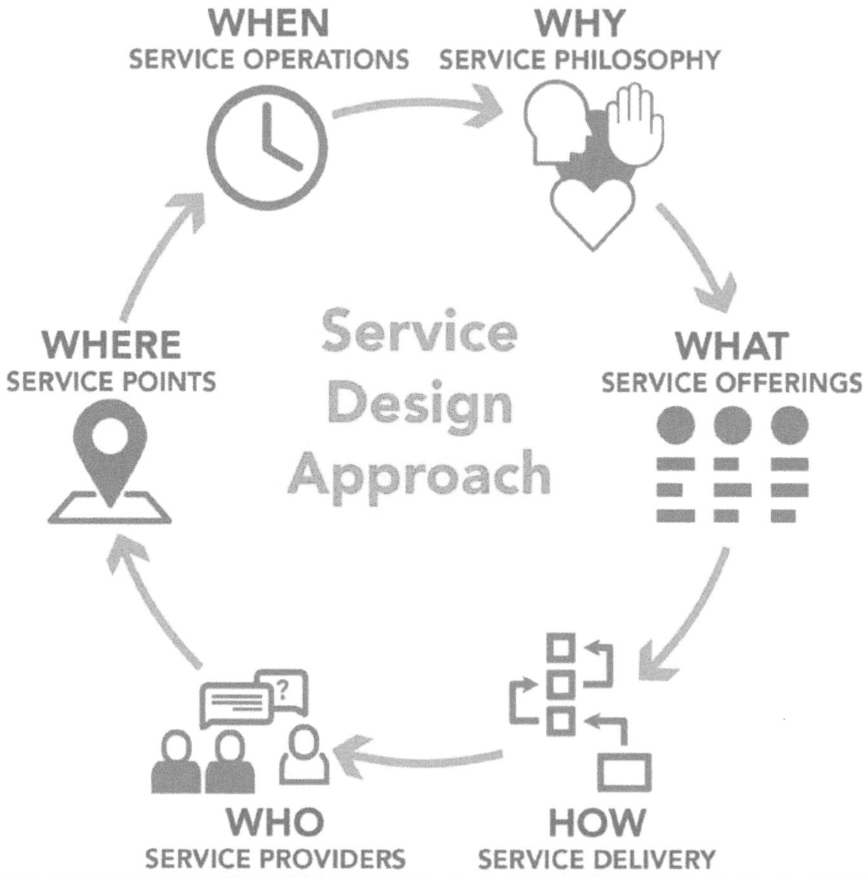

fig 14.9

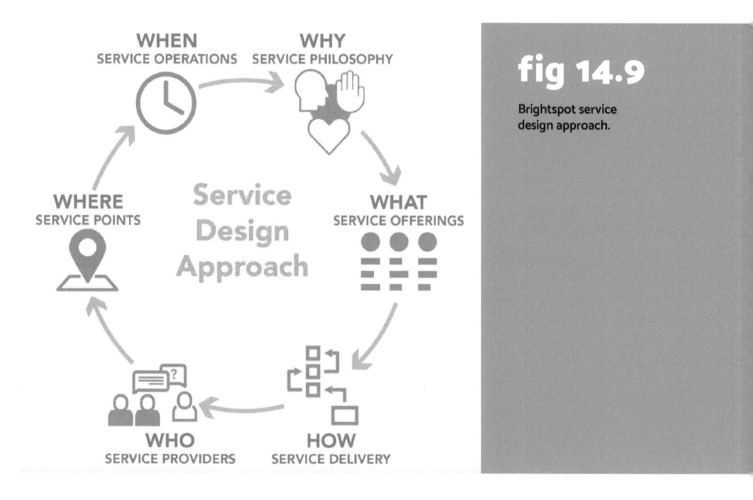

Brightspot service design approach.

Reimagining the Library Services

For "why," the service philosophy focused on "welcoming and collaborating" by being "predictive and proactive" to "engage and empower." This was guided by desired shifts: earlier involvement in research projects, more proactively pushing out services and outreach, enabling more self-service, providing technology-rich spaces, and selectively adding data services. The "what" of the service portfolio was organized into instruction, community engagement, advising, space management, information resources, technology, expertise, and general assistance, with each category including a mix of unchanged current services, future enhancements, and future new services. The "where" of service points included the central, integrated service point originally called the Library Store, and later changed to

Info Desk. This had been a deliberate attempt to reference the interactive showcase of the best retail models—along with service points for specialized spaces like the teaching studio, innovation and ideation studio, and consultation center. The "how" of service delivery was covered by creating four levels of support shared across services: help yourself, help me with, advise me on, work with me to. These were complemented by developing journey maps (figure 14.10) and service blueprints (figure 14.11) for each core service, mapping out the steps to deliver it along with the roles that frontline and behind-the-scenes staff and faculty play at each step and the resources required.

fig 14.10

User journey map.

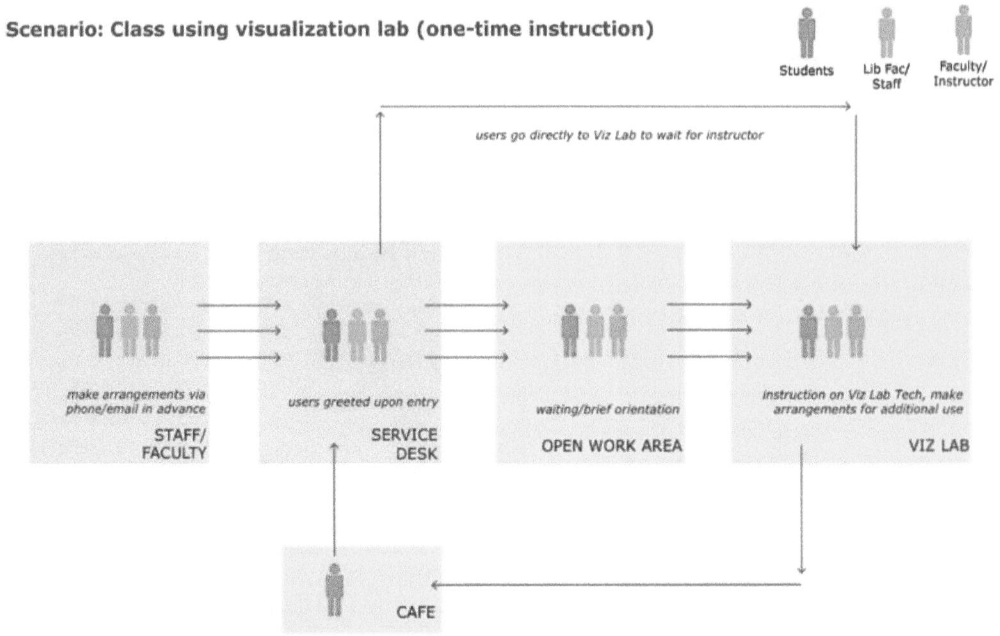

fig 14.11

Service blueprint.

Channels	Ideation	Physical	Digital	Exhibit Event
Physical Evidence or Communication Channels	• Develop exhibit concept • Do research • Plan scope • Plan budget needed	• Gallery space • Pop-up showspace • Event space	• Digital screen/mobile device or advanced technology	• Event space
User Actions	• Student/faculty wants to create an exhibit out of their artifacts or • Research	• Students/faculty/community attend and view physical exhibit • Perhaps participate • Provide feedback	• Students/faculty/community view digital exhibit and perhaps interact or • Participate with digital exhibit • Provide feedback	• Students/faculty/community attend event, listen to speaker • Perhaps eat at reception • View exhibit • Provide feedback
line of interaction				
Front-line Staff Actions	• Exhibits Coordinator meets with customer to discuss project and outline timeline and costs. • Communications/Event/ Financial staff may be present for meeting	• Exhibits Coordinator works with exhibit content creator to select materials to exhibit (student/ faculty/community)	• Digital Archivist may work with exhibit creator (student/ faculty/community)	• Meet with Events Manager
line of visibility				
Behind the Scenes Staff Actions	• Exhibits coordinator and/ or Library • Staff research exhibit possibilities based on GT research and/or traveling exhibitions	• Exhibits coordinator Archives staff • Prepares materials to install in display areas • Write label copy • Design interpretive graphics • Graphics production (printing) • Assess needs for security • Marketing by PR staff	• Digital Archivist may work with • Fedora/Hydra developer in creating digital exhibit • Archiving • Ongoing maintenance of digital exhibit	• Parking • ADA accessibility • Speaker set up • Catering/food/drinks • Set up & clean up • Back up contingency planning
line of internal interaction				
"Stuff" (Resources and Systems)	• Project planning software • Cost estimation software • Measurements • Test server space	• Exhibit display cases • Exhibit accessories ("kit of parts"/ showspace) • Graphics and interpretive labels • Museum/gallery infrastructure • Lighting/AV needs/power/data • Scheduling system for exhibit spaces	• Software repository (Fedora/ Hydra) to support system • AV for combined physical & digital • Devices to view exhibit • All the same resources that are in Physical exhibit channel	• Scheduling system • AV needs • Furniture Exhibit cases • Exhibit accessories ("kit of parts"/showspace) • Graphics and interpretive labels • Museum/gallery infrastructure • Lighting/AV needs/power/data

Applying Tools and Methods to Users and Staff

The "why," "what," "where," and "how" all depend on the right "who," and so the organization and operational planning for Georgia Tech Library staff and faculty was a critical part of the service innovation process. This included the development of staff and faculty personas, journey maps as previously noted, applying the space tools as with library users. Shifts in staff and faculty processes and workflows were also identified. New staff and faculty roles were also defined, such as the research navigator who could help library users negotiate administrative and other research hurdles across the spectrum of the research process, guiding them through the research infrastructure, assessing research needs, facilitating access to resources and tools. Finally, together, we created a staffing road map that identified training, piloting, and other activities to develop the organization in preparation to deliver the new and enhanced services and operate the renewed building (figure 14.12).

fig 14.12

Exterior view of renewed library.
(Credit: BNIM/Praxis 3.)

fig 14.13

"Library Store" service point.
(Credit: BNIM/Praxis 3.)

fig 14.14

Students working together.

(Photo by Elliot Felix.)

fig 14.15

Students studying individually.

(Credit: BNIM/Praxis 3.)

Lessons Learned

The purpose of this chapter is to describe user engagement techniques to align project goals with community needs at Georgia Tech as we transformed our library (shown in figures 14.13, 14.14, and 14.15). Over the course of the project, we learned a great deal about what worked well for us. First, we organized our work in teams of cross-functional working groups (six to eight persons) dedicated to each program concept. This approach helped to propel innovation and create a sense of ownership across the library organization. Additionally, using a data-driven approach leveraging Georgia Tech Library's long history of collecting detailed statistics was an important driver for gaining institutional support. A publicly facing library data dashboard capturing gate count was valuable to the engineering and design team in their goal to optimize building energy usage during peak load times.

Ultimately, Dean Catherine Murray-Rust did not waver from the overall vision of the project: to significantly reduce the footprint of print materials in the campus buildings, to build a strong partnership with Emory University as manifested in the Library Service Center, to make the work of information expertise more public and "on display," and to ensure library and user voices were represented when design moves were made. Additionally, the public-private partnership between Emory and Georgia Tech was significant in gaining support for the project among university leadership and within the state legislature. Finally, we took advantage of the extended period of construction to integrate robust videoconferencing tools and new processes to work across campus and with our partners at Emory University.

These new ways of working have been particularly valuable during the lengthy period of social distancing as a result of the global pandemic in 2020–21. For example, the library's popular data visualization workshops, public programs, and panel discussions were offered entirely online to a much broader global audience. We also discovered during our post-occupancy research that "Library Store" (figure 14.13) was simply too confusing, and that users required a more intentional descriptor for the main information point in a library. Finally, we learned a lesson about a key mistake made that led to less-than-optimal final service or architectural designs. Specifically, we performed the user research described above and much of the service design *prior* to bringing the architectural design team on board. This was due to perceived resource constraints but could have likely been avoided. Looking back, we would have preferred much more overlap between user research and design work. Ideally, the consultations with brightspot and the architectural design team would have been conducted in close coordination to maximize creative opportunities in the final building layout.

Notes

1. Elliot Felix and Martha Kyrillidou, "Library Design: How Many Seats Do We Need?" Brightspot, May 30, 2019, https://www.brightspotstrategy.com/library-design-seating-areas-utilization/.
2. Charlie Bennett, Wendy Hagenmaier, Lizzy Rolando, Fred Rascoe, Lori Critz, Crystal Renfro, Willie Baer et al., *Reimagining the Georgia Tech Library*, white paper, Georgia Tech Library, 2014, https://smartech.gatech.edu/handle/1853/51712.
3. Charles Forrest and Martin Halbert, eds., *Beyond the Information Commons: A Field Guide to Evolving Library Services, Technologies, and Spaces* (Lanham, MD: Rowman & Littlefield, 2020).
4. Edgar H. Schein, *Process Consultation: Its Role in Organization Development* (Reading, MA: Addison-Wesley, 1969).
5. Everett M. Rogers, *Diffusion of Innovations* (New York: Free Press, 2003).
6. Eric von Hippel, *Democratizing Innovation* (Cambridge, MA: MIT Press, 2006).
7. Ameet Doshi and Elliot Felix, "Lead Users: A Predictive Framework for Designing Library Services and Spaces." in *Proceedings of the 2016 Library Assessment Conference: Building Effective, Sustainable, Practical Assessment*, ed. Sue Baughman, Steve Hiller, Katie Monroe, and Angela Papplarado (Washington, DC: Association of Research Libraries, 2017), 439–45, https://www.libraryassessment.org/wp-content/uploads/bm~doc/71-doshi-2016.pdf.
8. Janel Davis, "Tech Drops $47M Building Request after Rebukes on Students' Due Process," *Atlanta Journal-Constitution*, August 28, 2016, https://www.ajc.com/news/local-education/tech-drops-47m-building-request-after-rebukes-students-due-process/1ihp3NdZctocJbShhh25bM/.

15

CHAPTER FIFTEEN

DESIGN INCLUSIVE SPACES WITH ACCESSIBILITY AND UNIVERSAL DESIGN

CARLI SPINA

As spaces that are used by a wide range of people, it is important that libraries be built with the needs of a diverse set of users in mind. Without this focus on usability for individuals with varied needs, libraries become spaces that exclude both potential patrons and employees. In addition, many libraries are subject to laws that set minimum legal accessibility standards to ensure that individuals with disabilities are not excluded from spaces and services. It is therefore both ethically and, potentially, legally imperative that libraries focus on inclusion throughout their design process. Unfortunately, all too frequently, topics of accessibility and inclusivity are sidelined during building projects, limiting the options available when they are finally considered.

Through thoughtful design, it is possible to build spaces that are comfortable, welcoming, and inclusive for users and meet any relevant legal requirements. To achieve this, it is important to understand accessibility requirements and best practices, as well as the principles of Universal Design. Taken together, these offer guidance for successful design projects. This chapter introduces these topics, explains how they can improve library spaces, and suggests best practices for integrating them into building projects.

What Is Accessibility?

Accessibility refers to the process of making a space open to and usable by people with disabilities. While other users may benefit from accessibility features, this is usually simply an extra benefit and not a significant and intentional part of the design process. Common accessibility features in building projects include ramps, push-button doors, elevators, Braille signs, and counters at a height that accommodates individuals who use wheelchairs, though there are countless design features that can contribute to accessibility. Accessibility features can be incorporated into the initial construction of a space, or elements can be retrofitted after the fact, though integrating them into the initial design phases is generally more successful and less expensive.

In many areas, laws and government regulations set minimum accessibility standards that apply to libraries. These can cover a wide range of requirements, from the design and positioning of signage to the size of doorways to the height of shelves. In some cases, these are absolute requirements, and in others, the standards can be met by offering alternative accommodations: for example, indicating that staff are available to provide assistance retrieving items from shelves that exceed the maximum height. These laws can be at the national level, such as the Americans with Disabilities Act in the United States, the Accessible Canada Act, or the Equality Act of 2010 in the United Kingdom.[1] In some countries, local laws can play a prominent role in accessibility as well, including state regulations, such as the state of Pennsylvania Department of Labor and Industry's Universal Accessibility Regulations in the United States or provincial laws such as the Accessibility for Ontarians with Disabilities Act in Canada.[2] Because the legal requirements can incorporate multiple different standards set by more than one lawmaking body, it is important to develop a full picture of the legal landscape.

Additional guidance, frequently set in regulations, is available to ensure that the requirements set by these laws are met. For example, in the United States, the Department of Justice has published the *2010 ADA Standards for Accessible Design*,[3] which provides more specific and detailed guidance. These standards cover everything from the minimum ratio of accessible parking spaces to total parking spaces in parking lots to the maximum pile for carpeting, which is set at 0.5 inch.[4] These standards are designed to ensure that the language of the laws, which tends to focus on broad statements that spaces shall not exclude individuals with disabilities, actually has its intended impact. Even those in jurisdictions without these sorts of specific requirements may find the rules of other jurisdictions useful in providing a benchmark for their designs.

The exact nature of the legal requirements varies significantly from location to location and can change over time, so it is important to integrate a review of these requirements into early stages of the project. In the absence of applicable legal requirements, best practices have been developed to guide a project to ensure that the final design is accessible. Often it is useful to identify an expert who can take the lead on this work, either internally from within the library team or an external consultant, though sometimes this may be a service provided by the architect or contractor. When looking to external team members to provide this expertise, it is important to ask about their qualifications and experience to ensure that they will be successful in identifying and resolving any accessibility issues that arise. In jurisdictions with accessibility requirements, a review by an outside party is often a required stage in the project, helping to catch accessibility issues early.

Accessibility is a vital part of any library construction, renovation, or expansion project. Without a focus on accessibility, the project will likely miss important details that can prevent patrons with disabilities from making use of one or more elements of the finished space. Though it may be possible to fix these problems when they are later identified, this approach is often costly and disruptive and can lead to bad publicity for the library.

What Is Universal Design?

Originating in architecture and industrial design, Universal Design is an approach that is focused on inclusivity. The term *Universal Design* is attributed to Ronald Mace, who was himself a wheelchair user.[5] It refers to "the concept of designing all products and the built environment to be aesthetic and usable to the greatest extent possible by everyone, regardless of their age, ability, or status in life."[6] It consists of seven principles that guide design choices and articulate priorities:

1. *Equitable use:* This principle focuses on ensuring that all users have equitable access no matter their needs. Specifically, the guidelines for this principle state that the design should "provide the same means of use for all users: identical whenever possible; equivalent when not."[7] This is important to ensure that users with specialized needs are not separated from other users, do not experience stigma around needing to use a separate accessibility feature or accommodation, and are not offered a lesser experience than other users. An example of equitable use in libraries would be installing an accessible automatic door at the main entrance so that all users can enter in the same way. This saves users who are unable to open the door themselves the inconvenience of using an alternative entrance or the stigmatization of asking for help.
2. *Flexibility in use:* This principle requires that the design be able to accommodate different approaches to use based on both need and preference. In particular, it is important that those using the space or tool in a variety of ways all have the same ability to get accurate and precise results. Ideally, a single means of use should not be singled out from others as either the best or worst approach. In the realm of product design, a quintessential example is scissors that can be used by both right-handed and left-handed users. However, this principle can equally apply to architectural, interior, or space design. Common examples in these realms are creating flexible use spaces through a mix of adaptable fixtures, integrating movable walls, or furnishing the space with modular furniture (figure 15.1). All of these can ensure that the full range of users will find a space usable and responsive to their needs.

fig 15.1

This classroom at Tri-County Technical College includes collapsible furniture on casters so that the space can be reconfigured for different needs and users can adjust the furniture as required.

(Photo by Brady Cross.)

3. *Simple and intuitive use:* This principle states that the design must be one that is straightforward and understandable by all users, even if they have limited experience, language skills, knowledge, education, or attention. Even more than some of the other principles, this principle is one of simple usability as well as access. If a design is confusing or requires a great deal of specialized knowledge or education, it will rarely be an inclusive choice. In general, the goal is to meet users' expectations and assumptions about how to make use of the space or item. Examples of simple and intuitive design abound, such as elevator up buttons always being above the down buttons or push button doors featuring a single large button with clear text and iconography to indicate its purpose and use.
4. *Perceptible information:* This principle considers how information is conveyed to users, the goal being to ensure that information is comprehensible by all users, regardless of surrounding conditions. This means that the information is often conveyed in ways that can be perceived by multiple senses. Examples of this are common in architectural and urban design projects, such as the use of yellow colored and textured (bumpy) floor materials to indicate when someone is approaching the edge of a street or train platform or a fire alarm using both sounds and flashing lights. An example found in many libraries is tactile maps that allow users to feel the layout of the library in addition to seeing it.
5. *Tolerance for error:* This principle ensures that if the user uses an item improperly or has an accident, there will not be significant adverse consequences. Though often thought of in the context of guardrails on ramps or stairs and caution signage, this principle can also be applied to designing spaces to avoid trip hazards or items that particularly tall, short, or distracted users might bump into while navigating through the area. The goal is to eliminate hazards where possible, provide warnings or protective features when hazards cannot be removed, and avoid any design that assumes or requires constant vigilance from users.
6. *Low physical effort:* This principle dictates efficiency and comfort in creating designs and, in particular, a focus on minimizing the amount of strength, dexterity, repeated motion, or effort needed to use an item or complete a task. Many examples have become ingrained in our world because they are so easy and efficient to use that they are now barely noticeable. For example, many spaces, particularly public spaces, have moved from doorknobs to lever door handles. Doorknobs require that users have an available hand, manual dexterity, and strength necessary to turn the knob, whereas levers can be pushed down with the side of a hand or even with an elbow, with no need to grip the lever. This makes them easy to use not only by users with varied needs, but also by those who encounter the door while carrying items or with their hands otherwise engaged.
7. *Size and space for approach and use:* This principle requires that "appropriate size and space is provided for approach, reach, manipulation, and use regardless of [the] user's body size, posture, or mobility."[8] It is focused on ensuring that there are appropriate sightlines, adequate space for users who rely on assistive devices (such as crutches or wheelchairs), and enough clearance for users of different sizes. It also points out the importance of providing space for an additional person who is assisting a user. A door that is wide enough to accommodate all types of wheelchairs can be an example of this. Two important examples in libraries are the layout of computer and technology hardware, such as computer stations, printers, and scanners, so that they can be approached and used by all users and the selection and layout of furniture to guarantee that it accommodates a range of needs and preferences.

These principles are constructed to focus attention on the key elements that can make a design inclusive or exclusive. Though the listing order is generally consistent, it is not intended as a ranking. Each principle brings equal weight to the pursuit of inclusion, and the best designs take all of them into account at all stages. Taken together, they can offer prompts to think about all of the elements of design that may be exclusionary. Their role in universal design is to take it from a broad statement that designs should be inclusive to providing guidance on how designers can actually achieve that goal. They are specifically written so that they are applicable to a wide variety of types of design, from architectural design to graphic design to web design. They are equally influential for the physical design of building spaces as for the interior design of a room, including furniture and fixtures.

The Difference between Accessibility and Universal Design

When applying Universal Design and accessibility in library building projects, it is important to understand how the two concepts relate to one another. While Universal Design is intended to improve access for disabled users, this is not its sole focus, as the principles demonstrate. Careful application of these principles can improve the experience for others as well, including older adults, those for whom the local language is not their first language, distracted users, and people of varied ages and sizes. As a result, Universal Design often has areas of focus and goals different from accessibility. Universal Design and accessibility are both important, sometimes overlapping, and often complementary concepts, but each has its own role, and often they can be applied side-by-side in the same project.

Though at times Universal Design and accessibility are treated as interchangeable, they are distinct. Accessibility is about the ability to access or use a space, service, or item, but does not generally focus as much on the user's experience. For example, a library that has a staircase leading into its main entrance and provides a separate backdoor entrance for visitors who use mobility equipment, such as wheelchairs, canes, or crutches, would be considered accessible. However, this space would not be considered universally designed because the main entrance is not designed so that it is equally usable by the widest range of possible users, instead relegating some users to an experience that is frequently inferior. This is one example of the fundamental difference in the approaches of accessibility and Universal Design, but it is important to remember that Universal Design does not necessarily mean universal access. Some users will always need accommodations to be able to use a library's spaces, services, and items. This is why accessibility, accommodation, and Universal Design need to work together. Adopting an approach that incorporates all of these concepts will ensure that any legal requirements in the local jurisdiction are met, that the library is prepared to provide additional assistance for patrons as needed, and that the library is designed to be inclusive for all users to the greatest extent possible.

Applying Accessibility and Universal Design in Libraries

Ensuring that accessibility and inclusion are stated goals of the project can prevent them from being overlooked at any stage. Too frequently issues around access and usability, particularly as they pertain to patrons with disabilities, are overlooked until the final stages of a project, which limits the options available to address any problems that are identified and increases costs. However, it can be very difficult to achieve an early focus on inclusivity. As Brady Cross, the digital initiatives librarian at Tri-County Technical College, notes,

> Unfortunately for librarians, the current model preferred by institutional decision makers is the design-build process. Design-build makes librarian input very difficult because the building design is almost finalized by the time it is presented to the institution's building committee. This means that the final design is made before any public input can be made.... [Libraries] need to have representation at the level where institutional planning occurs so we can have representation on the committees that input the project parameters in order to better influence the outcome at the design phase.[9]

Without this level of involvement in institutional decision-making, the needs of library patrons and employees may be overlooked, misunderstood, or improperly interpreted in the design process. This can have unfortunate consequences for all users, but it can particularly lead to a style of design that prioritizes the average user rather than understanding the full range of potential needs and uses among diverse users.

In addition to ensuring that the library has a seat at the table when the design process is being discussed, it is also vital that the library team take the necessary steps to understand their users. One of the most famous slogans of the disability rights movement is "Nothing about us without us," and this is instructive in how libraries can succeed in the design phase. In fact, a central element "of the universal design paradigm is user involvement in the process."[10] By bringing together diverse groups of users, it is possible to understand their needs and preferences while at the same time collecting requested features and suggested approaches. This means involving not just patrons with disabilities, but also employees with disabilities, as well as a diverse group of other individuals to ensure that the library is not just accessible, but is truly inclusive. This work should take place early in the design process to ensure that there is still an opportunity to make changes in response to the information collected. However, it should also continue throughout the entire process, from these initial phases to the evaluation of the final designs before construction begins, and to the final review of the finished project to catch any remaining issues before the space opens and in the early days of its use.

Involving users in this way is not, by itself, enough to ensure successful designs. While users bring an important and necessary perspective to the design, it is important to remember, particularly with respect to designing for users with disabilities, that it is not reasonable to assume that "anyone with a disability has expertise in all access or universal design issues."[11] For this reason, there is value in working closely with other departments and organizations that can combine expertise with deep knowledge of the needs of various users. For example, in cases where the focus is on accessibility and designing for disabled users, it can be helpful to partner with the campus disability services office or local disability advocacy organizations. Often these groups will have professionals who have training and expertise in accessibility and Universal Design but also have the ability to gather and share feedback from disabled users. Organizations that work with or represent other groups of users can similarly represent their needs and preferences.

It is also worthwhile to consider who will provide this expertise in the design team. While some architects and designers specialize in accessibility or Universal Design, many are not focused on this aspect of the project and may not have deep experience with these elements. A clear understanding of the level of expertise the design team is able to bring to the project is vital. If they are not specialized in this discipline, it is possible to bring in consultants who concentrate solely on these topics. They can combine their own knowledge of these topics with the information collected from users in a way that will maximize the ultimate usability of the space. Even in cases where a member of the library staff has experience with these topics, it can be useful to have an outside party dedicated to collaborating and coordinating directly with the building team so that no detail is overlooked. In many academic and civic settings, there may be architectural or capital planning specialists who have this expertise and can provide support throughout the project.

Regardless of whether there is expertise present within the design team, the library must be cognizant of how best to work with this team during the construction process. Of particular importance is the ability to prioritize requests, particularly if additional requests are made after the design is finalized. As Cross points out,

> My own experience has seen the person at the library's executive level become deliberately excluded from the entire construction process because their voice was too loud after the final design was announced. The lesson here is after construction begins, it is best to make only very small suggestions rather than demand changes.[12]

This necessitates a delicate approach focused on only the most important alterations to the design and proposing approaches that will maximize impact while minimizing disruption. Though a difficult balancing act, this is a skill that can make for a more productive working relationship with the design team throughout the project.

One way to avoid the need for design changes and also to future-proof the library is to incorporate Universal Design early in the process. Of the seven principles of Universal Design, flexibility and size and space for approach and use are particularly central to avoiding design changes and future-proofing the library. Flexibility has been particularly valuable during the COVID-19 pandemic as libraries find themselves looking to completely change the way that they use their existing spaces quickly and at a time when major construction is particularly unlikely. As architect Amanda Markovic noted when discussing the pandemic and library design in an interview with *American Libraries Magazine*,

There's a possibility that it will happen again. So I think [design] is about ensuring there's flexibility, making sure there aren't as many hard walls in these spaces to allow for the expansion and contraction [of our spaces] that will be necessary when these things arise.[13]

This is only one of many use cases for flexibility. Others include the ability to respond to changing technology needs, the opportunity to offer patrons more options to customize their use of the library, and the option to more quickly respond to the changing nature of library collections (figure 15.2).

fig 15.2

The Learning Commons Lobby at Tri-County Technical College has an open design, movable furniture, and a modular desk to maximize flexibility and options for reconfiguration.

(Photo by Brady Cross.)

In addition, building flexibility into the process makes it possible for the library to continue to meaningfully engage with its community after the building project is completed. Because users' needs change regularly, it is important to offer opportunities for ongoing feedback, suggestions, and user experience research. This ensures that barriers and annoyances are discovered quickly. If flexibility is at the core of the project, there are more options for addressing these discoveries effectively and at a low cost, which will improve inclusivity and ensure that users feel engaged with and enthusiastic about the library.

Examples of Accessibility and Universal Design in Libraries

There are myriad ways to successfully approach accessibility and Universal Design in libraries and to use these topics to focus on developing an inclusive environment. Many examples will be completely invisible to most users, such as designing spaces around graceful ramps where stairs would otherwise be necessary or integrating automatic doors into each entrance. In fact, some design elements that fulfill the principles of Universal Design are also extremely popular with users because they make the library space more usable and comfortable for all. Libraries have learned that their users are interested in customizable spaces where they can move the furniture to meet their needs;[14] that natural light, preferred by some users with low vision, is also popular with many other users;[15] that single use and universal gender bathrooms help foster inclusion in multiple ways;[16] and that flexibility is as much a priority for users as it is a beneficial feature for accessibility and future-proofing.[17] Overall, integrating a thoughtful approach to inclusion, accessibility, and Universal Design ensures a design that will meet the needs of the entire community in ways that are otherwise practically impossible to achieve, as demonstrated by the success many libraries have had with this style of design.

Modular architectural design is one excellent example of how libraries can apply the principles of Universal Design. These designs minimize elements that are built for narrow purposes or purely for decorative purposes in favor of more open and adaptable spaces. As Cross notes, "The very shape of the building can determine the level of flexibility allowed in the design process. Rectangular and square shaped designs are more modular than circular shaped ones because rounded edges are either more decorative or engineered for a singular purpose" and plans that use fewer load-bearing walls can similarly enable future alteration with minimum disruption.[18] For this reason, it is important to think about how the space's basic architectural plans will support multiple potential uses, both when the building first opens and in the future when plans may change. As Cross goes on to say, "If the building has an interior which allows spaces to be modified, then both temporary and permanent changes may be implemented without the cost of a major renovation."[19] The core structure of the library may not be as visible to the average user, but successful accessibility and Universal Design starts with a focus on these features.

Grand Valley State University (GVSU) Libraries offers another example of how flexibility can support inclusion. The library team strives to be very student-focused, as evidenced by both their design approach when building the Mary Idema Pew Library and their ongoing space assessment. As Annie Bélanger, dean of university libraries at GVSU, states, "For us, we see Universal Design of our space as the standard approach if we want to foster student success, inclusion, and student-owned spaces."[20] In particular, the library offers a significant amount of flexibility because of the way it uses expansive spaces and furniture. Kristin Meyer, user experience librarian and area lead for strategic planning at the library, notes, "We were really intentional about wanting to create flexible spaces and that probably has been the biggest success from my perspective."[21] The library has zones, such as collaborative and quiet zones, that are indicated by design choices such as color schemes and space configuration. Within these zones, students have access to movable furniture and even movable walls,[22] which allows them to "create a room on-the-fly in any of the collaborative areas."[23] The space offers not only the flexibility for the library team to decide to use it in different ways, but also for the users themselves to reconfigure the space to meet their current and changing needs. As former dean of libraries Lee Van Orsdel put it, "The furniture is all mobile and it goes where students want it—where it's going to be best for them at that time,"[24] with the caveat, as Meyer notes, that staff do regularly look for and move any furniture that is obstructing paths in ways that would limit accessibility for those using mobility aids.[25] They also offer a wide range of types of furniture to accommodate different needs, including "height-adjustable tables for library users who prefer or need to be working while standing, but may also be adjusted for seated users."[26] Though the accessibility implications of this particular decision may not be the first aspect that jumps out, in fact it means that virtually any space can be configured in such a way as to be accessible to a student's particular needs. Whether this is arranging a collaborative space that allows a student using a wheelchair to seamlessly participate or offering whiteboard access that can be taken to both noisy and quiet areas, each individual has the tools to configure the space to be more supportive of their needs (figure 15.3).

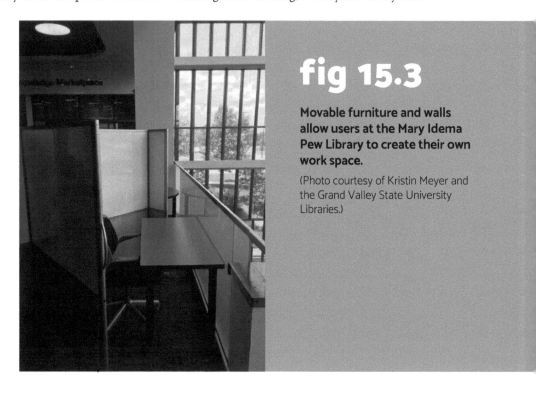

fig 15.3

Movable furniture and walls allow users at the Mary Idema Pew Library to create their own work space.

(Photo courtesy of Kristin Meyer and the Grand Valley State University Libraries.)

As part of its ongoing process to improve user experience, the library team has looked for ways to help all students use the space comfortably, including students with disabilities. Throughout the library, assistive tools that support focus are available for use by all students.[27] Examples include "weighted lap pads, noise-canceling headphones, reading overlays, fidgets and more," which it circulates (figure 15.4) because of feedback from students with a need for low sensory environments who "were able to identify that focus tools would be preferable to 'focus spaces' so that students could self-select where to be and how to be," and who offered "input into what tools should be included, [and] whether it should be individual tools or a toolbox for loan."[28] This also demonstrates the library's commitment to learning from its users on an ongoing basis, which is central to developing an inclusive community.

fig 15.4

Assistive tools that support focus available for checkout at the Mary Idema Pew Library.

(Photo courtesy of Kristin Meyer and the Grand Valley State University Libraries.)

After any project is completed, it can still be useful to complete an audit to ensure that the final product meets a high standard of accessibility and Universal Design. Jasmine Clark, the digital scholarship librarian at the Temple University Libraries saw the value of this and collaborated with the makerspace team within the Loretta C. Duckworth Scholars Studio.[29] Before the makerspace moved into a newly built space, she conducted an audit, which helped to identify access issues, including doors that were too narrow to meet accessibility standards and counters at a height that required users to climb up onto the seats. Finding these issues through the audit made it possible to remediate them before they presented barriers to users and before the library received complaints.

For those with less experience in these areas, there are a variety of checklists and support tools available from experts and practitioners that can help to guide this post-completion evaluation process. In particular, Dr. Sheryl Burgstahler of University of Washington's DO-IT has created a document called "Equal Access: Universal Design of Libraries," which provides important background and guiding questions for these types of evaluations.[30] The IFLA Library Buildings and Equipment section has published a post-occupancy evaluation checklist, which includes items regarding accessibility as well as some that correspond to Universal Design.[31] Each of these could serve as a template for developing a checklist or evaluation process for a newly completed construction, renovation, or expansion project.

In Summary

Regardless of the type of design project being done in a library, accessibility and usability for all users are important considerations that need to be a top priority at every stage of the work. Considering both accessibility requirements and the principles of Universal Design can ensure that the final space goes beyond minimum requirements to achieve greater inclusivity and offer a welcoming and enjoyable experience for all library patrons. Though often overlooked, this element of library design can have a significant impact on how the finished space is perceived by the community and how patrons use the space over time. It can also help to future-proof the space, which minimizes the need for additional renovation work and offers space for future innovation.

Notes

1. Americans with Disabilities Act of 1990, 42 U.S.C. Ch.126 § 12101 et seq. (1990); Accessible Canada Act, S.C. 2019, c. 10; Equality Act, 2010, c. 15 (U.K.).
2. Universal Accessibility Regulations, 52 Pa. Code §69.221 (1994); Accessibility for Ontarians with Disabilities Act, 2005, S.O. 2005, c. 11.
3. US Department of Justice, *2010 ADA Standards for Accessible Design* (Washington, DC: US Department of Justice, September 15, 2010).
4. US Department of Justice, *2010 ADA Standards*, 65, 104.
5. Wolfgang Saxon, "Ronald L. Mace, 58, Designer of Buildings Accessible to All," *New York Times*, July 13, 1998, https://www.nytimes.com/1998/07/13/us/ronald-l-mace-58-designer-of-buildings-accessible-to-all.html.
6. "Ronald L. Mace," Center for Universal Design, accessed June 29, 2017, https://www.ncsu.edu/ncsu/design/cud/about_us/usronmace.htm.
7. Bettye Rose Connell, Mike Jones, Ron Mace, Jim Mueller, Abir Mullick, Elaine Ostroff, Jon Sanford et al., "The Principles of Universal Design," ver. 2.0, Center for Universal Design, April 1, 1997, https://projects.ncsu.edu/ncsu/design/cud/about_ud/udprinciplestext.htm.
8. Connell et al., "Principles of Universal Design."
9. Brady Cross, e-mail message to author, January 13, 2021.
10. Laurie Ringaert, "User/Expert Involvement in Universal Design," in *Universal Design Handbook*, ed. Wolfgang F. E. Preiser and Elaine Ostroff (Boston: McGraw Hill, 2001), 6-1.
11. Ringaert, "User/Expert Involvement," chapter 6.
12. Cross, e-mail message.
13. Amanda Markovic, quoted in Lara Ewen, "Virus-Responsive Design," *American Libraries Magazine*, September 1, 2020, https://americanlibrariesmagazine.org/2020/09/01/virus-responsive-library-design/.
14. Sam Demas, "From the Ashes of Alexandria," in *Library as Place: Rethinking Roles, Rethinking Space* (Washington, DC: Council on Library and Information Resources, February 2005), 30, http://www.clir.org/pubs/reports/pub129/pub129.pdf.
15. Camille Andrews, Sara E. Wright, and Howard Raskin, "Library Learning Spaces: Investigating Libraries and Investing in Student Feedback," *Journal of Library Administration* 56, no. 6 (2016): 471.
16. Meredith Schwartz, "Inclusive Restroom Design | Library Design," *Library Journal*, May 2, 2018, https://www.libraryjournal.com/?detailStory=inclusive-restroom-design-library-design.
17. Susan Gibbons and Nancy Fried Foster, "Library Design and Ethnography," in *Studying Students: The Undergraduate Research Project at the University of Rochester*, ed. Nancy Fried Foster and Susan Gibbons (Chicago: Association of College and Research Library, 2007), 20–29.
18. Cross, e-mail message.
19. Cross, e-mail message.
20. Annie Bélanger, e-mail message to author, May 17, 2021.
21. Kristin Meyer (user experience librarian and area lead for strategic planning) in discussion with the author, May 2021.
22. Ian Chant, "Lee Van Orsdel Re-thinks Library Design," *Library Journal*, June 25, 2015, https://www.libraryjournal.com/?detailStory=lee-van-orsdel-re-thinks-library-design.

23. "Mary Idema Pew Library," Grand Valley State University, August 12, 2020, https://www.gvsu.edu/library/mary-idema-pew-library-21.htm.
24. Lee Van Orsdel, quoted in Chant, "Lee Van Orsdel."
25. Meyer in discussion with author.
26. Jen Taggart, "Inclusion Is More Than Accommodation: A Tour of the Mary Idema Pew Library," Adaptive Umbrella, April 16, 2019, https://adaptiveumbrella.blogspot.com/2019/04/inclusion-is-more-than-accommodation.html.
27. Jen Taggart, "Inclusion Is More Than Accommodation: A Tour of the Mary Idema Pew Library," *Adaptive Umbrella* (blog), April 16, 2019, https://adaptiveumbrella.blogspot.com/2019/04/inclusion-is-more-than-accommodation.html.
28. Bélanger, e-mail message.
29. Jasmine Clark (digital scholarship librarian) in discussion with the author, August 2020.
30. Sheryl Burgstahler, "Equal Access: Universal Design of Libraries," Disabilities, Opportunities, Internetworking, and Technology, University of Washington, https://www.washington.edu/doit/equal-access-universal-design-libraries.
31. Santi Romero, Karen Latimer, Dorothea Sommer, Jeffrey Scherer, Stefan Clevström, Inger Edebro-Sikström, Olaf Eigenbrodt et al., "Questionnaire about Library Buildings (Characteristics—Operation—Evaluation)," IFLA Library Buildings and Equipment Section, 2013, https://www.ifla.org/files/assets/library-buildings-and-equipment/Publications/poe_final_version.pdf.

V

SECTION V

COLLABORATIONS AND CONVERGENCE

16

CHAPTER SIXTEEN

COCREATING THE COMMONS

Campus Partnerships at the Heart of Two Library Space Design Projects at the University of Miami

KELLY E. MILLER,
ROXANE PICKENS, and
KINERET BEN-KNAAN

Introduction

Over the last six years, the University of Miami Libraries has formed two sets of strategic partnerships with campus units in order to reimagine how it supports the university's learning and research mission. These partnerships have played critical roles in the planning and design of spaces, services, and staffing positions. In the first case, UM Libraries is facilitating partnerships with academic service units in undergraduate education and other areas dedicated to student learning to create a learning commons on the first floor of the Otto G. Richter Library, the University of Miami's flagship library. In the second case, UM Libraries is facilitating a partnership with the Office of Research to create a faculty research commons on the third floor of Richter Library. How have these partnerships been formed? How have partners been involved in the planning processes? What are the benefits and challenges of these partnerships as they relate to space design? And what lessons have been learned?

About the University of Miami

The University of Miami is a private, secular research university in South Florida with approximately 11,000 undergraduate students, 6,000 graduate students, 3,000 faculty members, and 13,000 staff members. The university, located on three separate campuses (Coral Gables, Medical, and Rosenstiel), comprises 11 schools and colleges serving undergraduate and graduate students in more than 180 majors and programs, with libraries on each campus. The Otto G. Richter Library, which first opened in 1962, is located on the Coral Gables campus and serves as the central interdisciplinary library for the university. The learning commons is envisioned as a 21st-century transformation of the first floor, and the faculty research commons as a corresponding transformation of the third floor.

Learning Commons: Partnering to Improve Undergraduate and Graduate Education

LAUNCHING THE PROJECT

In 2014, the idea of developing a learning commons at the University of Miami began in conversation between the dean of the University of Miami (UM) Libraries and the dean of the College of Arts and Sciences. One of the drivers was pragmatic: find a new home for certain academic services, such as the Writing Center, which was inconveniently located in a building at the edge of campus; another driver was a sense of opportunity and possibility for renewing the library's space and services in relationship to student learning. The conversation expanded to include both the dean of Undergraduate Education and also the vice provost for Academic Technologies. A steering committee was established to guide the initiative. Composed of representatives from each administrative area, the university architect, and the lead for space management, the committee identified its overall goal: to colocate and coordinate the university's key academic services for students in a single convenient location on the first floor of Richter Library, a space occupied at the time by shelving that housed obsolete periodicals.

IDENTIFYING PARTNERS

Each of the administrative areas represented on the steering committee—College of Arts and Sciences, Undergraduate Education, Academic Technologies, and UM Libraries—is responsible for at least one academic services unit included in the commons: the Camner Center for Academic Resources, a peer-to-peer tutoring service, reporting to Undergraduate Education; the Writing Center and Math Lab, reporting to their respective disciplinary departments, English and mathematics, in the College of Arts and Sciences; and the Student Technology Help Desk, reporting to Academic Technologies. UM Libraries contributed its own relevant units to the commons, including the Creative Studio (a light makerspace), Digital Scholars' Lab, and a peer-to-peer reference and research consultation service. Importantly, the committee also determined that each unit would retain its unique service identity and existing structures for reporting, budgeting, and staffing. The UM Libraries agreed to provide leadership for hosting, coordinating, and stewarding the initiative.

THIRD-PARTY FACILITATION OF THE PLANNING PROCESS

Because of the complexity of the project and opportunity for innovation, brightspot strategy was enlisted to lead the planning process among relevant stakeholders. The subsequent user research and participatory planning process was conducted over a six-month period in 2015–16 and resulted in two detailed reports that have provided guidance for subsequent piloting and design. The first report, entitled "User Research Report," offers insight into student and faculty opinion.[1] The second report describes the "Service, Space, and Staffing Strategy" developed in sequenced workshops.[2]

FOSTERING RELATIONSHIPS DURING THE PARTICIPATORY PLANNING PROCESS

At the outset, a working committee was formed of representatives from each of the partners that manage their respective services on a day-to-day basis. These representatives included faculty members (both tenure-track and non-tenure-track), librarians (nontenured faculty), and full-time staff members. In several cases, they had not previously met one another, so the planning process helped stimulate new connections and relationships across campus. In other cases, representatives knew one another but had never worked so collaboratively before. The committee gathered in sequenced workshops to develop a vision, service model, and staffing strategy for the commons, as well as sharing detailed information about their units, including missions, goals, and needs. The planning process helped foster a spirit of cooperation and commitment to the overall learning commons initiative, while also exciting interest in the possibilities for improvement and growth in each of the individual services. The committee that formed during the planning process strengthened into an ongoing learning commons partners group that has continued to meet regularly.

fig 16.1

View into the largest of the flexible program spaces, with retractable glass walls, in the UM Libraries' Learning Commons (post-renovation; pre-occupancy).

(Credit: University of Miami Libraries.)

SHARED MISSION AND KEY PRINCIPLES FOR THE DESIGN OF THE LEARNING COMMONS

Led by brightspot and in consultation with the steering committee, the partners developed a shared mission for the learning commons that focused on creating opportunities for students to work individually and collaboratively, learn from both peers and experts, discover and explore resources and ideas, and create and experiment with one another. The partners also agreed on key principles driving the transformation of the first floor, including the need to coordinate services and resources across providers, foster creativity with technology, lead students to more advanced services, and showcase stories of learning, research, and creativity.

SERVICE CATEGORIES FOCUSED ON STUDENT SKILLS

Developed in response to the findings of the user research process and in workshops with the partners, the service model (figure 16.2) provides a unifying concept that focuses on the individual student learning experience. It answers the question "What do students need to be able to do in order to succeed in their studies?" The service model responds to this question by addressing students' needs to

- discover and explore resources;
- access resources and technology;
- conduct research;
- write, create, and communicate;
- publish, present, and promote;
- collaborate and discuss; and
- work with data in all its forms.

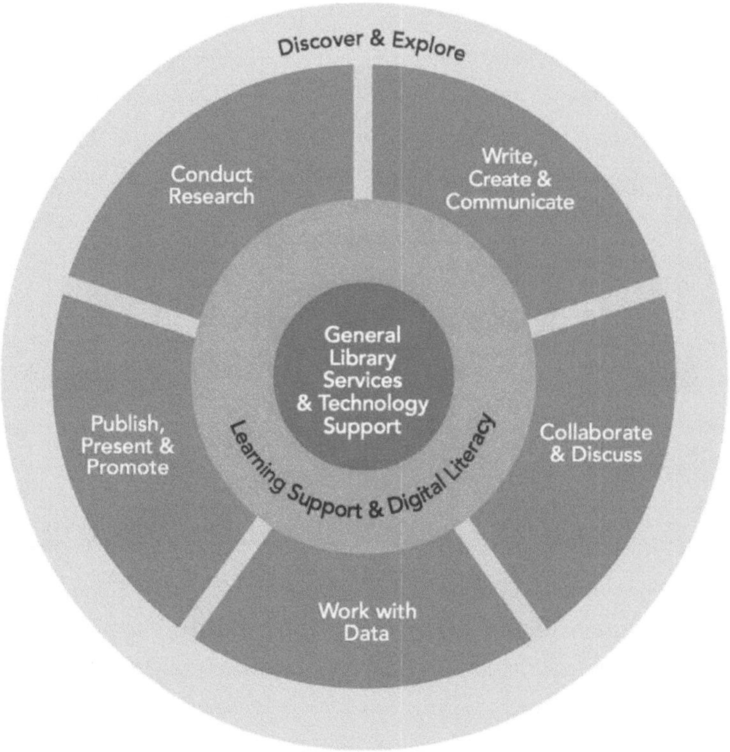

fig 16.2

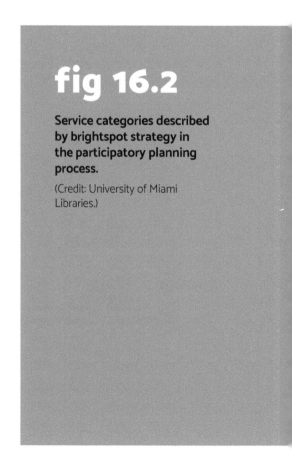

Service categories described by brightspot strategy in the participatory planning process.

(Credit: University of Miami Libraries.)

Each learning commons partner offers services that help students improve their skills in these areas. The physical platform for the service model is the library itself, providing a capacious, convenient, and flexible space for discovery and exploration. The library's core services offer access to collections, technology support, and information and digital literacy education. Other library units make it possible to help students with creative technologies, geospatial mapping, and data. The nonlibrary partners expand the service model by offering students help with writing, languages, disciplinary expertise (tutoring in individual subjects), and math. Working together, the partners provide a comprehensive set of coordinated academic services.

KEY SPACE TYPES SUPPORTING INQUIRY AND DIALOGUE

The planning process identified a set of key space types deemed essential to achieving the mission in the first phase of renovation:

1. a consultation zone providing small-group settings for appointments with staff and student experts from at least five participating academic service partners;
2. a service point for the consultation zone, where students can check in for appointments;
3. two flexible program spaces with retractable walls that can host scheduled programs and events, such as workshops and training;
4. an open study area featuring a variety of seating options and browsable shelving with new books; and
5. an office space for the new position of learning commons director (see figure 16.3).

fig 16.3

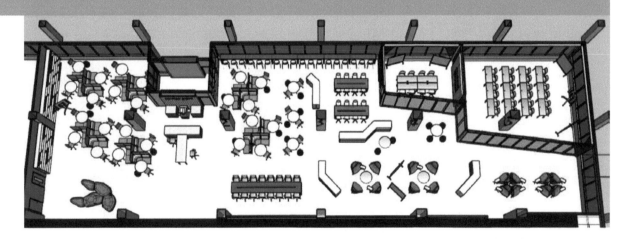

Floor plan design by G Alvarez Studio, Inc.

(Credit: University of Miami Libraries.)

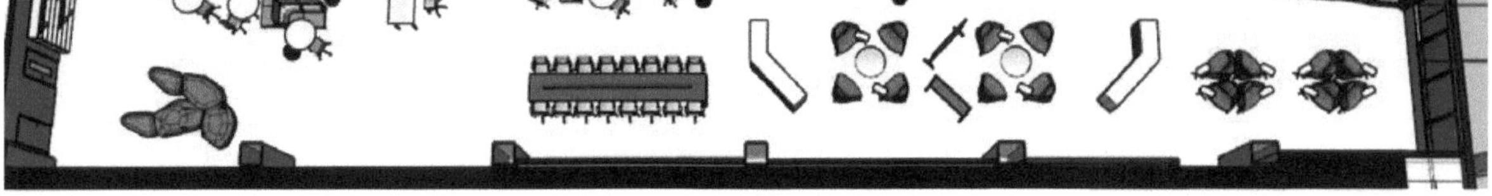

The signature space of the learning commons is the consultation zone (figure 16.4), where the academic service partners offer opportunities for students to meet with trained peers or experts for academic support. A staffed, facilitated space, the consultation zone has 24 "consultation stations," which are deployed for booked sessions during service hours and for open study after appointments have concluded. Ideal for conversations between two to four individuals, these stations are flexibly allocated for use by the partners based on usage trends and service needs. From semester to semester, as demand for services change, the stations can be reassigned to different partners.

fig 16.4

View of UM Libraries' Learning Commons' consultation zone and service point (post-renovation, pre-occupancy, wayfinding not yet installed).

(Credit: University of Miami Libraries.)

Designed by Miami architect G. Alvarez Studio, Inc., the learning commons offers a flexible environment that has made it possible to onboard new partners and thus expand the range of services provided for students. For example, following the renovation, the Modern Language Lab was invited to participate in the learning commons to offer opportunities for students to practice communication skills in languages other than English.

TYPES OF PARTNERSHIPS: HEADQUARTERED, SATELLITE, VISITING, AND SUPPORTING

Partners participate in the commons in a variety of ways. *Headquartered* partners deliver their full portfolio of services in the commons, which serves as their only location. *Satellite* partners deliver a selection of services in the commons but are headquartered elsewhere. *Visiting* partners offer services on a part-time basis: offering office hours, for instance. *Supporting* partners, such as Library Facilities and IT, provide behind-the-scenes support. These categories have helped define and frame the relationships that are facilitated by the UM Libraries. Importantly, the partnership framework is inclusive, valuing the contributions of each of the units.

DOCUMENTING AND AFFIRMING RELATIONSHIPS THROUGH MEMORANDA OF UNDERSTANDING

A written memorandum of understanding (MOU) was developed by the UM Libraries to define the parameters of the partnerships with the nonlibrary academic service partners. The introduction to the MOU summarizes the learning commons' purpose, background, vision and mission, and service model and the type of partnership. The core of the document describes library and nonlibrary partner responsibilities related to budget; staffing, orientation, and training; hours of operation; space and utilities; communication and promotion; technology and IT support; and supplies.

PILOTING AS OPPORTUNITY FOR PARTNERS TO LEARN TOGETHER

In 2016–17, prior to the release of any funding for renovation, the learning commons initiative was piloted in its designated space on the first floor of Richter Library that had been cleared of compact shelving and periodicals. The Writing Center, Math Lab, and reference service physically moved into the space using their existing furniture, and an experimental service point was established using repurposed and temporary furniture. Staff members offered coordinated services in the space and collaborated to develop solutions to challenges as they arose. Moreover, the piloting process gave UML's communications team a chance to test various wayfinding and promotional materials and strategies. The results of the piloting phase were encouraging. Students enjoyed having more space to learn on the first floor of Richter Library, and their readiness to use the piloted commons, even with outdated furniture, helped convince key administrators that the initiative could work.

STAFFING STRATEGY DEVELOPMENT AND RECRUITMENT OF NEW POSITIONS

The planning process also included the development of a staffing strategy. The partners were asked, "How should the commons be managed? What roles will be needed to make sure it runs successfully?" Ensuing conversations gave the partners an opportunity to discuss coordination and assessment needs, technology support, and other areas of concern. Importantly, the articulated strategy reflected the partners' willingness to rethink existing positions and adopt shared positions for the service point.

Successful searches were conducted for two new positions that were designated in the staffing strategy: a lead for the learning commons and a lead for assessment. These positions were funded through the UM Libraries by repurposing existing open positions. The new learning commons director guides the evolving relationships between the partners and coordinates expanding services and programs through activities such as holding regular partner meetings, liaising with UM Libraries' Facilities and IT employees, and developing workshops and programming.

SHARED ASSESSMENT STRATEGY

In collaboration with the learning commons director, the new assessment librarian developed an assessment strategy to evaluate the learning commons activities in light of its mission and vision. Assessment activities have involved participatory data gathering and analysis of data collected from all partners composed into reports that are presented annually to the steering committee. Collaborating around data and assessment has pivoted the learning commons partners from being solely concerned with their own unit's achievements to focusing on common overarching outcomes. The partners have agreed on mutual goals and set short- and long-term targets. In addition to data gathered from partners, the learning commons assessment activities include focus groups, feedback surveys, whiteboard polling, evaluation of space utilization, and user behavior observation both in the physical space and online. Insights from multiple data sources have been essential to measure progress, make changes, support ongoing engagement with partners, and communicate value.[3] Guided by data, the learning commons has documented an increase in student engagement with both its services and the libraries overall and demonstrated contribution to the university's teaching and learning efforts (figure 16.5). As a result, new conversations are underway about how the learning commons can contribute even more to university initiatives related to student success, retention, and graduation.

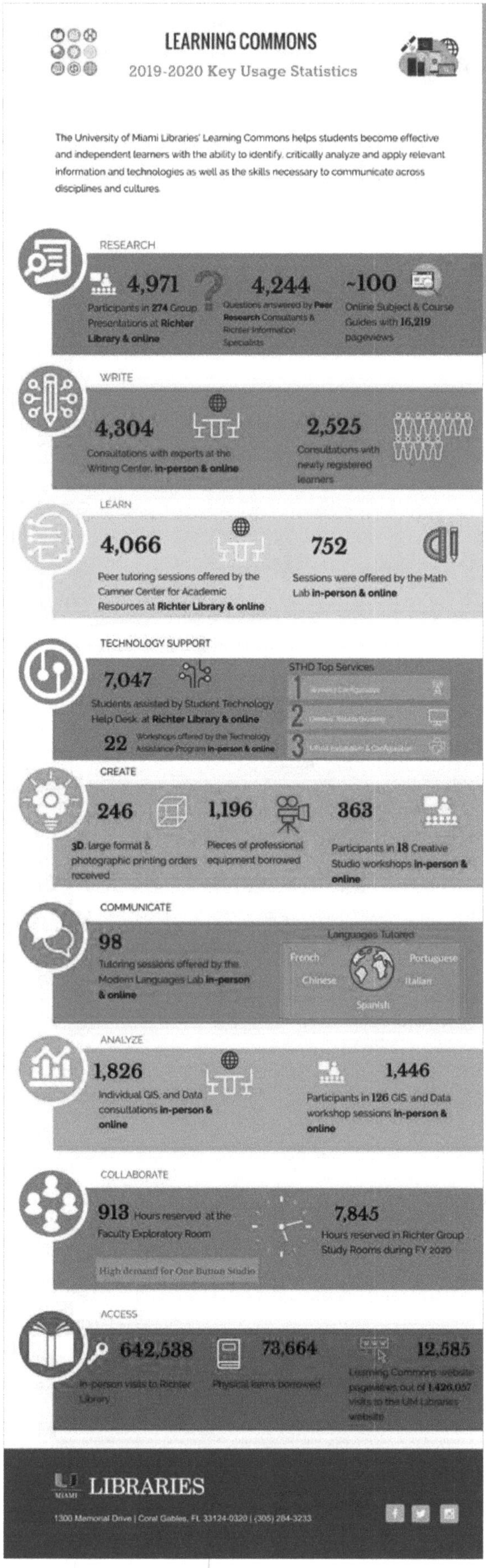

fig 16.5

The learning commons 2019–20 key usage statistics.

(Credit: University of Miami Libraries.)

SHARED SUCCESS IN THE RENOVATED SPACE

Due to the strength of the relationships formed between the partners themselves and skillful facilitation of these relationships by the director, the learning commons has proved to be an effective strategic initiative that fosters student engagement across multiple disciplines. In its first four years, participating academic services experienced increases in demand for consultations and tutoring appointments; new programming enticed both students and faculty to gather in the flexible, multipurpose rooms; and overall library occupancy increased following the renovation. In post-occupancy assessments, students have reported their approval of the space, services, and furniture; in fact, they would now like to see additional renovations that match the success of the 2018 project.

BENEFITS OF PARTNERSHIPS IN THE LEARNING COMMONS

Improved student access to academic services and resources across providers: One location for many academic services within the library provides students with convenient access to the support they need outside of class. Additionally, the learning commons consultation zone has made it possible for some satellite partners, such as the Camner Center, to extend its operating hours so that students have greater access to services than they had previously.

Increased use of the library overall: Student visits to Richter Library have increased with the opening of the learning commons. Use of the first floor has grown, and the variety of work activities among students on the floor has expanded.

Improved referral process: Service providers are more familiar with the other services offered in the commons and able to refer students to other services with greater ease and confidence.

Greater range and visibility of programming: The flexible program spaces adjacent to the consultation zone are frequently used for workshops, training sessions, orientations, and events that are open to the whole university community.

Coordinated assessment: The ability to gather and coordinate usage data from each of the partners on a regular basis has resulted in a clearer understanding of how students are using academic support services on campus and what additional help they need.

CHALLENGES

Managing flow of students into the commons: The open plan for the consultation zone, designed to be highly accessible and visible to students entering the library, presents challenges with managing the flow of students into the space. Learning commons staff have found it difficult, especially at peak times, to balance student demand for study space with the needs of students arriving for scheduled tutoring appointments across multiple service providers—the primary function of the consultation zone.

Service point design: The service point (figure 16.6), which offers stations for two full-time staff members and four student employees to be working simultaneously, was designed to be highly visible and enticing. However, the design is fixed and inflexible, and staff have identified the need for adjustments. A more flexible service point that would allow for changes and growth in the staffing model is desired.

fig 16.6

UML Learning Commons consultation zone service point.

(Credit: University of Miami Libraries.)

Comfort of expert service providers in consultation zone: The consultation zone was designed primarily with students in mind. As a result, some of the expert service providers, namely faculty members, have found it challenging to provide consultations in the renovated space, especially due to its permeable nature. These employees have identified the need for more visual and acoustical privacy for some consultations in the highly dynamic, collaborative space.

Balancing individual service identities with the skill-based service model: Promotion of the skill-based service model has been somewhat challenging to implement. Most of the participating academic service units already had well-established names for their services and associated branding that they wished to preserve going forward, and these names do not necessarily align with the service model categories. As a result, advertising for the learning commons includes both the terminology from the service model and the identities of the individual service providers, with the website reflecting this hybrid promotional approach.

Technology integration: multiple systems for appointment booking: One discovery in the planning process was the number of different types of specialized appointment-booking software being used by the various academic services. Students have to familiarize themselves with separate appointment-booking schedules and software for services, rather than using a single shared system. Work on resolving this challenge is ongoing.

LESSONS LEARNED

Mixed results of open, permeable designs: Student use of the space increases, but challenges occur in managing student flow into the space. The design of flexible, adaptable service points becomes especially critical.

Significance of ongoing cross-campus relationships: Strong relationships between service providers formed in the planning process are key to the stability and enduring success of the commons.

Librarians as facilitators of cross-campus partnerships: Librarians are providing leadership roles as connectors and community builders by facilitating relationships between the academic units, ensuring that partnerships are supported over time. This raises the visibility of the library and demonstrates its capacity to be integral in forming collaborative networks on campus.

Reflections Post-2020: The Learning Commons and DEAI Initiatives

With flexibility as one of its chief design principles, the learning commons has been successful in creating a platform for learning that complements the classroom and reaches beyond it. Additionally, flexibility allows it to be responsive to educational needs that arise from changing social contexts, as occurred with the increased attention to racial justice in the US during the summer of 2020. With outreach and engagement efforts that have centered diversity, equity, accessibility, and inclusion (DEAI) interests, the learning commons has become an important site for racial justice education and activity.

One example of creating avenues for community learning and growth in areas of social justice is the Spotlight Collection program, which connects themes from current events and culture, such as Black history and women's history, with selections from library collections (figure 16.7). Typically, these are physical displays of circulating materials located on browsable shelves in the learning commons consultation zone, a high-traffic area among students. With the shift to remote programming during the COVID-19 pandemic, the Spotlight Collection program began to feature digital collections. An example is the *Malaika* handbooks, a series of digitized campus guides for the University of Miami created and published in the 1970s and 1980s by the United Black Students organization.[4]

A second initiative central to the learning commons' DEAI work is its collaboration with the campus-wide common read program, One Book, One U, designed to build dialogue and community among students, faculty, staff, and alumni using texts centered in diversity and inclusion.[5] Its coordinators invited the libraries into collaboration soon after its spring 2018 launch. For three years, the learning commons has been an important partner with One Book, One U, hosting events like student-author conversations and book giveaways. In the fall of 2020, the learning commons became the administrative home for the program. Because One Book, One U centers on readings that speak directly to diversity and inclusion, such as the 2020–21 selection, Ijeoma Oluo's book *So You Want to Talk about Race*, the learning commons serves as a critical site for learning and exchange.[6]

fig 16.7

Learning commons includes browsing collections with adjacent comfortable seating. Spotlight Collections can be featured on the top surface of the shelves.

(Credit: University of Miami Libraries.)

The UM Libraries' exhibitions program has also provided the learning commons with an opportunity to engage students within a DEAI context. Because the entrance to the learning commons consultation zone is adjacent to a gallery space, it becomes possible to pique student interest by placing compelling materials on display. When the materials highlight and promote social justice themes, the potential for learning and civic engagement is amplified. This was the case in the summer of 2021, when two exhibitions, entitled *Hostile Terrain 94* and *Separated*, focused on the decades-long humanitarian crisis at the border of the United States and Mexico.

Faculty Research Commons: Partnering to Support Faculty Interdisciplinary Research

Thanks to the success of the learning commons, an idea emerged in 2018 to create a similar library environment addressing faculty needs to be housed in a reimagined, renovated third floor of Richter Library. The faculty research commons initiative has developed as a partnership between the UM Libraries and the Office of Research with the goal of providing improved spaces and services to support faculty research, particularly interdisciplinary, collaborative efforts. In early 2019, brightspot strategy was enlisted once again to lead a participatory planning process that included visioning exercises and the development of a space and service strategy.[7] This process drew upon data gathered from an Ithaka S+R Faculty Survey conducted at the University of Miami in the fall of 2018. At the conclusion of the planning process, brightspot produced a compelling report that offers guidance for how the third floor of Richter Library might be designed and outlines ideas for piloting key concepts.

The planning process engaged participants for several committees, including a working group consisting of representatives from the UM Libraries, the Office of Research, the University Architect's Office, the Faculty Senate, Faculty Affairs, Academic Technologies, the Graduate School, and others; a faculty advisory group with representative researchers from the 11 schools and colleges; and a set of interview participants that included the president of the university and other key campus leaders. Other participants included potential partners, such as the Center for Humanities, which may be headquartered within the commons or immediately adjacent to it. Together, these groups and individuals offered opinions and insights that helped shape the vision, service, and space strategy.

The vision for the faculty research commons emphasizes the cultivation of community among faculty members. During interviews and workshops with faculty members from the university's 11 disciplinary schools and colleges, one pressing need that faculty consistently identified was for more opportunities to connect to other researchers. Faculty members were particularly interested in ways to meet across different disciplines and the university's three campuses. They also expressed desires to be exposed to new ideas and technologies, share knowledge, and form new collaborations. Consequently, the faculty research commons began to be imagined as a library space where new relationships between faculty members could develop with the potential to catalyze innovative cross-disciplinary research questions and projects.

With this vision in mind, brightspot offered a "theory of engagement" based on the work of Mark Granovetter to help guide the service and space strategy development. This network theory posits that human relationships exist as "ties" and can be characterized as "strong" or "weak," both of which have advantages and disadvantages when it comes to sharing existing information and creating new knowledge. Brightspot argued that the design of services, programs, and events in the commons could be informed by careful consideration of what types of ties need to be cultivated between faculty, depending on the desired outcomes. This theory helped inform subsequent consideration of service design and space types.

Unlike the learning commons, with its focus on colocation and coordination of expert and peer service providers offering consultations, the faculty research commons concentrates on fostering connections between faculty members themselves. One articulated strategy to achieve this is to offer programs for faculty networking, matchmaking, sharing skills, and presenting and showcasing research. Another service model proposal is to facilitate connections with partner units responsible for research and grants administration on campus. Instead of having a fixed set of service partners operating within the commons, experts might be invited in for office hours with availability advertised ahead of time, thus encouraging a sense of faculty ownership of the space. Experts could include digital scholarship librarians and subject librarians, whose offices will be located adjacent to the commons; as members of the faculty themselves, librarians would also be participating actively in the life of the commons. Nonlibrary entities would operate as satellite partners offering services from time to time in the commons, but be headquartered elsewhere. Potential partners in this category included Government Relations, Corporate and Foundation Relations, and Business Intelligence.

Faculty envision the commons overall as having a "distinct and elevated atmosphere" that would both be inspirational and afford a sense of privacy for those seeking advice and help with research ideas and projects. In discussions, faculty also emphasized the importance of natural light, comfort, quiet, and personal control in the space design. Space types critical for supporting the vision and services in Richter include a welcoming entrance service point; enclosed meeting rooms and informal collaboration spaces for consultations and team meetings; a tech sandbox for emerging technologies and media production; a large flexible event space for presentations, lectures, and other programs; and a café and outdoor balcony space. Furthermore, the faculty expressed interest in the addition of places for rest and reflection, such as a meditation room.

Importantly, this new service and space model for the faculty research commons would require the UM Libraries to hire new staff members to achieve the innovative plan. Key areas of responsibility would include leadership, programming and event planning, reception, navigation and referral, communications and outreach, facilities operations, and technology support. Some of these could be accomplished by expanding roles of existing staff members; in other cases, such as leadership, new positions would need to be created. Just as in the learning commons, the role of the faculty research commons director in nurturing the development of partnerships is expected to be vital to the success of the overall program.

Over the last two years, since the release of brightspot's report in spring 2019, UM Libraries has begun experimenting with pilots of different services and space types using existing spaces, furniture, and resources. Piloting for the faculty research commons will continue until the project receives approval for design and renovation. Service pilots include the U-LINK Librarian Program, an embedded librarian program for university-funded interdisciplinary research team projects focused on societal problems; Research Sprints for U-LINK, involving targeted support for teams facing specific research obstacles or challenges; and networking events that match researchers interested in applying for U-LINK grants. Space pilots include the faculty exploratory, a meeting space for research teams; a renovated faculty reading room for individual study; and an XR/AR/VR lab, a collaboration with the Provost's

Office, for experimentation with spatial computing. Future design and renovation of the faculty research commons are anticipated, but currently on hold due to budget mitigation efforts resulting from the COVID-19 pandemic.

BENEFITS

Opportunity to check assumptions about faculty needs: The planning process revealed that faculty would like to have agency in the space and invite in services as needed, rather than have services colocated and coordinated in the space at all times. This shift in emphasis has important implications for the design of partner relationships.

Engaging with university leaders in conversations about the future of research and the role of the library: Interviews with key leaders helped inspire dialogue about the library's current and potential contributions to the university's research environment. The library is viewed as a key partner for the Office of Research and Provost's Office in strategic work to support interdisciplinary research, experiment with innovative technologies, and create a platform for connection making and collaboration on campus.

Learning from piloting experimental services: Creating programs like the U-LINK Librarian initiative has given the library the chance to explore new roles for librarians in the research process and gain insights into research needs of the faculty, especially as they relate to interdisciplinary research on pressing societal problems, such as racial justice and climate change.

CHALLENGES

Transitions in university leadership: Since the faculty research commons initiative began, changes in senior university leadership roles have necessitated new relationship building and adjustments to pilots in response to shifting priorities.

Need for greater attention to inclusivity: A challenge of the network model used in the faculty research commons planning process is that it did not sufficiently address the networking needs of underrepresented, marginalized members of the faculty given structural, systemic racism. Moving forward, the initiative must center engagement with BIPOC faculty members to ensure an inclusive environment. Additional partnerships need to be cultivated with administrative units that are working to support these communities and academic centers advancing relevant research agendas, such as the developing Center for Global Black Studies and the emerging Native American and Global Indigenous Studies program.

Designing Libraries in a Way That Fosters Community and Resilience

For the UM Libraries, the learning commons and faculty research commons initiatives are ambitious attempts to create more inviting, relevant, and supportive environments for students and faculty where they can engage in conversation with one another around questions of shared interest and with access to needed services and resources. In his book *Palaces for the People: How Social Infrastructure Can Help Fight Inequality, Polarization, and the Decline of Civic Life*, Eric Klinenberg writes that "despite—or maybe precisely because of—the fact that we spend so much time on screens and the Internet, we desperately need common places where people can come together, participate in civil society, and build stronger social bonds."[8] Klinenberg describes libraries as "among the most critical forms of social infrastructure" needed for building community.[9] In this 21st-century environment, libraries are serving an important function of connecting people not just to crucial information, but also, importantly, to one another. Located at the heart of the Coral Gables campus of the University of Miami, Richter Library—where both of these commons projects have taken shape over the last six years—now serves as a location for intentionally nurturing "stronger social bonds" among members of its diverse community.[10]

The UM Libraries has learned that the success of these community-building efforts depends a great deal on the quality of the relationships between employees themselves—the faculty and staff members who teach, research, and provide services in different administrative and academic areas across the university. Through active engagement in the participatory planning process for new library spaces, these employees have grown closer and more collaborative, more aware of one another's services and more attuned to the larger campus community. The result of these relationships has been the development of cocreated service models and pilots that would not otherwise have been possible.

The relationships established between employees have also strengthened the ability of the commons initiatives to transition effectively to online environments during the pandemic. Envisioned initially as primarily physical spaces for learning and research, the commons have evolved digitally, becoming virtual platforms for connection making, sustainability, and support in a time of crisis. As at many libraries, in the spring semester of 2020, the learning commons partners quickly shifted their consultations and tutoring appointments online. Students have appreciated the ability to meet with trained peers and experts remotely and hope that these options continue after the pandemic concludes. Online programs have also allowed for a broader range of participants than ever before, including alumni and community members in other states and countries, at a time when connection making is particularly vital for health and well-being. The partnerships developed prior to the pandemic have been critical to making this transition to online service delivery possible; the social infrastructure they embody ensures that the common places can thrive both in person and online.

As these initiatives demonstrate, designing new spaces and services in libraries provides extraordinary opportunities for fostering new collaborative relationships on campus or developing existing ones. Through participatory design processes, participants from multiple campus units can deepen understanding of one another's services and develop a stronger sense of shared mission. Such processes lead to cocreated spaces that enable ongoing relationships with students and faculty—beyond transactional encounters—and ensure that insights and innovations continue after initial planning has concluded. The communities of service providers that emerge are sources of expertise and resilience for the university as a whole, particularly in times of crisis.

Notes

1. Brightspot strategy, "University of Miami Learning Commons: User Research Report," October 2015, https://miami.app.box.com/s/v15bz6pm49eagcwlzsmad9ka1dt3m8dv.
2. Brightspot strategy, "University of Miami Learning Commons: Service, Space, and Staffing Strategy," February 2016, https://miami.app.box.com/s/clajg2i15344f9r82fgo5weq1ykpx7p7.
3. Association of College and Research Libraries, *Academic Library Impact: Improving Practice and Essential Areas to Research*, white paper, prepared by Lynn Silipigni Connaway,William Harvey, Vanessa Kitzie, and Stephanie Mikitish (Chicago: Association of College and Research Libraries, 2017), https://www.ala.org/acrl/sites/ala.org.acrl/files/content/publications/whitepapers/academiclib.pdf.
4. United Black Students of the University of Miami, Malaika Handbooks, digital collection, University of Miami, 1971–1985, https://cdm17191.contentdm.oclc.org/digital/collection/asu0161.
5. "One Book, One U," University of Miami Libraries, https://culture.miami.edu/programs/one-book/index.html.
6. Ijeomo Oluo, *So You Want to Talk about Race* (New York: Seal Press, 2018).
7. Brightspot strategy, University of Miami Faculty Research Commons Final Report, March 2019. https://miami.app.box.com/s/6dl8xr5126d2iuczmcswz0sng1brgk94.
8. Eric Klinenberg, *Palaces for the People: How Social Infrastructure Can Help Fight Inequality, Polarization, and the Decline of Civic Life* (New York: Crown, 2018), 217.
9. Klinenberg, *Palaces for the People*, 32.
10. Klinenberg, *Palaces for the People*, 217.

17

CHAPTER SEVENTEEN

A RENOVATION SOLIDIFIES A PARTNERSHIP

The Odegaard Writing and Research Center

JOHN DANNEKER

As a university library approaches a transformation of existing spaces and buildings, it is particularly critical to remember that a major renovation of a campus building may occur only once in several decades, so renovation planning must anticipate future growth while addressing current needs. Particularly in times of shrinking budgets and retrenchment in higher education, the renovation choices we make—and the related signals those choices send to library users, staff, and university administration—not only speak volumes about a library's priorities but also hold great potential to catalyze future change to transform our organizations.

In considering the effects of space planning and design on student learning and success, it has been argued that both a holistic view and intentionality are important factors:

> In higher education, there is a growing understanding that the layout of our campuses, the design of our academic buildings, and the quality of the education we provide all have an impact on academic culture and student experience. Today's marketing, student recruitment and retention strategies, and practices in higher education increasingly reflect an emphasis on the whole experience of learning. Understanding the potential of space to positively impact student learning and student success, intentional library space planning must be a priority.[1]

If libraries strive to be learning spaces that are holistically user-centered and student-supporting within our increasingly cross-disciplinary universities, it is then critical to insert into renovation conversations the possibility of realizing spaces for existing and future partnerships, particularly those that may most benefit our library users.

This chapter explores a partnership space that was realized during a major renovation, the Odegaard Writing and Research Center (OWRC) located in the Odegaard Undergraduate Library, a bustling 24-5 student hub on the Seattle campus of the University of Washington (UW). Planning for and completing a major renovation of Odegaard in 2012–13 led to a deeper examination of the ongoing writing and research partnership and, ultimately, a lasting commitment to a colocation of services. In the past eight years of operations, both the shared space itself and the stronger cross-staff relationships that colocation requires have helped to sustain and grow the partnership through leadership changes, organizational shifts, and, more recently, national conditions that have tested it. When looking back, if surviving the year 2020 teaches us the importance of both resilience and flexibility in student-facing library services, examples like the user-focused partnership engendered by the OWRC space are poised to endure.

This chapter begins with a brief examination of select literature about library partnerships (both general, and academic libraries and writing centers specifically) and previous writing about the OWRC partnership. Then, after discussing the 2012–13 renovation and concepts of learning guiding the work, it illustrates key design choices that help situate the shared space of the OWRC in the greater context of the renovation and mentions a few areas for improvement. The chapter next considers lessons learned through organizational changes and choices that have occurred and ways that collaboration encouraged by the OWRC physical space renovation have helped the partnership to endure. The chapter concludes by looking ahead from early lessons of the year 2020 to anticipate future staffing and delivery of services of the OWRC and how those may further test the partnership and the space.

Key Literature on Partnerships

Much has been explored about the value of partnerships and collaboration in serving library users effectively, including countless variations of partnerships in university libraries. While the body of literature is too vast to be surveyed effectively in the span of this short chapter, key concepts from a few authors over the past decade have proven to be influential touchstones regarding the views on partnerships in Odegaard.

From a perspective of academic libraries and partnerships, a team from the University of Wisconsin–Madison explored partnerships as a force to redefine the traditional roles of the library within campuses. They apply Lippincott's framework defining types of partnerships (colocation, cooperation, collaboration) that may exist within a department's span of control,[2] and they explain how their examination of those relationships led to a more strategic alignment of effort invested by the UW staff. They advise that "understanding the benefits of partnerships can help libraries better understand their role within our institutions and help guide the library through the changing landscape of higher education."[3]

Similarly, a team from Cornell University Libraries described assessment tools that they used to determine the viability of partnerships as part of a greater strategic planning effort and, ultimately, to help define whether partnerships are a worthwhile investment of limited resources. They illustrate the importance of regular assessment to potential and existing partnerships, and they remind readers that a standard tool helps you to assess partnerships more objectively.[4]

Finally, there exists a complex history of partnerships between university libraries and writing centers. New publications build on the rich body of literature annually, focusing on topics of information literacy, pedagogy, organizational models, writing and learning theory, and more. Still, the survey authored by Ferer in 2012—which summarizes much of the available literature consulted by UW teams at the time of the Odegaard renovation—remains an invaluable resource as a jumping-off point for exploring these collaborations.[5]

The OWRC Partnership and the 2012–13 Renovation

Both great opportunity and challenge exist in strategically chosen and regularly assessed partnerships, and a regular consideration of the benefits to both users and staff is critical if we are to sustain these partnerships. At the UW, a partnership between the College of Arts and Sciences and the libraries extends back across two decades, with a version of the writing center being housed in Odegaard officially since the 2004–05 academic year. A previous publication about the OWRC partnership focused on the relationship between the areas of writing and research expertise and the ways in which the staff from the college and the libraries, who jointly staff the OWRC, collaborated to articulate underlying values and shared vocabularies to guide continued services across the center. This included a grounding of services in the ACRL *Framework* and shared conversational consultation models drawing on the affective in interactions.[6] It was argued that this cross-divisional partnership and lessons learned through it have broadened the capabilities of both writing tutors and librarians, and that by demonstrating "leadership to our campus constituencies—through excellent services achieved by a combining of disciplines and working across cultural divisions, we model the very learning we hope students will achieve in our undergraduate environment."[7]

While the previous article also illustrates the OWRC space as a manifestation of organic partnership relative to the active learning classrooms that were also realized during the 2012–13 renovation, there is little doubt that underlying principles that guided the entire renovation—namely the creation and activation of spaces for 21st-century student learning and academic success—were critical to the physical choices in design, build, and finishes that made the project successful. The Odegaard project presented a rare opportunity to explore explicitly the creation of space for partnerships within an existing loved and heavily trafficked building.

The 2012–13 renovation resulted from a UW provost–commissioned report from the Odegaard Undergraduate Library Building Vision Steering Group, which in 2010 pointed to directions in teaching and learning outcomes, academic student success, and social functions that could be realized through a renovation of this facility. Writing in that report, the group expressed that "the vision and resulting revitalized facility will serve as a powerful demonstration of the University's commitment to a high-quality undergraduate experience" and "will be a direct and visible demonstration to students that they come first."[8]

The libraries then worked with the capital planning offices in UW Facilities to complete a feasibility study and successfully proposed the renovation of Odegaard as a capital project with major funding from the state of Washington, to which additional funding from UW and libraries' endowments was added. A challenge, however, was the expected turnaround from the award of state funding in 2011 to the expected completion of the work in mid-2013.

Accomplishing the scope of work within this timeline required creativity and innovations in processes. Project lead contractors Mortenson Construction and architects the Miller Hull Partnership worked closely with UW Facilities, incorporating the libraries and stakeholder partners, and completed the entire project, from planning to occupancy, in 20 months, with a successful delivery in summer 2013 for an autumn 2013 reopening.

> The university was strategic in selecting its design and construction partners together before programming was even completed. By integrating the project delivery team early in the process, the team capitalized on the time to understand its customer's business, and improve it through increased usable square footage and a higher-quality student experience. The collaborative process enabled the team to complete the project in just under one year, while allowing students to continue to use the space for their studies. The renovated library is equipped to serve students in a more social and sustainable learning and study setting.[9]

A Miller Hall partner and design lead on the Odegaard project who regularly presents about learning spaces, Ruth Baleiko, has written about the renovation:

> The way we were able to transform Odegaard Undergraduate Library's existing structure into an award-winning, 21st century landscape of spaces allows the university to better accommodate today's academic expectations and restore itself as the "heart" for students of all disciplines. Peer-to-peer and active learning is now tangibly on display.[10]

The activation and maximization of usable space in the renovated building's open first floor serves to foreground learning as both a collaborative and social process that is the building's focal point. As this is a critical space for student learning, and particularly a high-volume hub of daily activity, Baleiko explains that the concept of serving as the "students' office on campus" guided the work and

> suggests a stronger relationship between student learning outcomes and the library. Our team seized this and worked with the university to identify a series of behaviors or learning experiences that global citizens should have as part of their university education. This list acted as the driver for design interventions within the building: all the elements we added were directly related to accomplishing and expressing those learning outcomes.[11]

Placed within the overall learning space concept of the Odegaard renovation, and especially within the context of a floor that also features two large active learning classrooms and a smaller instruction/computer lab, the OWRC comprises a complementary service and collaboration space on the redesigned first floor where learning is visibly occurring in various modes, including active, group, and individual learning across formal and informal spaces.

The OWRC Space

The 2012–13 renovation resulted in the OWRC space as a central focal point of the dramatically improved first floor. In creating the footprint of the OWRC, a physical space that combines the functions of research and writing support emerged:

> We created a shared service space that allows numerous simultaneous consultations and requires a blending of our work cultures and models, [combining the staff employed by the College of Arts and Sciences and the libraries] in a learning environment that blurs false divisions between research and writing. Our joint belief is that research and writing are intertwined and iterative processes occurring

> within ongoing academic conversations, and having them play out in a shared physical space promotes better support of the many needs that a student may have when they approach our staff.[12]

The physical footprint of the OWRC sits on the center rear of Odegaard's first floor open atrium (figure 17.1) and occupies a space with much higher visibility than the writing center had prior to the renovation, when it was housed in a very large study room on the building's third floor. The increased visibility of the OWRC, coupled with an increase in the number of student writing tutors, led to a dramatic increase in appointments in the years that followed the renovation—writing appointments rose to an all-time high before plateauing and (later) falling due to budget constraints resulting from Seattle minimum wage increases that greatly impacted the total working hours of student hourly staff. The shared space has created an ease of referrals and collaborations among the writing and research staff within the center, who are no longer separated by several floors.

fig 17.1

View of the OWRC from the first floor atrium.

(© Lara Swimmer Photography.)

In consulting broadly with users, staff, and stakeholders, the renovation architects and project managers made several key design choices that serve to link the OWRC with the overall look and feel of the building while creating a space that is a manifestation of the shared vision.

Glass walls envelop the center on three sides and duplicate renovation design choices throughout the project, including the glassed-in silent study/stacks floor and the three new classrooms elsewhere on the first floor. From the outside, the glass "open kitchen" concept allows users to see in and creates interest in the ongoing consultations, thus marketing the services (figure 17.2). At the same time, clients and staff enjoy visual connections to the bustling open atrium and natural lighting, and they feel part of the goings-on of the whole building.

The visual accessibility of the space is critical for another reason: on a large R1 campus where many undergraduate students may otherwise feel overwhelmed or lack connection with and knowledge of academic supports, it is particularly important that a renovation create spaces that further a sense of belonging by establishing the approachability of academic support services, like those offered in the OWRC. One simply cannot overstate the value of centrally locating critical academic supports in a familiar setting that destigmatizes and normalizes—and, when successful, even celebrates!—the process of reaching out for assistance. The act of coming into a visually welcoming and easily accessible environment like the OWRC feels less like a punishment or a weakness (a deficit model) than an opportunity for clients to work with staff and contribute their own knowledge to cocreate their success (a strength model). To reinforce this, students are consistently encouraged to come to the OWRC at any stage of the writing and research process.

fig 17.2

The front wall of the OWRC.

(© Emily Ruder/UW Libraries.)

Within the OWRC, options of several seating arrangements create a nonhierarchical space in which clients choose either seating at round tables or a "genius bar" type interaction. Both setups allow for close interaction, including easy screen sharing or paper sharing, between the service provider and the client. The positioning of these options across the open space also allows for a more public or private conversation, depending on a client's needs and comfort. In addition to client support via librarians and peer tutors, the OWRC and Odegaard directors agreed to jointly fund hourly student administrative support in the form of a walk-up concierge and intake/follow-up assistance, which serves as a welcoming presence to demystify the service. Also notable within the space is the inclusion of several computing options (including laptops and fixed workstations) for interactive co-researching and workshopping (figure 17.3).

fig 17.3

View through side windows of ongoing writing and research help appointments, showing seating options, concierge station, computing options, with conference room at rear.

(© Emily Ruder/UW Libraries.)

Besides the technology options, also critical are several whiteboard paint walls (figure 17.4), which create surfaces for clients and staff to collaboratively map out ideas, brainstorm research and writing topics, create mind maps and word webs, or simply doodle. This simple, yet effective, maximization of limited space allows for the working out of ideas in ways that activate spatial and tactile connections that differ from collaborating on computer screens alone. The choice of orange color carries through a major visual accent of the entire renovation, and it serves not only to warm the space but also to form a visual connection with many other writing surfaces spread throughout the building.

fig 17.4

Students collaborate at a writing wall.
(© Emily Ruder/UW Libraries.)

Beyond the consultation spaces for research and writing help, it was necessary that dedicated space be provided for the Arts and Sciences professional staff of the OWRC. Utilizing a small footprint at the very back of the space, the renovation incorporates one private office for administration, a small semiprivate conference room, and an informal staff alcove space for student tutors. (A notable limitation of combined air circulation and egress concerns prevented the conference room from being fully enclosed.)

Despite overall positive responses to the OWRC, as is often the case with major renovations, a few challenges with design and finishes have since arisen:

- The open floor plan of the space, which allows for variety in seating choice during regular service volume periods, can become a challenge in noise and distraction for clients and staff during periods of high occupancy, such as the weeks leading to major project and paper deadlines when 10 or more concurrent appointments are occurring. Additionally, noise from the partially enclosed conference room sometimes affects appointments on the floor of the main space. Potential solutions of partial divider walls and noise-dampening surfaces have been considered, in addition to moving research consultation appointments into private librarian offices, if clients request.
- The value-engineered whiteboard paint walls, which took the place of pricier enameled metal or glass surfaces, have not withstood years of use and abuse. Similar to other public parts of the building, these surfaces will be addressed with a more durable replacement treatment, likely glass boards.
- Due to changes in center permanent staffing, there is a lack of sufficient dedicated office/administrative space to accommodate back-of-house functions. An additional underutilized corner space near the present single office is being considered for a cubicle addition, which would eliminate one or two tables previously available for client consultations.

Post-renovation: Ongoing Organizational Transformation

If post-renovation architectural awards (including recognitions from the American Institute of Architects, the American Library Association, and *Library Journal*) and generally positive assessments from periodic libraries user surveys are good indicators, the building's transformation has been a broad success.[13] Both clients and staff have benefitted from the new location of the OWRC space, but the successes have not been without challenges in the ensuing eight years.

The most immediate benefits of closer partnership in the OWRC, including an ease of cross-staff referrals and interactions, a shift to a more conversational model of research assistance, and a standardization of the use of ACRL *Framework* as shared principles across the writing tutors and librarians, were realized within the first few years of the combined space.[14] A related offshoot of the renovation that points to a broadened successful partnership is the creation of new outposts of the writing center in two other libraries spaces—one geared toward general graduate students in the Research Commons in Allen Library, and one in the Health Sciences Library that serves students in related disciplines. These locations, which are staffed and administered through the OWRC, resulted from the higher visibility of the center and the ongoing success of the writing and research partnership as a direct result of the Odegaard renovation.

Numerous organizational transformations have occurred since the opening of the OWRC space in 2013, and for the partnership to thrive, both the OWRC writing tutoring staff and the libraries research staff have relied on the partnership's strong foundations that were forged through the collaborative space planning, execution, and occupancy. One notable shift has been a greater investment on the part of the units' administrative leadership in ongoing regular meetings and shared visioning and planning regarding the OWRC space, through regular monthly meetings between the directors and in ongoing operations meetings among the administrative staff from Arts and Sciences and the heads of libraries Curriculum Support and Odegaard Access and Building Services. These regular discussions, coupled with a memorandum of understanding (MOU) that formally outlines the service and space expectations across the partners, have heightened a sense of trust and cooperation among the partners from the top down. Additionally, leadership has examined the MOU at regular biennial intervals to ensure that the present operational agreements are reflected and to address any needs or areas of concern before reaffirming the partnership. While spelling out such an agreement may, at first glance, feel counterproductive to building trust, the MOU has proved a useful tool in defining and ensuring common understandings and has provided stability through several changes in organizational leadership.

Additionally, through a libraries organizational review and staffing realignment in 2017, the libraries personnel housed in Odegaard Library became the core of the new four-unit Learning Services department, which incorporates online learning and (new) student success units to complement curriculum support and Odegaard Library operations units. This new departmental structure, finalized in mid-2018, has driven improvements and assessments across a breadth of services and projects, defined departmental initiatives, and cemented the importance of the teaching and learning enterprise to the libraries. With librarians and graduate students of Learning Services continuing to serve as the research help providers within the OWRC, this departmental transformation has further foregrounded student learning and academic success in the ethos of the OWRC.

Looking Ahead: Resiliency, Flexibility, and the Future

The shocking realities of the COVID-19 pandemic and the resulting unknowns in higher education are numerous, and it is through a mix of resiliency and flexibility that the combined staffs of the OWRC survived the 2020–21 academic year. As this article looks to the future, it feels critical to acknowledge that great learning occurred in 2020 that has implications for the future of this partnership and the OWRC space. At the time of this writing in spring 2021, UW Seattle has been operating mostly remotely since March 2020, and the renovated Odegaard remains closed to users and staff. Out of necessity, the libraries grew and strengthened capabilities to support online learning, research, and programming dramatically during the last 15 months.

Despite the myriad of challenges, two important examples of positive transformation have occurred, thanks in part to the ongoing partnership ethos among the staff of the OWRC. The first transformation has been a move to synchronous online appointments for both research and writing consultation—these services had been offered only in person in the OWRC before the pandemic. Prior to the March 2020 closure, the research help librarians of the OWRC were planning a pilot of synchronous remote appointments using Zoom as a strategic move toward a more equitable option for off-campus students, adult learners, and caregivers. When the UW announced its spring quarter 2020 classes (beginning late March) would be online, and with many campus buildings closing, the research help staff accelerated that pilot and experimentation. The Learning Services' instructional design team created training modules and best practices for online appointments in Zoom, and the ID team led held numerous synchronous workshop sessions for both librarians and writing tutors because it was decided that all services of the OWRC would need to move online. Because librarians and tutors were able to train with each other rapidly to learn a new modality to support clients through synchronous online appointments, the services have continued for all academic quarters in some capacity.

Additionally, in the 2019–20 academic year, Learning Services began a serious feasibility study for a peer mentoring/consultation program as a model to radically change the student employee experience, specifically by creating a cohort of undergraduate peer tutors and mentors who would supplement librarian and graduate student teams, working in both undergraduate instruction and research help capacities. Although a lack of on-site work during the pandemic has greatly impacted the student workforce numbers during the present academic year, the Learning Services peer mentoring implementation team continued their work and created a pilot of the peer consultant program that began in April 2021. A critical piece of this team's work included the interrogation of existing peer-to-peer service models in a variety of university settings, including the model of the OWRC writing tutors. The student writing tutor team from the OWRC, who function as peer consultants, were supported by their director in sharing training materials during this academic year and in engaging with the libraries' implementation team to share their experiences in focus groups. Some writing tutors also served to critique possible staffing materials and make further recommendations for services moving forward.

Beyond these two examples, the administration of Learning Services/Odegaard and the OWRC are engaging in further discussion about post-COVID reentry and additional transformation that will influence the future of the OWRC space and the ongoing relationship. Among the key conversations will be determining the mix of on-site and online synchronous appointments for both services and planning changes to the physical space of the OWRC to better accommodate on-site tutor engagement with remote clients online, which is assumed to continue in some capacity. Additionally, assuming a peer tutor model for libraries' research help begins to supplement (and possibly replace) librarians in the center during the 2021–22 academic year, there might be additional opportunities for cross-staff growth and development among the students themselves. A combined cohort model for writing and research assistance may also be explored, which might be a creative solution to potential future budgetary reductions that are predicted post-COVID.

While it is impossible to predict the exact state of writing and research assistance in Odegaard in the COVID-affected future, the spatial and organizational changes that have affected the OWRC in the past decade—especially the sense of collaboration strengthened through the planning and execution of the 2012–13 renovation and through subsequent years of OWRC-based services—have provided a strong foundation for the staffs to tackle future challenges together as partners. The ORWC serves as evidence that a space renovation realized with mutual organizational investment can both transform organizations immediately and, when the partnership continues to be beneficial to library users, support future organizational growth.

Notes

1. Mary Ellen Spencer and Sarah Barbara Watstein, "Academic Library Spaces: Advancing Student Success and Helping Students Thrive," *portal: Libraries and the Academy* 17, no. 2 (2017): 398.
2. Joan Lippincott, "Linking the Information Commons to Learning," in *Learning Spaces*, ed. Diana G. Oblinger (Boulder, CO: EDUCAUSE, 2006), https://www.educause.edu/ir/library/pdf/PUB7102.pdf.
3. Rosemary Bodolay, Steve Frye, Carrie Kruse, and Dave Luke, "Moving from Co-location to Cooperation to Collaboration: Redefining a Library's Role within the University," In *Space and Organizational*

Considerations in Academic Library Partnerships and Collaborations, ed. Brian Doherty (Hershey, PA: IGI Global, 2016), 247.

4. Zsuzsa Koltay, Xin Li, Curtis Lyons, Danielle Mericle, and Gail Steinhart, "Partnerships: Assessing When to Start, When to Hold, and When to Fold," *College and Research Libraries News* 77, no. 2 (2016): 65.
5. Elise Ferer, "Working Together: Library and Writing Center Collaboration," *Reference Services Review* 40, no. 4 (2012): 543.
6. John Danneker and Amanda Hornby, "Leading from Unexpected Places through Collaboration: Undergraduate Libraries in the Research University," *Library Leadership and Management* 31, no. 3 (2017): 10.
7. Danneker and Hornby, "Leading from Unexpected Places," 11.
8. Odegaard Undergraduate Library Building Vision Steering Group, "Report to the University of Washington Office of the Provost," March 2010, 20. Internal document.
9. Rob Warnaca, "Library Overhaul Was Fast, Cheap, and Efficient," *Seattle Daily Journal of Commerce*, November 21, 2013, http://www.djc.com/news/co/12059584.html.
10. Ruth Baleiko, "Libraries of Today and Tomorrow: How Architecture Can Help Craft a Responsive New Language," *Public Library Quarterly* 38, no. 4 (2019): 377.
11. Ruth Baleiko, quoted in Phil Morehart, "The Future, Today," *American Libraries* 46, no. 3/4 (February 26, 2015): 42.
12. Danneker and Hornby, "Leading from Unexpected Places," 8.
13. Emily Puckett Rodgers, "Odegaard Undergraduate Library | New Landmark Libraries 2016 Winner," *Library Journal*, September 13, 2016, https://www.libraryjournal.com/?detailStory=odegaard-undergraduate-library-new-landmark-libraries-2016-winner; "User Feedback Surveys," Assessment, University Libraries, University of Washington, https://www.lib.washington.edu/assessment/surveys.
14. Danneker and Hornby, "Leading from Unexpected Places," 10–11.

18

CHAPTER EIGHTEEN

THE CONVERGENCE OF KNOWLEDGE AND CULTURE

Collaborations Creating a New Footprint for the Future

TOM HICKERSON

Academic institutions are engaged in redefining their mission and goals. Faced with evolving public expectations to be active contributors to societal and cultural values, existing organizational, professional, and functional roles are being reenvisioned. It is an exciting and a challenging time when both entrepreneurial innovation and economic and cultural equity must be pursued simultaneously—a time for creating new models.

Libraries are active participants in this process of institutional change. Features contributing to their potential as campus and community leaders include libraries' trusted role as stewards of the intellectual, artistic, and social record of peoples worldwide and their neutrality in serving the needs of all disciplines, departments, and diverse categories of users, local and international. Their users now include communities accessing their holdings from anywhere at any time.

While remaining trusted stewards and maintaining a spirit of neutrality, they have adapted to rapid technological development, changing relevance and use of their print collections, and an age of open access, open data, and open science.

As libraries' previous model for support of learning and research has been transformed, it is opening the door for a range of expanding partnerships on campus and beyond. Operationally, primary functions like collection housing, access, and management are being conducted via new models. Libraries must now be prepared to serve the changing needs of their institutions by employing both traditional and emergent strengths in new roles and in creating new organizational, professional, and spatial footprints.

Convergence of Knowledge and Culture

Through the ongoing convergence of knowledge and culture, our understanding of human identity and experience is manifested in a multifaceted environment beyond the published literature. Our efforts to understand and preserve cultural heritage are broader than the printed record. Terms such as LAMP (libraries, archives, museums, and presses) and GLAM (galleries, libraries, archives, and museums) are in increasing use in referencing new organizational and curatorial aggregations. These consolidations are being driven by new functional alignments but also by increased expectations of universities as societal contributors. In this process, libraries are expanding their roles as cultural institutions, as well as learning and research enterprises.

Libraries have long served their institutions as cultural repositories. Their holdings commonly include extensive collections of paintings and photographs and audiovisual collections ranging from oral histories to artistic performances, video productions, and popular music. Three-dimensional artifacts, from cuneiform tablets to statues, are also held. Now these resources are being more directly incorporated into teaching, research, and public engagement, and similar objects are often held elsewhere on campus. While this convergence is historical, it is growing and is impacting library practice and spatial design.

Archives and Special Collections

Among the range of new campus and community roles now evolving, a prominent one is an expansion and a reconceiving of a very traditional aspect of libraries. As the centrality of the printed collection of books and journals has substantially declined, the significance of archives and special collections has not.

Although the term *archive* is used in diverse ways, in academic libraries, archives are often grouped with special collections. While archives are often textual, numeric, or graphic, they can include almost any information format and are increasingly generated and retained in electronic form. Responsibility for the institutional records of their universities is a common archival role.

Special collections are combinations of rare books, literary manuscripts, and personal correspondence, but they also include subject-based aggregations and corporate archives.

The term *archives and special collections* is used in academic libraries to include all of the above, and they can all be characterized as primary sources. Their unique nature contributes to their authenticity and value as records of human experience. It makes them particularly valuable for teaching and research in diverse fields. As intrinsic evidence of cultural heritage, they generate a broad spectrum of public interest, contributing to public education and engagement. Critically, these archival holdings may contain the record of Indigenous peoples, racial minorities, and other underrepresented sectors of society, further amplifying their importance.

Archives and special collections are an increasing priority for academic libraries. In past years, they were often located on upper floors or in basements, separated from principal user spaces. Today, more prominent and publicly accessible spaces are being employed. When in the city of Calgary, stewardship of the Glenbow Museum's extensive archival holdings documenting western Canadian history was transferred to the University of Calgary, it provided the library with an opportunity to also move the existing archives and special collections reading room and exhibition area from a low-visibility location on the fifth floor to a prominent space on the second floor immediately adjacent to student learning spaces and nearer the building entrance.

As the prominence of the general collection diminishes, archives and special collections naturally align with an expanded sense of societal mission and with the collaborative reenvisioning of other cultural programs on the campus and in the community.

Museums

There are three general types of museums common on university campuses. Biological museums maintain a diverse range of specimens and are commonly associated with various fields of the sciences. Anthropological museums sometimes align closely with archives and special collections in their documentary role. Art museums are increasingly aligning organizationally with libraries and their collections, but shared roles in teaching and research must be developed. Most importantly, what all three types of museums share with libraries is *curation*. This is a critical similarity shaping their ethos and professional definition, and it has significant implications for space.

In the case of biological collections, similarities contribute to the employment of technologies common to libraries. High-resolution imaging is a good example, along with enhanced metadata and preservation. At the University of Calgary, Libraries and Cultural Resources (LCR) is systematically digitizing plant specimens held in the University Herbarium. The resulting collection now includes images and information for 1,700 plants native to the province of Alberta (see figure 18.1).

fig 18.1

Herbarium director Jana Vamosi, right, with digital special projects associate Rob Alexander, who oversaw the creation of the new online Flora of Alberta collection.

(Credit: Photo by Riley Brandt, University of Calgary.)

Partnering in a multidisciplinary biodiversity project at the University of Calgary, three-dimensional, high-resolution images of bees were produced by LCR digitization staff. Extending this approach, a multidisciplinary team, including biology and engineering faculty and LCR's digitization manager for special projects, has received 2021 funding from the university's Taylor Institute for Teaching and Learning to conduct student-led digitization of zoological specimens.

Makerspaces are proving valuable in illustrating biological specimens, and visualization capabilities are also valuable for both teaching and scholarship. These organizational and technological synergies significantly enhance transdisciplinary approaches to both research and curation.

In their organizational, operational, and cultural models, anthropological museums are similar to archives and special collections, and sometimes their content overlaps. Anthropological and archaeological museums combine evidence of cultural behavior, cultural meaning, and material culture. They provide a record of human experience paralleling that provided by libraries and archives but illuminating cultures in very different ways, often enhancing the spectrum of academic interest. These museums are particularly critical in documenting the experience of Indigenous cultures and can dramatically expand on and elucidate the written record within libraries and archives.

Today, organizational collaboration between art museums and libraries is expanding significantly.[1] Libraries have long conducted roles commonly associated with art museums, acquiring and maintaining three-dimensional objects, paintings and photographs, and audiovisual records. Libraries often include exhibition galleries, and with the digitization of images, recordings, and artifacts, dissemination can be worldwide. But moving from coexistence to true convergence also requires changes in professional identity and practice. Convergence can be spatial, but it must also be programmatic in its effort to combine resources in support of integrated outcomes, to seek new complementarities among professional roles, and to engage all staff in achieving collective success.[2]

At the University of Calgary, the university's art museum had been organizationally administered as part of the library, but in 2006, the library was rebranded as Libraries and Cultural Resources to clearly signal a broadened sense of a shared cultural mission. When a new central library was built there, a multi-floor exhibition space was incorporated, art storage was constructed both in the new building and in the high-density storage facility, and the museum was fully integrated into a newly articulated teaching and research role (see figure 18.2). Operational realignment was also necessary, and a new organizational and service model was explicitly incorporated into planning for the new building.[3]

fig 18.2

Nickle Galleries, Taylor Family Digital Library, University of Calgary.

(Credit: Photo by David H. Brown, University of Calgary.)

Libraries and Cultural Resources also includes an art gallery and a library and archives as part of a Canadian federal Military Museums facility located elsewhere in the city of Calgary. The mandate of the Founders' Gallery at the Military Museums is to explore human conflict worldwide through projects by local and international artists that challenge and expand viewers' knowledge and perceptions of warfare. Public exhibition and educational programs, long a staple of museums, further enhance the library's capacity to contribute to the university's role in the community.

New media art has expanded the potential for collaborations. In some cases, like the Rose Goldsen Archive of New Media Art, a program founded and curated by Cornell University professor Timothy Murray (comparative literature and English) and sponsored by the Cornell University Library Division of Rare and Manuscript Collections, the collecting, housing, and exhibit of art are united digitally. Library/art museum partnerships reflect organizational and spatial efficiencies and a more holistic curatorial vision. At the University of Delaware Library, Museums and the Press, its division of Special Collections and Museums includes two art galleries and a mineralogy museum.

These kinds of synergistic partnerships are growing. Exemplary is the statement in February 2021 by the Emory University interim provost, Jan Love, announcing that the university was creating a new position of vice provost for libraries and museums. "Uniting the two areas will strengthen academic programs and is in perfect alignment with our aspirations for research eminence," said Love. "This restructuring is about preparing for future investments and alignment with our strategic priorities."[4] These rapidly emerging realignments within universities reflect a heightened appreciation for their cultural role and an understanding of inherent synergies across the campus and with the broader community.

University Presses

While not embodying the characteristics of curatorial programs, a similar vision for efficiencies and aligned roles with libraries is inspiring growing synergies in publishing. Libraries are now actively involved in publishing in many forms, and it is a primary area of growth and partnership with research and learning administration and with individual scholars. Open-access publishing and open educational resources (OER) are programmatic areas in which libraries are expanding their skills and technological capacity. This makes libraries ideal participants in addressing public funders' demand for open scholarship and the need to reduce the cost of textbooks for students. Within this growing arena of involvement, a specific area of expanding partnership is with university presses.

In the publishing and distribution of academic monographs, university presses exercise the lead role, aligning closely with their university mission to disseminate scholarship. It is increasingly common for university presses to be organizationally incorporated into the university library. This provides alignment with the university's investment in knowledge dissemination and reflects administrative efforts to better manage presses and to employ operational efficiencies.

The University of Michigan Press is an integral component of the University of Michigan Library's Michigan Publishing, which is the principal academic publishing division of the university. This type of functional alignment is increasing. New publishing software and open repositories have dramatically enhanced library capacity to distribute scholarly research, and libraries are well positioned to exercise leadership in such endeavors.

At the University of Calgary, the press had been organizationally located in the library since the mid-1990s, but in 2010, it began to align its practices with the library's commitment to open access, publishing its first OA title later that year. This dramatically increased the impact of the press. In the following 10 years, books published by the press were downloaded more than a million times by viewers worldwide without cost to the reader. In late 2020, the establishment of BSPS Open was formally announced. This international open-access book series for monographs in the philosophy of science is an innovative collaboration by the British Society for the Philosophy of Science with the University of Calgary Press.

Like galleries and museums, university presses, through their marketing and events such as book launches, connect with diverse campus and community audiences. While sharing technological and operational efficiencies and synergies in copyright administration and financial management, their spatial presence is frequently enlarged beyond that of typical press facilities, including high-visibility spaces for author colloquia and media display. Critically, libraries and presses working together are also advancing their universities' ethical commitment to open scholarship.

These new curatorial and publishing partnerships are only a few of many new collaborations now underway, and more new initiatives are evolving. In combination, these changes have resulted in the need for a very different approach to architectural design. In planning for the future of libraries, fully incorporating both interior and exterior space, a new imagining of the scope and nature of the spatial footprint for libraries is essential.

Planning for Collection Housing and Management and More

Both convergence and partnerships will exert substantial impact on the library's spatial planning. Similarly, housing of the physical collection and the locating of associated functional roles are a critical element of such planning. Today, a central aspect of the vision for any new library or for a renovated or expanded library is the decisions regarding evolving models for information access and where and how an institution's general collection and archives and special collections will be housed. Although certain portions may be housed in open stacks, it is likely that a significant portion will be housed in high-density storage, often located beyond the main campus.

High-density housing of books, journals, and other holdings began slowly in the late 1980s, but it is now commonplace. Yet an appropriate means to address this need and the potential for other operational efficiencies beyond the central campus is not always included in initial planning. It should be, and the plan should extend beyond just storage and be an integral part of a newly evolving vision of collection management and other strategic realignments.

The physical size of a library's collection was long viewed as a determinant of the quality of a library and seen as reflecting on the status of an institution. In the 20th century, it was widely assumed that the utility of that collection was influenced by the extent to which these holdings were housed in open stacks. Floor upon floor of open stacks characterized prominent libraries, and often the structure of these libraries was designed to align with the structure of those stacks.

This principle regarding collection size and open stacks persevered well into the 21st century. Throughout the 1990s, the majority of new or renovated library space was constructed to address collection growth despite growing awareness that much of the print collection was seldom used, but a transformation has now occurred.[5] With the arrival of the World Wide Web in the mid-1990s, the transition began, first providing remote desktop access to bibliographic information and rapidly followed by full-text access to an increasing portion of academic literature. Today, spatial needs for digital scholarship centers, makerspaces, and visualization studios must also be addressed. Having the physical collection housed immediately nearby has lost its centrality for students and even more so for faculty.

Many libraries had been housing portions of their collections in closed storage areas for a long time, but automated storage and retrieval systems (ASRS), allowing high-density storage within libraries, and the building of off-campus storage facilities expanded rapidly. And as off-campus storage facilities have become common, the design of the stacks and storage and retrieval methods have become ever more efficient, and a range of additional services are now being incorporated into these facilities.

In most cases, off-campus facilities were initially designed to support the needs of a single university, but cooperative endeavors serving multiple libraries within a state or provincial system or regional partnerships are increasingly common. The Big Ten Academic Alliance has brought together 15 universities in ongoing strategic conversations focused on their "BIG Collection." They are committed to managing their separate collections as a single collection and employing associated services in building a shared "Knowledge Commons."[6] Digital access to print via

HathiTrust is also contributing to an emerging vision of the "Collective Collection." In combination, a much more nuanced understanding of library collections and their component parts has evolved.[7]

Collection Housing

It is critical to the vision statement for a new library space to have initial projections in place regarding the quantity and nature of resources to be housed in the new space. Assuming it includes printed books and journals, what other physical media will be housed, and will all these items be self-serve? Will rare books and archives be housed there? Will art and artifacts be included? What hours of the day will the various materials be accessible, and under what conditions?

Beyond the various types of materials, what types of stacks, map cases, and containers will be employed? What types of viewing and reproduction technologies are necessary? Will compact shelving be used? What floor-load capacity will be needed to support such housing? These questions should be addressed in a systemic manner incorporating a new vision for the role of collections, the impact of shared print and digital programs, and the roles that a remote storage facility can play in achieving integrated solutions. And these solutions must be approached using permeable thinking and design incorporating the likelihood of future changes.

In designing a new or renovated library building, its location and campus logistics are also critical issues. Libraries often occupy a relatively large spatial footprint, and therefore such structures must align well with the campus master plan and reflect placement appropriate to their envisioned mission. Such planning must incorporate the exterior features of the new or expanded building and will also focus on walkways and principal connecting paths used by students, staff, and faculty and on proximities to public transportation and parking lots.

Also vital are campus transit ways. Do you expect that portions of the collection will be delivered to and from the library daily? Do you expect that shipments of books and journals will arrive from vendors there? Will large archival acquisitions or artworks arrive there? Campus planners consistently strive to limit vehicular traffic through the campus. Can driveways and loading docks be appropriately located to facilitate movement to the building and within the building? What future challenges can be envisioned? How did the pandemic impact such transit and opportunities for drive-by pickups and drop-offs?

Innovative Solutions

The design of high-density storage solutions must be addressed creatively with both short- and long-term goals considered. Normally, these facilities are largely comprised of circa 30-foot-high shelving with retrieval conducted via forklifts. Inventory control is based on item size and storage efficiencies. Custom-designed environmental conditions improve long-term physical preservation. And physical storage is not the sole capacity to be considered. Often a small reading room is included onsite, and early on, conservation programs were incorporated into new storage facilities. This reflected the expansion of preservation initiatives but also technical factors such as the need for cold storage capabilities and to ensure that chemicals used in book and document repair and fumigation were not off-gassed in mid-campus.

Now many other programs and services are being incorporated. The following three illustrations are indicative of the panoply of possibilities to be considered.

GEORGIA INSTITUTE OF TECHNOLOGY AND EMORY UNIVERSITY

At Georgia Tech, redesign of multiple libraries was conducted over several years, and it was assumed that a significant portion of the print collection would be moved from the central campus. This was deemed essential to the programmatic and architectural vision being pursued. Similar planning was beginning at nearby Emory University, and the organizational solution chosen was the sharing of a high-density storage facility.

Emory and Georgia Tech had long shared areas of common interest in neurosciences and biomedicine and partnered in establishing a 501(c)(3) nonprofit biotechnology business incubator, EmTech. When a common need for library collection storage was identified, EmTech was restructured to provide a collaborative umbrella for planning, construction, and operation of a shared storage facility. Because Georgia Tech is a public institution and Emory is a private university, this capital partnership provides an essential structure for shared ownership and administration.

The new joint Library Service Center was dedicated in March 2016, and the new 55,000-square-foot building employs state-of-art technology for optimal housing of both general and special collections of both institutions. In the first year, almost all of Georgia Tech's print collection was moved into the center, and Emory's holdings are being transferred as renovations evolve there. From the beginning, most of the holdings in the center are being managed as a singular resource serving the faculty and students of both universities, as well as the larger scholarly community.[8]

UNIVERSITY OF BRITISH COLUMBIA

At the University of British Columbia (UBC), in addition to several branch library renewals, three major building projects were conducted over a period of 25 years. Each evolved in response to changes in the programmatic mission of libraries and in evolving collection housing strategies. These changes provide an illustrative timeline for the ongoing conceptual rethinking of the role of collections as a component of library services. As characterized by Demsey, Malpas, and Sandler, "library space is being configured around engagement rather than around collections, the long-term stewardship costs of print materials are being recognized, and the role of books in research and learning is changing."[9]

The initial new library was the Walter C. Koerner Library, opened in 1997, the construction of which was in significant part seen as addressing collection growth and was planned as the first component of a multiphase building solution. But with the transformative vision for new technologies and collaborative learning spaces underway in the early 2000s, a very different solution was adopted. The existing Main Library built in the 1920s was designated for this transformation, with totally new wings constructed around a revitalized historic core, resulting in the new Irving K. Barber Learning Centre. This fundamentally new building reflected a new emphasis on campus partnership and on public programming.

The Learning Centre includes a learning commons, classrooms and study rooms, theaters, and technology supporting varied uses. It also houses the UBC School of Information (iSchool) and the Centre for Teaching, Learning and Technology. In one wing, library services and bookstacks remain, but with most of the collections concentrated in an ASRS, and with the libraries' special collections programs located adjacent to the ASRS. This new building is now a hub for campus and community interaction, but to accommodate continued collection growth and creation of more public space, an additional facility for book and archival storage was needed. In response to this need, a high-density storage facility was built at the periphery of the UBC campus.

Opening in 2015, the new facility addressed principal book and journal storage needs, but a significant portion of the building is designed for archival storage. In cooperation with the library's University Archives program, the building serves as the University Records Centre. UBC's Records Management Office (RMO) immediately launched an initiative to move all records from its external records storage supplier, Iron Mountain, to the new on-campus Library Preservation and Archives (Library PARC; http://about.library.ubc.ca/changes/libraryparc). This move quickly provided substantial cost savings to administrative offices and faculty departments. The RMO reported that in less than four months, over 3,300 boxes associated with the Finance and Operations portfolio were either safely destroyed or transferred to Library PARC, with estimated savings of $9,000 per year in storage costs for this one office. Additionally, a multipurpose teaching and reading room has been constructed there, and the building was also designed with a flexible space available to house other collection stewardship functions in the future.

UNIVERSITY OF CALGARY

With the initiation of design planning for a new central library in 2006, the new university provost and new university librarian jointly committed to a vision in which most of the public space would be devoted to learning and research supported by collaborative spaces and new technologies. It was also envisioned that the university's art museum and the University of Calgary Press would be housed in the new library. In realizing this vision for the convergence of knowledge and culture, a high-density storage facility, where the majority of book, journal, and archival holdings would be housed, was made a primary element of the construction project. This allowed coordinated planning for those portions of the library's collections to be maintained both on and off campus and for art museum storage to also be incorporated into the off-campus facility.

The new high-density storage facility (HDL; see figure 18.3) opened in 2010, shortly before the opening of the new Taylor Family Digital Library (TFDL) in 2011. In addition to housing for books, journals, archives, artifacts, and artworks, it included a small reading room and a cold storage vault. The facility immediately proved its utility, soon thereafter becoming the ingestion point for the multi-year arrival of the huge Capitol-EMI Music Canada Archive.[10]

fig 18.3

Blair Cherniawsky (center), facilities manager, conducting a tour of the High Density Library, University of Calgary.

(Credit: Photo by Leonora Crema.)

In 2016, the government of Canada announced $160 million in funding for eight key infrastructure projects at the University of Calgary as part of its national Post-secondary Institutions Strategic Investments Fund. LCR staff had planned carefully for an expansion of the HDL, and the university selected a $30 million (combining federal and institutional funding) expansion of this facility as a principal project. With this expansion, the library was able to realize the full extent of the original vision for the TFDL and to address evolving change.

The expansion of the HDL emphasized expanded housing of archives and special collections through the adoption of mobile compact shelving for the 30-foot-high stacks. This additional space allowed the University of Calgary to double the size of its archival holdings, taking custodial responsibility for the entirety of the Glenbow Museum's archive documenting the history of western Canada.[11]

Additional capabilities incorporated included a custom-designed audiovisual reformatting studio, expanded cold storage space, and a conservation lab. Most important, however, was an expanded archival processing area and a new work space for Metadata Services staff, who moved from an older building in central campus.

Via this expanded vision, the HDL now became LCR's primary point of ingest, with new deliveries of books and new archival acquisitions first arriving there for initial processing and subsequent housing for most items. Those materials selected for housing on campus are then moved there. This new single point of ingest generates new efficiencies in the processing, management, and preservation of collections. It also reduces vehicular traffic on campus.

Designing housing for the university's physical collections is a critical component in the design of new or renovated libraries and must be incorporated into programmatic and architectural design from the beginning of the project. The idea of a single point of ingest remote from central campus where initial processing of most new acquisitions can be conducted is a powerful concept to be considered and aligns well with new organizational and spatial visions for a variety of campus operations.

Balancing Critical Roles

New creative visions for the library's evolving role as a cultural organization will be manifest in a new model. As this happens, innovative strategies must be employed to align with the changing mission and operation of the library. As libraries adapt to future roles, the focus must change from maintaining existing functions to the articulation of new capacities. In this process, traditional expertise and values will be incorporated into a new organizational, professional, and spatial presence, shaped in part by newly developing partnerships.

Libraries are among the principal education and research programs of their institutions and also serve as stewards of scholarly monographs and academic journals. Through efficiencies in the retention and housing of existing physical collections of books and journals and the technologies and purchasing agreements enabling digital acquisition and use of most current academic literature, libraries have created a globalized model in which most collections funding is devoted to licensing electronic publications. And most of what is being bought is being bought by everyone. While many libraries hold regionally focused special collections, the larger profession has embraced a vision that casts libraries primarily as portals to a globalized and commercialized online knowledge system.[12]

In expressing his concerns regarding what he sees as "serious crises" in current trends in scholarly communication, Clifford Lynch wrote,

> I think that academic and research libraries need to be spending a lot more time considering the changing nature of the scholarly record, the broader cultural record that underlies it that enables future scholarship, and how we can collectively exercise effective long-term stewardship over this.[13]

Curation of archives and special collections, art, artifacts, and material culture remains a primary means for exercising a distinctive cultural role in documenting the human experience, including artistic achievement, science, industry, agriculture, government, politics, and religion, through preservation of items of international distinction as well as regional resonance.

As colleges and universities seek to reshape their societal impact, they must establish creative new partnerships on campus and beyond. Libraries in their role as cultural institutions have outstanding potential to realize new kinds of community roles. They are well suited to such endeavors through both their services and their collections. With growing attention to place-based scholarship and commitment to societal inclusion, libraries can realize both traditional and transformative values.

In achieving a balance between participation in the global information network and their roles as cultural institutions, libraries are reshaping the learning and research environments in which they operate. Systemic realignment is essential in realizing new contexts for partnership and collaboration. New kinds of spaces, interior, exterior, and remote, will all be necessary, and permeable thinking will enable evolving change. It is the opportunity to think creatively about today's library and its evolving footprint for the future.

Notes

1. Mary Lee Kennedy, "Collaborations among Galleries, Libraries, Archives, Museums Explored in Research Library Issues," Association of Research Libraries, June 19, 2020, https://www.arl.org/news/collaboration-among-galleries-libraries-archives-museums-explored-in-research-library-issues/.
2. Wendy M. Duff, Jennifer Carter, Joan M. Cherry, Heather MacNeil, and Lynne C. Howarth, "From Co-existence to Convergence: Studying Partnerships and Collaboration among Libraries, Archives and Museums," *Information Research* 18, no. 3 (September 2013), https://files.eric.ed.gov/fulltext/EJ1044683.pdf.
3. Tom Hickerson, "Organizational Design for 21st Century Convergence: Realignment at the University of Calgary" (presentation, World Library and Information Congress: 76th IFLA General Conference and Assembly, Gothenburg, Sweden, August 10–15, 2010), https://www.ifla.org/past-wlic/2010/106-hickerson-en.pdf.
4. Jan Love, quoted in "Emory to Include Libraries and Museums under New Leadership Structure," Emory News Center, Emory University, February 22, 2021, http://news.emory.edu/stories/2021/02/er_libraries_museum/campus.html.
5. Rick Lugg, "Benchmarking Print Collections: A Beginning," *Next* (blog), OCLC, May 10, 2016, https://blog.oclc.org/next/benchmarking-print/.
6. "The BIG Collection Introduction," Big Ten Academic Alliance, https://www.btaa.org/library/big-collection/the-big-collection-introduction.
7. Oya Y. Rieger, *What's a Collection Anyway?* issue brief (New York, Ithaka S+R, June 6, 2019), https://sr.ithaka.org/wp-content/uploads/2019/06/SR-Issue-Brief-Whats-A-Collection-06062019.pdf.
8. Charles G. Forrest, "The Library Service Centre: A Collaborative Partnership for Legacy Collections and Programme Innovations," in *Library Design for the 21st Century: Collaborative Strategies to Ensure Success*, IFLA publication 179, ed. Diane Koen and Traci Engel Lesneski (Berlin/Boston: de Gruyter, 2019), 133–42.
9. Lorcan Dempsey, Constance Malpas, and Mark Sandler, *Operationalizing the BIG Collective Collection: A Case Study of Consolidation vs Autonomy* (Dublin, OH: OCLC Research, 2019): 1-2. https://doi.org/10.25333/jbz3-jy57.
10. Bram Gonshor, "Universal Music Canada Donates EMI Music Canada Archive to University of Calgary," Music Canada, March 31, 2016, https://musiccanada.com/tag/emi-music-canada/.
11. Laura Beauline-Stuebing, "U of Calgary Offers a New State-of-the-Art Home for a Massive Collection of Western Canadian History," University Affairs, University of Calgary, October 28, 2020, https://www.universityaffairs.ca/news/news-article/u-of-calgary-offers-a-new-state-of-the-art-home-for-a-massive-collection-of-western-canadian-history.
12. Amy Brunvand, "Re-localizing the Library: Considerations for the Anthropocene," in "Libraries and Archives in the Anthropocene," ed. Eira Tansey and Rob Montoya, special issue, *Journal of Critical Library and Information Studies* 2, no. 3 (2019): 2–9, https://core.ac.uk/download/pdf/234708091.pdf.
13. Clifford A. Lynch, "Updating the Agenda for Academic Libraries and Scholarly Communications," *College and Research Libraries* 78, no. 2 (2017): 128.

VI

SECTION VI

LEADERSHIP, ORGANIZATIONAL CHANGE, AND NEW STAFF ROLES

19

CHAPTER NINETEEN

EFFECTING TRANSFORMATIONAL CHANGE LEADS TO TRANSFORMATIONAL SPACES

MARY ANN MAVRINAC

Introduction: Transformational Change

At heart, our spaces are *only* spaces without the programs, services, expertise, scholarly content, and technology that enable and infuse these spaces to drive the transformational experiences that we aspire to create for our students, faculty, and staff. To activate our spaces, our staff must be the drivers, unleashing their talent, creativity, and expertise to continuously make improvements in anticipation of or in response to user needs and changes in the environment. Enabling and empowering staff to accomplish this requires progressive leadership that provides foundational elements and structures to support staff, increasing organizational capacities for change and thereby transforming spaces.

What is transformational change? According to James MacGregor Burns in his work, *Transforming Leadership: A New Pursuit of Happiness*, transformational change "causes a metamorphosis in form or structure, a change in the very condition or nature of a thing, a change into another substance, a radical change in outward form or inner character."[1] To achieve transformational change, an organization's culture must be examined, evolved, and changed, including its structure, operations, processes, and reward systems. All organizational elements, such as vision, mission, strategy, and values, must be in alignment. This can take years to achieve, as culture, especially in mature organizations, is extremely persistent. Achieving transformational change is painstaking yet inspiring and rewarding work.

Transforming organizations and transforming spaces are iterative, dynamic, and codependent processes. This chapter will discuss foundational elements to achieve transformational spaces, such as the importance of anchoring space design in an organization's strategic and facilities master planning and ensuring that users obtain learning spaces that support their scholarly work by placing them at the center of planning. A number of other elements set the stage for a process of ongoing development and change: situating learning as a central organizational asset; understanding the importance of the individual and the critical role of senior and middle managers in leading change; providing governance structures that foster regular and iterative user feedback and assessment; and cultivating mindsets and competencies that nurture risk-taking, agile decision-making, and creative problem-solving that push the boundaries of library roles and expertise. The alchemy among these creates culture, builds capacity, and engages the hearts and minds of all organizational members.

Anchor and Align: Strategic and Facilities Master Planning

Strategic and facilities master planning are essential foundational processes that serve to provide a compelling vision and a road map for transforming organizations and transforming spaces. The process and engagement used to develop these planning blueprints are as important as the outcomes that are achieved. Ideally, these plans are robust, coherent, and aspirational. They provide staff with overarching direction, context, and the rationale for change most effectively if staff are engaged and have agency in the planning process. Staff become drivers of change when they understand and contribute to achieving the aspirations of the organization.

In recent years, the River Campus Libraries (RCL) at the University of Rochester have developed two strategic plans for the organization and a strategic facilities master plan for the main library to guide organizational and space planning priorities and direction over the long term. Research libraries exist to support and add value to the research, teaching, and learning mission of the university or institution they serve. Anchoring and aligning space planning within university priorities and the library's strategic plan provides coherence and rationale for developing new learning spaces and the commensurate staff competencies needed to realize the vision for these spaces.

The RCL's vision is purposefully confident, articulating the unique value the library brings to the academic enterprise:

> With its unique expertise, collections and spaces, the River Campus Libraries provides transformational experiences for students and faculty to achieve their scholarly aspirations.[2]

This vision states that we provide "unique spaces" to the university community, and "Enabling Spaces" is one of five strategic priorities in our strategic plan. These align and anchor space planning and design into our primary planning documents, signaling the importance of library spaces to our staff and to the broader university community. They also convey that the library is uniquely positioned to develop learning spaces to support the university's mission.

Developing a 10-year strategic facilities master plan for our main campus library, Rush Rhees, was essential to the success of our learning space planning.[3] It also drove user engagement and staff development. The library was built in 1930, with its classic architecture designed in service to the main stack tower, and the strategic facilities master plan continued to emphasize the importance of scholarly collections, providing a road map for the transformation required to ensure Rush Rhees Library's ongoing relevance as a state-of-the-art research library in the 21st century. The plan articulated the different types of spaces, much like an urban master plan: spaces for general and specialized learning, collections, and staff. This provided a blueprint for planning that was robust yet coherent, allowing a series of discrete projects to unfold as programs evolved and funds were available. For instance, Evans Lam Square was the first project to be realized from the strategic facilities master plan. Its origins grew out of a series of staff working groups that reimagined the work and the competencies required for access and reference services. Form, which was Evans Lam Square, followed function, the design of which reflected the programs and services that would be provided in this space.

Strategic facilities master plans are, by their very nature, aspirational. Yet it is essential that actions occur to realize these plans. It is important to align these plans with broader university priorities. They also serve to obtain support and coherence, answering the question "Why are we doing this?" Staff and users understand why we are heading in the direction in which we are headed when a comprehensive and inclusive planning process (figure 19.1) has occurred, and a robust planning blueprint provides a road map for the future.

fig 19.1

Rush Rhees Library strategic facilities master plan, design charrette with students, led by architect Andrew Frontini.

(Photo credit: Perkins&Will.)

Early in the 2000s, aligning a new library building project at the University of Toronto Mississauga with the priorities of the campus was essential in obtaining the administrative and funding support to proceed. The campus's strategic plan aimed to double student enrollment in the near term. Aligning the vision for a new library to provide enough study space for the planned enrollment growth meant that the vision, "people space over collection space,"[4] resonated with users, administration, and funders, leading to the success of the Hazel McCallion Academic Learning Centre.

At Rochester, developing Studio X as the hub for extended reality to foster cross-disciplinary collaboration, exploration, experimentation, and experience to drive innovative research and teaching in immersive technologies was in direct response to over 50 researchers engaged in extended reality (XR) technologies across the university.

User Engagement

As important as it is to engage and involve staff in the process for library space planning, it is equally important to involve users. User engagement informs the functional program of a space, the absence of which can result in a generic renovation that could be situated in any setting. Users who are meaningfully engaged in the planning process immediately recognize the fruits of their labor. The learning space resonates, and it is ready to be activated by the community that is already engaged in its success.

User research is a time-intensive, inclusive, iterative activity that places users at the center, taking them through the stages of the planning process, the outcome of which is a detailed functional plan. A functional plan articulates the programs, services, spaces, technology, and expertise needed to realize the project. It becomes a blueprint for architects to develop a detailed design for the learning space. It is essential to involve as many types of users—faculty, undergraduates, graduate students, staff, and donors—as makes sense for a particular project. This engagement, much like the importance of strategic facilities master planning, will drive the program, build a ready-made community of users and advocates, be a catalyst for fundraising, and create a meaningful buzz for the program and space. User engagement also lays the groundwork for organizational change as it communicates to staff that new skills, competencies, and mindsets are needed to realize the functional program developed in the course of user research. Staff are more inclined to learn new skills and competencies and adapt to a new state when the need comes from users. As a result, users drive organizational change through an inclusive design process.

The Barbara J. Burger iZone—imagination, ideas, and innovation—a new program and space in the RCL, aspired to recreate the essence of the ancient Alexandrian Library where scholars gathered to explore and discuss ideas, use scholarly resources, and create new knowledge. iZone is a 21st-century expression of this concept of a research library. In spite of students' full backing and involvement in this project, the creation of iZone was a shift for the library and the university, with many wondering why the library would be involved in a pre-incubator for idea generation and innovation?

User research was an essential component in the success of iZone. It spanned six months, engaging administration, staff, faculty, and students. The outcome was a detailed functional plan, including a vision, use cases, personas, journey maps, services, programs, staffing, and space needs, all grounded in data that emerged during the process of engagement. The functional plan also depicted the skills and competencies needed to work in this space, skills and competencies that were not yet readily available in the library marketplace. Hiring a director with a background in innovation and start-ups and a team that was gifted in working with students has resulted, over time, in a suite of niche services that are being used across the university. The functional program provided the incoming director with a planning guide and a ready community of users from which the program took flight. Now there is rarely a question about why iZone is located in the library. It is now a given that the library would provide services and expertise in idea generation, creative problem-solving, and design thinking. These methodologies are used in academic programs from art and art history to neuroscience, as most, if not all, disciplines require a creative and agile mindset, risk-taking, and problem-solving skills and abilities, as does the marketplace.

In developing Evans Lam Square, user engagement yielded mixed opinions in embracing a new form of service for access and reference services. Users loved the feel of this traditional space and were cautious about changes that might undermine its look and feel. Library staff, on the other hand, recognized that the existing space would not allow the flexibility required for the dynamic services and programs they envisioned. The vision, in this case, drove Evans Lam Square, which symbolized a town square for the university, where students, staff, and faculty would come to find information, engage in research consultations, experience new technologies, touch down between classes, and participate in pop-up programs (figure 19.2) that exposed them to library collections and services and student research. The notion of a town square resonated with users. They were convinced even more when photos pulled from the University Archives told the story that Evans Lam Square would be at least the eighth time this area of the library had been renovated since the building opened in 1930. This was a dynamic space that evolved to meet the needs of users and the broader environment. User engagement was essential throughout; however, it demonstrated that organizational change is not solely an internal matter. Functional planning is a bidirectional exchange of expertise and data where library expertise is as important as user expertise. Exposing users to environmental trends, best practices in research libraries, history, and data provides essential ingredients to the planning process without which results would be suboptimal. Evans Lam Square has resulted in new forms of engagement with library users and an inclusive space. It is an example of the dynamic and codependent manner with which transformational change can occur.

fig 19.2

Evans Lam Square, pop-up program, music and healing, featuring the music of Joanne Shenandoah, Oneida artist; the Native American Cultural Center performing music and dance, discussing treaties, and showcasing wampum reproductions and books.

(Photo credit: Adam Fenster.)

Learning: A Central Organizational Asset

It is vital to position learning as a central organizational asset to ensure staff are equipped to respond to and anticipate changes in the environment, an environment that, if anything, continues to change at an exceedingly rapid pace. Where before, transformational change in technological innovation would take hundreds and even thousands of years, transformational changes are now occurring exponentially.[5] Environmental change can include technologies, academic programs, research focus, diverse perspectives, and fiscal constraint, to name a few. In Edgar Schein's classic work, *Organizational Culture and Leadership*, he states,

> My sense is that the various predictions about globalism, knowledge-based organizations, the information age, the biotech age, the loosening of organizational boundaries, and so on have one theme in common—we basically do not know what the world of tomorrow will really be like except that it will be different. That means that organizations and their leaders will have to become perpetual learners.[6]

Schein underscores the importance of library organizations being in perpetual learning mode, where learning is at the heart of organizational life.

Robert Darnton's article "The Library in the New Age" chronicles the great technological shifts in how information has been communicated through the ages.[7] This underscores the need for ongoing learning, in particular, in knowledge-based organizations such as a library. Darnton chronicles technological change from 4000 BC, when humans learned to write. In AD 3, the invention of the codex allowed pages to be turned rather than scrolls unfurled. Movable type or the printing press was invented in 1450, revolutionizing access to print materials. Electronic communications in the 1970s led to the democratization of information through websites and search engines in the 1990s. The pace of transformational change has accelerated unrelentingly. Adding to this has been the growth of social media and smartphone technologies in the early-to-mid-2000s and a decade later, inventions such as virtual reality and artificial intelligence that no longer seem futuristic. The ways in which we communicate are increasingly graphical, instantaneous, fluid, and machine-driven.

Library staff must stay abreast of new technologies to ensure the library's relevancy in communicating and engaging with users and deploying services, spaces, and collections. Functional specialists will always hold deep expertise to drive innovation, yet it is incumbent upon us to ensure that all staff have the opportunity to be exposed to new technologies and to develop a basic level of competency and understanding about their application in relation to teaching, learning, research, and collections. Positioning learning as a central organizational asset is a strategic imperative given the riveting pace of change. Learning must be part of the fabric of the organization. The broad-based Learning and Development Committee at the RCL provides experiential learning opportunities across the spectrum, including learning new technologies, cultural competencies, project management, and design thinking. Translating an immersive, multiday learning experience that would occur at an institute into a mini-version that is accessible to all staff equips interested staff with skills and awareness they might not otherwise achieve. An example of this occurred with the Digital Scholarship Institute (DSI), when the RCL played a leadership role in its development through the Association of Research Libraries.[8] Staff who attended the five-day institute subsequently became instructors for a mini-DSI developed to encourage anyone interested to learn and become conversant in the basics of digital scholarship, including geographic information systems, textual analysis, and more.

Community of practice is a process of collective learning that provides the opportunity for organizational members to explore and immerse themselves in a functional domain of interest. Etienne and Beverly Wenger-Trayner believe that a community of practice has an identity defined by a shared domain of interest and that the community engages in activities, discussions, discovery, and information sharing to enable learning and the development of a shared practice that builds competency and understanding about that domain.[9] Experimentation and exploration are important attributes of a community of practice, where practice is informed going forward. Inviting all organizational members who are interested in a community of practice communicates that all organizational members are welcome and encouraged to join and learn.

Providing learning opportunities that are rooted in the values of equity and inclusion expands organizational capacity. Positioning learning as a central organizational asset incorporates learning into the everyday fabric of the organization and not something that is episodic and reserved for special circumstances. Cultivating a culture of perpetual learning embeds learning as strategically important for transforming organizations and, thereby, spaces. As more staff become conversant in the organization's learning curriculum, greater understanding and cohesiveness in the direction of the organization is likely to occur. Rather than an "us versus them" or "those in the know" and "those not" bifurcation, inclusive learning provides opportunities to all organizational members.

The library's focus on immersive technologies through Studio X (figure 19.3) includes staff who have deep expertise in these technologies and tools; however, it is incumbent upon the library to share and expose any interested organizational member to these technologies to encourage learning. For instance, inviting staff to try out VR goggles and experience the 15th-century Elmina Castle in Ghana is an example of work being done by the library's Digital Scholarship department in collaboration with faculty and students.[10] Developing learning opportunities that map to the library's strategic priorities heightens staff understanding of and engagement with these priorities. This increases organizational capacity and diversity of perspectives that serve to inform practice. And, at heart, learning *is* change.[11]

fig 19.3

Studio X, an extended reality workspace in Carlson Library.

(Photo credit: Stephen Dow.)

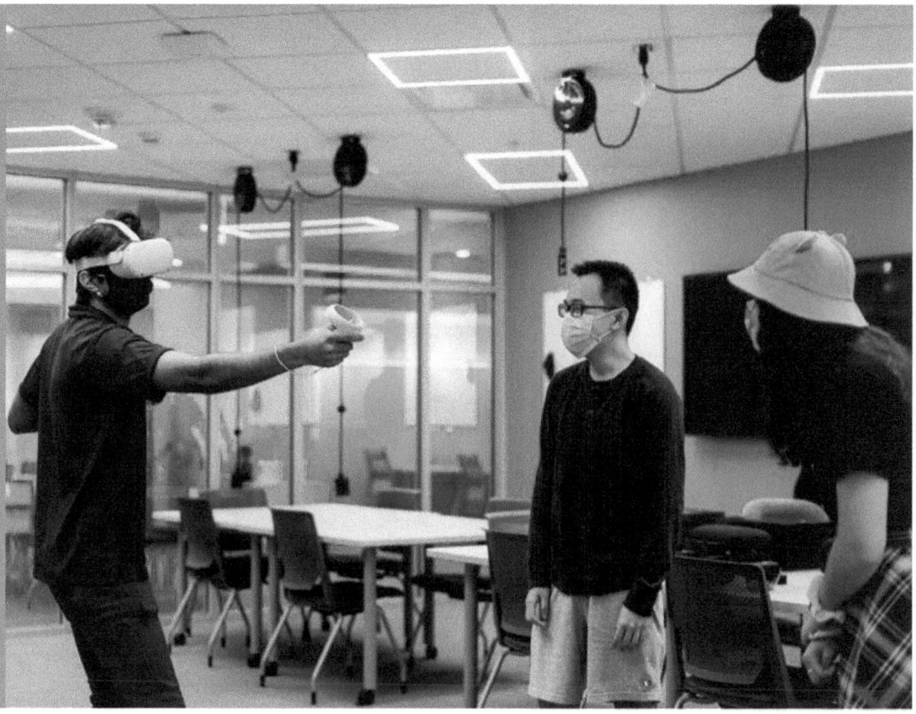

Importance of the Individual in Transformational Change

The importance of the individual cannot be overstated when embarking upon transformational change. This includes the critical role that the middle management leadership team plays in developing staff talent. Nurturing and providing support for staff development, leadership development, and creativity and innovation increase the organization's capacity and the likelihood it will achieve transformational outcomes. Participative leadership and inclusive practices are critical to the meaningful engagement of all organizational members. This builds organizational capacity, provides diverse perspectives that lead to better decision-making, and ensures, as much as possible, that all employees understand, embrace, and contribute to the direction in which the organization is headed.

It is important to understand the basic premise that organizations are comprised of individuals, each of whom embodies a self. Individuals have wants, needs, fears, aspirations, values, identities, experiences, and history that they bring to the organization. This dynamic and complex chemistry of individuals is essential to the success of the organization. Investing in individual staff members, inviting their participation and ideas, and realizing their needs and aspirations are critical in achieving organizational goals. When change is afoot, the central question for most individuals, whether stated consciously or unconsciously, is "How will this impact me?" Staff, in turn, determine whether they will support the change. Meaningfully engaging staff in any change initiative, more often than not, will result in a better outcome. In addition to meaningful participation and engagement in organizational change, it is also vital to listen, empathize, and be respectful and compassionate to those who are experiencing change, as not all change is welcome, nor does each of us internalize or accept change at the same pace.

Plans are only plans if they do not engage staff to enliven and drive the planning process. Similarly, a renovation is only a renovation if it is not undergirded by a strong program that reflects the needs of users. Programs and services drive space development, and programs and services must be driven by staff and users. Involving staff and users in the development of strategic and master plans is critical. The benefits of providing staff with the opportunity to participate or, better, to lead planning are endless. Planning activities inherently develop the capacity of staff as they learn new skills, competencies, and mindsets to respond to and anticipate new programs, technologies, and services. Engaged staff heighten diversity of perspective and shared ownership of the process and outcomes, and engaged staff develop an esprit de corps within planning teams, especially important if these teams are cross-functional and pull from departmental units across the library and beyond. Staff are happier, more motivated, and more confident when they are doing meaningful work.

The leadership team plays a vital role in organizational talent management. Talent management supports the life cycle of an employee's time in the organization, from onboarding to departure. Nothing can be achieved in an organization without the hearts and minds of all organizational members. New learning spaces will be flat and uninspiring without the creative brainpower of individuals and teams.

Developing a culture of leadership where all organizational members are viewed as leaders is essential for a healthy work environment and necessary when striving to achieve transformational outcomes. Individuals supported and empowered to be leaders are invited to solve problems, explore ideas, and create opportunities, the success of which occurs within a structural framework such as the library's strategic priorities and functional work. Developing leadership capacity is generative, resulting in a multiplier effect in relation to the breadth and depth of organizational outcomes. The RCL invested in its leadership team, and the full organization, through a multi-month leadership development program using the appreciative inquiry methodology. Appreciative inquiry focuses on an organization's strengths and opportunities. In their article "Positive Problem Solving: How Appreciative Inquiry Works,"[12] the authors cite research that indicates that positivity builds resilience, contributes to our ability to cope during challenging times, develops connections, and fosters teamwork.[13] This was essential leadership development work during the pandemic when the organization was in flux, staff were under extreme stress personally and professionally, budgets were cut and constrained, and the future was unknown. Yet organizational members were being called upon to produce some of the most creative work in their careers in order to support faculty, staff, and students in an increasingly digital and virtual world. This was absolutely the time to invest in our leadership team to manage tumultuous organizational change, and appreciative inquiry was a methodology that focused on our strengths, which was imperative for us to remember and build upon. During this vexing time, the program, user engagement, and skills and competencies for Studio X, for instance, were advanced. Building upon its strength when the capital project was paused due to COVID-19, Studio X capitalized its virtual assets to drive the program forward, to develop its brand, and to engage and expand its community.

An example of inclusive, progressive leadership has occurred in the Barbara J. Burger iZone. With a small team of three full-time staff, the staffing model relies heavily upon student employees. iZone broke out of the mindset that only full-time staff can lead workshops, develop programs, and solve problems. iZone views students as integral to its success. Students provide creative energy, unique perspectives, and necessary diversity that mirrors the student body, contributing to innovative programming that resonates with their user base.

When everyone, including students, are empowered to lead, structures to support their success are essential. These structures are enabling. They are not controlling. Structures include iZone's strategic plan, its mission and vision, a commitment to iterative feedback, the concept of failing fast, and the enabling guidance of the director and full-time staff. Students have created and led design challenges, workshops, user research, creative programming, and more (figure 19.4). Unleashing the creative energy and leadership capacity of all organizational members, including students, has been transformational for iZone. iZone's student employee ethos has spread to other areas of the organization and contributed to a donor-supported library fellowship program called Karp Library Fellows, where undergraduate students are provided with the opportunity to lead projects in learning spaces such as iZone and Studio X, with a focus on collaboration, creative thinking, and leadership meant to prepare students for their careers. This is a transformational program for the RCL that is infusing learning spaces with the unique talent and contributions of undergraduate students. The intentional use of undergraduates is strategic, as it increases the capacity of the library to create transformational experiences in a variety of learning spaces, both virtual and physical.

fig 19.4

Barbara J. Burger iZone campfire program created by Dewey Bazirake, iZone Student Fellow.

(Photo credit: Zoe Wisbey.)

Continuous Improvement

Creating learning spaces, new programs and services, and evolving roles, skills, and competencies are not once-and-done activities. Libraries that are providing transformational experiences for their users are committed to continuous improvement. Structures to support a spirit of continuous improvement are needed, ones that are rooted in an ethos of service excellence. These structures help codify mindsets that foster creative problem-solving, experimentation, risk-taking, and exploration. Basic yet essential structures such as the creation of advisory groups for learning spaces, for user groups, or, more generally, for the library at large are mechanisms by which the regular flow of feedback can occur, much of it iterative. How is a new space being used? What went well? What needs addressing? What are unexpected outcomes? Learning spaces should not languish after construction is complete. Intentional pursuit of user input ensures that learning spaces will evolve over time and stay in sync with current needs. At times, protracted use or striking changes in the broader environment occur that warrant a more intensive retrofit of a learning space. For instance, a very popular 24-hour study space, the Gleason Library, has undergone a major refresh after over 14 years of intensive use. The fundamental premise of this space has not changed, yet user research and a review of best practices at other institutions has delivered a collaborative study space that meets the current needs of undergraduate students and thus has refreshed this learning space for another decade or more.

In addition to formal and informal user input, transformational spaces occur when staff are eager to experiment and take risks. iZone's ethos of "failing fast" means staff focus on outcomes. They are encouraged not to fall in love with an idea or a program. If something is not working, they embrace failing fast and moving on to something that will hopefully yield better outcomes. This mindset is difficult to cultivate. Going back to the importance of the individual in organizational change, no one wants to be seen as failing, yet cultivating a trusting environment for failure is essential. Methodologies and practices such as project management, design thinking, user research, and pilots and prototypes provide a framework for staff to develop programs, services, and learning spaces that will be, more likely than not, successful simply because staff members have done their homework and invested the cognitive energy and research into the project.

For instance, a project management framework demands a thoughtful articulation of the project—its base assumptions, intended outcomes, risks, stakeholders, timeline, resources, scope, and so on—essentially ensuring that a project is well thought out before it is launched. Regular review of the project plan holds project members accountable and wards against scope creep, a phenomenon that can result in a project's failure. Pilots and prototypes can occur out of a project plan to try something over a short duration to see if it resonates with users. Knowing a pilot is not meant to be the final product allows staff the psychological safety to experiment. Piloting and prototyping are part of the organizational fabric of the RCL.

Over the course of three years, Studio X engaged stakeholders in user research and, in turn, piloted and prototyped several workshops and programs, rigorously committing to a continuous process of assessment. Staff also took this opportunity to learn new platforms and technologies, build their brand, and hone their offerings. Through these processes and stages, Studio X built a community, supporters, and momentum before the physical space had opened. This experience informed the nature of the physical space so much more than would have occurred if this preparation had not taken place.

Design thinking is a methodology that approaches problem-solving from a user's perspective, fostering an empathetic approach to understanding the problems each faces. By working with a diverse team, design thinking encourages the generation of many outside-the-box solutions. Rapid prototyping brings ideas to life to obtain user feedback (figure 19.5). An example of this occurred during the pandemic. A Collaborative Study Design Challenge occurred to find creative solutions to address the lack of collaborative study space options due to the restrictions of physical distancing. Solutions were generated for easy, medium, and big ideas, some of which flowed into the Gleason Library Refresh Project as we adjusted the bid documents at the eleventh hour to accommodate new ideas. A design thinking mindset includes a bias toward action, use of play as a means to creative problem-solving, failing fast, and developing the creative confidence to generate unexpected and valuable solutions.

fig 19.5

Barbara J. Burger iZone design thinking workshop.

(Photo credit: Julia Maddox.)

Methodologies, tool kits, user advisory groups, and formal and informal feedback mechanisms provide scaffolding for staff to gain comfort with continuous improvement and the need to adjust or to stop something because it is not working. Mindsets that embrace problem-solving and failing fast will infuse the organization with creativity and innovation and will reduce the inclination to feel that one failed. With a philosophy of failing fast, one's propensity to personalize failure is greatly reduced. These are important mindsets and approaches for an organization that pursues transformational outcomes.

Dynamic Organizations Lead to Transformational Change

Transforming organizations and transforming spaces are rooted in a dynamic organizational culture, and organizational culture is created by each and every organizational member. Staff must be supported and empowered by the leadership team, providing structures to support learning and staff development, inclusion in the development of organizational plans and goals, and the provision of methodologies, tool kits, and practices that unleash creativity that can lead to transformational change. These also contribute to the development of a vibrant, creative, confident, and healthy organization, one that creates the conditions for students, staff, and faculty to achieve transformational experiences in their scholarly work and pursuit of excellence, including that which occurs in learning spaces. Transformational change, nonetheless, is complex, dynamic, and, at times, messy. It is essential that staff be engaged and have a stake in the library's future. When that has been done, the library has increased its capacity to exceed expectations and create the conditions for transforming spaces.

Notes

1. James MacGregor Burns, *Transforming Leadership: A New Pursuit of Happiness* (New York: Atlantic Monthly Press, 2003), 24.
2. River Campus Libraries, "River Campus Libraries Strategic Plan, 2018–2025," University of Rochester, 2018, https://www.library.rochester.edu/sites/default/files/documents/strategic_priorities_2018-2025.pdf.
3. Examples of learning spaces and planning initiatives are for the River Campus Libraries, University of Rochester, unless otherwise stated.
4. This is an abbreviated version of the vision that was easy to remember and communicate.
5. Raymond Kurzweil, "The Law of Accelerating Returns," *Kurzweil: Tracking the Acceleration of Intelligence* (blog), March 7, 2001, https://www.kurzweilai.net/the-law-of-accelerating-returns.
6. Edgar H. Schein, *Organizational Culture and Leadership* (San Francisco: Jossey-Bass, 1992), 361.
7. Robert Darnton, "The Library in the New Age," *New York Review of Books*, June 12, 2008, https://www.nybooks.com/articles/2008/06/12/the-library-in-the-new-age/.
8. "ARL Digital Scholarship Institute," Association of Research Libraries, accessed May 28, 2021, https://www.arl.org/category/arl-academy/arl-digital-scholarship-institute/.
9. Etienne Wenger-Trayner and Beverly Wenger-Trayner, "Communities of Practice: A Brief Introduction," Wenger-Trayner.com (blog), April 15, 2015, https://wenger-trayner.com/introduction-to-communities-of practice/.
10. "Elmina Castle," River Campus Libraries, University of Rochester, accessed May 28, 2021, https://www.library.rochester.edu/spaces/studio-x/xrur/elmina-castle.
11. Mary Ann Mavrinac, "Transformational Leadership: Peer Mentoring as a Values-Based Learning Process," *portal: Libraries and the Academy* 5, no. 3 (2005): 391–404, https://doi.org/10.1353/pla.2005.0037.
12. Sallie Lee, Margaret Henderson, and Gordon Whitaker, "Positive Problem-Solving: How Appreciative Inquiry Works," *ICMA Press* 43, no. 3 (2011), https://cplg.sog.unc.edu/publication/positive-problem-solving-how-appreciative-inquiry-works/.
13. Barbara L. Fredrickson and Marcial F. Losada, "Positive Affect and the Complex Dynamics of Human Flourishing," *American Psychologist* 60, no. 7 (October 2005): 678–86, https://doi.org/10.1037/0003-066X.60.7.678.

20

CHAPTER TWENTY

IT'S NOT A SPACE, IT'S A PHILOSOPHY

Designing a High-Purpose Culture within Your Learning Environment

BRIAN MATHEWS

You can dream, create, design, and build the most wonderful place in the world ... but it requires people to make the dream a reality.

Walt Disney[1]

When planning a new library space, there are many components to consider. Whether it is a renovation, an addition, or an entirely new building, countless variables compete for your time and attention. Architects imagining the flow of people and the functionality of the environment. Vendors showcasing a wide range of technologies and furniture possibilities. Designers presenting endless options of colors, patterns, and textures that weave together a spatial narrative. Facilities managers focusing on electrical capacity, heating and cooling, asbestos, and cleaning schedules. Building officials referencing state codes on egress and seating capacity. It's a lot to take in.

I've worked on over 30 construction projects and have experienced a certain joy in the act of shaping an initial concept into a physical reality. But honestly, the grand opening is just the beginning. How we infuse that space with an inspiring spirit and sustain that over time is the real challenge. As much as I enjoy selecting furniture and dabbling with new technologies, stewarding that environment is the real work. This chapter will outline a set of components that I recommend for nurturing a high-performing culture for your high-purpose learning space. But first, we'll begin with a story.

Something's Missing

I distinctly recall visiting a newly renovated library and feeling surprisingly underwhelmed. Millions had been spent on the effort. The space looked great: shiny, clean, modern. It had everything I expected to see, yet something was missing. I couldn't pinpoint it at that time, and in fact it would take several years before I completely understood my reaction. This experience stayed with me. Libraries were heavily investing in their facilities, and I wanted to figure out why some clicked and others didn't. Perhaps it boils down to personal preference, just as art connects with certain audiences but not others. Regardless, this exploration into the heart and soul of library spaces was the journey I felt compelled to undertake.

A Glimpse

The mystery began to unravel, of all places, at a grocery store. As I became more familiar with built environment philosophies, I was always attempting to decode my experiences in the world around me. I noticed that one particular store felt different from the others. It wasn't necessarily its inventory, pricing, or the layout that struck me, but something intangible.

As I moved through the aisles, staff offered friendly greetings. I observed several small nuances, such as unexpected displays, generous food samples, and subtle innovations including a refrigerator near the front for quickly grabbing milk and other staples. The cashiers were conversational, personifying small-town southern hospitality. And if a checkout line ever grew beyond five customers, a new register would open.

Engagement, responsiveness, efficiency: these are qualities that we aspire to layer throughout our libraries. I found it interesting to observe them here within a different context. This grocery store became a living case study for me. When I visited, I felt cared for and connected to the space and employees. There was never just one standout thing, though; my experience was more about how it all coalesced. The way I describe this today is that I felt the environment was propelling me forward, effectively supporting my goals. This is the same emotion that I want library visitors to experience. Somehow our combination of technologies, collections, expertise, and furniture should harmonize to inspire and empower people in a deeply satisfying manner.

Distilling Culture

Over the years, I encountered this driving force in other locations: a museum, a botanical garden, a car dealership, a hair salon, a gym, even an airport. The sensation wasn't necessarily about the particular activity, but more so about the configuration of attributes enabling me to accomplish tasks. There was a thoughtfulness toward the sequence of the encounter that made it harmonious. I would describe this as feeling as though I were swimming with the current, rather than against it.

This phenomenon is hard to measure. It doesn't appear in our assessment metrics, annual reports, or architectural drawings. It's intangible and amorphous and intensely personal. So, what is it? *Culture.* After years of experiments and many mistakes, I affirm that the culture of a place, this binding dynamism, makes or breaks the experience for customers, patrons, or guests. And of course, there are an ever-growing number of books, theories, and models on this topic.[2] I've distilled this concept down to three key components based on my work over the years.

Component One: An Interdisciplinary Team

"The more complex the problem, the more help you need to solve it," counsels Tim Brown, former CEO of the global design firm IDEO.[3] Our libraries are becoming increasingly more complex, and we need new expertise. Take for example my team at Carnegie Mellon, which includes colleagues with PhDs in archeology, cultural geography, art history, computer science, data science, media studies, American studies, and English. This eclectic group intertwines together with librarians, archivists, software developers, an MBA, and other talented staff to offer a wide array of services.

So how does this all come together? How do we blend a host of different preferences, personalities, and methodologies into a harmonious faction? What enables a group, particularly an interdisciplinary one, to operate effectively?

Two studies shaped my thinking: Google's Project Aristotle and the MIT Human Dynamics Lab's sociometric badging research. The motive behind these explorations was to uncover, quantitatively, which aspects empower groups. Google's study followed 180 of its project teams over the course of a year.[4] Researchers took into account a variety of attributes including personality types, hobbies and shared interests, educational backgrounds, gender, age, diversity, previous experience working together, and so forth. They also factored in group configurations such as hierarchal and flat structures. After 12 months, the researchers ended up more confused than when they began; they could not detect any logical patterns. In fact, the *who* didn't seem to matter at all. Based on the descriptive and demographic data collected, the researchers could not determine why some groups were more successful than others.

Reviewing their materials again and comparing them with decades of academic studies, Google researchers started to piece together an understanding. Their conclusion: it wasn't a group's composition that mattered; instead, it was the presence of group norms. They had hoped to reveal which norms or collective behaviors mattered most but couldn't determine an optimized list. Some successful groups centered around consensus, while others relied on majority rule, and some deferred to a team lead. Some met every day, some only once a month. Some were extremely organized, while others were more ad hoc. There was no definitive best way to operate. Instead, the study found that what mattered most was whether the group members were on the same page in terms of how they would perform and interact. The most successful groups arrived at a shared understanding: how they would make decisions, handle disagreements, set priorities, divvy up demands, and essentially function as a team. The key takeaway: success is not achieved solely by tackling objectives efficiently—it also involves a sense of unity around how a group will accomplish those tasks.

MIT's Human Dynamics Lab adds another dimension. Researcher Alex Pentland discovered that the most productive groups have a very distinctive data signature.[5] Using electronic badges that collected information on communication behaviors, Pentland could predict a group's success regardless of *who* they were or *what* they were working on, simply by examining *how* they interacted. In a nutshell, when everyone in the group talks and listens in roughly equal measure, it correlates to a higher probability of success. The finding suggests that conversations flowing across all members, rather than just between a few, resulted in better team alignment and productive outcomes.

Libraries may have unique cultural dynamics in terms of introvert and extrovert ratios, but this kernel of insight is helpful. As an administrator, I'm mindful of conversational monopolies and consciously step back and encourage discussions around the table, not just with me. Secondly, when starting a new project or launching a new team, I invest time up front to talk about the group dynamics. The process can't be prescribed; that is, the leader should not dictate the rules. And we can't simply import norms from one group into another. Instead, it's beneficial to establish the mode of operation openly together considering the objectives at hand and the composition of the team.

This might sound simplistic, but an important first step for a *group* is to make a commitment to becoming a *team*. Semantics perhaps, but it's a symbolic gesture that can be accomplished by setting norms. This pledge activates a psychological shift in identity from a group of individual contributors into a purpose-driven collective. Their commitment generates buy-in beyond merely checking off action items on an agenda and morphs into goals around mutual progress and overall success.

A game-changing tool to consider is Belbin's *Team Roles* model.[6] This framework articulates nine roles or functions that teams need to successfully balance and execute work. These include identities such as shapers, implementers, finishers, and resource investigators. In most instances, team members will need to take on multiple roles. In fact, this act of wearing several hats not only advances progress but also reinforces the team character.

I once served on a campus-wide committee with some creative faculty members. We spent hours talking about big ideas. It dawned on me after the third meeting that we didn't need more ideas, but, in Belbin's terms, we lacked a coordinator. We needed facilitation instead of more ideation.

Reviewing the team roles model when groups are formulating norms enables you to determine strengths as well as deficiencies, perhaps indicating a need to bring in other skill sets or to encourage existing members to stretch their commitment. I always find myself asking "What does this team need?" and then challenging myself to fill the gap or inviting someone to take on a particular identity for that project. For example, someone who is usually an idea person tries their hand at logistics. It's a bit like becoming a character in a play, but it ensures all the roles are covered.

Some teams need a creative spark to get things going, while others have plenty of ideas, yet require structure and organization. Some have good plans in place but might be distracted with interpersonal matters, and other teams just need a little push or encouragement to wrap things up. From a leadership standpoint, the team roles model is insightful for determining why certain groups might be stuck: What's missing? Personally, I am always looking for opportunities where I can experiment by taking on different roles beyond my comfort zone; ultimately, this makes me both a better team player and a more conscientious administrator, which is vital for fostering a high-performing culture.

Component Two: A Guiding Philosophy

"The Internet isn't really a technology, it's a belief system—a philosophy."[7] This is the visionary opening sentence in an essay by entrepreneur Joi Ito. While we might consider our digital infrastructure in terms of hardware and software, supported by routers, servers, web browsers, and mobile apps, those are just attributes of a larger paradigm. Ito explains, "The belief system of the Internet is that everyone should have the freedom to connect, the freedom to innovate and the freedom to program." This ideology of an open, accessible, networked architecture was the foundational root that blossomed into what we have today.

In this regard, our libraries are also a manifestation of a belief system. With each decision, you're enacting a philosophy. Let's say you are planning a new addition and are considering artwork for the walls. Do you display work from students and faculty members, or do you select regional, statewide, national, or global artists? Maybe you choose pieces that amplify your university's prestige and reputation or perhaps, instead, works that are socially and culturally inspiring or provocative. Is the space more aligned with a traditional stately scholarly temperament, or does it have more of a vibe conducive to edgy themes and a bold palette? Whatever choice you make is representative of a guiding philosophy.

Another way to consider this is by exploring your service perspective. Is your objective to encourage self-service or to offer full service? Are books placed on hold picked up in a grab-and-go manner, or are they retrieved through a help desk employee? Anticipated procedures are important to know during renovation planning because they set in motion decisions about physical design, staffing, and workflows.

Let's apply this to 3D printing. One library purchases a fleet of machines that it keeps in a back office and develops an efficient process for users to submit files for staff-mediated on-demand printing at a nominal cost. Another library offers a handful of machines in a makerspace lab that is open to anyone to use and handle freely. Both libraries support 3D printing, but they approach it through two different belief systems.

Having a clearly stated philosophy is vital for the design and management of learning spaces because it helps staff understand what's truly important and how to engage with patrons. Organizational culture researcher Daniel Coyle claims that a clear sense of purpose "isn't about tapping into some mystical internal drive but rather about creating simple beacons that focus attention and engagement on the shared goal."[8] Coyle emphasizes that successful cultures create engagement around a set of priorities that function as a lighthouse, orienting behavior and providing a path forward.

Libraries struggle with this. We feel pressure to be everything to everyone, resulting in misunderstanding, miscommunication, and conflicting priorities that hamper our success. This misalignment feels like swimming against the current, to use my analogy from before. Instead of trekking further along this unhelpful path, a shared purpose can congeal a team and transform a library.

Here is a thought experiment. Let's say your university wants to improve student retention and time-to-graduation rates. In a bid to secure major renovation funds, you propose the library as an academic success center, which is an underdeveloped resource at your institution. This decision would set you on a clear trajectory. It would impact not only portions of your physical footprint but also your hiring needs and other decisions. This "library as success center" model would stimulate new partnerships and programming. You might bring in a writing center and build presentation rehearsal spaces. Perhaps you would begin offering floating office hours for tutors, advising, financial aid, counseling, and proctoring. Your instructional strategy would need to expand beyond information literacy to include topics such as study skills, time management, and methods for effective group work. If you moved the library forward in this direction, you would need to better understand the multitude of challenges that students are encountering and then situate the library as part of the solution. You may also need to invest in curriculum support and instructional design to aid faculty and enhance teaching across your institution. And there would be new alliances with colleagues working across thematic areas including ESOL, first-generation students, disability services, diversity and equity programs, and student affairs, to name a few. As you can see, outlining a unifying purpose suddenly brings clarity and direction. You can see the path forward unfolding.

The Virginia Tech Libraries developed a guiding philosophy to bring focus and intentionality as a series of new services, studios, and commons areas were designed over the course of several years.[9]

STUDIO PHILOSOPHY

The Studios exist because we believe that creativity is as critical a skill as literacy. We recognize that students require new ways to create, collaborate, and engage with emerging technologies in order to be successful in the 21st century. We also believe that well-designed learning spaces can be tools to shape meaningful interactions, make innovation tangible, and spark community.

STUDIO VALUES

- *People-centered.* The Studios are designed to help our users solve problems, so we keep their needs front and center in everything we do. Empathy informs every service we provide. We are in the business of saying yes.

- *Accessible.* The Studios are for everyone, regardless of academic affiliation or skill level. There is no cost for students, staff, or faculty to use a Studio, and no previous experience with a technology or subject is required. We lower barriers and open doors.
- *Hands-on.* Recognizing that the process of learning is just as important as the finished product, the Studios emphasize hands-on, informal learning driven by thoughtful human interaction and, whenever possible, peer-to-peer teamwork. We aspire to provide expertise and to make experts.
- *Playful.* Believing that good ideas often happen while not taking yourself too seriously, the Studios encourage prototyping, experimentation, trial and error, and risk-taking. Breaking things in the process of figuring out how they work is OK. And having a sense of humor helps.
- *Community.* The Studios nurture connections between people and ideas. As much as they are physical spaces, the Studios are embodied in the community around them and the stories our users have to tell. We actively seek opportunities to build partnerships across and within the Studios and encourage collaboration whenever possible. We recognize that creativity is a collective endeavor as often as it is an individual pursuit.
- *Adaptive.* Needs change. Technologies change. Accordingly, the Studios themselves are spaces of continuous iteration and evolution. We think of the Studios as true learning environments: designed with intentionality, yet flexible enough to adapt to the diverse work being carried out within them.

The premise of this example is that creativity is a vital form of literacy. The objective then is to use the library's learning spaces as a testing ground for that belief. This purpose impacts the allocation of positions, the selection of furniture and technology, the content and pedagogy of workshops, the development of policies and workflows, the demeanor of interactions at service points, the metrics for assessment, and so forth.

Whether you are beginning a space project or you are looking to revitalize an existing one, articulating a purposeful theme provides a guiding thrust that enables pieces to fall into place. Here are a few ideas to jump-start your thinking:

- Wonder, Awe, Curiosity, Exploration
- Well-being, Mental Health, Concentration, Contemplation
- Productivity, Efficiency, Life Hacking, Self-Improvement
- Learning, Achievement, Academic Success
- Production of Knowledge, Scholarship, Open Research
- The World as Data, Computational Thinking, Systems Thinking, Interconnectedness
- Challenge the Status Quo, Think Different, Rebelliousness
- Designing a Better World, Sustainable Futures, Interdependence, Global Impact
- Social, Civil, Civic Engagement, Change-Makers, Inclusivity
- Innovation, Entrepreneurship, Ideation, Enterprise
- Art, Imagination, Expression, Design
- Service, Volunteering, Acts of Compassion, Community Building
- Tinkering, Experimentation, DIY, Maker Ethos

This list offers a range of possibilities that would result in widely different approaches to libraries. It might be helpful for your team to consider a few of these themes as a brainstorming exercise. How might a library focused on student success look, feel, and operate compared to one focused on research and knowledge production? Likewise, what are the differences between a library that is guided by imagination and design compared with one focused on productivity and efficiency? This is the power of purpose; it helps formulate intention and fosters a sense of identity. And most importantly, it provides you and your staff with a clear sense of shared values and priorities. A guiding philosophy helps us explain who we are as an organization and where we're heading.

Component Three: Innovating Processes

"'Tain't what you do, it's the way that you do it" is timeless advice that Ella Fitzgerald belts out from the 1930s.[10] This lyric gets to the heart of the third cultural component. After you have a team in place and a guiding philosophy, you need processes to inhabit growth. In short, this is how you steward your learning environment. Architects provide beautiful renderings. Engineers, contractors, and designers build amazing spaces. Once they are done, it becomes an ongoing organic metamorphosis. Libraries are not static; our job isn't simply to maintain what's been built, but rather to help that environment evolve and thrive.

I draw a parallel to virtual worlds. Consider a large game such as *World of Warcraft* that constantly introduces new features, characters, quests, and challenges.[11] Developers regularly adapt content based on how players engage with it. The version of the game today looks and operates much differently than when it launched in 2004. The same principle applies to libraries and learning environments. Similar to game designers, we need mechanisms to help us understand how services, spaces, and collections are being utilized and how to adapt based on changing needs and preferences.

There are many competing tools, frameworks, and theories for innovation. It can be confusing and intimidating to adapt those for libraries. But as Ella Fitzgerald encourages, it's more about "the way" we approach things: our intention. I know from experience it's easy to get caught up in following specific methodologies to the detriment of focusing on a more generative and serendipitous outcomes-based journey. After much experimentation, I've found three concepts that can be integrated and scaled into most organizations.

Plussing. This is a term that Walt Disney coined when referring to taking a good idea and making it better: *How can we plus it?*[12] The phrase emerged while building Disneyland and had less to do with the ideation or development phase and more connection with the postlaunch stage: after something is built, how to make it better. Long lines for a ride? How can we make waiting a more entertaining experience? Parking lots are a long walk? How can arrival and departures be made more enchanting?

I've experimented with this approach around mobile furniture and challenging my team to explore different configurations. What's the result if tables and chairs are arranged in one manner compared with another? What happens when we introduce portable monitors and mobile whiteboards? There are obviously many ways to mix and match furnishings and accessories, and depending on your philosophy you're going to get different outcomes. The key piece is fostering an R&D mentality and encouraging team members to be vigilant, constantly exploring and experimenting. *How can we plus it?* Similar to an amusement park or an online video game, library spaces are not finished, but instead present a constant opportunity to evolve. Remember: progress, not perfection.

Road maps. There is often so much activity going on that you need a dashboard or a visual tool to keep track, especially if there is a lot of plussing. I use road maps because they offer a lightweight framework to understand where you are, where you're going, and how you intend to get there.

Differing from a typical project management chart, road map tools don't dictate precise steps or track exact timelines, but instead envision work across three broad categories:[13]

- What are you working on NOW? (This month or this semester)
- What are you working on NEXT? (Next semester or the one after that)
- What are you working on LATER? (Next year and beyond)

Generating a flexible list like this for all services in your portfolio is game-changing. It allows your team to consider and batch short- and long-term projects and enables colleagues across the library to understand the direction and aspirations.

Let's return to 3D printing. Maybe right now you're working on streamlining the file submission process. Next semester you want to improve the notification process and the related data tracking. Next year you want to consider different ways to showcase creative works and establish some type of annual award or celebration. Down the road you may want to explore course integration, but right now the focus is on procedures and efficiencies.

Generating road maps for all library services provides staff with empowering insight. It makes the intention tangible and transparent, aiding decision-making, assessment, and outreach. It lays out future plans and homes in on what's happening currently. Structured road map lists open the landscape beyond silos, keeping everyone in sync while also inviting collaboration.

Sprints. A detailed to-do list is helpful, but without a supportive structure in place, it likely won't get finished. Innovating our learning spaces requires an adaptive, iterative framework. Yet that's not how we typically operate.

Most libraries I've worked at tend to follow a traditional one-hour-a-week meeting schedule sandwiched in between other engagements. At this pace the work inches along over a 16-week semester. What if we envision a different way to get things done?

Library teams could benefit from adopting agile practices, particularly sprints. Software developer Jake Knapp outlines an approach that could be used for any type of project, even nontechnical ones, by essentially combining information sharing, idea sketching, prototyping, and initial testing into a condensed intensive period.[14] Instead of stretching out that task force every Monday for four months, what if you did the work in three days?

Let's return to our 3D printing scenario. Imagine a small team is working on improving the file submission process. They commit to doing a three-day sprint where they explore and develop a handful of workable solutions. After a few intensive days they wind up with two potential models. The team deploys each one over the next month, enabling live field-testing and making any appropriate adjustments. Eventually they select the most feasible option and host a one-day sprint to improve (*plus!*) that model and draft flowcharts and the related documentation.

To foster an innovative and iterative culture, we must consider different ways to bring diverse sets of people together to collaborate more productively. Sprints can help unlock that potential. Instead of weekly meetings, imagine weekly sprints. This shift helps strengthen a library's creative muscle as well as its social capacity. Sprints could also align with your road maps so that your organization is routinely developing, testing, and deploying new ideas that directly enhance services. Of course, there isn't a one-size-fits-all solution for operationalizing sprints. It can be difficult for staff to step away from core responsibilities and other duties, but finding ways to scale this modality for your team, department, or organization can help accelerate innovation, recognize efficiencies, and create a stronger team bond.

Conclusion: Creating Conditions

At the beginning of this chapter, I mentioned visiting a library and feeling underwhelmed. The reason I had that response was due to my expectations. It was described as a *transformation*, yet it seemed more like a *refurbishment*. The same service design and structures were in place. Yes, it looked stylish, but conceptually speaking, it operated in the same manner as it did decades prior. My disappointment had nothing to do with aesthetics. Rather, my reaction was to the unseized potential. This library had a chance to transform itself—to actualize a new guiding philosophy—and it missed that opportunity.

When I started working on library renovations, I focused on students and designing inspiring spaces and services for them. Over the years my motivation shifted inward. Today I am far more interested in developing spaces that inspire library staff. It's a subtle shift, but it was a powerful revelation for me. Our colleagues are the ones managing and operating the labs, studios, commons areas, classrooms, exhibit spaces, and service desks. If I could spark their creative interests and foster their excitement for the environment, then they will embrace it with ownership and ensure that the space is maintained and improved upon. As a by-product of staff enthusiasm, the students receive a far better experience then I could ever dream up myself.

Library spaces offer the chance to develop a high-purpose culture and a deeply engaged workforce. It starts with forming an interdisciplinary team. Bring together a swirl of interests, expertise, approaches, and perspectives and give them a large canvas to work with. Establishing group norms and delineating clear roles are essential. This team also needs a philosophy: a belief system and guiding vision. This helps them understand priorities, direction, and what success looks like. They recognize how to effectively interact with each other and with library visitors. None of this can just be words on a page. In practice, it should serve as a living, breathing credo translating directly into daily conversations and actions. Lastly, we need processes for innovation. Your learning space can't remain static; your job is to help it evolve. I suggest plussing, road maps, and sprints as a starting place. A noticeable impact results from integrating all of these aspects. A compounding effect occurs with each piece propelling the culture further.

In the end, all we can do is create the conditions for success. The experience I noted about swimming with the current can't be forced or manufactured. It arises from the convergence of factors that reinforce and layer upon each other, resulting in something remarkable. If we try to overdesign it, we'll fail. The leader's role is to inspire staff with a compelling vision and then to empower them with the autonomy to fulfill it. When they have a purpose that they believe in and the freedom to create, then their work becomes artistry. Remember, you're not building and managing a learning space, you're enacting a philosophy.

Acknowledgment

Thanks to the Virginia Tech Library's Studio Team and particularly to Patrick Tomlin for always being ready to try something new and for stretching my imagination into new possibilities.

Notes

1. Walt Disney and Dave Smith, *Walt Disney: Famous Quotes* (Lake Buena Vista, FL: Walt Disney Company, 1994), 80.
2. Three classic organizational culture books that I found enlightening: Edgar Schein, *Organizational Culture and Leadership* (San Francisco: Jossey Bass, 2010); Gareth Morgan, *Images of Organization* (London: SAGE, 1997); Lee Bolman and Terrence Deal, *Reframing Organizations: Artistry, Choice and Leadership* (San Francisco: Jossey-Bass, 2013).
3. Tim Brown, quoted in Daniel Coyle, *Culture Code: The Secrets of Highly Successful Groups* (New York: Bantam, 2018), 160.
4. Charles Duhigg, "What Google Learned from Its Quest to Build the Perfect Team," *New York Times*, February 28, 2016, https://www.nytimes.com/2016/02/28/magazine/what-google-learned-from-its-quest-to-build-the-perfect-team.html.
5. Alex "Sandy" Pentland, "The New Science of Building Great Teams," *Harvard Business Review* 90, no. 4 (April 1, 2012), https://hbr.org/2012/04/the-new-science-of-building-great-teams.
6. R. Meredith Belbin, *Team Roles at Work* (New York: Routledge, 2010).
7. Joichi Ito, "In an Open-Source Society, Innovating by the Seat of Our Pants," *New York Times*, December 5, 2011, https://www.nytimes.com/2011/12/06/science/joichi-ito-innovating-by-the-seat-of-our-pants.html.
8. Daniel Coyle, *Culture Code: The Secrets of Highly Successful Groups* (New York: Bantam, 2018), 180.
9. "Studios," Virginia Tech University Libraries, accessed January 15, 2021, https://lib.vt.edu/create-share/studios.html.
10. Ludovic Hunter-Tilney, "'Tain't What You Do (It's the Way That You Do It)—Ella Fitzgerald Popularised This Classic Swing Tune," *Financial Times*, November 11, 2019, https://ig.ft.com/life-of-a-song/taint-what-you-do.html.
11. Philip Kollar, "Behind the Scenes of World of Warcraft's Biggest Patch Ever: Blizzard's Devs Explain Everything That Went into the Massive Patch 7.2," Polygon, March 31, 2017, https://www.polygon.com/2017/3/31/15139962/world-of-warcraft-wow-patch-7-2-tomb-of-sargeras-legion-biggest-ever-developer-interview-blizzard.
12. Theodore Kinni, *Be Our Guest: Perfecting the Art of Customer Service* (Disney Editions, 2011), 137.
13. C. Todd Lombardo, Bruce McCarthy, Evan Ryan, and Michael Conners, *Product Roadmaps Relaunched: How to Set Direction While Embracing Uncertainty* (North Sebastopol, CA: O'Reilly Media, 2017), 81.
14. Jake Knapp with John Zeratsky and Braden Kowitz, *Sprint: How to Solve Big Problems and Test New Ideas in Just Five Days* (New York: Simon & Schuster, 2016).

21

CHAPTER TWENTY-ONE

REIMAGINING THE LIBRARY WORKFORCE

CATHERINE MURRAY-RUST

The Challenge

When I retired from the Georgia Institute of Technology (Georgia Tech) in the summer of 2020, two beautifully renovated buildings beckoned to an eerily silent campus. In e-mails with the architects, I expressed my sadness that there would likely be no grand opening, no joyful giving back of the buildings to the students and the faculty after several long years of construction. The pandemic prevented us from celebrating, but it also reminded us that reinventing library services and spaces does not end with a certificate of occupancy.

During the years we worked on the renovation of the Georgia Tech Library, my colleagues and I experimented with new structures and work processes to support our commitment to engaging the community in reimagining the library. We started out creating cross-functional teams to write a new strategic plan and deal with the severe budget cuts, hiring freezes, and furloughs during the Great Recession. To guide us through the long-awaited building renovations and collaboration with Emory University Library to create a shared collection and build a state-of-the art storage facility, we worked with Georgia Tech consultants and outside firms to establish stronger connections to the community. We experimented with transitioning from traditional, specialized departments to a project portfolio structure with teams leading and managing renovation and service programs. We brought in consultants to help us change the organizational culture, but it was always a struggle to align resources with long-held values and new priorities. Despite our best intentions, when the pandemic shut down the campus, we still had a long way to go toward transforming the organization to complement the physical renewal of the library buildings.

I have continued to reflect on organizational transformation since Georgia Tech hosted the Designing Libraries Conference in October 2019. What follows is not an academic paper or a how-we-created-the-perfect-library story. My recommendations are based on what I learned from the strategies and programs that my Georgia Tech colleagues and I tried. It is a call to action to revitalize the library workforce to better support diverse communities now and in the future.

Knowing that every library is different—different people, different culture, different parent organization—I focus here on the most critical element of any transformation: building a coalition of willing people who are deeply invested in moving their library from content-centric to community-centric. This chapter includes ideas for energizing current library workers and designing a more diverse, action-oriented workforce for the future. Mindful of our library values, we have an imperative to change the culture in which we work, the behaviors we encourage, and the achievements we reward. Without fundamental organizational transformation, we will never enjoy diverse, creative, productive organizations in which people want to spend their time and energy as part of an engaged community.

S. I. Ranganathan, the hero of the University of London library school when I was a student there, warned in his 1931 classic, "An organism that ceases to grow will petrify and perish." In his Fifth Law of Library Science, he explains, "The library, as an institution, has all the attributes of a growing organism. A growing organism takes in new matter, casts off old matter, changes in size and takes on new shapes and forms."[1] I would add that libraries are first and foremost human organizations—imagined, created, and built by people. Libraries thrive, struggle, or fail to achieve the future they want because of the people who lead them, work in them, and support them. Just as people create beautiful, functional buildings, they also animate and enhance those spaces to calm, educate, and inspire. Dazzling libraries, like gorgeous homes, are just buildings without people to bring them to life.

The very best libraries are closely linked to their communities. They are dedicated to helping people individually and collectively meet their aspirations. They adapt to the changes in their environment. Their employees are happy to be the guide, not the hero of the story—Obi-Wan Kenobi, not Luke Skywalker. They offer not one or two but four key benefits to their communities: curated content; inspiring physical and digital environments; information expertise; and excellent services. All four are required, and all four depend on the passion and commitment of the library workforce.

When I think about how people contribute to organizational transformation, I think about structure, roles, and hierarchies both official and unofficial. I think about strategic alignment. How well do employees understand the organization's challenges and priorities, its strengths and weaknesses? I think about human resources or talent. Are individuals in the correct roles that allow them to use their skills, learn, and grow? Are the roles being performed the most important for the library right now and in the future? I think about behaviors. How do people interact with each other individually and in groups? Do people go along to get along, or do they speak truth to power and value honest discussion and respectful disagreement? Are employees siloed and inward-looking, or enthusiastic team members focused on growing their audience and supporting their community?

In libraries, we typically have little control over the external environment in which we operate. We have limited negotiating power to set the price and terms of access for content, especially digital materials. We have few sources of income and philanthropic support independent of our governing bodies. Most of us work in organizations overseen by larger organizations, specifically schools, colleges, universities, and local governments. Especially in public institutions, our fate is tied to complex budget priorities, rigid human resources policies and procedures, and fierce competition for resources sometimes with our own customers. We do not have price and earnings or market share reports to force us to make difficult decisions, address our organizational culture, and push us forward to change and grow. Our long history of stability, both a strength and a weakness, is reflected in the current composition of the library workforce.

The Library Workforce

Despite frequent, heartfelt calls for increasing diversity, equity, and inclusion, library workers continue to be White, female, middle-aged, and poorly paid. According to the United States Bureau of Labor Statistics (BLS) *Occupational Outlook Handbook*, libraries and related organizations employ fewer than one percent of the labor force in the United States. The US Census Bureau's Current Population Survey reports a decline in library and related jobs from 395,000 in 2006 to 308,000 in 2019. Women hold 80 percent of all librarian positions, and 82 percent of all library technicians and assistants are women, more than 60 percent of whom work part-time. The mean annual salary for librarians in 2019 was $61,920, while the mean hourly wage for library technicians was $17.76 and $14.34 for library assistants. Salaries vary widely by state and library type, but female librarians working full-time continue to be paid 92 percent of median salaries earned by men.[2]

Over the past 20 years, several studies about the composition of the library workforce were commissioned by professional organizations seeking to understand the expected wave of retirements. In 2009, the American Library Association's (ALA) Office for Research and Statistics hired Decision Demographics to conduct a workforce study that would inform ALA's strategic plan. That research, published in *Planning for 2015: The Recent History and Future Supply of Librarians*, followed the aging of the cohort of librarians born between 1946 and 1964 and predicted that 28 percent of ALA members would retire by 2020.[3] In Canada, organizations motivated by the same retirement concerns as ALA produced a series of studies between 2005 and 2020. Researchers analyzed the library workforce and called for training of early career employees and reskilling in such areas as management and leadership, core research competencies, and technology.[4]

Despite the good intentions and efforts by professional organizations, educational institutions, and library practitioners, little has changed in the composition of the workforce in decades. Current enrollment data in library education programs is not encouraging. The Association for Library and Information Science Education (ALISE) 2020 report provides data for about 51 US library schools, seven Canadian programs, and one overseas degree-granting institution. Fall 2019 enrollments totaled 30,579 students, of whom 18,239 were female (33 percent White) and 12,340 were male (18 percent White). In the same year, ALA-accredited master's degree students were 62 percent White and 80 percent female. Of the 6,686 degrees awarded that year, 5,002 were earned by women and 60 percent of all degrees were awarded to Whites.[5]

The lack of progress creating a more diverse, inclusive library workforce was a major theme of a forum sponsored by the Institute of Museum and Library Services (IMLS) in 2017. The report, *Positioning Library and Information Science Graduate Programs for 21st Century Practice*, addresses several issues, including the value of an LIS education, diversity of LIS students, and the continuing disconnect between library practitioners and educators. The recommendations focus on strategies for recruiting students, including rebranding for community-based librarianship, going where the diversity is, and considering radical changes to the MLIS degree. Forum attendees stressed the need to balance theory and practice, teach and assess interpersonal skills, and promote practical experience opportunities for LIS faculty. They emphasized that countering prevailing stereotypes about librarians and the work they do and encouraging libraries to create organizational cultures that value diversity, inclusion, and equity are crucial to transforming the library workforce.[6]

Meanwhile, the ongoing conflict between LIS educators and library administrators over who is to blame for the mismatch between the skills of library school graduates and the workforce needs of academic and public libraries flares up at library meetings and in publications. Library administrators complain that some new employees do not have a clear understanding of what working in a library entails and are unprepared for the demands of their jobs. As a library administrator, I complained to LIS deans and faculty as well as professional colleagues about the unrealistic work expectations of early career librarians. I particularly worried about those who have left other occupations such as teaching and law hoping to have a quiet, contemplative work life surrounded only by books and people who care about them.

Library educators complain that practitioners' expectations are impossible to meet. They are frustrated that the number of competencies and skills employers want never stops growing and the requested skills are difficult to teach in the classroom. Not only LIS faculty, but also university faculty generally, are discouraged by these demands. A list of the top 15 skills for 2025 compiled by the World Economic Forum illustrates the problem. Number one is analytical thinking and innovation, followed by active learning and learning strategies; complex problem-solving; critical thinking and analysis; creativity, originality, and initiative; leadership and social influence.[7]

Librarians publish similarly daunting compilations. Roisin Gwyer, a university librarian in the UK, used content analysis, focus groups, and trend reports to come up with her unranked list published in the *New Review of Academic Librarianship*. She includes change management, proving value, influencing and negotiation, creativity and innovation, supporting research in a digital world, digital literacy, marketing, digital information management, developing and managing space, and collaboration.[8]

LIS educators are discouraged by these lists, and so are current and potential employees. In 2016, *Library Journal*'s careers column featured the top skills for tomorrow's librarians. Most were contributed by public library leaders. The unranked list included advocacy/politics, collaboration, communication/people skills, creativity/innovation, critical thinking, data analysis, flexibility, leadership, marketing, and project management. Three university library directors added teaching, active faculty support, and rapid resource response. One reader going by the name pigbitinmad, responded, "Thanks, I think I will just go kill myself now."[9]

The most troubling accusation by library school faculty is that they do their best to prepare early career library workers to meet the growing list of demands by employers, but when new recruits join the library workforce they are treated badly by their bosses, colleagues, or customers. Early career librarians often complain to mentors and friends that their ideas for new services and programs are dismissed by their supervisors and senior leaders, who either do not listen to their proposals or never hear about them from middle management. Some library employees give up trying and silently go along to get along. Others change jobs or leave the profession they worked so hard to join.

In my 40-plus years in libraries, I have worked for bad bosses, felt discrimination, and left jobs that I otherwise enjoyed. To my great regret as an administrator, I sometimes failed to listen, pay attention to dismissive behavior, and deal with it quickly. I was shocked, but not surprised, by the results of Kaetrena Davis Kendrick's low morale studies in academic and public libraries.[10] I applaud efforts to make these dysfunctional work situations known, help people cope, create effective remedies, and prevent such toxic behavior in the future. Speaking this kind of truth to power reminds us that we all have the responsibility to change library culture to be honest, respectful, inclusive, and equitable. Every person who flees from a library because of bad treatment is a tragic waste of potential that we in libraries should not accept and cannot afford. Losing these employees not only harms our reputation as an employer and community partner but also endangers our future.

Librarians and library educators have made slow progress in changing curricula and offering training to ensure current and future employees learn needed skills. The IMLS, through its Laura Bush 21st Century Librarian Program, has funded training and development grants for the past 15 years. ALA, the Association of College and Research

Libraries, the Association of Research Libraries, and the Canadian Association of Research Libraries (CARL), as well as other professional organizations and private companies, offer a wide variety of books, webinars, and courses about all aspects of library work, including leadership development, project management, and technical skills. In recent years, some library leaders implemented programs to hire workers with PhDs, JDs, MBAs, and subject master's degrees to address the technical and research skills gaps. In coming years, libraries, like other organizations faced with skilled labor shortages, must not only strongly advocate for better salaries and employee benefits, but also pivot away from requiring expensive and time-consuming degrees toward workplace training and grow-our-own programs that help employees develop professionally.

Stop Hoping for a Miracle and Start Being More Explicit

Despite the progress the library community has made transforming library spaces and services, sustaining our progress is not guaranteed. Although financial support for libraries is uncertain, the major threat today is our capacity to reskill and reenergize the library workforce. Unlike pigbitinmad, I do not want to end my life when I read the long lists of skills and abilities that library workers must have to be employable. At worst, I find them annoying and unhelpful. At best, they make me think of the Sidney Harris cartoon with two scientists in lab coats standing in front of a large blackboard filled with equations. "A Miracle Happens" is scrawled in a cloud in the middle. One man is saying to the other, "I think you should be more explicit in step two."

Most economists will tell you that there are only two ways to grow the economy of a country, an industry, or a company—put more people to work or make the current workforce more productive by investing in education, training, and infrastructure. People do their best work when employers make work convenient, challenging, and well-compensated. As Patty McCord, the former chief talent officer of Netflix, insists,

> Most people want from work to be able to come in and work with the right team of people—colleagues they trust and admire—and focus like crazy on doing a great job together. People want to join organizations knowing that people there are proud of where they work and what they do. They enjoy a heady mix of responsibility and freedom.[11]

Where can we learn practical ways of transforming the library workforce, especially how to create an organizational culture that supports us on our path forward? One place to start is to learn about the details of successful library renovation projects that model team building, complex problem-solving, and community engagement. Outstanding library buildings are the achievements of passionate, innovative, technically proficient, diverse teams of people. These projects involve people inside as well as outside the library sharing their perspectives and expertise. The reimagined buildings and services that garner recognition as well as financial and political support are creative endeavors among architects, planners, designers, technologists, and library employees in close collaboration with the communities they serve.

At Georgia Tech, we were fortunate to be included in the long process of designing and renovating the libraries, which is not always the case in universities. We earned our seat at the decision-making table over several years. We managed the long and challenging 10-year reaffirmation of accreditation for Georgia Tech. We piloted projects and user studies that inspired the design of Clough Undergraduate Learning Commons, a classroom and lab building attached to the library, and enthusiastically agreed to manage its building operations. We expanded our outreach programs and vigorously engaged with the campus community and major stakeholders to understand how research and teaching were changing. The time and energy we put into major university projects earned us what I call social credit. Our efforts convinced campus leadership and senior faculty that we could balance our advocacy for the library with the needs of the campus as a whole and we had the talent, expertise, and deep commitment to make a significant contribution to Georgia Tech. We were, in short, a good investment in the future.

In addition to learning from successful library design projects, we can look to other professions and organizations for guidance on how to manage successful transformations. Some business sources, such as William and Susan Bridges's classic *Managing Transitions*, provide useful advice about scaffolding change to avoid the "hoping for a miracle" gap between the present and the desired future.[12] Better yet are rare studies about the experiences with transformations in industries undergoing major upheaval.

One of the most useful recent books on the disruption of traditional journalism over the past 20 years is *Transforming Newsrooms: Connecting Organizational Culture, Strategy, and Innovation*. Although we in libraries have not been forced to fight for our survival like newspapers, we have the same pressures to engage with our audiences, thrive in a digital-first, 24-7 world, and attract employees with technical and media skills who also understand our mission and uphold our values. To make changes that last, the authors, both journalism professors, recommend beginning with a comprehensive review of the organization's values and culture. Only then should organizations move on to articulating the organizational strategy and getting buy-in at all levels. After those two areas are addressed, organizations can turn their attention to generating innovation and building teamwork.[13]

Although we started with strategy, not organizational culture, at Georgia Tech, we achieved many parts of our agenda. Two old, crumbling buildings became two beautiful, light-filled places for people, not warehouses for books. Now, offices and work spaces bring people together physically and online systems bring them together virtually wherever they are in the world. The library looks and feels community-focused, not content-focused. It is no longer an aging, badly maintained building filled with books few people use, but a growing, responsive organism of the kind Ranganathan described.

We used project portfolio management, teamwork, and skill building to internally manage the renovation, services, and technology. Projects and resources were connected in meaningful ways for the first time. Carefully assessing service gaps and discussing them with the campus community resulted in new public programs and teaching opportunities. Moving more than 95 percent of the physical collection to a shared facility with Emory University Library and coordinating services required a variety of enhanced skills—cross-institutional collaboration, teamwork, initiative, and project management.

Even so, in hindsight we would have benefitted from a deep dive into the library's values and culture at the beginning of the reimagining process, as the authors of *Transforming Newsrooms* recommend. When we circled back later to these issues, we had conversations about mission, vision, and values, but we made the mistake of not including everyone in the discussion. We did not ensure we all had the same understanding of the values we professed, what they meant to us as individuals, and how they impacted everyday work. Although we made some positive changes in refocusing the library from content to community, improving efficiency, enhancing customer service, and reskilling the workforce, we did not create lasting cultural change to support the reimagined spaces because we did not pay attention first and foremost to understanding organizational culture before we tried to change it.

Bringing It All Together

If we are to successfully transform our libraries and keep changing to meet the needs of the communities we serve, we need a reimagined workforce that thrives in an environment of freedom and responsibility. In the spirit of being more explicit about what we can do to create successful change, here are some suggestions for transforming today to ensure that our libraries are ready to take on the challenges of tomorrow.

CULTURE AND STRATEGY

- Champion a study of the culture of the library by an outside researcher using focus groups and other in-person techniques. Share and discuss the findings widely.

- Form a coalition of people from all levels who are committed to planning and action for organizational transformation.
- Ensure that everyone in the organization has the opportunity to provide input into the library's strategy for engaging the community, broadening its audience, and serving its customers.
- Assess and communicate strengths, weaknesses, threats, and opportunities that impact the organization's ability to serve its community.
- Update everyone regularly about the library's financial and political situation, especially issues that may impact individual work lives.
- Build a culture of honest communication and responsible discussion at all levels.
- Model working with others with respect and civility and insist on these behaviors from everyone.

PAY AND CONDITIONS

- Advocate for higher pay and better benefits for everyone in the library workforce.
- Improve day-to-day working conditions, including building repairs, supplies, and equipment.
- Hold everyone accountable for interacting with each other about performance throughout the year. Discontinue annual reviews in favor of more frequent performance discussions, not tied to salary if at all possible.
- Change job descriptions to reflect what each individual is actually doing to support the library's vision and mission. If replacing existing job descriptions is not feasible, work with employees to develop informal, internal job descriptions and job titles.

SKILL BUILDING

- Champion learning opportunities and training that encourages everyone to solve problems with colleagues and team members.
- Develop an environment that supports curiosity and exploration.
- Encourage innovation and risk-taking by trying out team-based techniques for rapid innovation and fast-paced service development.
- Build digital-first strategies to engage and expand the library's audience.

FUTURE WORKFORCE PLANNING

- Market working in a library as an opportunity to serve the community in collaboration with talented, skilled people who are educators, artists, and innovators.
- Advocate for paid internships and practicums to help people find a job in which their contribution is valued.
- Work with LIS educators and professional organizations to decrease the cost required to earn library credentials and make the time to gaining credentials shorter.
- Consider hiring people with diverse educational qualifications and community engagement experience to broaden the library's skill base and strengthen teamwork.
- Break down the barriers to people moving among kinds of libraries and library specialties, especially between public and academic libraries.
- Ramp up grow-our-own programs for new employees, as well as internships and volunteer opportunities.

- Forge alliances with cultural institutions including museums, galleries, and archives to share expertise and talent.
- Increase programming to demonstrate and strengthen the library's interaction with the community.
- Create a strong digital-first mentality through a robust website, effective social media, user involvement, and quality programming.

A Call to Action

Despite all the changes we have made in recent years to educate, support, inspire, and enliven our communities, libraries are still undervalued and underfunded. Beautiful spaces, well-used collections, educational programming, and even Wi-Fi hot spots and streaming services help meet pressing needs, but true community engagement depends on reimagining and reenergizing the library workforce. We must develop a sense of urgency about diversity, equity, and inclusion. Dedicated, passionate employees—who they are, what skills they have, and how well they work together—will determine whether libraries thrive in the future. To honestly earn social credit that we can translate into new services, content, and outreach, we must attract the best, brightest diverse workers, pay them the compensation they deserve, offer them training and continuing education, support their ideas and dreams, and send them out to remake libraries and through our libraries remake our communities.

Notes

1. Shiyali Ramamrita Ranganathan, *The Five Laws of Library Science* (London: Edward Goldston, 1931), 382.
2. US Bureau of Labor Statistics, "Librarians and Media Specialists," *Occupational Outlook Handbook*, 2020, https://www.bls.gov/ooh/education-training-and-library/librarians.htm; US Bureau of Labor Statistics. "Library Technicians and Assistants," *Occupational Outlook Handbook*, 2020, https://www.bls.gov/ooh/education-training-and-library/library-technicians-and-assistants.htm; US Bureau of Labor Statistics. "Archivists, Curators, and Museum Workers," *Occupational Outlook Handbook*, 2020, https://www.bls.gov/ooh/education-training-and-library/curators-museum-technicians-and-conservators.htm; Department for Professional Employees, "Library Professionals: Facts and Figures," AFL-CIO, June 10, 2021, https://www.dpeaflcio.org/factsheets/Library+Workers+Facts+&+Figures+2020.pdf.
3. Denise M. Davis, comp., *Planning for 2015: The Recent History and Future Supply of Librarians* (Chicago: ALA, 2009), http://www.ala.org/tools/sites/ala.org.tools/files/content/librarystaffstats/recruitment/Librarians_supply_demog_analys.pdf.
4. Vivian Lewis, "New Skills for the Academic Library Workforce—A Canadian Experience," Proceedings of the 2017 IATUL Conference, paper 3, https://docs.lib.purdue.edu/iatul/2017/challenges/3; CARL Competencies Working Group, *Competencies for Librarians in Canadian Research Libraries* (Ottawa: CARL-ABRC, 2020), https://www.carl-abrc.ca/wp-content/uploads/2020/09/Competencies-Final-EN-1-2.pdf.
5. Association for Library and Information Science Education, *2020 Statistical Report: Trends and Key Indicators in Library and Information Science Education* (Estford, MA: ALISE, 2020), https://ali.memberclicks.net/assets/documents/statistical_reports/2020/ALISE%202020%20Statistical%20Report%20Summary%20Final_Revised%2020210106.pdf.
6. Ashley E. Sands, Sandra Toro, Teri DeVoe, Sarah Fuller, and Christine Wolff-Eisenberg, *Positioning Library and Information Science Graduate Programs for 21st Century Practice* (Washington, DC: Institute of Museum and Library Services, 2018), https://www.imls.gov/sites/default/files/publications/documents/imlspositioningreport.pdf.
7. World Economic Forum, *The Future of Jobs Report 2020* (Geneva, Switzerland: World Economic Forum, October 2020), https://www.weforum.org/reports/the-future-of-jobs-report-2020.
8. Roisin Gwyer, "Identifying and Exploring Future Trends Impacting on Academic Libraries: A Mixed Methodology Using Journal Content Analysis, Focus Groups, and Trend Reports," *New Review of Academic Librarianship* 21, no. 3 (2015): 269–85, https://doi.org/10.1080/13614533.2015.1026452.

9. Meredith Schwartz, "Top Skills for Tomorrow's Librarians: Careers 2016," *Library Journal* (digital access edition), March 9, 2016, https://www.libraryjournal.com/?detailStory=top-skills-for-tomorrows-librarians-careers-2016.
10. Kaetrena Davis Kendrick, "The Public Librarian Low-Morale Experience: A Qualitative Study," *Partnership: The Canadian Journal of Library and Information Practice and Research* 15, no. 2 (2020): 1– 32, https://journal.lib.uoguelph.ca/index.php/perj/article/view/5932/5977; Kaetrena Davis Kendrick and Ione T. Damasco, "Low Morale in Ethnic and Racial Minority Academic Librarians: An Experiential Study," *Library Trends* 68, no. 2 (Fall 2019): 174–212, https://muse.jhu.edu/article/746745.
11. Patty McCord, *Powerful: Building a Culture of Freedom and Responsibility* (Silicon Guild, 2017), 19.
12. William Bridges and Susan Bridges, *Managing Transitions: Making the Most of Change* (Boston: Da Capo Books, 2016).
13. Carrie Brown and Jonathan Groves, *Transforming Newsrooms: Connecting Organizational Culture, Strategy, and Innovation* (New York: Routledge, 2021).

VII

SECTION VII

PROGRAMMING FOR RESEARCH, LEARNING, AND COMMUNITY

22

CHAPTER TWENTY-TWO

FOREGROUNDING USERS IN HUMANITIES-CENTRIC LABS

CATHERINE DeROSE and PETER LEONARD

In *Digital Humanities and the Library*, Anu Vedantham and Dot Porter write that "libraries are associated primarily with a sense of place. We 'go to the library,' a physical building that contains resources to help us think, read, find materials, and conduct research. The appearance and functionality of the library can affect our research productivity as well as our metacognition—our perception of our own productivity."[1] Does this sense of place hold for digital forms of scholarship as well? In their introduction to "Lab and Slack: Situated Research Practices in Digital Humanities," Mila Oiva and Urszula Pawlicka-Deger note, "There is a threat that we will forget how the place is also entangled in the digital. DH scholars work together in a physical place—a center and a laboratory—in which an infrastructure, facilities, and equipment determine the knowledge creation practices."[2] How can we acknowledge the role of place and create welcoming spaces that inspire and support digital research?

Questions around place and digital practice informed an architectural and service design team that transformed a Tudor-themed reading room in the heart of a 1930s library into a space for humanities-inflected digital scholarship at Yale University (see figure 22.1 for an early depiction of the room). Throughout the design process, library staff and external architects reflected on this interplay of infrastructure and support programs in reimaging the space so that it foregrounded humanities scholars. In so doing, we explored how—in the words of Vedantham and Porter, the "colocation of library expertise near collaboration spaces can help faculty and students draw connections between traditional library capabilities (collections, subject specialists, bibliographers, catalogers) and newer capabilities (scanning, digitization, data analysis and visualization, new media creation, web/blog design, audio/video editing)."[3]

fig 22.1

Sterling Memorial Library Reserve Reading Room, circa 1950s.

(Yale University, Photographs [RU 696]. Manuscripts and Archives, Yale University Library.)

This chapter focuses on the intersection of architectural design and service programming in the Franke Family Digital Humanities Laboratory (FFDHL), a 5,000-square-foot space in Sterling Memorial Library. A dramatic glass cube enclosing specialized hardware anchors the room, flanked on either side by new staff offices and an ever-expanding print collection of digital humanities (DH) volumes. With visualization screens, flexible furniture, and reconfigurable space, the design of the FFDHL supports innovative and varied programming in a historic room: an opera composed by a neural network, graduate students meeting with staff to discuss teaching DH to undergrads, and K–12 students interacting with a map of 120,000 photographs from the Great Depression. As the main hub for DH work on Yale's campus, the FFDHL aims to showcase the potential of humanities computation while also providing guidance to researchers looking to undertake their own projects.

Architectural Design Principles

Apicella + Bunton, a New Haven–based architectural firm behind many renovation projects in Sterling Memorial Library, was selected for the design of the FFDHL. Partner J. Bunton, present from the beginning of the project, set a tone of trying to understand as much as possible about the scholarly and professional practices that would take place in the space, with the goal of "creating a space that allows you to do what you do best."[4] Project architects wanted to know how lab staff would teach, consult, assist, and otherwise engage with clients in order to articulate architectural principles that would help the design process succeed.

Throughout the ideation, design, and refinement processes, we worked together to stay faithful to two guiding principles: that the space would be defined by *openness* and *transparency* and that it would be *flexible* and *adaptable*. Although they would be manifested in the physical realms of architecture, finishes, and furniture, these principles also represented values that guide the DHLab in its delivery of services to patrons.

OPENNESS AND TRANSPARENCY

The range of DH development on most campuses presents unique opportunities for showcasing the diversity and breadth of new forms of scholarly practice. The FFDHL would need to be a physical space that encouraged intellectual exploration—of scholarly practice as much as books or data sets. The room would have to welcome all patrons, not just those who self-identify as having explicit DH interests or abilities. The existing layout of the room offered, for the most part, an open canvas.

As the architects observed, the notion of a welcoming space starts with access to the room. Like much of the first floor of Sterling Memorial Library, the FFDHL does not have ID-based access restrictions. No proof of Yale identity is required to come into the space, which has proven useful in facilitating events that include public as well as campus participants. From high school students enrolled in STEAM (STEM plus arts and humanities) workshops to curators from the Smithsonian Institution, diverse audiences gather in the FFDHL without the need to obtain special identification or privileges. Even within the campus community, the lack of access control or other gatekeeping features ensures the space welcomes as many as possible, regardless of how familiar they are with a traditional research library.

Once inside, the visual appearance of the room itself plays a central role in how first-time visitors and habitual users alike perceive the space. We made the decision to foreground print collections in the design of the room. This decision is in keeping with the historical purpose and, indeed, infrastructure of the reading room itself: originally designed to hold 10,000 volumes, the walls already consisted of built-in bookcases. In alignment with our values of openness and transparency, we wanted to change how the bookcases functioned, presenting volumes with their covers, instead of their spines, facing the user. The architecture and millwork teams found ways to reuse the 1930s brass hardware to support new L-shaped wooden shelves, which cradled books at an angle facing up and toward the user. The overall effect was more like a book display than a library shelf—and mirrored trends in other display contexts, such as Amazon's physical bookstores, which foreground book covers. The architects also noted the digital inspiration for this very analog solution: "Taking cues from webpages and curated image platforms like Instagram, Pinterest, and Tumblr, the bookcases encourage a more intuitive approach to browsing, responding to the changing ways researchers have become accustomed to looking for relevant sources online."[5] Stained to resemble their flat predecessors, the new shelves had an overall effect of visual continuity with the carved wooden bookcases, paired with eye-catching displays of color and typography on volumes such as *W. E. B. DuBois' Data Portraits*, *Data Feminism*, *How to Lie with Maps*, and *Teaching Digital Humanities*. Each book in the 250-strong collection is a window into the data, theory, and practice of its authors and plays its own role in exposing the room's users to a broad range of DH practice in a visually appealing way.

While print monographs represent one scholarly tradition that we wished to highlight, we felt equally strongly that the walls should showcase digital work as well. The architects designed spaces for an alternating pattern of bookshelves and high-resolution monitors, woven together in a repeating pattern 12 times throughout the room (figure 22.2).

fig 22.2

Graduate students in the Franke Family Digital Humanities Laboratory, 2018.

(Photo Mara Lavitt.)

Positioned at eye levels, these screens display past and current DH projects by Yale professors and students: dominant colors extracted from multiple editions of William Blake's hand-colored manuscripts, the growth and intertwining of Yale's campus with maps of New Haven, networks of photographers and editors from the Magnum photo agency, and 360° photography of the late poet John Ashbery's house.

Although colorful and engaging, the interplay between digital screens and analog book covers might not be the feature of the room that most stands out to first-time visitors. Offset from the center of the room, large panes of glass are supported by a metal structure that encloses several work areas grouped together in what would come to be called the special projects cube. This largest modern intervention in the room aims to highlight the axial view corridor of the space: the transparent glass filters light in a modern interpretation of the leaded-glass windows that flank the walls. People can walk directly through the center of the structure without obstruction (figure 22.3)

fig 22.3

The special projects cube in the Franke Family Digital Humanities Laboratory, 2018.

(Photo Mara Lavitt.)

The special projects cube stands as the most concrete manifestation of the principles of openness and transparency in the FFDHL. The three work spaces house specialized equipment, such as VR/AR goggles, microfilm scanners, and large-scale disk arrays, that—thanks to the glass walls—are always visually on display, even when not in use. Rather than being locked away in a closet or basement, the means of encountering and transforming data are highly visible. And when scholars are using these same pieces of equipment to perform their work, their activities and practices are similarly framed and highlighted to everyone who enters the room (figure 22.4)

fig 22.4

The special projects cube in the Franke Family Digital Humanities Laboratory, 2018.

(Photo Mara Lavitt.)

Reserved for DHLab-sponsored project activity, the special projects cube might contain an English professor exploring a poet's house in VR, a research assistant digitizing a historic African American newspaper, a graduate student spelunking through terabytes of licensed electronic data, or a programmer configuring deep learning hardware to generate new texts from literary source material. With 10-gigabit fiber optic internet connections, high-capacity disk storage, and high-resolution monitors, the special projects cube places the hard work of data cleaning, metadata remediation, exploratory data visualization, and other crucial phases of DH projects at the core of the room, in a space that is simultaneously secure and transparent.

Due to the centrality of the special projects cube in the room, the team wanted to create a decorative program for the glass walls that celebrated the properties of the transparent material itself. The result was an active collaboration between lab programmers and designers and the architects to produce a repeating variegated pattern of rectangles that rise from the floor and dissipate roughly five feet above. Each rectangle is the exact proportion of the holes in punch cards used in early mainframe computing. This analog form of binary input/output references a famous image of Jesuit priest Roberto Busa inspecting a digitized text of Thomas Aquinas, converted into punchcard form for computational processing. Reflecting on the design, Apicella + Bunton wrote:

> An animating and meaningful visual element in the space, [the abstracted punchcard design] primarily serves a real practical need: addressing privacy needs of those seated at the Cube's workstations and partially obscuring the power and IT cordage supporting its equipment. Our team saw an opportunity to meet this need with a thoughtful and personalized solution that elevates the aesthetic of the space and draws in the history of digital humanities itself.... Working with the DHLab staff to design the abstracted punchcard pattern taught us more about the history of the digital humanities and helped us bring that history into the project in a novel, beautiful, and practical way.[6]

The ability of glass to communicate principles of openness and transparency extends to other design elements in the room, such as the treatment of new staff offices that were introduced in a former back-of-house space that originally held reserve book shelving. Five new openings were created in a load-bearing wall to house DHLab team members such as a UX designer and programmer. These openings in the wall were designed as glass apertures, so that one entire side of each office is visually open to the room. The design was influenced by lessons learned during the 2012 renovation of Yale's Center for Science and Social Science Information (CSSSI), where the glass apertures increased the visibility of library staff to patrons and made them feel more integrated into the larger space. In Apicella + Bunton's renovation of the mid-century CSSSI, located on Yale's Science Hill, chemistry and sociology librarians' offices were designed to be open visually to a large central patron space via glass walls and doors. In the FFDHL, the same principle is adapted to a 1930s Tudor reading room, which required a nuanced understanding of how to join the sleek new glass to the older parts of the wall. Apicella + Bunton noted that such a solution took advantage of what they call "borrowed light," illuminating the staff offices and connecting them to the vast space of the main reading room (figure 22.5)

fig 22.5

Staff office in the Franke Family Digital Humanities Laboratory, 2018.

(Photo Mara Lavitt.)

FLEXIBILITY AND ADAPTABILITY

Strong design elements characterize the transformation of the FFDHL into a space connoting the values of openness and transparency: digital screens showcasing projects interwoven with books, the large glass cube in the middle of the space, added support staff offices where a solid wall once stood. But just as important to the goal of foregrounding users are the values of flexibility and adaptability. We felt we were designing a room for which the ultimate range of uses would become clear only in the future. Overcommitting to a certain space division, furniture strategy, or anticipated activity would run the risk of prematurely aging the space. Many electronic classrooms, after all, were built in the 1990s under the assumption that computers would always have large CRT monitors—not to mention the expectation that computing would remain a desktop, as opposed to mobile, activity.

To manifest the values of flexibility and adaptability in the FFDHL, the team agreed that the space would need to be as reconfigurable as possible. The large size of the main floor (4,000 square feet) led to the possibility of modular subdivision, in which certain areas would be delineated not by hard walls that stretch from one side to the other but by design elements of the renovation (figure 22.6) A primary example of this is the way the special projects cube is positioned: centered in the shorter axis of the room, but offset in the longer axis, it forms a visual scrim and acoustic screen between the larger open space that welcomes visitors into the room and the smaller area beyond it, toward the far end.

The FFDHL was designed well past the point of most students on campus needing a lab for access to computing resources. The trends of decentralization and miniaturization have seen mainframe terminals of the 1960s and 70s replaced by desktop computer labs of the 1980s and 90s, which were themselves obsoleted by laptops becoming more affordable in the 2000s. With the advent of tablets, smartphones, and other high-powered devices that can fit in a purse or pocket, some campus spaces have been reimagined to de-emphasize technological equipment completely, such as Columbia University's Butler Studio.

fig 22.6

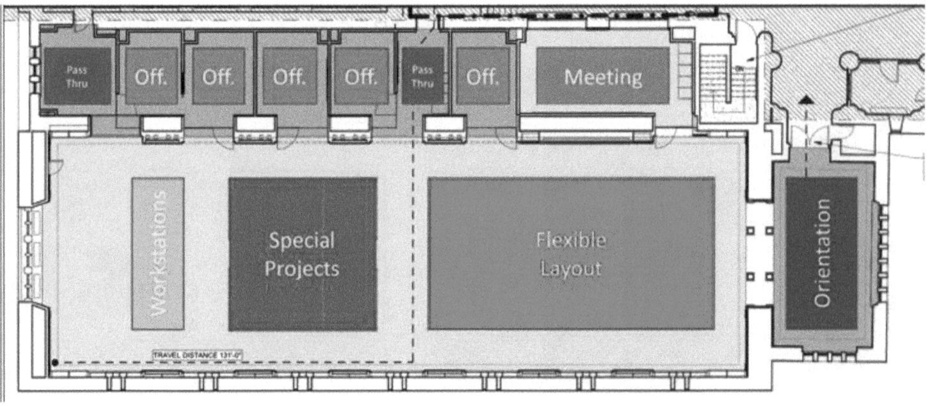

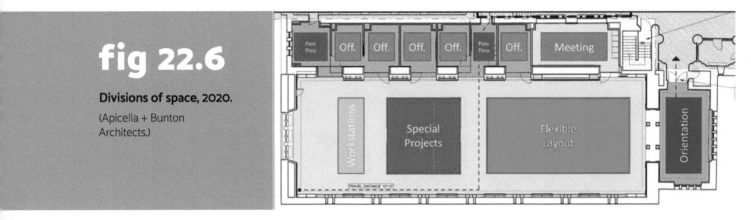

Divisions of space, 2020.

(Apicella + Bunton Architects.)

Despite these advances, we still needed to grapple with the question of walk-up access to certain types of computing resources that many students would not otherwise be able to access. While the special projects cube would house specialized equipment on a reservation basis, this still left a gap between the iPad a student might have in her backpack and what might be required for a data-intensive project. Certain kinds of software, such as statistical packages, visualization tool kits, or programming environments, certainly benefit from full-fledged desktop computers with large screens, capacious memory and storage, and hardwired connectivity. For this reason, we set aside some of the space flanking the special projects cube for a relatively traditional lab setup, with eight high-end workstations capable of dual-booting into both Windows and Mac OS. We have seen this equipment used quite often by students who need a particular tool (optical character recognition software or GIS packages, as two examples) and perhaps a place to use that tool in a concentrated way. Intriguingly, these users have often come from social science or science disciplines.

This small lab space, together with the special projects cube, is one of the only non-movable objects in the room. The rest of the furniture is wheeled and may be deployed in a variety of configurations depending on the activity taking place. The architectural team devised a number of hypothetical arrangements of the chairs and tables, from scattered groupings that support multiple simultaneous consultations to traditional lecture-style arrangements. With time, we have settled on common deployments that suit frequent uses, such as a workshop configuration with tables in a U shape opposite the room's largest screen, our "data canvas." Special events, such as conferences, provide an opportunity to reimagine the room for much greater occupancy levels on a temporary basis. Conversely, when safety-related considerations required de-densifying the room after March 2020, we were able to create distanced seating arrangements that still enabled the use of the room as part of the library's seating capacity.

From Architectural Plans to Service Design

The principles that guided the FFDHL's renovation—openness and flexibility—are further reflected in the DHLab's support model, which includes four components tied directly to the physical space: instruction, consultation, projects, and events. Each type of support comes with its own needs and opportunities, which the collaborative design process aimed to satisfy and address.

INSTRUCTION

The FFDHL's flexible, open design supports a range of ways to learn, from large-group workshops and class visits to small-group exchanges. DHLab staff regularly teach technical workshops that are open to students, faculty, and staff from across campus. Held near the entrance, these workshops are highly visible to anyone walking into the space. This visibility was important to the DHLab team, as it helps foreground different methods, tools, and use cases to wider audiences, from the people who registered for the workshop to the people who just happened to be in or passing through the space. For passersby who have their interest piqued, they can (and often do) sit at one of the tables nearest to the workshop so they can follow along; those seats at nearby tables also provide backup space for registrants on the wait list.

The open space and wheeled furniture allow for quick room reconfigurations tailored to the needs of any particular workshop (figure 22.7). By default, tables are arranged in a U shape facing the data canvas, beside which we wheel out a podium for staff. This arrangement gives all participants a clear view of the screen and speaker, while also ensuring they have peers near them to whom they can also turn for assistance. Additionally, it means staff are able to easily reach any participant who might be having an issue on their local machine. For power sources, we have two power strip towers we wheel to either side of the U so that all participants have ready access to an outlet; there are also sets of outlets on the wall with the data canvas for presenters and participants seated nearest the wall. For workshops with more than 20 participants, we add a row or two of tables behind the U. For more group-oriented activities, we group tables into pods.

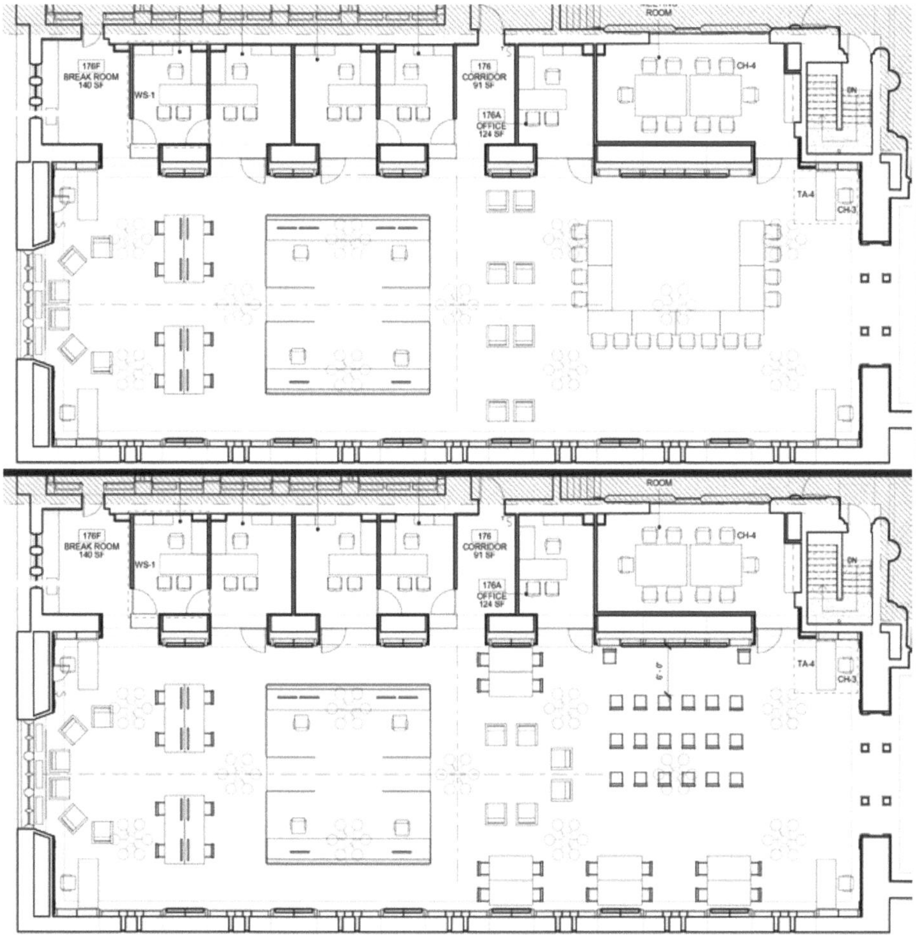

fig 22.7

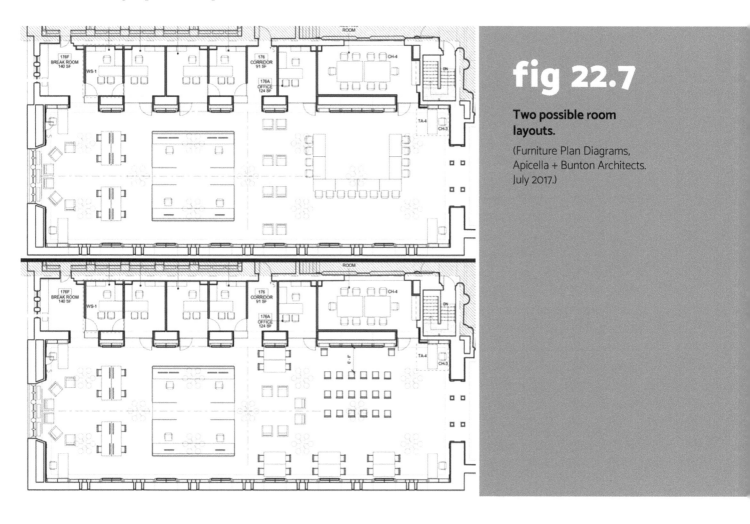

Two possible room layouts.

(Furniture Plan Diagrams, Apicella + Bunton Architects. July 2017.)

Along with teaching workshops in the main space, DHLab staff also give lectures for visiting classes. For these, the FFDHL serves as an active "set" that highlights DH methods and technologies, along with available lab services. During their lectures, staff can reference books along the shelves (situated on the wall opposite the data canvas) that thematically or methodologically tie into the class. They can gesture to the special projects cube to underscore the labor and equipment underlying DH projects. They can point at the front desk and staff offices, where students (and faculty) can reliably find support. Visiting classes provide another opportunity for happenstance DH exposure, where other students working in the space can glimpse the use of network graphs in a 19th-century literature class or discover platforms for creating multimedia presentations on social movements in New Haven.

While the open work space lends itself well to large-group, technical instruction, the meeting room works better for teaching smaller groups that are more discussion-based and may have privacy concerns. Each semester, the DHLab awards DH teaching fellowships to graduate students who are interested in incorporating DH methods, tools, or theories into their classrooms. During the fellowship, the graduate student cohort meets periodically with DHLab staff to discuss their individual classes and participate in a combination of lab-led pedagogical and technical workshops, with the goal of preparing the fellows to teach their students. The meeting room—with its door and solid wall facing the lab (contrary to the staff offices)—provides more privacy for such discussions, encouraging students to be open with questions they might have. Furthermore, given that the agenda for the cohort meetings is subject to change based on what is happening in fellows' classes around that time, the meeting room's whiteboard, which facilitates impromptu workshopping, is an additional advantage of the space.

CONSULTATION

The reading room the DHLab moved into originally contained a circulation desk that physically and functionally moderated entrances and exits. In an effort to convey that all are welcome into the space, we collaborated with the architects to repurpose the desk, relocating it to the front lobby, where it now serves as a welcome point, a place where visitors can ask questions about the lab or DH more generally.

The high visibility of the front desk makes it the ideal meeting spot for the DHLab's weekly drop-in office hours. Open to anyone on campus, office hours provide an opportunity to meet with a DHLab team member to discuss DH, from nebulous ideas and software recommendations to advice on project management. The lobby itself has a dramatically lower ceiling than the main room—no doubt an architectural trick from the building's original design to heighten the drama of entrance—and this more intimate space can feel welcoming to those who are just beginning their exploration of DH. The length of the desk comfortably allows for up to three consultations at a time, which is especially helpful in moments where two students might be asking related questions. Consultants can then combine their expertise, and students find a peer engaging in similar work with whom they can follow up beyond office hours. If instead of at that front desk the consultations were held in staff offices or at separate tables, those connections would not as easily be made in real time.

In addition to the desk in the lobby, the FFDHL also has two corner desks in the front of the main room that serve as consulting stations for complementary expertise. One desk is reserved for consultations with the geographic information system (GIS) librarian and her team. The other is available to DH teaching fellows for their class office hours. Outside of open consulting times, both desks contain signs that promote the respective services, with information on how to schedule a meeting.

PROJECTS

DHLab-supported projects generally fall into two categories: those that are using or making minor modifications to existing web software and those that entail custom development. Each has different spatial requirements. Projects built with existing tools can often be accomplished in real time on personal laptops around a shared display screen. (Even the shared screen is optional in most cases.) For projects with such requirements, the DHLab's open work space, meeting room, or offices all work well. However, projects needing custom-built software generally have more technological—and by extension, spatial—constraints. To run most efficiently, they may require specialized hardware, monitors, external hard drives, or wired internet connections. Moreover, they likely include code that needs to churn for days or weeks on end, meaning they need a dedicated computer on which programs could run without risk of interruption. Such projects necessitate a more stable and secure workspace: the special projects cube.

Distinctive in both its look and function, the special projects cube provides a work space that is physically locked but visually open (figure 22.8). DH labor—from scanning and OCRing to preparing, analyzing, and visualizing data—is on display. People can walk between the two halves of the cube to get a closer look at the work underway at any given moment. One half of the cube foregrounds the scanning and preparation stages, the other half the analyzing and visualizing. Along with fulfilling its technical purpose, the high-powered equipment is eye-catching. People walking from one end of the lab to the other have to pass by the cube, and as they do so, they often stop to discuss the equipment or projects on display. It is common for staff, when they're working in the cube, to field questions from interested students, faculty, or campus visitors. When staff leave work for the day, they don't need to remove the equipment and secure it behind a locked door out of view; rather, the cube's glass doors provide security while still showcasing the projects and equipment to students who continue to study in the space even after the staff leave. Similarly, the designated workstations ensure that computing tasks can run as long as they need to with minimal risk of interruption.

fig 22.8

The Franke Family Digital Humanities Laboratory, 2018.

(Photo Mara Lavitt.)

DHLab staff moderate access to the special projects cube through an internal award process, with exceptions for researchers who are technically self-sufficient but who may require specialized hardware for a short period of time. Students, faculty, and staff submit proposals through the DHLab, which—if awarded—could include access to the cube's equipment. Along with a key to the cube, recipients also receive training from DHLab staff on the code, equipment, or methodology relevant to their project. The limited access to the cube ensures the space remains secure and available to the projects that most need it. Furthermore, by adjudicating access to the cube through the award process, staff can better understand the technical requirements of the projects that will be making use of the equipment and can set up computing environments accordingly.

The special projects cube enables the lab to have a subset of computers with changeable configurations and user permissions that differ from the lab's more standard machines, which are managed by library IT. As Miriam Posner writes:

> It is easy to see why [libraries] place a premium on information technology infrastructure that is secure, scalable, and does not require a lot of fiddly maintenance. Alas, many DH projects require customized support, or at the very least, server-level access for collaborators. If a DH scholar needs to file a support ticket every time she, say, wants to install a Drupal module, a project is virtually guaranteed to languish.[7]

Tying cube access to projects lets staff reconfigure a subset of the lab's computers based on project needs; oftentimes, this step includes giving the researcher—who must first sign a terms of use statement—the ability to install software packages without needing to go through an approval process for each package or update. The cube's computers are then reset after the award term.

EVENTS

In an effort to promote community and bring visibility to DH happening on and off campus, the FFDHL also serves as a venue for DH-related events. As with our workshops, we typically stage these events in the front third of the main room beside the data canvas. Once again, this highly visible location attracts attention to the activity while also providing an opportunity for those who did not preregister to participate. The openness of the space and flexibility of the furniture mean we are able to accommodate events ranging in scope from a one-hour presentation by an invited speaker to a two-day symposium that brings visitors to campus to discuss, debate, and collaborate on DH work. For such events, the lobby's front desk extends its purpose, becoming a place to display name tags and promotional materials.

Especially for events, the FFDHL's location on the first floor of Sterling Memorial Library has proven invaluable. Located to the left of the main entrance to the building, the lab is easily found and accessed. Furthermore, adjacent to the FFDHL is an open room that library staff may reserve. This room can serve as a staging area for events that require more logistical support or as an overflow room for events that surpass occupancy limits.

The digital display screens interwoven with bookcases around the FFDHL's perimeter further equip the space for hosting a variety of events (figure 22.9). We can change the feel of the room by swapping out our normal demonstrations of DH projects for images that reflect the underway event—faces and biographies of speakers or material that supplements a talk being given in the room. In addition, notices of upcoming events and workshops lend an air of contemporaneity to the space. When planning for the reopening of library spaces in August 2020, we updated all of our digital signage to add COVID-19 safety information to the rotation of images.

fig 22.9

Yale-Smithsonian Symposium at the Franke Family Digital Humanities Laboratory, 2019.

(Photo Mara Lavitt.)

Lessons Learned and Future Plans

After only a few months in the renovated space, the successes and a couple of lingering challenges of design decisions became apparent. Having already reflected above on the successes, we would like to conclude by pointing to some of our reconsiderations and future planning. While many students are drawn into the workshops and talks that we hold in the main space, the sound levels can be disruptive to students who were looking for a quieter place to work. In response, we have begun to place signs on the tables that give advance notice of when the space will be used for an event so that students can make alternative arrangements, if desired. Additionally, sound carryover from collaborations underway in the space may also be distracting. In an effort to be transparent about the space and its expectations, we have added placards to all of the tables that encourage talking and make note of quiet reading rooms available elsewhere in the building for work that requires silence.

We are also exploring how we can accommodate increasing demand for reservable work space by affiliates—postdoctoral researchers, visiting scholars, and so on. One option entails repurposing existing desks in the room's corners, which seem well suited for occasional and repeat visitors who wish to secure small belongings or equipment on an ongoing basis. The challenge would be in visually distinguishing the desks from the open work spaces so that they remain available to the visitor.

Similarly to other library facilities, we confronted questions about capacity, service, and safety during the coronavirus pandemic. As for many, it was a complicated experience to inhabit a new space for a short period of time only to move all consultations, training, and patron engagement online; however, the experience reaffirmed the role of place in building and maintaining a community around DH on campus. In addition to providing access to resources, labs as physical spaces provide in-person opportunities for people to gather, collaborate, and learn in expected and serendipitous ways. It is important that we design such spaces so that they are accessible and responsive, able to grow with users and DH.

Notes

1. Anu Vedantham and Dot Porter, "Spaces, Skills, and Synthesis," in *Digital Humanities in the Library: Challenges and Opportunities for Subject Specialists*, ed. Arianne Hartsell-Grundy, Laura Braunstein, and Liorah Golomb (Chicago: Association of College and Research Libraries, 2015), 180.
2. Mila Oiva and Urszula Pawlicka-Deger, "Lab and Slack. Situated Research Practices in Digital Humanities—Introduction to the DHQ Special Issue," *Digital Humanities Quarterly* 14, no. 3 (2020), http://www.digitalhumanities.org/dhq/vol/14/3/000485/000485.html.
3. Vedantham and Porter, "Spaces," 180.
4. Apicella + Bunton Architects, interview by authors, January 6, 2021.
5. Apicella + Bunton Architects, "Digital Humanities Lab, Yale University" in *Apicella + Bunton Architects* 201 (2020): 17.
6. Apicella + Bunton Architects, "Digital Humanities Lab," 17.
7. Miriam Posner, "No Half Measures: Overcoming Common Challenges to Doing Digital Humanities in the Library," *Journal of Library Administration* 53, no. 1 (2013), 47-48, https://doi.org/10.1080/01930826.2013.756694.

23

CHAPTER TWENTY-THREE

ON THE EDGE

Balancing Space and Services in a Digital Scholarship Program

LIZ MILEWICZ,
JOEL HERNDON, and
BRITTANY WOFFORD

This case study of the Edge at Duke University considers how service development concurrent with renovation planning, and the different stakeholder interests involved, can challenge priorities and resources for a digital scholarship program. In particular, this chapter discusses the tensions of program and space and competing priorities when fulfilling the needs of a broad user base. Many libraries renovating spaces and creating digital scholarship programs will likely face similar challenges.

Duke University is a private Research 1 university located in Durham, North Carolina. Of 15,551 students, 6,542 are undergraduates and 9,009 are enrolled in graduate or professional programs.[1] While interdisciplinarity has been a signature feature of Duke for decades, the 2000s saw an increased focus on interdisciplinary e-research across all levels of education and scholarship, and institutes and services across the university were launched to provide specialized research or IT support.[2] A heightened emphasis on research as an integral part of the undergraduate experience encouraged multiple programs offering team-based, cross-disciplinary research opportunities, from summer intensives to credit-bearing courses. Duke Libraries responded by opening the Edge: the Ruppert Commons for Research, Technology and Collaboration (figure 23.1)—a unified space and program to highlight its existing digital scholarship services and resources and debut others while meeting increased demand for interdisciplinary, collaborative research.

In the following sections we first situate development of the Edge in various assessment activities involving different stakeholders and in the recent history of Duke Libraries' space and service development and address some of the space and service tensions we encountered during design and launch. We then consider how implementation of the Edge—a program meant to push researchers to explore new ways of conducting research—also challenged libraries staff involved in the program as they took on new roles and new ways of assessing and communicating impact of both services and spaces. We conclude with the Edge in 2021, when consultation, instruction, and much of the software used in digital scholarship has moved online, and reconsider what it means now to create programs that support 21st-century research.

Defining a Program among Stakeholders, Spaces, and Services

Duke Libraries launched the Edge in response to a succession of campus initiatives to expand and support innovative research and their own assessment of space and service needs for Duke's research community. Harmonizing stakeholder interests, service requirements, and space expectations was an ongoing activity for those involved in the Edge's planning and development. The following provides a brief timeline of efforts that preceded development of the Edge and traces space, service, and stakeholder considerations throughout.

Creation of the Edge roughly began in 2011 with gathering information from campus stakeholders and exploring trends in library research commons and in our own services. Data from research consultations and public service points showed trends prevalent at other academic libraries: researchers sought in-depth and project-long consultations on a wider range of topics, such as data management and curation; data analysis and visualization; e-research tools and methods.[3] Interviews with faculty and administrators (conducted as part of Duke Libraries' participation in the 2011 ARL/DLF E-Science Institute) also showed research trending toward more collaborative, interdisciplinary projects.[4] This exploratory phase also included librarian-led ethnographic studies investigating the cultures of research within different departments.

An exploratory committee conducted an environmental scan of research commons and digital scholarship centers and interviewed program coordinators.[5] In early 2012, the committee proposed a research commons–based service model to meet emerging digital scholarship needs at Duke.[6] Services were seen as critical, and thus preliminary efforts focused on consolidating and promoting existing services virtually (e.g., a centralized website for promoting instruction and consulting) while also planning for subject liaisons' increased role in digital scholarship support (e.g., a summer boot camp on project management for skilling up librarians).

Simultaneous with service consolidation and development, the libraries pursued plans for dedicating library space for digital research services. In summer 2012 an architectural firm was enlisted, a visioning workshop was conducted that August with numerous campus stakeholders in order to define priorities for the space, and then libraries staff formed a space planning committee to develop design priorities.[7] Many of the same individuals interviewed for the E-Science Institute were included in the visioning workshop, but this time they were prompted to answer how *space* could support *both research and learning*—an emphasis that also reflected Duke's integration of research into the classroom.

While the year began with developing digital research services, by year's end, program development was grounded in space supporting research and learning. Work to develop and expand digital research services continued, but the decision to move forward with space development, the design priorities developed by the visioning workshop, and the momentum and gravity created by regular meetings with architects, facilities managers, and administrators meant that the focus of conversation expanded to include, and at times shifted to emphasize, the physical space of the program.

fig 23.1

The Edge logo.

(Image Credit: Official Collection of Duke University Libraries Flickr Images: https://www.flickr.com/photos/dukeunivlibraries/21903679443/.)

The space chosen for the Edge was the main floor of the Bostock Library, which adjoins a pedestrian thoroughfare connecting Abele Quad (the main campus quadrangle) and the medical and sciences areas of campus. In contrast to other library spaces considered for renovation, Bostock level 1 offered a high-traffic, high-visibility location for the Edge program as well as a large footprint of over 16,000 square feet. The Edge was designed to have over half of the floor space open, enabling high visibility with no lockable doors. With most furniture on wheels and with partial walls and support pillars covered in writeable material, the emphasis was on ease of access and collaboration. Programmed areas included a workshop room (accommodating upward of 50 people), nine project rooms of varying sizes, and two labs—the Murthy Digital Studio and the Brandaleone Lab for Data and Visualization Sciences. The Murthy Studio featured software commonly used in the digital humanities, while the Brandaleone Lab provided mapping, statistical analysis, and visualization software, plus three Bloomberg terminals. All enclosed rooms had hallway-facing glass walls, and the project and workshop rooms' interior walls were writeable surfaces (figure 23.2).

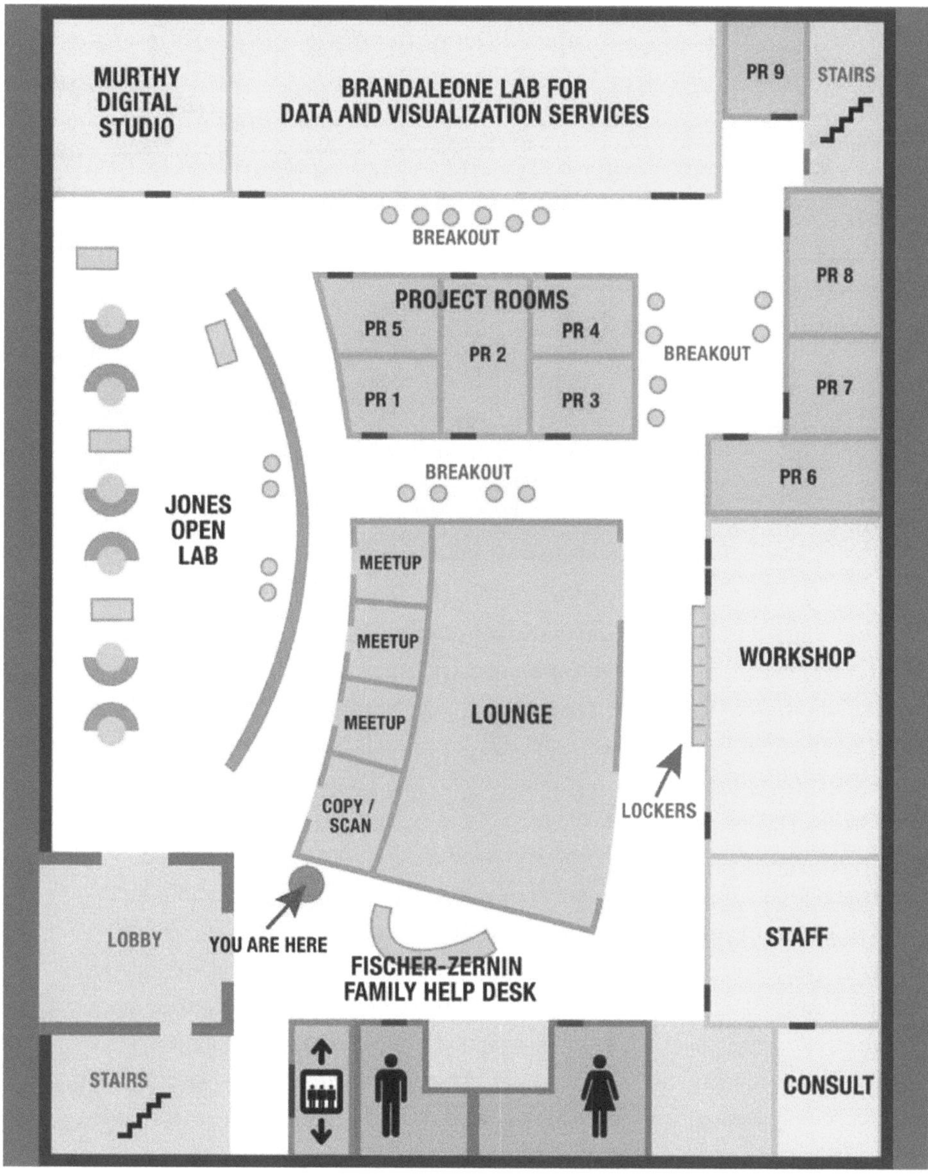

fig 23.2

Edge floor plan 2015.

Our exploration of other research commons and digital scholarship spaces pointed to the value of making the research program visible, and so space development focused on ensuring this visibility. Yet as we soon learned in practice, our research program (consultation, instruction, technology, experts) was often hard to see amid the open space of the Edge (tables, chairs, project rooms), which, if not actively animated by our staff and program, communicated unspecific services and possibilities to users.

"SMALL PEG, BIG HOLE" AND THE EXPECTATIONS GAP

At its launch in 2015, the Edge opened with the publicly stated mission of promoting interdisciplinary, data-driven, digitally reliant, team-based research. Within its first year, the Edge and its bright, modern design quickly attracted a large audience: not just advanced researchers but also various groups searching for project and event spaces. Duke undergraduate students, who had formerly used Bostock level 1 for traditional individual study, also quickly reinhabited the space for that purpose (figure 23.3).

fig 23.3

Jones Open Lab in the Edge.

(Image Credit: Official Collection of Duke University Libraries Flickr Images: https://www.flickr.com/photos/dukeunivlibraries/22337237918/.)

Siting a digital scholarship program in a highly visible, high-traffic area can raise questions about who the intended users are. Specialized services and resources intended for a particular set of users (small peg) can be difficult to scale to meet programming and use expectations implied by the larger space (big hole). We focused on providing specialized research consulting, infrastructure, instruction, and spaces, especially for interdisciplinary teams of graduate and research faculty. Yet the design and launch of the Edge faced strong demand to meet general research and study space needs for undergraduate students. While the Edge program did surface and engage some of the advanced digital research projects we'd envisioned, the high visibility of the space sharply increased undergraduate requests for individual consultations and access to digital research tools. Office hours, instruction, and more general digital research support frequently took priority over focused and time-intensive partnerships on advanced digital projects.

The high value of space, especially in a centrally located campus library, means that there will be many interests driving space design—some competing, and not all necessarily aligned with the original service priorities. In our experience the stakeholders in space development were a larger, more varied group than the researchers whose needs originally animated questions about innovating our service model. Disconnects emerged as we attempted to incorporate the smaller group's specialized research interests within a physical space intended to accommodate general use. For example, digital scholarship tools, such as high-resolution scanners or high-performance computers, require greater security as well as staff on hand to assist with their use. But a locked and staffed space for providing

fig 23.4

Edge project room.

(Image Credit: Official Collection of Duke University Libraries Flickr Images: https://www.flickr.com/photos/dukeunivlibraries/22536054281/.)

access to these tools did not conform to the flexible and open space design encouraged in architectural discussions. A locked room, regardless of the software and hardware within it, doesn't meet the needs of users who see access to space as the primary service. This tension was particularly acute around use of the Edge's project rooms (figure 23.4), which, when reserved for long-term use by digital scholarship teams, raised strident objections from undergraduate students seeking short-term study rooms.

Also, not all stakeholders had equal weight in setting program objectives and defining impact: influential stakeholders on campus, such as vice provosts, deans, presidents, and funders, often had greater ability to shape program goals and direction. For instance, an administrator's directive that the Edge should be open to all users ran counter to faculty and graduate students' requests for spaces and services available only to them. Scoping the Edge to include undergraduate researchers also departed from other research commons and digital scholarship centers we visited whose constituents were graduate students and faculty. Reflecting on this phase of the Edge's development, we also see a disconnect between those who planned the space and those who used it: undergraduates, who are the heaviest users of the Edge space, were not part of the visioning workshop and only nominally involved in the planning process.

MANAGING SPACE THROUGH MISSION-DRIVEN POLICIES

To navigate these gaps between space and service and stakeholder expectations, we developed policies that reinforced the values underlying our program and that were critical to its success, such as encouraging interdisciplinary research collaborations and supporting broader engagement in data-driven and digitally reliant research. Policies for space use in the Edge are a particularly good example of how we created rules based on researchers' priorities, and also how these policies enabled us to balance competing desires for readily available spaces versus reserved and reliable spaces. The August 2012 visioning workshop with campus stakeholders surfaced a desire for both readily available, easily reservable team space and also recurring or dedicated meeting space for longer-term projects. Accordingly, this desire was prioritized in design decisions, as we worked to ensure that the majority of our physical space was programmed as either "open" (non-reservable) or "project rooms" (reservable immediately or in advance, for short or recurring use). Within both open spaces and project rooms we planned for a variety of movable chairs, tables, and whiteboards to better support ad hoc work groups. At a policy level, we set up rules to ensure project rooms could be reserved without significant advance planning: for instance, reservations could not be placed more than seven days in advance, and individuals could reserve no more than three hours per day total.

Our policy of requiring proposals for recurring or dedicated project space also helped support our mission while meeting researchers' desire for recurring or dedicated workspace. Space was awarded based on whether requested use reflected the type of activity the Edge was designed to support, namely digitally reliant, data-driven, interdisciplinary, team-based research. This policy helped us ensure that projects working out of the Edge reflected and were well served by its program and also helped support researchers' expressed desire for more reliable access to project space.

COMPLEMENTARY RELATIONS WITH CAMPUS PARTNERS

As a way to help coalesce research support, the Edge management team actively sought relationships with other campus groups that could provide complementary services.[8] Ideally, such partnerships would benefit the Edge and other digital programs by raising the profile of all digital programs on campus while extending services beyond any one program's capacity. Because some of our services were still nascent (e.g., provisioning project room space for ongoing use; providing a lab for experimenting with text analysis tools), we also sought to ensure that our offerings did not compete with other campus services or confuse our users.

For instance, one floor below the Edge, the College of Arts and Sciences technology support unit ran the Link—a center for innovating teaching and learning, with technology-enhanced classrooms for courses, reservable study rooms, and technology lending, such as laptop chargers, for students.[9] We were careful to distinguish our mission as focused on *research* (rather than on teaching and classroom support) and to set policies for room use that emphasized this difference (e.g., not for teaching classes, office hours, or study groups). We also saw our proximity to the Link service desk as an asset, since it made it easier for researchers in the Edge to borrow computer peripherals or get tech support.

While in theory the Link and the Edge served different audiences and purposes, in practice the permeable boundary between research and teaching at Duke meant that many Duke courses were especially eager to take advantage of new research spaces in the Edge for course-based project teams and learning groups. Our proposal process helped in sorting out some of these "edge cases," but often the reality was that our campus research culture made it difficult and sometimes counterproductive to delineate digital pedagogy projects from digital research projects. Still, without drawing these clear distinctions, we faced challenges in defining the scope of our program and increased pressure to use the Edge spaces for purposes unrelated to our mission.

Other campus partners helped generate a steady stream of programs and events that the Edge could promote and sponsor and that directly supported our research focus. One such partner was the Office of Information Technology, which provides centralized campus technology services and support. The Edge management team worked with OIT's training coordinator to offer the Learn IT @ Lunch series in the Edge workshop room (figure 23.5). This series became a consistent feature of the Edge program, with staff trainers introducing OIT-supported tools and services. This type of relevant programming helped bring people to the Edge who were likely to make use of its services.[10]

fig 23.5

Edge workshop room.

(Image Credit: Official Collection of Duke University Libraries Flickr Images: https://www.flickr.com/photos/dukeunivlibraries/22524907665/.)

Staffing a Place-Based Digital Scholarship Program

Effectively implementing and sustaining a digital scholarship program, especially one grounded in a physical space, requires adequate staffing. Logistical, technical, administrative, and communicative aspects of the program may require responsibilities and skills that differ significantly from those required for core services. In our case, a number of program needs translated into additional roles and responsibilities for those already involved in developing and supporting the Edge's services. For instance, as much as we tried to build user autonomy into the space through features such as movable furniture and touch interfaces for reserving rooms, other aspects of the program still required dedicated staff to ensure the space functioned as intended, such as providing technical assistance or troubleshooting help or ensuring additional custodial support for day-long catered events.

The Edge management team and their staff took on *event management* (e.g., scheduling and preparing rooms, managing registrations), *marketing and outreach* (e.g., creating marketing materials, promoting information through lists and digital flyer systems), *assessment* (e.g., recording and reporting data on events and consultations), and *internal communication and training* (e.g., reports and presentations to libraries staff and administrators). *Program coordination* was written explicitly into the position of one staff member who worked with campus partners to schedule events and workshops, provided on-site support for project teams, and hired and supervised student desk staff. Beyond student workers, no new staff were hired; we absorbed this work into our existing responsibilities.

Engaging Existing Staff in the Program

While the above roles and responsibilities helped support the space and program, the foundation for digital scholarship services is functional expertise. When the Edge opened, nine full-time staff members offered a range of instruction and consulting to support data-driven, digitally reliant, team-based research, from project planning and management, to copyright and fair use, to data visualization and text analysis methods. We sought to expand this base of support for digital scholarship by working with libraries staff to develop skills and knowledge for digital scholarship work.

Yet even if staff are sufficiently skilled and eager to engage in the digital scholarship program, we found that other organizational factors can interfere. For instance, do existing models for librarians' work conflict with the model imposed by the space? Will staff participation in the program be "visible"? The liaison model at Duke Libraries, following similar trends across academic libraries, was to provide consultations and instruction within academic departments, not to ask faculty and students to come to a specific library space. If the liaisons provided digital scholarship–adjacent instruction for a class, offered advice on a digital project, or joined a project team that was *not* physically based out of the Edge, the general perception was that such activities didn't count as being part of the Edge's work. Despite the fact that such activities were demonstrably part of the libraries' broad base of support for digital scholarship, the conflation of program with space frequently interfered with staff's ability to see themselves as part of and participating in the work of the Edge.

Our experience has taught us to consider carefully the service model and staffing needs for a space-based digital scholarship program. What aspects of the space require staffing? Are there proposed services that may not be possible without commitments to more staffing? Beyond just providing digital scholarship expertise, running an effective digital scholarship program involves a number of activities that, while not necessarily requiring specialized skills, nevertheless require significant time, attention, and effort and that need to count as part of someone's work.

Making Digital Scholarship Visible

Making research visible was an animating concept throughout the Edge planning, from the glass-walled project rooms and researcher-centered events to situating this space in a high-traffic area. A few years after the Edge's launch, we came to see the question of visibility in more nuanced ways: *how* is our digital scholarship program visible, and *for whom*? Making visible all aspects of a program is a constant challenge. Pre-pandemic, the Edge's large footprint and openness resulted in the blurring between programmatic and general use. When undergraduates flooded the Edge immediately upon opening, they created an impression of engagement in the Edge's program but also complicated the task of disambiguating and assessing activities that actually realized the Edge mission. Are those students sitting at a table working on a shared research project or just friends studying together? In some cases, users were able to mark their participation in the Edge by formal means (e.g., applying for a project room and registering for workshops and events), but this clearly defined use was in the minority.

Further, stakeholders' priorities can have a strong influence on how a digital scholarship program's impact is evaluated. Choosing measures that align campus users' expectations with the libraries' assessment practices and priorities can prove a difficult balancing act. Assessing and communicating about a digital scholarship program means deciding what counts as success and how to measure that impact while simultaneously dedicating staff to perform this assessment and report the results.

DIFFERENT ASSESSMENT STRATEGIES FOR DIFFERENT GOALS

From the beginning, familiar metrics such as gate counts and event attendance didn't readily translate into signs of our program's success. For example, if heavy usage of the space were the defining measure of success, the Edge succeeded immediately without the need for any digital scholarship services or events. Though simplistic, this example demonstrates the limits of empirical measures to measure the goals of a digital scholarship program and the need for clear goals and thoughtful measures for gauging success.

Initial assessment of the Edge covered users' experience navigating the space and use of some of its features, such as room reservation software and self-service lockers. Though not program-related per se, it helped in making early arguments that work by other libraries staff, especially those concerned with space and technology use, was necessary to keep the Edge up and running on all days and hours of operation.

Other early efforts centered around quantitatively measuring the interdisciplinary aspect of research in the Edge. For instance, collecting data on project team members' and event participants' affiliation with campus departments, schools, and programs allowed us to track and show disciplinary involvement. These metrics were especially valuable in reports demonstrating library use by different schools and departments particularly because, outside of library consultations and instruction, this data on interdisciplinarity is rarely collected.

Later evaluations focused on specialized aspects of the program, with mixed results. A survey of teams that reserved project rooms showed satisfaction with the nuts and bolts of space (e.g., ease of accessing markers and erasers for writable walls), but produced no data on how specialized spaces and access to library staff and resources impacted their work. However, similar assessments of specialized services (e.g., instructional workshops) were more useful in surfacing what researchers wanted and appreciated in our digital scholarship program. For example, participants from a text analysis workshop were invited to attend a focus group lunch where they offered perspectives on why they attended the workshop, what aspects connected most readily to their current or planned research, and how they expected to continue this work; for example, whether they were likely to consult with libraries staff or use libraries-based resources.

The open space and use of the Edge, while complicating assessment of the program, still succeeded in raising the profile of services, resources, and events in the Edge. The openness of the floor design displayed labs and library staff working with users, creating awareness of the Edge's offerings among a general population of users. The heavy use of the space and the visibility of the brand made it possible to extend the program outside of the physical location. For instance, as part of a series of events on open publishing, the Edge hosted the screening of a documentary on open access publishing in the Rubenstein Arts Center; while the event itself was not in the Edge, use of the logo allowed us to reinforce the connection between this externally hosted event and the libraries' digital scholarship program. Thus, activities could be understood to be *of* the Edge program, even if not *in* the Edge space.

Even so, we found that library administrators and other stakeholders could often miss programmatic work when it occurred outside of the Edge. Active and targeted promotion, along with regular assessment and reporting, were necessary to give the whole picture of the digital scholarship program.

REASSESSING OUR ASSESSMENT STRATEGIES

The breadth of the Edge's mission speaks to the challenges and opportunities of assessing the program as a whole: a broad mission makes success easier to claim, but concrete progress is difficult to measure without a well-defined focus. In measuring discrete activities, we found that numbers demonstrating success in digital scholarship support must be contextualized if they are to be meaningful alongside other assessment data. Knowing that 10,000 students visit the Edge in an average month offers one impression of success; knowing that dozens of interdisciplinary project teams worked in the Edge project rooms in a single month provides a much more nuanced and relevant evaluation of the success of the Edge program. Of course, context is also important for deciding how or whether to make changes based on assessment: knowing that a lot of people are using Microsoft Word in the data and visualization lab is not a cue to turn it into a writing studio.

We also found that multiple indicators helped us to disambiguate the use and value of space and services. In our case, including both qualitative and quantitative measures was especially important for specialized services where the number of people and projects using those services was low but the impact (and often effort!) loomed large. For instance, we took a more holistic view of staff involvement on digital projects by soliciting targeted feedback, asking teams about libraries resources and expertise that were especially valuable to their work and how these could better serve their needs. Reporting this qualitative feedback to library administration added an important dimension to the quantitative data, made more visible the research taking place in the Edge, and demonstrated the necessity of collaboration across multiple library units to support advanced project-based research.

Rethinking Spaces and Programs for 21st-Century Research

As we reflect on the past several years of planning, implementing, and adapting the Edge, a key lesson for us is that *space*, while ideally reinforcing and promoting a digital scholarship program, can become its own service. If the offerings and expectations of the space are not well aligned with the digital scholarship program—its mission, its size and planned growth, its target audience and primary stakeholders—staff may find themselves dividing limited time, attention, and resources between competing priorities, making expedient choices rather than strategic ones. In the context of 21st-century digital scholarship, which in 2020 became rapidly and almost entirely remote, the service dimensions of space take on new implications: When we take away the space from the program, how does that shift our focus and resources? And what might that tell us about services essential for supporting digital scholarship?

As part of the university's pandemic response, the Edge, along with other libraries' spaces, was physically closed in March 2020, then repurposed in August 2020 for more general uses (namely, socially distanced and reservable study seats) to support the campus's limited reopening. In-person meetings were restricted, and staff whose work did not require being physically present were discouraged from entering the building. With digital scholarship support staff working from home, the Edge was no longer a space encompassing a digital scholarship program, let alone visibly evidencing that work.

Yet with much of our campus population working remotely and in-person instruction limited, the core elements of our program followed our community online: synchronous training shifted to online platforms; consultations happened over those same platforms as well as e-mail and chat; and we continued to work with many of the same web-based tools that we'd used before, such as Box, Omeka, and OpenRefine. To those just beginning the process of conceiving a digital scholarship program, or even those reconceiving in light of new logistical realities, we offer a key insight as the starting point for planning: *people make the service*. This becomes especially clear when spaces are closed, and programs tied to those spaces, such as consultations and instruction, have moved online. If we see 21st-century research as primarily reliant on instruction and assistance in order to succeed, physical space is secondary to that aim. Knowledgeable staff are essential, followed closely and assisted by technology.

That said, some tools are now out of reach for those researchers who relied on lab-provisioned software, and some tools simply cannot be virtualized, such as high-resolution scanners. As tightened budgets and travel restrictions made it harder (or impossible) for researchers to avail themselves of technology in physical spaces on their campuses, the need for a virtual commons increased. If anything, the challenges to access imposed by the pandemic and the subsequent economic fallout should draw our attention to the ways that libraries' IT licensing agreements and negotiations need to take into account a broader community of users than those who can be physically limited within a space. Provisioning lab software online is possible and can provide researchers a more convenient means for undertaking research.

As of the writing of this chapter in summer 2021, we anticipate that both virtual and physical services, including space, could define our program going forward. Many resources and services, such as virtual computing environments, some types of staff consultations, and programming, may continue to be offered online. Virtual services can provide greater convenience and accessibility for users, such as closed captioning and audio controls, multiple ways to ask questions or engage in discussion, no travel time to join events, and higher quality recordings for sharing out. Other activities, such as tool-based training requiring hands-on assistance or specialized software, may be more successful when based out of our physical space.

Physical space continues to be a valuable service for our users—a place for interactions and engagement with others—and a resource for our campus partners, especially so after the seismic shifts of a year of pandemic. Already our campus appears eager to resume in-person activities and use of the Edge space for workshops and events, with partners and staff making requests to reserve workshop and meeting spaces. In our desire to meet users' needs and our own desire to resume familiar work, we nevertheless find ourselves asking, "Do we want to return to 'normal' (our program before the pandemic), or do we want to pause and reassess? Is this a moment to rethink how we provide digital scholarship support and *where*?" For ourselves, as we reenvision and restart our program, and for anyone about to embark on developing space and programs to support digital scholarship, we offer these considerations: "*Who* is being served by our digital scholarship program, *how* can we best meet their needs *now*, what is our *capacity* to offer that support, and what is our *priority*?"

Notes

1. "Duke at a Glance," Duke University Communications, accessed June 8, 2021, https://facts.duke.edu/wp-content/uploads/sites/31/2020/01/duke_at_glance.pdf (page discontinued).
2. "Timeline: Interdisciplinary Studies at Duke University," Duke University Office of Interdisciplinary Studies, accessed April 30, 2021, https://sites.duke.edu/interdisciplinary/about/timeline-interdisciplinary-studies-at-duke-university/.
3. Duke University Libraries, "ARL/DLF e-Science Institute: Planning Support of e-Research (Executive Summary)" (unpublished internal report), Microsoft Word file.
4. The institute (https://www.arl.org/resources/overview-of-the-arldlf-e-science-institute/) was a multi-month exercise, undertaken by numerous libraries staff members, to discover and analyze research trends at our institution and develop a strategic approach for addressing these.
5. The committee was chaired by the Research and Instructional Services department head and included, among others, heads of the Digital Scholarship and Production Services and the Data and Visualization Services departments. These departments were persistent partners in designing and implementing the Edge.
6. Duke University Libraries Research Commons Exploratory Committee, "Research Commons: Exploration, Findings, and Next Steps (Executive Summary)" (unpublished internal report, February 2012), Microsoft Word file.
7. Shepley Bulfinch, "Library Planning Study—Research Commons Report (Duke University Libraries)" (unpublished internal report, February 23, 2013), Microsoft Word file.
8. This team included department heads for Research and Instructional Services, Digital Scholarship and Publishing Services, and Data and Visualization Services, as well as the Edge coordinator, the head of

the Core Services department (IT), and later a representative from the Office of Copyright and Scholarly Communication.

9. "Link Teaching and Learning Center," Duke University, accessed June 8, 2021, https://link.duke.edu/.
10. Stephen Schramm, "A New Way to 'Learn IT' at Lunch," Working@Duke, August 27, 2019, https://today.duke.edu/2019/08/new-way-%E2%80%98learn-it%E2%80%99-lunch.

24

CHAPTER TWENTY-FOUR

REIMAGINING SPECIAL COLLECTIONS

MIMI CALTER

Introduction

Special collections have long been a defining feature of a research library. Rare, valuable, and otherwise exceptional collections can define a library's mission and draw researchers, scholars, and other users to its doors. Special collections materials, by definition, require higher levels of security and supporting services than regular library collections, and that is especially true in 21st-century libraries.

Special collections have always come in a wide variety of formats. Today, the types and formats of material that constitute special collections are dramatically expanding, and many new special collections are born digital. Special collections programs must provide technologies and services to support these new formats, and digital collections demand new workflows. In addition, physical special collections materials are being digitized, both as a preservation tool and as a way to increase their accessibility. That brings new opportunities and ways of working with collections but also requires physical and digital versions of items to be managed in tandem. This demands integration of technology and related support services into special collections spaces.

In parallel with these technological changes, special collections programs, long thought of as exclusive and restrictive, are recognizing the importance of increasing their accessibility and inclusiveness, reaching out more actively to researchers, integrating collections with student learning, and providing opportunities for community building and knowledge sharing. Thus, special collections spaces more than ever must be welcoming, open, and flexible even while increasing the integration of technology.

The David Rumsey Map Center

Stanford Libraries' David Rumsey Map Center is an example of a special collections space that was designed from the ground up to address the changing needs of special collections in a contemporary library. It offers a useful case study of the concerns and considerations of designing for special collections.

The center is one of three units within the Stanford Libraries that work together to purchase, curate, transform, and serve geospatial materials to the Stanford community. The Branner Map Library supports current cartographic materials; the Stanford Geospatial Center supports digital mapping and analysis; and the David Rumsey Map Center supports both historic and digital maps and provides transformational services. The integration of these programs is important to ensure that those services are available across the spectrum of cartographic resources.

The center is home to a collection of maps, globes, atlases, cartographic tools, historical survey instruments, and related materials, many of which have both print and digital incarnations, as well as a suite of technologies that allow digital and physical materials to be used effectively together. It provides a flexible and rich environment for research and teaching, incorporating high-resolution screens equipped with interactive tools for viewing and analyzing digital images, and is supported by expert staff. The center's resources lend themselves to interdisciplinary work, which is critical for maps and the very nature of contemporary scholarship especially in the humanities and the social sciences.

Building the Vision

THE DONORS

The David Rumsey Map Center, not surprisingly, starts with David Rumsey, a collector, author, entrepreneur, philanthropist, and pioneer of geospatial techniques. Rumsey's remarkable map collection is comprised primarily of rare 16th- through 21st-century maps and includes a broad spectrum of formats from flat maps to atlases, wall maps, globes, school geographies, pocket maps, and maritime charts. If you count the individual maps in the atlases, the David Rumsey Map Collection itself has over 150,000 items, which would be a highlight of any library's special collections. The center also houses historic cartographic collections from other libraries, and so it holds several other smaller but important collections. These include Glen McLaughlin's Collection of Maps of California as an Island and a significant collection of maps of Africa.

David Rumsey leveraged technology to support scholarly access to his collection long before bringing the collection to Stanford. He has made significant strides toward digitizing the collection himself and developed a website (https://www.davidrumsey.com/home) to host and distribute those images. He drove the development of digital asset management software (LUNA; https://www.lunaimaging.com/) to improve the accessibility of the digital collection and used those digital resources in creating historical map projects in Google Earth (https://www.davidrumsey.com/view/google-earth), Google Maps (https://www.davidrumsey.com/view/google-maps), and the virtual world of Second Life (https://www.davidrumsey.com/view/second-life).

Abby Smith Rumsey, also a lead donor on the project, brought her own perspective as a historian to the management and use of special collections for research. Together David and Abby Rumsey articulated a vision for a center focused on the interdisciplinary use of maps and cartographic resources and the integration of technology into that scholarship.[1]

STANFORD LIBRARIES

The center is now an integrated part of the Stanford Libraries program of geospatial services, but that integration, and the development of the broad suite of geospatial services that Stanford Libraries provides, took time to develop. The roots of the center's development go back more than a decade before its opening to a conversation between David Rumsey and Michael Keller, Stanford's university librarian. Stanford Libraries, under Keller's leadership, had demonstrated success in integrating technology into research processes and improving access to collections through digitization. Stanford Libraries' commitment meshed well with the Rumseys' interest in technology-enabled research, and the libraries' success helped David and Abby Rumsey to see that Stanford Libraries had the capacity to effectively support and maintain their vision for a map room that integrated technology into the study and use of its collections.

WORKING TOGETHER

During the decade between the initial conversations and the opening of the center, the concept of a space providing the technology and the physical infrastructure to enable the most effective use of both digital materials *and* archival collections was developed and refined. Collections were digitized and technological developments were monitored to understand what was possible and what would be the most useful. Together the Rumseys and the Stanford Libraries built a shared vision and a program that addressed both of their needs.

For any library working on a donor-funded project, it is important to define the library's goals and interests and revisit them regularly to ensure that the interests of both parties are being met. Most critically, both parties need to be aware of the concerns and interests of library users and researchers and ensure that they are central to the planning process. Take the time to define the users' needs up front. This can be challenging for innovative services! Also, be sure to think critically about the cost of any donation or donor-funded project in terms not only of cosponsorship but also of cost share and staff time. Offers of funding and new collections are always attractive, but the project will not succeed if the library does not understand the full cost of implementing the program or have the capacity to address all program needs. Consider not just construction costs but staffing costs, equipment and technology costs, and the requirements to refresh and maintain both the technology and the space itself. Particularly where innovative technologies are central to the program, a regular effort to refresh technology will be important. Finally, be patient and think carefully about timing. Ideally libraries and donors will develop long-term relationships and can collaboratively find the right time to initiate a project.

Articulating the Vision

The vision for every capital project is formally codified in its program statement, and every project should have one. As noted above, this is particularly true where a donor and library may have differing interests and perspectives. The program statement development process is a platform for many critical discussions and gets everyone on the same page. The document will then serve as a basis for architects and designers to build out their plans and act as a touchstone for decision-making when the inevitable implementation challenges arise.

The program statement for the center went through at least five revisions over two years, but the final version articulates its purpose well:

> **Program Overview**
>
> The David Rumsey Map Center will be a unique collections-based research center in the Stanford University Library for the use of cartographic information in all forms—from paper to digital—that enables and promotes interdisciplinary scholarship. Centrally located in the Green Library and planned to be housed on the 4th floor of the Bing Wing, the Center will occupy dedicated space that provides access to original historical cartographic material in multiple ways, from direct service of the items and exhibit spaces that begin at the entry and staircase leading to the main entrance of the room; to innovative use of digital displays, interactive tools, and GIS applications. The space will serve faculty, researchers, and students, with seminar space, group study and collaborative spaces.
>
> Here physical and virtual spaces will be collocated to facilitate and leverage geospatial research in ways never before conceived by combining rich and unique collections of physical maps and other cartographic artifacts with their digital derivatives in a one-of-a-kind technology-rich environment. The Rumsey Map Center is being designed from scratch as an incubator and accelerator for collaborative and interdisciplinary work that embraces the arts, humanities, sciences and professional disciplines. It will be a unique resource for the Stanford community and the region and will serve as a new model for twenty-first century collections-based digital research and teaching.

The program statement, as well as a number of subsequent publications, also describe the four separate, though interrelated, programmatic functions of the center. The single public room would function as

- an exhibit space
- a special collections library supporting research
- a classroom and learning space—the "geo-laboratory"
- a meeting and conference center

The integrated technology that is core to the vision of the space supports all four aspects of the program.

Implementation

In the visioning stage, plans can grow quite grand, but ultimately any project must fit in the available space and budget, and implementation is where goals are put to the test. This was certainly true for the David Rumsey Map Center. The project had to deal with a challenging location, four competing program elements, and integration of cutting-edge technology.

LOCATION

Stanford's main library, Green Library, was already a fully programmed and active building when the vision for the center was being developed, so identifying a location for the center was a challenge. Real planning began after the libraries were able to relocate some back-of-house processing operations to an off-campus location. However, the 3,500-square-foot space was on the fourth floor of the building with the primary entrance being up two flights of stairs. It also had significant plumbing and ductwork running through it. Figure 24.1 shows the room that would eventually become the center before any renovations began.

fig 24.1

Future home of the David Rumsey Map Center.

(Credit: Gabrielle Karampelas for Stanford Libraries.)

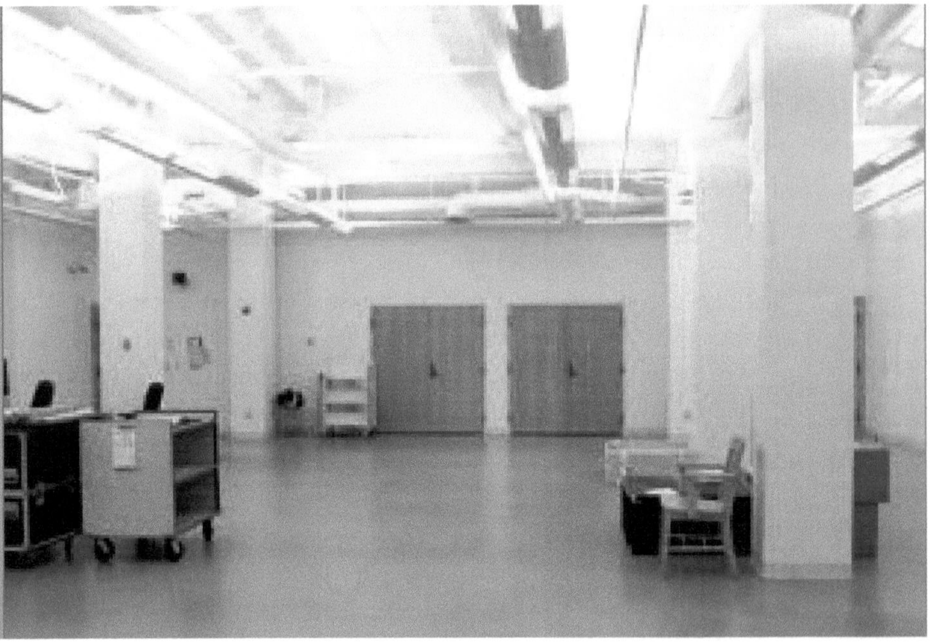

The project team took several steps to make the best use of a difficult room. First was finding creative ways to work around ductwork. The largest bit of ductwork limited the ceiling height of a portion of the room dramatically. This area was converted to storage and also adapted to provide backing and support for the central high-definition screen. Figure 24.2 shows the entry to that storage area. The low-ceilinged area over the storage room doors houses the ducts.

fig 24.2

Storage area built in behind screen and under ductwork.

(Credit: David Rumsey Map Center Staff.)

A second area of large ducts was incorporated into the exhibit space that is central to the program of the room. Figure 24.3 shows the casework, currently housing globes, that was built in under large ducts.

fig 24.3

Casework built in under ducts.

(Credit: Wayne Vanderkuil for Stanford Libraries.)

While every effort was made to use the designated room effectively, ultimately there was not enough space for the level of collections storage needed to support the program. Stanford Libraries dedicated an additional 1,650 square feet of stacks space to center collections and ran a separate project to add security to those stacks. Storage, movement, and careful management of physical materials remain a critical function and integral to all four of the room's programmatic functions, and so the provision of additional storage space was determined to be necessary for the success of the room.

The most inspired, and most popular, creative solution to space challenges is in the main entry stairway. In order to keep visitors entertained (and hopefully distracted) as they walked up two flights, maps from the collection were converted into wallpaper and laid out to line the staircase. David Rumsey's knowledge of the collection was very helpful here as he picked the maps, determined the layouts, and oversaw every detail of installation. Figure 24.4 shows a plan of the staircase maps.

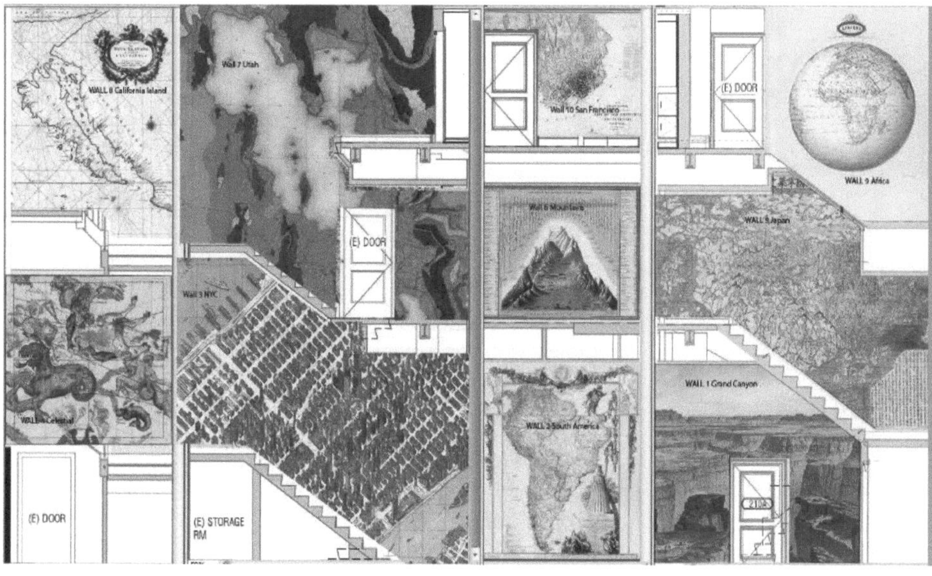

fig 24.4

Maps line the staircase to the David Rumsey Map Center.

The staircase opens into the main rotunda, and the maps have proven to be an effective way, along with signage in the rotunda itself, to draw visitors to the center.

While the entry staircase is now a popular feature, it nevertheless raises accessibility concerns. Beyond the main entrance the center has two additional doors, one of which can be reached via elevator. The elevator is a requirement not only for accessibility but also for movement of materials and so was an important consideration in both the physical design of the space and the development of a security program.

ONE SPACE, FOUR PROGRAMS

A number of tools were built into the center to allow it to meet its four-fold purpose. Most clearly visible are the built-in exhibit cases, which were a significant planning focus for the construction project. The fixed cases mean that the exhibits are the most permanent of the four functions of the space. There is always attention to be paid to the cases, which typically support both print and virtual exhibits.

The remaining three functions—research, teaching, and meetings—are somewhat in competition. To fully support all three, the center makes use of time shifting along with very flexible furniture!

Research

In general, the room is open to the public for research and study from 1:00 to 5:00 p.m. on weekdays. During that time users can view previously paged materials, receive support from the staff, and collaborate with each other. The screens can be very popular during public use hours, and thus staffing is always a concern. The room must be monitored, but when materials are being viewed a minimum of two staff members need to be present and others may also be called on to assist in the use of equipment or to answer questions about materials.

Teaching

Mornings in the center are generally dedicated to teaching, including classes and workshops. The room can be configured lecture style if needed, or the large but collapsible worktables that are used in the reading room configuration can also be retained. For example, a professor may want to conduct a seminar-style session that requires a long table. In other words, the furniture is modular by design and multipurpose in function. Specialty equipment may also be made available for teaching.

David Rumsey Map Center librarians and staff work regularly with both faculty and graduate students to help teach classes in the space, providing expertise on collections as well as the use of technology, with varying degrees of involvement depending on the needs of the class. In some cases, center librarians may be co-teaching with discipline faculty, planning and laying out class content in advance, including hands-on interaction with the physical maps and their digital surrogates on the big screens. In other cases, experienced faculty use the center's technology to enhance the more cartographic-heavy class periods with minimal librarian support.

When classes are not in session, or when the day's classes do not require active participation, mornings are also a time that center staff work individually or on ongoing projects—for example, consideration of materials for an upcoming exhibition.

Conferences

Talks, symposiums, and conferences often happen in the center on evenings or weekends, though occasionally the research and teaching programs may be suspended to accommodate larger conference programs. Conference content is typically also used in exhibits, so those two functions complement each other.

In all cases, having multiple furniture options and the ability to store and swap furniture is important. While this is an effective approach, it's important to consider the staff time associated with furniture changes when building this flexibility into a space. You'll need to be prepared to allocate changeover time and to have staff dedicated to regular furniture moves and changes.

TECHNOLOGY FOCUS

Integrated technology that allows physical and digital collections to be used in tandem is central to the vision and all program aspects of the David Rumsey Map Center, and thus technology is central to the space. The most visible of these technologies are the two large display screens in the main room.

Figure 24.5 shows the high-resolution presentation screen that is, literally, at the center of the center. It is 16 by 9 feet, and 7,680 by 4,320 pixels, and at the time of installation was the only one of its kind in the United States. Put together by Cinemassive of Atlanta, Georgia, it is actually an array of 16 state-of-the-art LG monitors. The screens have a combined bezel of only 3.6 millimeters, which means the seams between the monitors effectively disappear and the array acts as one large screen. A Creston configuration controls the screens' multiple configurations and runs on two high-powered computers called the alpha and the bravo. The alpha is the computer that maintains the communication, and the bravo is the main computer behind the screen. It runs on a Windows 10 operating system, so it has similar functionality to a PC but one with an exceptional monitor.

fig 24.5

High-resolution presentation screen.

(Credit: Wayne Vanderkuil for Stanford Libraries.)

There is a second large screen in the center that features touch control. The touch screen functions exactly like the presentation screen but can be manipulated with hands on the screen itself. It is like a very large iPad and is *very* popular for both teaching and exhibits. The screen is 12 by 7 feet, which is just small enough to allow most users to use the touch feature effectively even at the top. The configuration is done by the same company, Cinemassive. Figure 24.6 shows the screen as it is installed, integrated into exhibit casework.

fig 24.6

Large touch screen and exhibit cases.

(Credit: G. Salim Mohammed for Stanford Libraries.)

The center has an additional touch screen that is located not in the main center but near its entrance in the Green Library rotunda. It's an Ideum 65-inch Drafting Table Touch Screen, 3,840 by 2,160 pixels, and features 60 touch points. The location and built-in interactivity of this screen is intentional, particularly as the center is open in the afternoons. The Ideum allows visitors to get a sense of what the center is all about and serves as a digital ambassador to the center upstairs.

There are a number of other technologies that the center uses that are not built into its infrastructure. These include four Oculus Rift stations, a couple of Microsoft HoloLenses, and a set of iPad Pros that can hold content related to exhibitions. The center also coordinates with the Stanford Libraries map digitization program to digitize collection materials on an ongoing basis.

Karl Eikenberry, a retired lieutenant general and a US ambassador, has visited the center and described the technology as "like nothing he had ever seen." Maintaining that cutting-edge level of technology is a challenge, but also a priority for the center. To that end the center has incorporated a technology refresh budget into its capital plan. Technology upgrade requirements are an important consideration for any program with a technology focus and should be incorporated into any planning for special collections space renovation.

Operations and Ongoing Adaptation

The center opened in April of 2016, and in the first few years of operations has learned some lessons about what works and what does not. Overall, the center is a success in all four of its programmatic areas, though there have been challenges in each case.

SPECIAL COLLECTIONS LIBRARY

The center is well used as a location for personal study, use of its collections, and use of the integrated technologies, and its high occupancy is one marker of its success. Beyond the basic reading room function, the center aspires to be a geo-laboratory where users can tinker, build, and explore what cartography has to offer. There are markers of success here as well. One example is a student project to convert the Turgot Atlas of 1739 into a virtual reality program for the Oculus Rift headsets. The original atlas carefully details the streets of Paris; using the students' program you can walk those streets virtually (figure 24.7). Having tools available for tinkerers requires careful thought for staffing, as support for the use of these tools is necessary, but the results are noteworthy.

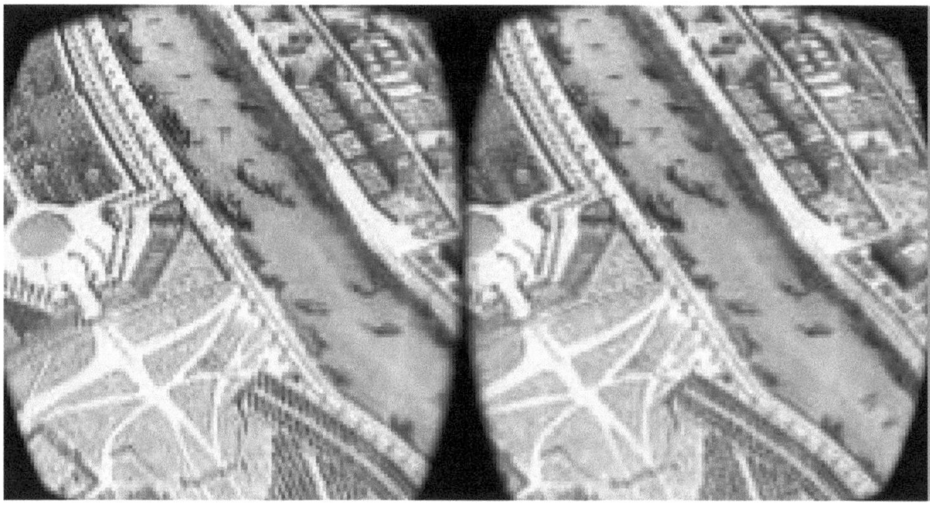

fig 24.7

A VR walk through the streets of 1730s Paris.

CLASSROOM

The David Rumsey Map Center is not an ordinary classroom space, and center staff, rather than the university's registrar, are responsible for managing the center's limited capacity to support teaching. The focus is always on programs where faculty and graduate students leverage the technology in the room to intersperse spatial-based sources in their scholarship, and those openings always fill very quickly!

That high occupancy is seen as a marker of success and a demonstration of the demand for technology-enabled and -supported spaces. Also noteworthy is the variety of classes that are taught in the center, which come from all schools in the university and demonstrate the interdisciplinary nature of cartographic materials. Karl Eikenberry, former ambassador to Afghanistan, teaches regularly in the room. His class uses the integrated screens to present maps of Afghanistan, examine the country's topography, and look at buildings and locations in 3D. A different example comes from history professor Karen Wigen, who has also taught multiple classes in the center. Professor Wigen's class uses unique maps of Japan and San Francisco to study their history. The sciences also make use of the space and collections, and recently the center hosted a class on Antarctic marine geology and geophysics. This class used the high-definition screen to study ice cores, which are very large but hold critical information in millimeter-size sections. The high-resolution screens allowed the class to focus in on individual sections of the digitized ice cores in a way that allowed the whole class to see and discuss the material (figure 24.8).

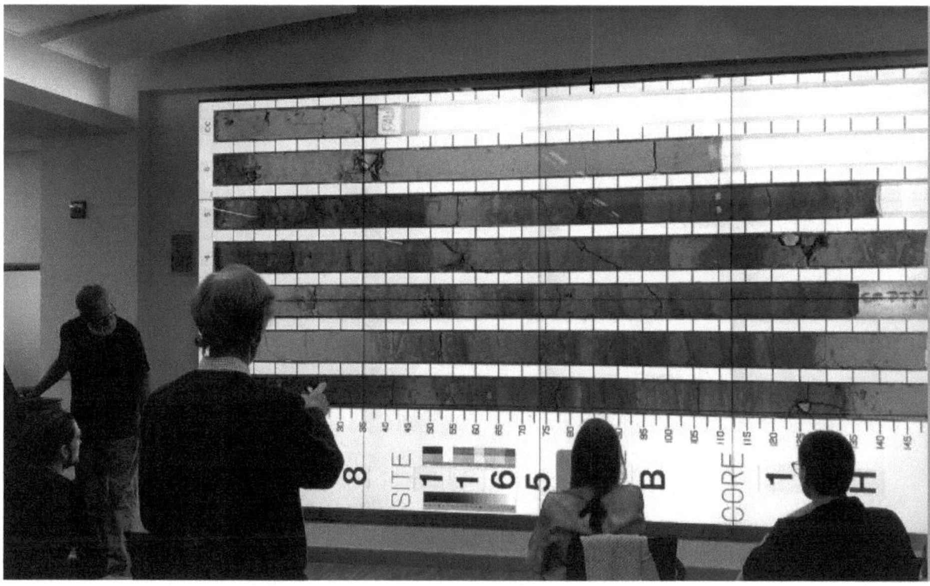

fig 24.8

Studying ice cores in the David Rumsey Map Center.

(Credit: G. Salim Mohammed for Stanford Libraries.)

CONFERENCE AND EVENT SPACE

The center has proven popular, and quite successful, as an event space. Before COVID-19, the center typically hosted at least one event a month, often two, and also hosted two major conferences each year. On more than one occasion the center has hit its fire-marshal-imposed occupancy limit of 177 and has had to turn people away, which speaks to the quality of the programming that the team has been able to put together as well as the popularity of the center itself.

Entering the COVID-19 lockdown period, the center had a significant advantage—most of its collections are available online. The center immediately pivoted to an online presence, by holding online office hours, workshops, classes, and events including digital exhibition openings, talks, and a mini-symposium. Attendance at these events has been high, with up to 600 attendees from all over the world.

Whether physical or virtual, the conference program for the center is tied to partnerships that were cultivated and formalized well before the center opened. There are two partnerships providing annual funds: the Barry Lawrence Ruderman Conference on Cartography and an annual essay and speaker series sponsored by the California Map Society (CMS). The Ruderman Conference, held every two years, brings in cartographic scholars from all over the world for three days of extraordinary programming. The David Rumsey Map Center/CMS partnership brings one renowned speaker to give a lecture at the center and in locations in Los Angeles and San Diego and also supports a competition for essays using cartographic materials from Stanford Libraries. Both these programs are administered by the center. The conference program is an opportunity to be very collaborative with related organizations and to build community and connectedness. It also brings new users to the center and its collections.

The conference program and its community-building role drove one of the major post-opening changes made to the center infrastructure. The initial design did not have integrated technology for content capture, and it was quickly apparent that there was a lot of public interest in the presentations being made in the center. Since there was already a program for virtual exhibits that was tied to the physical exhibit program, and there were often presentations tied to the exhibits, there was a need to capture presentations for integration into those exhibits. To address this need, it was determined that an integrated audio system including microphones and video capture should be the first major upgrade. In February 2019, a fully integrated video system with a suite of new microphones as well as an Epiphan camera was installed, giving the center's staff the ability to automatically record events. This included a direct feed from the screens themselves. Subsequent to the installation, the center has been recording and making its talks available to the public on its YouTube channel.

EXHIBITS

The center itself has 22 cases, in a variety of sizes and formats, to house physical exhibits. The location, format, and structure of those cases was an important planning and discussion point in the design of the space. All exhibit cases are glass enclosed and secure. The hanging exhibit cases incorporate a metal backing that allows maps to be hung using magnets in a way that will not damage the paper. Getting the magnet strength right required careful coordination with members of the Stanford Libraries Conservation team. This system greatly reduces costs and time taken to install and uninstall exhibits.

The center typically hosts two to three exhibits per year, usually connected to events. The center's exhibit program is separate from the larger program that the Stanford Libraries manages, though efforts are made to coordinate the programming between the two. In particular, the rotunda space that typically houses the libraries exhibits may be used by the center to accommodate larger exhibits, and it is important to ensure that those schedules do not conflict. The center's opening exhibit was a great example of that, encompassing over 200 maps spread over 25 cases. Like the conference program, the center's exhibits program seeks opportunities for collaboration and partnership. A great example of this is a collaboration with Helen and Newton Harrison on the exhibit Terraforming: Art and Engineering in the Sacramento Watershed as well as the exhibit Leonardo's Library unveiled in May 2019, where materials from the center were used in the Munger Rotunda and Peterson Gallery Exhibition.

MANAGING TECHNOLOGY

While the integration of technology is one of the features of the space, it has also presented some operational challenges. The high-resolution screen is very new technology and the first implementation of its kind. It's exciting to be on the bleeding edge, but it also means you bleed occasionally, and the center has had a screen failure during an important conference. This was a learning opportunity for the center staff, who have become much more adept at switching between the high-resolution screen and the touch screen in an emergency—including switching video capture. This has also demonstrated the importance of having multiple technologies available and being able to change platforms quickly. In fact, the center is also now home to a large mobile screen that serves as an additional backup. Center staff have also built out maintenance skills for all of the unique equipment, including sending staff to train at the Cinemassive headquarters in Atlanta. Because this equipment is not part of the package of tools the library's technology support team regularly manages, it is necessary to have specialized skills within the center staff. It also requires a maintenance contract with Cinemassive, which is a significant budget item for the center.

One surprise was the physical challenges that users face in working with the high-resolution screen. Faculty teaching a two- or three-hour class using the screen have reported eye strain as well as hand and neck pain related to moving back and forth between the presenter kiosk and the screen. A confidence monitor has been integrated into the kiosk to reduce the number of times instructors must turn toward the screen. And center staff continue to experiment with laser pointers and other equipment to reduce strain and stretching in using the screen.

Finally, note that it is important to think about file management. Most presenters in the center are using lots of high-resolution graphics to take advantage of the high-resolution screen. This has required the addition of network ports to allow efficient file uploads.

STAFFING

The staff of the center are its heart and what keeps it vibrant and active. They have been highlighted repeatedly in the above review of programs because the infrastructure and technology associated with a special collection cannot be used to full effect if staff are not available to support and manage their use. Any space design is going to need to be thoughtful about the necessary staff for a space and how they are accommodated and able to work effectively. The David Rumsey Map Center incorporates an office for the head of the center, G. Salim Mohammed, and has a separate work room off the main space that accommodates the three to five additional staff of the center. These additional staff include a map librarian and service supervisors.

One interesting staffing challenge for the center was managing through its popularity. When the center first opened, staff were quickly overwhelmed with requests for tours. Tour requests are now funneled to a monthly tour date, which was successful until put on hold by COVID-19. Staff do occasionally make exceptions for VIPs, but limiting public tours has been important for managing staff and meeting other demands. Similarly, the center has started doing scheduled workshops for technology training for those who want to use specific technologies in the room. Consider carefully the demands on staff in managing popular spaces.

Conclusion

The changing nature of special collections necessitates changes in the spaces that support those collections; spaces must integrate technology to support born-digital collections and also to enable new ways of working with digital collections. The David Rumsey Map Center provides a model for such technology integration and shows how technology can adapt over time as programs change or concerns arise. However, the true success of the center is not the availability of technology alone but the integration of the center's program into the larger teaching and research work of Stanford University and its capacity to bring together the diverse community of users of cartographic resources.

The flexibility of the space supports its community-building role and takes important steps toward making special collections an accessible tool that is valued across the organization.

Acknowledgment

Thanks to G. Salim Mohammed, head and curator of the David Rumsey Map Center, and to David Rumsey for their contributions to this chapter.

Note

1. You can hear David and Abby Rumsey describe their vision for the David Rumsey Map Center in their own words here: Stanford University Libraries, "David Rumsey Map Center at Stanford Libraries," September 22, 2015, YouTube video, 4:55, https://youtu.be/QLmKt_XEpT4.

25

CHAPTER TWENTY-FIVE

SUPPORTING THE RESEARCH EXPERIENCE

Creating a Hub for Interdisciplinary Collaboration

JOHN BROSZ

With the predominance of online resources, from the library as well as the internet in general, researchers are seen in the library less and less. This can lead to academic libraries being perceived as of limited relevance to campus research or as simply the negotiators of contracts with academic publishers. Academic libraries are responding by adapting to the changing nature of research by providing access to unique tools and software, creating new spaces for collaboration, and developing programs and expertise to support new approaches in research. These developments are promoting new and exciting interactions between students, scholars, and library staff, positioning the library as an important hub for research collaboration and interdisciplinary inquiry on campus.

Lab NEXT at the University of Calgary

At the University of Calgary's Taylor Family Digital Library, a new space called Lab NEXT provides specialized software, analysis tools, collaboration spaces, and unique spaces such as the visualization studio and facilitates access to services such as the copyright office, spatial and numeric data services, and digitization. However, the challenge remains that libraries are not always first to mind for scholars when it comes to managing data sets, data visualization, or makerspaces. Additionally, since these functional research supports are at times new areas for libraries and with services varying between different libraries, it can be challenging for scholars to recognize all the different areas in which the library can support their research or who to approach in the library to do so. This chapter describes the creation of Lab NEXT, a focal point for a constellation of functional services that provides an example of how to make these library resources more easily discoverable and navigable for your institution's scholars.

Within the University of Calgary Libraries and Cultural Resources, Lab NEXT provides a central point of service (virtual and physical) to support scholars and their research. Services connected by Lab NEXT include research data management, spatial and numeric data services, metadata services, the copyright office, data visualization, virtual reality, digitization, repositories and publishing, scholarly communications, A/V edit suites, and a makerspace (figure 25.1). Lab NEXT's mission is to improve researchers' experience with the library. It provides a central entry

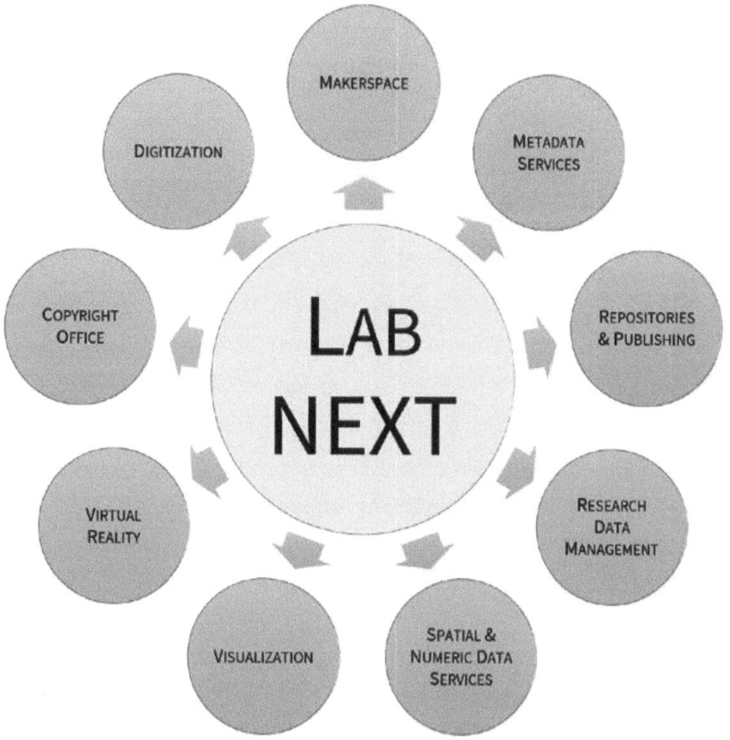

fig 25.1

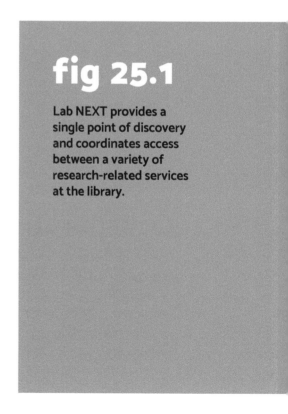

Lab NEXT provides a single point of discovery and coordinates access between a variety of research-related services at the library.

point where library specialists can work with scholars to identify all ways in which the library can assist with their projects and help coordinate access to the library's specialized research services, expertise, and resources.

The development of Lab NEXT was shaped by the research project Academic Research and University Libraries: Creating a New Model for Collaboration (ARUL), led by Thomas Hickerson and funded by The Andrew W. Mellon Foundation. This project explored the instantiation of a research platform for supporting campus research, enhancing campus-wide partnerships, and repositioning libraries within the research endeavor.[1] This research platform is envisioned as a suite of common services, technical infrastructure, and expertise that will enhance campus research efforts. This platform, realized through Lab NEXT, was explored and developed by the ARUL project, which funded competitive grants from the library of up to $40,000 each to 12 multidisciplinary research projects involving 53 scholars from nine faculties and 25 departments.

A benefit of Lab NEXT's approach is that it provides a focal point for a constellation of research resources: the services, infrastructure, and expertise that scholars would otherwise need to seek out individually. While colocating all of these entities would be optimal, it often is not practical due to building and space constraints. Serving as a hub, Lab NEXT is staffed by personnel with in-depth familiarity with the varied roles the library can play in supporting research efforts and able to make suggestions to assist beyond immediate needs.

As a physical space, Lab NEXT is approximately 1,800 square feet primarily configured as a flexible, collaborative space with chairs, tables, and digital displays all equipped with wheels to allow for easy reconfiguration (figure 25.2). Groups of up to 40 can be accommodated as a whole or divided into smaller groups. Lab NEXT also features a small makerspace (~350 sq. ft.), three glass-wall collaboration rooms, and a group of six high-performance workstations.

Lab NEXT is operated by a team of research specialists: the director of the lab and digital initiatives librarian, a metadata librarian, a visualization coordinator, and an emerging technology specialist. On-site service at Lab NEXT is provided by digital media mentors—primarily graduate students recruited to bring new technology and research skills to expand the library's expertise and offer mentorship and training.

fig 25.2

The Lab NEXT space in the Taylor Family Digital Library.

(Photo by David H. Brown, University of Calgary.)

Collaboration Process

Scholars approaching Lab NEXT begin with a consultation with one of the aforementioned research specialists chosen based on the nature of the project and the availability of personnel. In this consultation, the nature of the project is explored and additional library resources that the scholar may not have been aware of are described to see if they can strengthen the project. For example, in the context of discussing data management planning, the specialist would mention the potential of working with the metadata librarian and staff members to develop metadata templates, train research assistants in applying the templates, and assist with quality assurance. One finding that was made through the ARUL project was that having Lab NEXT personnel assist in creating (or at a minimum reviewing) the data management plan often revealed a variety of areas where additional library resources could be brought in to benefit the scholar's efforts.

After this consultation and as the project gets started, the specialist introduces the scholar to the library collaborators to set up the collaboration and lines of communication and to ensure that the scope and timelines of all contributions are understood. Working with the scholar's preferences, project management applications such as Trello, Asana, or Basecamp are used to assist in maintaining communication and project awareness throughout the life span of the project. The Lab NEXT research specialist continues to provide an easy-to-find point of contact for the scholar as challenges occur.

Organizationally, within the library, Lab NEXT coordinates efforts between the different units listed in figure 25.1. A key aspect is that this is not a reporting structure; rather, Lab NEXT specialists, using their knowledge and contacts throughout the library, coordinate between the various units and personnel, saving the scholar from this task. The individual units and personnel support research projects to the extent possible given their capacity. Where this capacity is exceeded, additional support can be pursued with the scholar through funding from research grants or through internal funding from the library, campus research administration, or other areas.

Lab NEXT focuses on aspects of research beyond what is traditionally known as "the collection." Rather, the focus is upon providing functional support. That is, Lab NEXT provides supports that are useful across a variety of disciplines (e.g., data visualization); that lend expertise in novel or specialized techniques and tools (e.g., digitization); or that help scholars deal with the predominance of data across all areas of research (e.g., metadata services).

Units

This section describes the various library units that form the research platform connected by Lab NEXT. These descriptions focus on the research activities of the units, but note that all of these units also contribute to student learning, public outreach, and other library activities.

COPYRIGHT OFFICE

The copyright office often acts in a consultative role in research projects. This is particularly the case in projects with a digitization component, but this office also assists with issues such as meeting funders' licensing requirements and guidance for embedding web assets and web scraping, as well as advice on procedures for securing image (and other intellectual property) permissions.

DIGITIZATION

Beyond standard contracting to digitize materials, the digitization group also offers training to research teams so that they can book time with the equipment to perform the digitization themselves. This minimizes costs to researchers, provides research assistants and students more hands-on time with the materials, and provides greater control over the digitization process. Digitization also works closely with metadata services to ensure high-quality records are established and assists in quality assurance testing on outputs. The digitization group can also assist in establishing online digital collections or offer guidance in using digital scholarship platforms.

MAKERSPACE

The Lab NEXT makerspace provides a variety of tools and technologies common to other library makerspaces: 3D scanning and printing, laser cutting, CNC (computer numerical control) milling, automated embroidery, vinyl cutting, and several different technology kits, including Arduino and Raspberry Pi. This is one of several makerspaces on campus, but within the Lab NEXT context, it has provided a venue where research teams can book the entire space for significant periods, months in advance. The makerspace has supported a variety of research projects, including a qualitative user study examining the use of and learning techniques involved in user makerspaces and 3D printers; 3D scanning and photogrammetry to produce high-quality digital reproductions of archaeological materials; creation of wearable arts via Arduino and the embroidery machine; 3D printing prototype devices for use in labs; and 3D printing dinosaur fossils to test theories about the soft organs next to the bone material. Digital media mentors are available to provide group or individual training on 3D modeling, 3D scanning, and other technical makerspace skills.[2]

METADATA SERVICES

As noted by Cooper and Rieger, scholars are collectors and often need support in managing and organizing these collections.[3] The metadata services unit plays a key role in this by applying the library's metadata and cataloging expertise to assist scholars in efficiently creating high-quality metadata for their data and other research materials. As a result, individuals in this unit can take on a variety of roles, such as embedding themselves with the research team to guide the data creation/capture process; creating and applying metadata templates, schemata, and controlled vocabularies; creating metadata records or training project staff in metadata record creation; and performing quality assurance testing. This move into direct research support has led metadata services personnel to adapt their cataloging-focused skills into the more data-centric areas that are frequently needed by research projects.

REPOSITORIES AND PUBLISHING

Repositories are frequently incorporated into Lab NEXT research projects by ensuring research outcomes are preserved and made publicly available. Similarly, a web-archiving service is available for scholars to preserve websites in a long-lasting archival format. This unit operates two repositories: PRISM for handling texts and media and PRISM Dataverse for data sets. These repositories can be important elements of research projects. In several projects, Lab NEXT established web links between the data repository (PRISM Dataverse) and the research project's active website, ensuring research materials are preserved while simultaneously improving the search visibility of the research websites. This group also manages a journal publishing system that is of use to scholars in creating publications and peer-review processes.

RESEARCH DATA MANAGEMENT

Research data and data management are critical elements of almost every research project across campus. Consequently, research data management provides the opportunity to engage with scholars from the start of the project (data management planning) to its conclusion (data publishing, deposit, and archiving). At the University of Calgary, the research data management librarian works closely with liaison librarians to support scholars in developing data management plans. In this capacity, this group works closely with campus IT to highlight data management software and storage offerings. It also works closely with metadata services and digitization to ensure research teams are trained to produce quality data and with repositories and publishing to ensure project outputs are deposited in the repository and preserved according to the scholar's needs.

SPATIAL AND NUMERIC DATA SERVICES

Spatial and numeric data started as a map and aerial photograph library, but in recent decades has taken on the role of assisting students and scholars with geospatial information systems and finding related data sets. This team is made up of a geospatial librarian, a data analytics librarian, and a data and geospatial resource specialist who helps scholars find needed data sets from Statistics Canada's open data sets, Canadian Community Economic Development Network (https://ccednet-rcdec.ca/en), the city of Calgary's open and restricted-use data sets, and other open data sources. Assistance is provided with this material in data preparation, software assistance, guidance in mapmaking, and research team training in these areas. More recently, spatial and numeric data services has moved into greater support for qualitative data through individual and group training in NVivo for qualitative data analysis.

VISUALIZATION

The visualization studio is a space that features a large 16 foot by 6 foot (4.9 m by 1.8 m) digital display wall. This display wall features a resolution of 9600 by 3600 pixels, making it extremely well suited for visualizing large, complex data sets. The display is supported by a high-performance Windows computer running standard software through mouse and keyboard as well as multi-touch interaction on the wall. This display is also well suited to exploring heterogeneous information sources such as spreadsheets, documents, websites, and videos, which can all be placed on-screen at the same time, allowing small groups to work together synthesizing information (figure 25.3). The display wall is also used beyond data visualization. It is frequently used for showcasing research to media and other visitors; for detailed analysis such as working with extremely large spreadsheets or exploration of high-resolution imagery and maps; and for presentations including graduate oral examinations. Rajabiyazdi and colleagues have provided a detailed examination of researchers' uses of the visualization studio's display.[4]

fig 25.3

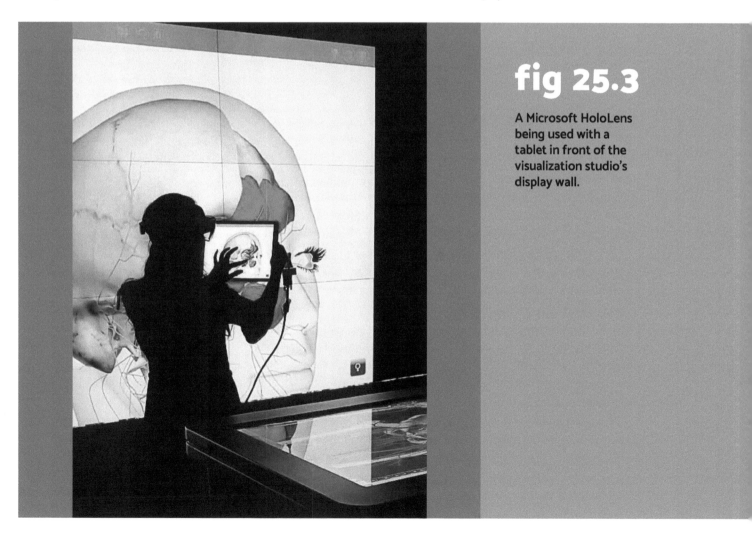

A Microsoft HoloLens being used with a tablet in front of the visualization studio's display wall.

Expert advice for data visualization is provided by the data visualization coordinator, available to consult and help develop research data visualizations, collaborate on research projects, recommend software, and train or mentor graduate students and research assistants.

VIRTUAL REALITY

The virtual reality studio is an exciting new space that is often used to expose students and scholars to the experiences possible with new virtual reality (VR) equipment. The VR studio is composed of two rooms. One, designed for the development of VR applications, is equipped with a high-performance workstation and several VR headsets and is available for long-term bookings. The other, larger room is where people can come to experience VR and make use of existing applications and games over shorter periods.

The operation of the VR studio is challenging due to the rapid progression of this technology. To keep up with the latest developments, one should expect to refresh equipment every two to three years. Thankfully, this equipment continues to be less expensive over time. However, this lowering cost often motivates scholars that become dedicated to VR research to buy this equipment themselves and stop using the library's facility. To maintain connections and share expertise with these groups, Lab NEXT personnel have organized a campus-wide community of practice to help scholars keep up with recent developments and promote awareness of virtual reality activity across the university.

Lab NEXT has seen several VR research projects at the library: a user study on differences in memory retention when experiencing information through VR, film, and museum exhibit modalities; an exploration of 3D haptics for telesurgery; and serious games developed within and for the library's VR environment. Lab NEXT has also developed an artist-in-residence program to encourage artists to develop VR-based digital art and have this art publicized across the library's digital displays.

COLLABORATIVE SPACE

A common concern noted by scholars at the University of Calgary is the lack of available space, particularly for cross-discipline collaboration.[5] It is challenging to find collaborative working spaces to hold recurrent meetings that bring together teams from different academic departments. It can also be difficult to find larger spaces suitable for events (figure 25.4) or high-traffic areas in which exciting research can be highlighted or in which user studies can take place. Lab NEXT research specialists work with scholars to find library spaces that can best fit these varied needs.

Technology-enabled collaboration is available through Lab NEXT's consultation rooms, the visualization studio, the virtual reality studio, and other library meeting rooms. These spaces support 5 to 20 people working with digital displays or whiteboards. Key considerations that make these spaces useful for scholars include the ability to book recurring sessions months in advance or to pursue specific technologies or room configurations (e.g., rooms without windows suitable for working with confidential data, or rooms with large numbers of whiteboards for design sessions). Larger groups may make use of the Taylor Family Digital Library's Gallery Hall (capacity of 90), fourth-floor classrooms (seating for up to 144), or Lab NEXT's main space (capacity of 40). The larger spaces have been used by scholars for small conferences, project launches and announcements, and a variety of presentations, workshops, and design sessions.

Being positioned at the center of campus, the Taylor Family Digital Library's main floor features large numbers of people using the facility and passing through—up to 10,000 a day in the fall and winter terms when the campus is operating at full capacity. Consequently, it is useful for scholars to feature research demonstrations and user studies either in person or through the library's prominent digital media wall. This is another type of access that Lab NEXT propounds and facilitates for scholars.

fig 25.4

Use of the Lab NEXT space for the public launch of a research project.

Case Studies

The following are two cases of collaboration with research projects, illustrating Lab NEXT in operation.

DIGITALLY PRESERVING ALBERTA'S DIVERSE CULTURAL HERITAGE

The project Digitally Preserving Alberta's Diverse Cultural Heritage (figure 25.5), led by Professor Peter Dawson in the department of anthropology and archaeology, set out in 2017 to establish an online archive of digital models of cultural heritage sites captured by Dawson's research team. Through Lab NEXT consultation, this project grew to engage the library on several fronts.

To both create an online presence and preserve this data, library staff put forward the strategy of depositing the captured data into the PRISM Dataverse repository and contracting the library's software development team to build a WordPress-based website that would allow the research team to feature the remarkable capture methodology, two- and three-dimensional imagery, and historical context of these heritage sites. The metadata librarian was provided with samples of the heterogeneous data: images, videos, 3D scans, geospatial information, building information models, and other materials. Based on this material a metadata template was developed. The metadata librarian trained the research team in the use of the template and assisted in quality assurance on the creation of the initial records. With this knowledge of the data set, the metadata librarian collaborated with the development team to develop the website based on Professor Dawson's design requirements. The repositories and publishing unit engaged with the metadata librarian and research team to establish procedures for depositing the data sets and a fixed mapping between the metadata template and the PRISM Dataverse metadata fields. With the completion of the website, documentation and training were provided to the research team members on how to update and enter new heritage projects on the website and deposit their data sets.

The research project's website, shown in figure 25.5, can be found at https://alberta.preserve.ucalgary.ca/.

fig 25.5

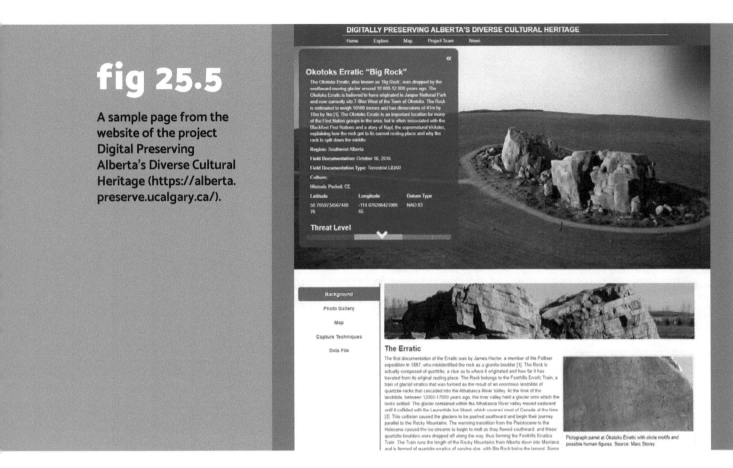

A sample page from the website of the project Digital Preserving Alberta's Diverse Cultural Heritage (https://alberta.preserve.ucalgary.ca/).

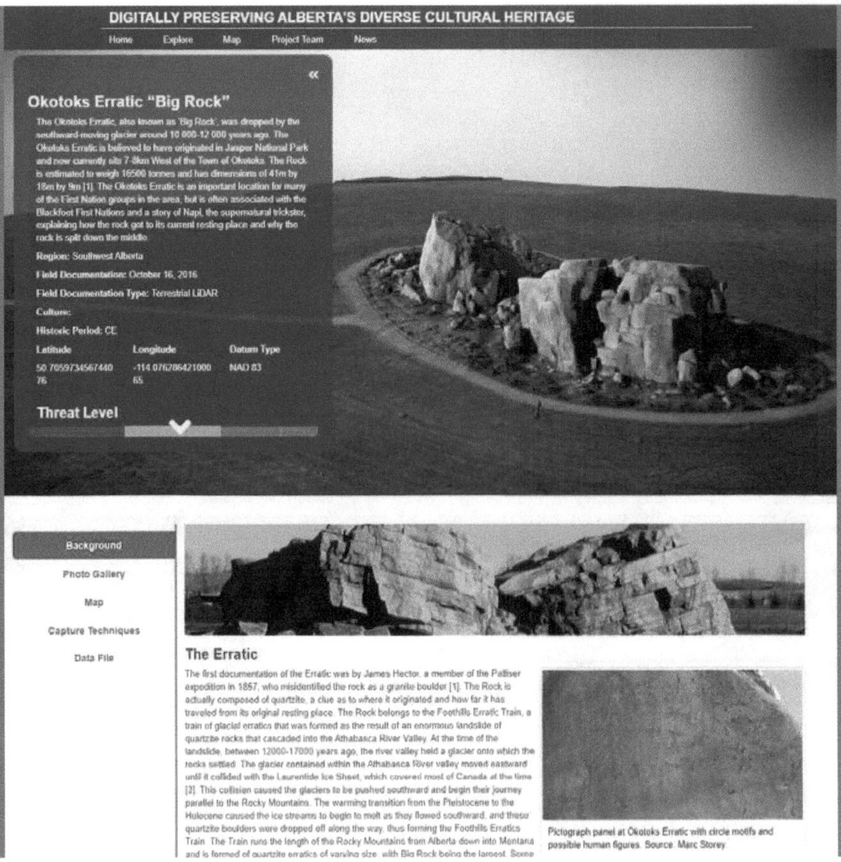

MAPPING AND VISUALIZING VICTORIAN LITERARY SOCIABILITY

In 2018, professors Karen Bourrier (English) and Dan Jacobson (geography) set out to examine how propinquity (proximity of people to one another) affected the careers of Victorian authors, editors, artists, and publishers. A major challenge in this project was relating historical addresses, buildings, and other place names to modern places, including latitude and longitude. To accomplish this, the research team worked closely with spatial and numeric data services where the geospatial librarian, Peter Peller, researched, developed, and trained the research team in a workflow (figure 25.6) for performing this historical geolocation process.

Based on the positive experience with the project Digitally Preserving Alberta's Diverse Cultural Heritage, the library's web development team was contracted to develop a project website with a map to display the entries in the produced data set, create a submission form for crowdsourcing additional Victorians and historical addresses, and provide access to the data set. The resulting website is https://victorians.ucalgary.ca/.

The research team worked with the metadata librarian, Ingrid Reiche, to develop appropriate metadata fields to encode the data set as TEI XML. Her work specifically focused on preserving the relationship between historical and current geographic names.

The team also worked with the data visualization coordinator, John Brosz, to extract a seed data set from a database provided by the Orlando project's (http://orlando.cambridge.org/) records on literary Victorians. Later the data visualization coordinator developed exploratory visualizations of the completed propinquity data set for analysis by the research team.

The digital initiatives librarian, Christie Hurrell, worked with the research team in hosting an event for the Victorian Studies Association of Western Canada conference at the library's gallery hall and visualization studio. The conference featured a session where Peter Peller trained conference attendees in the developed historical geocoding workflow, while the research team instructed attendees on submitting additional Victorians and locations with the website.

fig 25.6

Workflow illustrating the challenge and multiplicity of sources used to establish a link between a historical address and modern latitude, longitude, and place name.

(Image courtesy of Peter Peller, University of Calgary.)

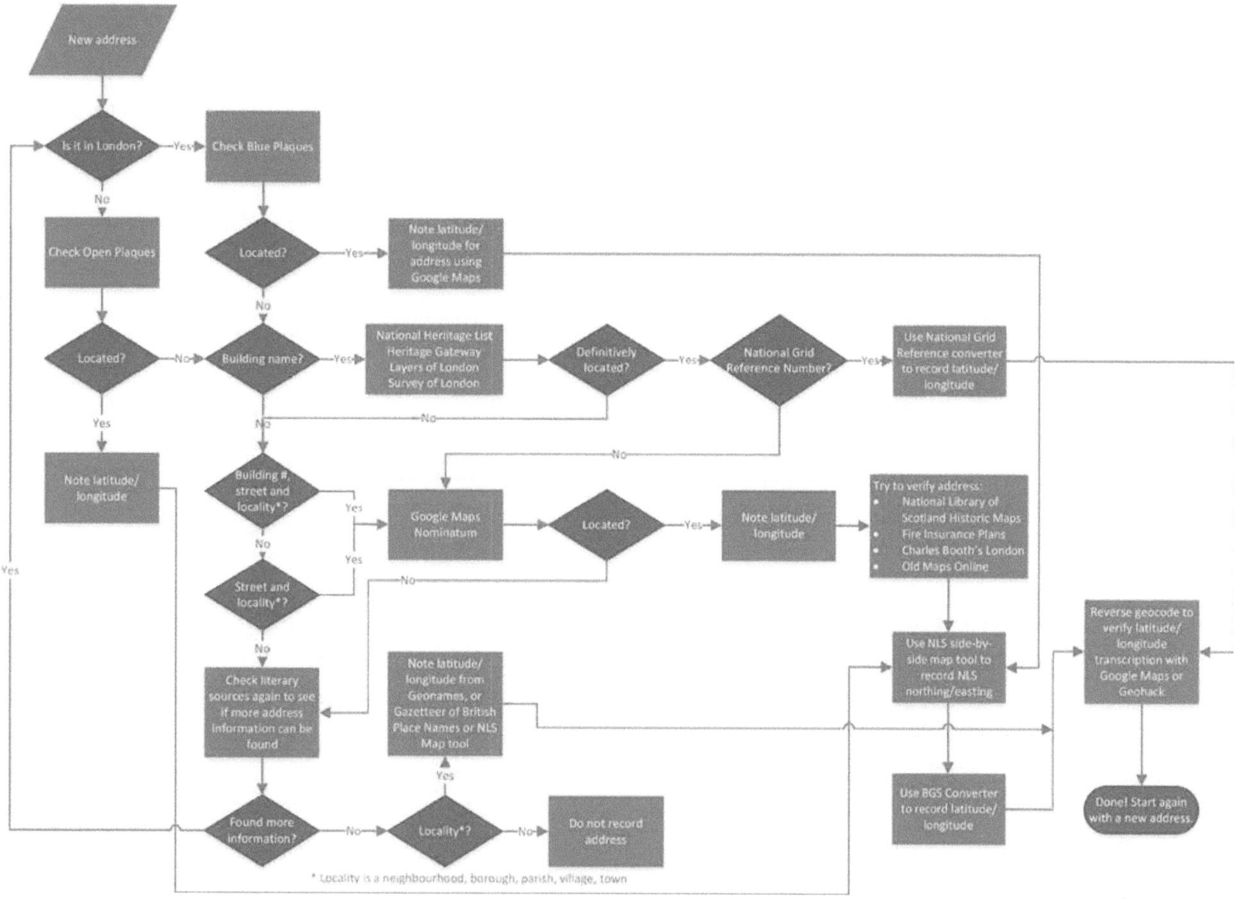

Conclusion

With the proliferation of online services and resources, scholars are less frequently visiting campus libraries. Lab NEXT is a model that provides scholars with a central point of engagement for conducting research in collaboration with services, personnel, and infrastructure distributed throughout the library. This model provides a space to draw in scholars where their specific needs are met by expert library personnel. It provides the opportunity for the library to present a coordinated research experience exposing scholars to new and exciting library capabilities. This is far superior to having scholars hunt down the people, services, and distributed resources they need across various library departments, locations, and teams—it saves scholars' time and ensures that they find all the library resources they need. Ultimately this approach can provide the mechanism for the library to become a collaborator in scholars' research projects—forging relationships, working with scholars throughout the entire research life cycle, coordinating timelines and resources, and sharing project knowledge among library staff. It avoids scholars' interactions with the library being inefficient or piecemeal and gives library staff direct insights into a research project's goals and objectives.

Lab NEXT provides much-needed multidisciplinary, collaborative research space on campus. This leverages the libraries' long-standing role providing shared spaces and resources, often located at the heart of campus, in which multidisciplinary research teams can meet, work, and promote the products of their research. A key aspect of this research hub is that it draws upon the services, infrastructure, and expertise that already exist within academic libraries. By building upon these resources and connecting with others across campus, libraries can serve as vital components of the local research ecosystem and support the increasing interdisciplinarity of academic research.

Notes

1. Thomas Hickerson and John Brosz, "Remaining Relevant: Critical Roles for Libraries in the Research Enterprise" (presentation, World Library and Information Congress, 85th IFLA General Conference and Assembly, Athens, Greece, August 25, 2019), https://prism.ucalgary.ca/handle/1880/111632.
2. Renée Reaume, "Survey of the Digital Media Mentors at the Taylor Family Digital Library," in "Engaging Students in Reimagined Spaces: Successful Peer Mentor Programs and Experiences" (panel discussion, Designing Libraries 6: Designing Libraries for the 21st Century, Raleigh, NC, September 17–18, 2017), video, 17:35–25:35, https://vimeo.com/234532936.
3. Danielle Cooper and Oya Rieger, *Scholars ARE Collectors: A Proposal for Re-thinking Research Support*, issue brief (New York: Ithaka S+R, November 28, 2018), https://doi.org/10.18665/sr.310702.
4. Fateme Rajabiyazdi, Jagoda Walny, Carrie Mah, John Brosz, and Sheelagh Carpendale, "Understanding Researchers' Use of a Large, High-Resolution Display across Disciplines," In *ITS '15: Proceedings of the 2015 International Conference on Interactive Tabletops and Surfaces* (New York: Association for Computing Machinery, November 2015), 107–116, https://doi.org/10.1145/2817721.2817735.
5. Christie Hurrell, "Aligning the Stars: Understanding Digital Scholarship Needs to Support the Evolving Nature of Academic Research," *Partnership: The Canadian Journal of Library and Information Practice and Research* 14, no. 2 (November 2019), https://doi.org/10.21083/partnership.v14i2.4623.

26

CHAPTER TWENTY-SIX

AN ACADEMIC "ECOTONE"

The Wilmeth Active Learning Center, Purdue University

JAMES L. MULLINS

In 2012, Purdue University was in discussion with the Arthur C. Clarke Foundation about locating a research center on campus that would be committed to the philosophy of Arthur C. Clarke. Many entities on campus made presentations to the visiting committee because the intended scope of the center was quite broad. The center would also house the Clarke papers, hence the invitation to Purdue Libraries to participate in the presentation and proposal.

Over a period of several days, Purdue representatives made presentations. It fell to me, as dean of libraries, to make the presentation for the libraries. I attended all of the presentations; however, one particularly fascinated me, the one given by the biologists. Their presentation centered around the concept of an ecotone in nature and how that would be applicable to what Purdue would propose for the Arthur C. Clarke Center, by bringing together his many interests into a whole that would be more innovative than focusing on any one part of his legacy. As I listened, I could see how this concept could apply to what was being proposed for the construction of a combined engineering and science library with a classroom building.

In environmental science, an ecotone is used to define the area in which two different ecosystems touch or overlap, such as woodlands and savannah, or growing seasons such as a Zone 4 or Zone 5.

In an ecotone, the flora develop characteristics necessary to survive in both, thereby creating an entity stronger and more resilient with new characteristics. This concept was applied when we conceptualized the design for what would become the Wilmeth Active Learning Center (WALC) at Purdue University (figure 26.1).

fig 26.1

Daytime view of WALC with Bell/Clock Tower in foreground.

(Permission of: Photos: Trevor Mahlmann.)

The program statement for WALC took the ecotone concept and applied it to the intent and design of the building. That is, take what is typical of a classroom, in this case an active learning classroom, combined with what is typically found in a library—access to collections, services, and research and study space—and unite them in a seamless whole that allows spaces to serve one role during the day and morph into another role later in the day. In this concept, the physical space gains an efficiency that appeals to university administrators, funding agencies, and donors.

Background: Libraries at Purdue

As a land-grant university focused on agriculture, engineering, and science, Purdue University was chartered in 1869 to complement the more traditional liberal arts role of Indiana University, founded in 1820.

In 1913, the first building dedicated solely as the University Library opened. Built in a modified Greek Revival/Romanesque/Renaissance style, its layout was consistent with the principles of library design at that time. The second floor Reading Room (figure 26.2) was designed to be a place where demeanor was serious and focused. The Reading Room, finished in the Arts and Crafts style, was flooded with sunlight through large windows facing south, east, and west.

fig 26.2

1913 Library Reading Room.

(Courtesy of Purdue University Libraries–Archives and Special Collections.)

In the 1920s, engineering and science faculty lobbied to have research materials closer to their offices and labs. This set in motion explosive growth of departmental and disciplinary libraries. In the 1960s, there were over 40 branch libraries listed in the libraries' annual reports.

After WWII, a change occurred in the concept of library design. The idea that stacks should be closed and accessible only to library staff was challenged when, in 1948, the first "supermarket" style library opened at the University of Iowa without the typical large, grand reading room.

In the early 1950s lobbying began at Purdue for a new library that would serve as the central library, augmenting or replacing the 1913 Library. Completed in the late 1950s, known today as Stewart Center, the building was conceptualized as both a conference center and a library designed in the supermarket style. The plan called for the new building to be attached to and surround the 1913 Library on the south and west sides. The 1913 Reading Room had most of its windows covered over, and the room was modernized and no longer served as a reading room.

When Stewart Center opened in 1958, the concept of integrating a library and conference center was well ahead of its time—unfortunately, too far ahead of its time for logical and effective management of library collections. It was not long before access to all floors of the library created a collection security nightmare. The university librarian is reputed to have said, "I asked for a library, instead I was given a &#% sieve!" The library access points on the second and third floors were closed and used only as emergency exits, and that practice continues to the present day.

In the 1970s, the initiative to consolidate branch libraries began. A major consolidation occurred when the Siegesmund Engineering Library opened in 1978, consolidating six engineering libraries. In the 1980s the undergraduate library was constructed and opened in 1982.

In 2004, when I arrived on campus, the transition from print to digital access had progressed to such an extent that it required a major rethinking of Purdue's 15 libraries, most of which were science and engineering. The need for a central, combined engineering and science library was obvious.

The Link between Active Learning and Libraries

In 2010, Purdue faculty and administrators became concerned about the level of student success in the large first-year lecture courses. It was determined that lectures to five hundred students in a lecture hall were not conducive to learning, but what was the alternative?

The renovation of the Business Library provided insights into how information literacy instruction could be delivered. The Learn Lab (figure 26.3) in the Business Library was a new concept in Purdue instruction.

fig 26.3

Parrish Library Learn Lab, Teresa Brown Collection.

(Courtesy of Purdue University Libraries–Archives and Special Collections.)

In the Learn Lab, libraries faculty taught classes with each student sitting at a computer. The Learn Lab enabled an individual student or teams of students to share with the class the results of their individual or collaborative work. In addition, the instructor could view the work of each individual or team at his or her station. Visual display on three walls allowed students to be facing different directions while always having a clear line of sight to a screen. Since libraries faculty collaborated with disciplinary faculty in the information literacy instruction, it exposed faculty throughout the campus to this new classroom design. It did not take long before disciplinary faculty were requesting the Learn Lab as their assigned classroom.

When the vice provost for undergraduate academic affairs experienced the Learn Lab, he recognized the possible impact this classroom design could have on instruction throughout the university and the potential for improving the success of first-year students.

Active Learning

Pedagogists have long known that students learn more quickly and more deeply when they can apply what they are learning. When students work in teams, there is a benefit because one student may grasp a concept that she or he can then teach or explain to fellow students, possibly even more effectively than the instructor. Students participate in their own instruction; hence, "active learning."

Active learning requires classroom design that optimizes collaboration (figure 26.4). In the past, a typical classroom was arranged with rows of tablet armchairs in order to create maximum efficiency of the space. The tablet armchair arrangement requires between 12 and 15 square feet per seat. In contrast, an active learning classroom furnished with tables and technology, requires, depending upon configuration, approximately 25 to 30 square feet per seat.

fig 26.4

WALC active learning classroom.

(Photo by author.)

The Office of the Provost created and funded a program called Instruction Matters: Purdue Academic Course Transformation, or IMPACT. IMPACT is a university-wide initiative with the goal of incentivizing faculty to explore new ways to teach. Faculty were given a reduced teaching load for a year while enrolled in IMPACT and provided with tutors in various areas to help integrate new teaching methods into their instruction. The lecture previously given once in a large lecture hall would now be recorded and accessible online anytime by a student and as many times as desired. The class session time—that is, formerly the large lecture—would now be committed to active learning with students in multiple locations.

To support the instructor in learning this new teaching methodology, pedagogists from the Center for Instructional Excellence (CIE) assisted instructors in mastering new methods of teaching; Information Technology at Purdue (ITaP) professionals instructed faculty on the use of newer hardware and software; and libraries faculty collaborated with instructors to integrate information literacy into the course. IMPACT was rolled out in 2011.

An immediate challenge was the need for additional classrooms to accommodate the IMPACT program because classroom utilization at Purdue was nearly 100 percent. So where will these active learning classes be held?

Active Learning Classroom Space Provided by Libraries

Two members of the libraries faculty, Tomalee Doan and Beth McNeil, approached me about giving up a room in the basement of the Undergraduate Library so it could be reassigned as an active learning/IMPACT classroom. My first reaction was "No," because once it moved from the libraries' space inventory to that of the registrar, libraries would lose use and control of the space and it would mean that the room was no longer available for students to study. In addition, the room was the only one in the libraries that was large enough to accommodate a staff meeting. However, upon reflection and considering the needs of the university, I agreed to give over the room for this new purpose with the stipulation that if, in the future, the room was no longer needed by the registrar, it would revert to the inventory of the libraries.

The Office of the Provost provided $1,000,000 to renovate the room with new lights, carpet, furnishings, new instructional technology, and more robust wireless access. Beginning in fall 2011, IMPACT courses were offered in this reconfigured room in the Undergraduate Library. The courses included subjects as wide-ranging as communications, genetics, soil sciences, psychology, basic mechanics in engineering, political science, and biology. These classes, primarily taken by first-year students, had an immediate impact by introducing them to the Undergraduate Library.

With the IMPACT classes, students came to the Undergraduate Library to attend various classes beginning as early as 7:30, continuing until the end of the class day at 5:30. It did not take long before libraries faculty and staff began to witness a positive, win/win situation. The IMPACT classroom, which had been underutilized during the day prior to IMPACT, was now being heavily used once the class day ended. In the evening the IMPACT classroom became a highly desirable collaborative study space with state-of-the-art furniture and technology—a natural extension of library study space.

The plan was to roll out IMPACT-designed courses in year one, then add a new cohort of faculty and courses the second year, and each year thereafter. Therefore, it was understood that for the next academic year the need for additional active learning classrooms would grow. Concurrently, the libraries had made the decision to reintegrate the book and periodical collections from the Undergraduate Library into the disciplinary libraries, thus making space available to be repurposed to student study and collaborative spaces. This availability of space within the Undergraduate Library also provided areas that could be used to create two additional IMPACT classrooms. The renovation and creation of two additional active learning classrooms was completed during summer 2012.

During fall semester 2012, the libraries faculty and staff observed that students were meeting in teams before class in the Undergraduate Library; going to their class in one of the three classrooms; and after class returning to the Undergraduate Library to continue working as a team. Sometimes the instructor would join the teams, thus continuing the active learning beyond the class session. This extension of the class into the library had never been observed before because classrooms and library spaces were never so integrated. This new dynamic of library and classroom integration intrigued us and needed to be explored.

The Ecotone Solution: Additional Classrooms and Consolidation of Libraries

The old power plant, built in the 1920s on what was then the north edge of the campus, was a large and imposing structure. It was decommissioned in the 1980s. In the early 2000s it was in a state of deterioration and an eyesore. At one time its smokestack, in pre-pollution-awareness days, had been a beloved unofficial icon of Purdue University. By the 1990s the smokestack had been removed and the official icon, the Bell Tower, was erected opposite the old power plant.

In 2005, I presented a plan to the provost to renovate the old power plant, now in the center of campus, into a central science and engineering library. Her response was that the site had to be cleared and a classroom building built to meet the need for more classrooms.

Understanding this obvious need, the libraries collaborated with the registrar and director of space planning to develop a program statement that would define a facility that would house classrooms and a library—however, with a clear demarcation between the two.

In 2005 the university began a multimillion dollar project to remove the old power plant from the grid that it had fed power and heat to for over 50 years. However, from 2005 to 2012 there was little progress on obtaining approval and funding for the classroom/library building as it was then conceptualized; always toward the top of the list of priorities for building projects, it was often bumped in favor of a privately funded project.

In 2012, the growth and initial success of the IMPACT program created an urgent need for more classrooms, specifically active learning classrooms. Combining the need for additional classrooms and a new, state-of-the-art engineering and science library created the opportunity to apply the concept of an ecotone to the program statement: that is, creating a building that would have active learning classrooms and a consolidated engineering and science library, albeit with a twist. During the day 40 percent of the building would be dedicated library space with nearly 60 percent committed to active learning classrooms, but after the end of the class day, the active learning classrooms would become library study and collaborative spaces, making the entire building's 174,000 square feet more or less a library supervised by staff of the libraries. Therefore, the building would be an excellent classroom building while preserving and expanding the role of the academic library into the instructional space of the campus: hence, an ecotone in the academic setting where the whole is stronger and more adaptable than its parts. This ecotone scenario drove the vision for what would become the Wilmeth Active Learning Center.

Innovative Integration of Library/ Classroom Space Study

In 2013, I retained Dr. Nancy Fried Foster, an anthropologist who had undertaken research on how students viewed and used library space at the University of Rochester, as a consultant to the Libraries Users Study Group comprised of Purdue Libraries faculty and staff. Dr. Foster integrated anthropological research methodologies in order to determine what Purdue students wanted in a library. Additionally, team members were instructed by Dr. Foster on how to observe and record how students were using library spaces.

Key points that students wanted in a new library facility were identified. A list was created that included, among other things, large windows with views of the campus; natural light as much as possible; a central location allowing for quick and easy access to and from class; food service within the library; integration of state-of-the-art technology and wireless support; a variety of study spaces; a dedicated quiet space or spaces; visibility of books upon entering the building; a variety of individual study spaces including carrels or cubicles; collaborative spaces to work in teams; and artwork that highlighted the history of Purdue.

One of the findings of the Libraries User Study Group was that, although an empty classroom in the evening was on the list of places where students would consider studying, they also admitted—primarily women—that there was a level of concern about security since classroom buildings were not monitored during evening or night hours.

The primary issue to be addressed was the central location of the building on campus. As in real estate in general, "location, location, location" was a defining factor. The registrar and director of space planning emphasized the 10-minute rule for transition to and from classes. The site that met that need was the site of the old power plant (figure 26.5).

Once the decision was made that the classroom/library facility project, identified officially as the classroom/ library building, was a high priority, program planning began in earnest. The program plan defined the vision for and what the building would comprise, including active learning classrooms, learning/library spaces, and informal areas including a café. The program planning committee consisted of the vice provost for undergraduate academic

fig 26.5

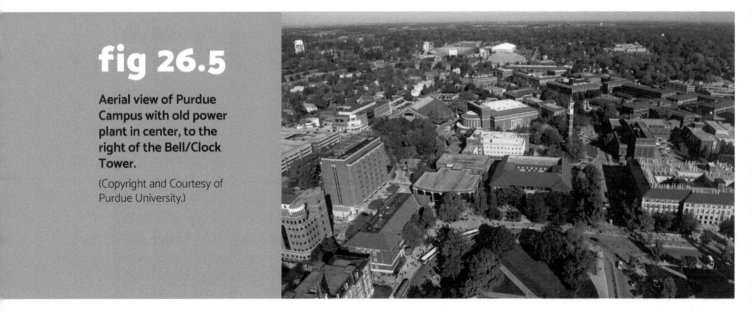

Aerial view of Purdue Campus with old power plant in center, to the right of the Bell/Clock Tower.

(Copyright and Courtesy of Purdue University.)

affairs, the director of space planning, and the dean of libraries. An important member was the project manager assigned by the facilities department. This was not an easy collaboration because the director of space planning, who was responsible for all classroom design and support, opposed any change in traditional classroom design.

A specific issue was the use of windows to the outdoors or to an atrium or hallway because he argued windows and views into the classroom would be distracting for students. Since these classrooms at the end of the class day would become library study spaces for individuals and groups, the ability to see into the rooms by libraries staff was imperative to ensure a safe and secure space to study or collaborate. Typically, the vice-provost did not attend the planning meetings, but when there were stalemates between what the libraries and space planning wanted, he would intercede to resolve the problem. There were other critical members of the planning team, including the university architect and representatives of the academic and administrative information technology units. Graduate and undergraduate students and faculty were brought in as the planning progressed.

Ranking and Funding of the Classroom/Library Building

During summer of 2012, the classroom/library building project was chosen as the capital project with the greatest likelihood of receiving funding by the state of Indiana. Since the Indiana General Assembly had not approved bond authority for a capital project at Purdue since 2007, it was determined that the project had to excite and convey Purdue's commitment to the learning and success of its undergraduate students. Of all the projects considered, the classroom/library facility was ranked first and most likely to receive support and funding from state legislators.

Before the final decision was made, a group of senior administrators met to discuss how this proposed project should be submitted to the Indiana General Assembly. One senior administrator said asking for funding for this project with the name "Classroom/Library Building" was a surefire way to be denied funding. The name conveyed no excitement, appeared to be out of date, and was not in step with the changing environment of higher education. Since the building was being designed to support active learning, it became obvious that it should be called the Active Learning Center—a name that would generate interest and require imagination to understand its intent.

The request for support to the Indiana General Assembly was for $50,000,000, in bonding authority, of the estimated total cost of $79,000,000. The university administration committed $13,000,000 up front. Libraries accepted the responsibility to raise $16,000,000.

Project Challenges and Fundraising

On the last day of the Indiana General Assembly, April 30, 2013, the request from Purdue for $50,000,000 to help fund a substantial portion of the Active Learning Center was approved. Typically, funding for capital projects at Indiana's chartered universities is given through bonding authority. Instead, the General Assembly approved the $50,000,000 in cash! As far as anyone could determine or remember, this was the first time a capital project at Purdue had been funded with cash from the state.

The challenge given me as the dean of libraries by the president of Purdue was to have 50 percent of the $16,000,000 committed before he would give approval to move forward on the project. The deadline for the 50 percent was May 1, 2014, with scheduled demolition on the old power plant to begin summer 2014. The 50 percent goal was met.

Working with the libraries' director of advancement, we approached individuals who were interested in the project and committed to furthering the goals of the libraries as well as undergraduate education. The chair of the libraries dean's advisory council committed a lead gift toward the goal; the Lilly Endowment contributed a multimillion dollar gift to the project; and the Wilmeth Family made the gift of $8,000,000 in memory of the two Wilmeth brothers who graduated from Purdue in 1935 and 1940. In recognition of the Wilmeth gift, the board of trustees agreed, in April

2015, to name the building the Thomas S. and Harvey D. Wilmeth Active Learning Center (WALC). The remainder of the needed funds were provided by numerous alumni and donors. The goal to have 100 percent of the funds raised or committed by May 1, 2015, was achieved. The entire cost of WALC, just under $100,000,000 (including extensive exterior site and landscaping), was paid off within two years after WALC opened in August 2017.

Design Concept for the Wilmeth Active Learning Center

Since the location of the Wilmeth Active Learning Center (WALC) was at the center of the campus—and the surrounding architecture reflected "Purdue style"—it was determined that WALC had to blend with surrounding buildings in mass, design, and construction materials; that is, red brick, Indiana limestone trim, and red tile roof. Even though the exterior design would be traditional, it was not so for the interior. The interior would have a postindustrial theme consistent with the engineering and science focus of the university. The 170,390-square-foot facility would house the Library of Engineering and Science (LoES) and 27 classrooms designed for active learning.

The university embarked on the process of selecting an architect for what would become WALC in 2013. A request for proposals was made to architectural firms around the country. Four firms were chosen to make a presentation to a university committee. From those presentations, the decision was made to select BSA Life Structures of Indianapolis. The committee was impressed by the work completed at two universities, the University of Notre Dame and Indiana University.

Since BSA had not designed an academic research library, Purdue required BSA to visit with a Purdue team universities that had libraries or other facilities that reflected aspects of the proposed building. A cohort of seven included two BSA architects and its interior designer; the library consultant; Purdue facilities project manager; a student representing the Undergraduate Student Libraries Advisory Council, as the student viewpoint was critical; and myself.

Four universities were visited: North Carolina State University, Duke University, the University of Georgia, and the Georgia Institute of Technology. Each facility was considered from different vantage points, but primarily assessed how students were using and not using various spaces. NC State provided insights into the use of space and transition. At Duke, there was an opportunity to see classrooms with glass walls and to determine if visibility into the room bothered the students or instructor—the students did not appear to notice us peering into the room; this was confirmed when we asked if they had noticed us watching them through the glass, and they hadn't. We were able to use this information to eliminate the resistance of the director of space planning to glass into the classrooms.

At Duke, I particularly wanted the architects and the student representative to see its beautiful reading room. I was determined that Purdue students would have a space similar to the one lost when the 1913 Library Reading Room was remodeled in the 1950s. My vision was that the Reading Room would be two stories, with large windows overlooking the iconic Bell Tower at the center of campus.

At Georgia Tech we stood on a bridge that connected two study areas filled with students on the second floor of the Clough Undergraduate Learning Commons during a class change. Hundreds of students passed below us talking and laughing. We looked to see if the studying students took notice, and they did not. I asked our student member what he thought. His answer was that the activity in the building helped to create a dynamic atmosphere. The Miller Learning Center at the University of Georgia provided an opportunity to assess the impact of the adjacency of classrooms and study spaces in one building.

Over the next six months, the architects worked with the libraries' administrators, faculty, and staff as well as classroom design staff, technology staff, and students (figures 26.6–26.8). Tomalee Doan, a Purdue Libraries division head, had become particularly knowledgeable in the requirements and design of active learning classrooms. She, along with a colleague in space management, designed the building's classrooms, which had both movable and fixed furniture, to accommodate differing numbers of students. The total number of assignable classrooms was 27, ranging in capacity from 40 to 180. Another room was a theater that could seat 320.

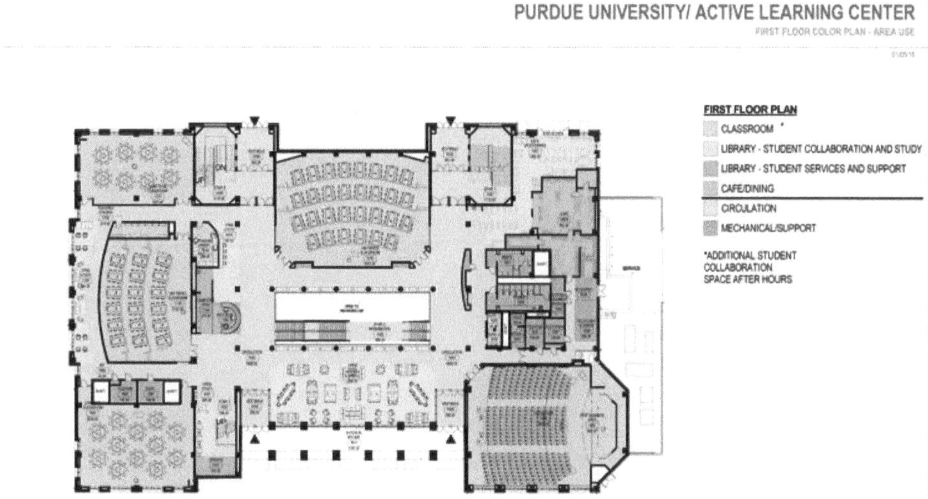

fig 26.6

WALC first-floor plan.

(Courtesy BSA LifeStructures.)

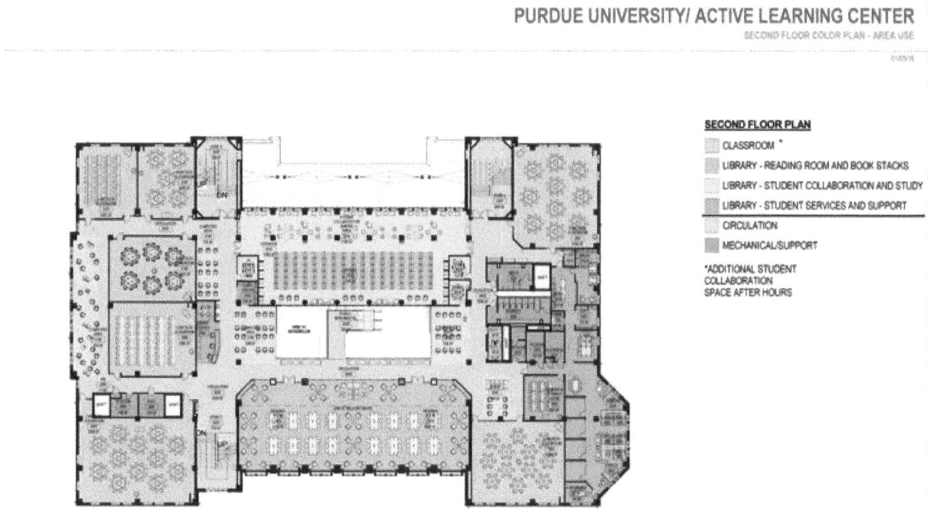

fig 26.7

WALC second-floor plan.

(Courtesy BSA LifeStructures.)

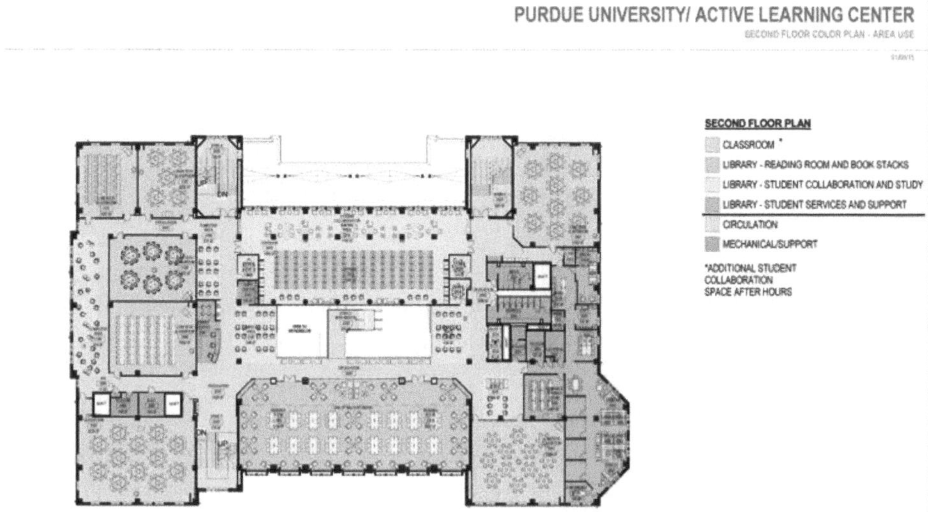

fig 26.8

WALC third-floor plan.

(Courtesy BSA LifeStructures.)

One particular challenge was to provide a semi-lecture-style space that could seat 180 students while still providing the opportunity to have students work in teams. The solution was to create a series of platforms within the room that could accommodate tables, perpendicular to the front of the room, that could seat six students each. This arrangement allowed students to turn to the instructor and the front of the room when needed, while also allowing them to work in team collaboration during the class. This model was so unique it has been called the "Purdue Classroom" (figure 26.9).

fig 26.9

"Purdue Style Classroom" designed to seat 180 for active learning.

(Photograph by author.)

The design of the Wilmeth Active Learning Center is postindustrial style. The central atrium with an open staircase connects all floors and allows daylight from the clerestory into the center of the building (figure 26.10). The classrooms are clustered in one wing of the building; dedicated individual and group study spaces are interspersed among the classrooms.

fig 26.10

WALC stairway and atrium, second floor, engineering and science stacks on the left and Reading Room on the right.

(Permission Dean Lingley.)

The center of the building is the primary focus of the dedicated library space. On the west side of the second floor is the Reading Room, and on the east side is the dedicated stack space for engineering and science print materials. Upon reaching the second floor using the central staircase, one can see the Reading Room through glass walls on the left and the book stacks on the right.

The Reading Room was originally designed to continue the postindustrial design. However, when the university was offered the only authorized full-scale copy of *Washington Crossing the Delaware* by Emanuel Leutze, it was decided it would be displayed in the Reading Room. Therefore, a style change was dictated to create an atmosphere more consistent with the painting. The choice was made to finish the room in an Arts and Crafts style, similar to the original 1913 Reading Room. This brought a more traditional atmosphere into the Reading Room. The two-story windows overlooking the iconic Bell Tower at the center of campus foster connections between students and the campus while they are studying in a quiet, beautiful setting along with others (figure 26.11 and 26.12).

fig 26.11

WALC Reading Room on second floor.

(Photo by author.)

fig 26.12

View of Bell/Clock Tower from WALC's Reading Room.

(Photo Courtesy of Purdue University Libraries–Archives and Special Collections.)

Opposite to the Reading Room is the engineering and science stack area. Prior to the planning for the building, the engineering and science librarians reviewed what print collections must be available in the new library. The six libraries that were to come together had a combined total of nearly 800,000 volumes, primarily journals. With the acquisition of nearly all back files available, all titles available digitally were weeded, and those deemed necessary were sent to off-site storage. The science and engineering librarians determined the optimal number of print materials in the stacks would be 35,000 volumes. The stack area is the only place in WALC that has Tattle-Tape door security.

D-VELoP (Data Visualization Experience Lab of Purdue) provides visual support for geographic information systems (GIS). The Viz Wall and Lab provides a full wall to visualize data.

The Wilmeth Active Learning Center is the locus of the libraries' faculty and staff in the engineering and science areas. At Purdue, librarians are full members of the faculty with the expectation of teaching and research. To facilitate their work, space is allocated for graduate assistants within the libraries faculty office area.

In order to ensure the old power plant was not overlooked for its many years of service and its identity with the campus, artifacts were removed from it prior to its demolition. Working with interior designers, these artifacts were installed throughout the building. Life-size photos of past Purdue students listening to faculty describe the functions of the boilers in the generation of heat and electricity, with plant employees looking on, provide a visible historical record of engineering at Purdue (figure 26.13). An audio tour of the artifacts and photos was created so the WALC visitor could also be an active learner.

fig 26.13

WALC photo mural of students, professor, and old power plant staff: "active learning" in the 1940s.

(Photo by author.)

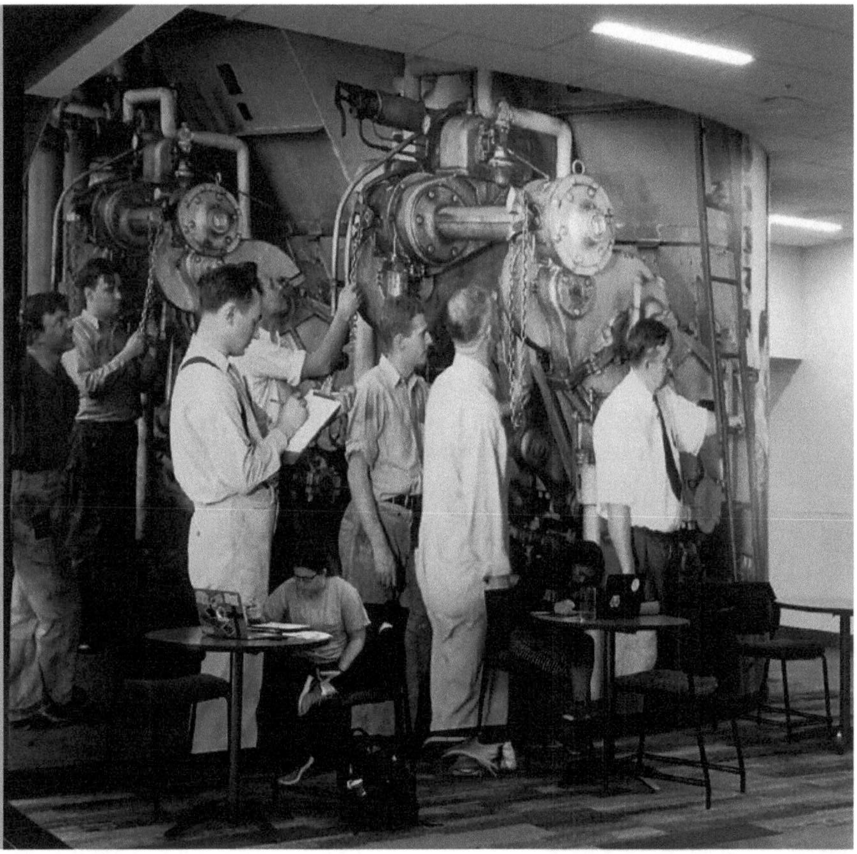

One element that resonates with older alumni is the information desk on the first floor. It is semicircular in shape, faced with bricks from the old power plant, and made to evoke the smokestack that had for so many years marked Purdue University's location.

Conclusion

A project as complicated and massive as WALC required many, many people to make it happen. No one person can be identified as making this project come to fruition; rather, it was the collaboration of individuals who have unique skills, talents, and knowledge who made this project successful.

Ultimately, it is the students and faculty who use this building daily for years to come who will decide if the work committed to this project was on target or not. The hope is that this building was designed in a manner that will allow it to be modified to meet changing needs in the future while maintaining a presence on campus that is consistent with the design ethos of Purdue, just as the old power plant provided the heat and power as well as an active learning laboratory for well over 60 years. At the heart of campus, the Wilmeth Active Learning Center is a worthy successor at this important location.

At the dedication on September 22, 2017, Purdue's president, Mitch Daniels, stated that the Wilmeth Active Learning Center was the new hub at the center of campus. He also announced that the Reading Room would be known as the Mullins Reading Room to recognize the commitment I made to make this building a reality. In December, 2017, an oil portrait commissioned by the university, was unveiled to hang in the Mullins Reading Room where it appears, I am glad to say, I look approvingly on the students diligently studying. The Wilmeth Active Learning Center represents an academic ecotone through the integration of classroom and library space that morph in function during the day—60 percent classroom and 40 percent library—and night (figure 26.14)—100 percent library—thus creating a whole stronger and more adaptive than its parts.

fig 26.14

Night time view of WALC with Bell/Clock Tower in foreground.

Permission of: Photos: Trevor Mahlmann

27

CHAPTER TWENTY-SEVEN

SERVING THE BROAD NEEDS OF COMMUNITY THROUGH A PATRON-CENTERED, PARTNERSHIP-FOCUSED, INCLUSIVE APPROACH

SARAH MEILLEUR

Calgary Public Library opened a transformational new Central Library (figure 27.1) on November 1, 2018. This project was years in the making. Need for a new Central Library was identified by the library board in the 1980s. The site was selected and confirmed by Calgary's city council in 2011, and the design of the new building, by world-renowned architects Snøhetta and Calgary firm DIALOG, was shared with the public in 2014. By the time the building opened, the entire library system had been transformed to meet the new standards that were promised by the innovative and inspirational design of the building. In the over two years since opening day, the new Central Library has seen over 2.4 million visitors and hosted thousands of programs, events, and outreach activities. It is clearly a center of community that resonates with Calgarians and visitors, as demonstrated by the citywide use of the facility in a data set released by the library in 2019.[1] This chapter will focus on three key reasons for the success of the building and the library system as a whole: the human-centered strategic vision and approach, the focus on partnership and inclusion, and the inspiring and versatile design of the building. These elements of success provide a framework to highlight examples of these principles in action and how they combined to create the impact of a library internationally recognized by *Time* magazine, the *New York Times*, and *Architectural Digest*.[2]

fig 27.1

Exterior of Central Library.

(Credit: Michael Grimm.)

Human-Centered Strategic Vision

Calgary Public Library ensures that user needs are at the forefront of decision-making through a patron-centered perspective. This foundational approach involves mapping of a customer's journey through their multiple interactions with the library space (both virtual and in person). This also includes a design thinking approach that considers the entire user experience, targets different patron personas, and significantly impacted decision-making for the new building. It was critical that there be something in this building for everyone to connect with, and this was delivered through the collection experience, through early literacy and play, through a dedicated space for quiet and reflection, through self-serve meeting rooms, and through a service on the floor model.

COLLECTION EXPERIENCE

It is common for people to think of, or remember, libraries of the past as full of high shelves, crammed with thousands of books, hard-to-see titles, and little natural light. The intention here was for a dramatically different experience. Public libraries invest millions of dollars yearly in new collections, and Calgary Public Library wanted these collections to be highlighted and celebrated in the new library, and in all library locations. Working with the architects, a decision was made to minimize the shelf height, invest in lighting in all the shelving, and include plenty of room for display shelves to highlight collections and titles. Bookstores have been merchandising their collections well for years, and the library wanted to learn from their best practices. Time was spent testing different shelving configurations at the other community libraries before the decision was made on which shelving to purchase for the new library. Library staff also worked with the shelving vendor to develop a system for the shelf lighting that would be as clean and neat as possible (figure 27.2). Additionally, the layout was designed to minimize books on the bottom shelves, when necessary having tilt stands so bottom shelf books are easier to see and retrieve. Room was left for growth in the collection, and no shelf is more than two-thirds full. Additionally, all the shelf end signage in the system was updated, ensuring a consistency in the experience across all library locations, since many patrons regularly visit multiple libraries in the city.

fig 27.2

Lighted shelving.

(Credit: Michael Grimm.)

Additional focus was paid to the collection experience in the children's area. Picture book art is beautiful, and children love it and are drawn to it, but for years libraries have shelved picture books spine out to make it more convenient for adults (library staff and parents), who were putting books away in order or looking for specific titles. A patron-first perspective, considering children first, resulted in a decision to purchase low bins and display picture books face out, with the picture book art front and center (figure 27.3). This approach transformed the children's

fig 27.3

Children's collections in face-out bins.

(Credit: Calgary Public Library.)

library because it became designed for children to choose their own titles based on the images that intrigued them. Circulation increased and children felt more independent in choosing their own reading materials. This approach was trialed and tested at community libraries, and then implemented at Central, along with all library locations.

Additionally, staff identified that they regularly spent significant time helping children and caregivers find princess books, dinosaur books, and animal books. Identifying these common requests, combined with a human-centered design approach, resulted in library staff curating books with these themes into separate bins so that children could independently find the books they liked best. This project resulted in additional work and investment on behalf of staff, including the collections department (assigning themes to the books when ordering and processing) and the support staff (knowing where to put the books away when shelving, and finding books in bins to fill holds), but the impact on patrons was immediate. With the standard picture book collection at Calgary Public Library, an average of 35 percent of it is checked out at any given time. For the picture-book-themed collections, an average of 75 percent of them are checked out at any given time. And children and caregivers appreciate the feeling that this area of the library was designed for their needs and interests.

The Local History collection was another significant collection area that was transformed in the new library building. Previously, this collection was accessible only with staff assistance, behind locked doors, in a separate room. The patron experience of this was an impression that this collection was only for serious researchers and that a good reason was required to explore. And yet this is a collection about the history and development of Calgary and Southern Alberta, and it belongs to everyone, as the most publicly accessible local history collection in the city. In the new building, this collection was freed from the confines of a locked room and highlighted in new ways. These collections are on the highest shelves in the building, and the shelf ends highlight images from photographs and postcards that are available within the digital library. It has also been reimagined as Calgary's Story, presented by Walt and Irene DeBoni (figure 27.4). It is on the fourth floor of the building and now includes the Elders' Guidance Circle and the Indigenous Languages Resource Centre to acknowledge and celebrate the tens of thousands of years of history of Indigenous peoples and the land. Open map cabinets highlight an incredible collection of historical maps, old phone books, and Henderson's directories, all accessible to everyone, and regularly changing displays highlight the breadth and depth of the collection. There is also a vintage media lab and a story studio, encompassing the Williams Harris Shared Story Studio, celebrating historical art forms and new media. This is a collection for all, and use and value of the collection has increased enormously now that it is more open and accessible. It is also a favorite stop for school-age children to learn more about the history of the place they call home.

fig 27.4

Calgary's Story collection.

(Credit: Calgary Public Library.)

EARLY LITERACY AND PLAY

Libraries have traditionally been considered places where children needed to be quiet and focused. And yet we now know that children's development is multifaceted and learning to read is a part of whole child development. With over 90,000 kids under the age of five in Calgary, the Calgary Public Library developed an early learning strategy in 2017.[3] This work resulted in piloting and testing early learning centers (figure 27.5) in multiple library locations.[4]

These included opportunities for unstructured play, including loose parts (crayons, light tables, and building blocks), imaginative elements (scarves, costumes, and puppet theatres), and baby/toddler areas for younger children with sensory elements and crawl tracks. The Central Library provided the opportunity to add active play to the list of early learning center elements. Calgary is a winter city, and there was a demand for indoor spaces for parents and caregivers to bring their babies, toddlers, and preschoolers during the winter months. Collaboration with early learning experts and architects resulted in a fully interactive early learning center, including a large-scale playhouse with a net, a climbing wall, colorful windows, and all the things that a family would require for an outing, including a nursing room, a dedicated children's washroom with a child-size toilet, a baby/toddler space within view of the larger full-body play space for preschoolers, and a café close by with coffee and snacks for parents and hungry children. The results are that the Central Library is a destination for families during all months of the year, for play, learning, programming, and books.

fig 27.5

Early learning center.
(Credit: Neil Zeller.)

QUIET AND REFLECTION

In direct contrast to the noise and busyness of the children's area is the TD Great Reading Room (figure 27.6). As Calgary Public Library experimented with early learning centers in libraries throughout the system, patrons voiced many concerns that the space for quiet and reflection, which they had always valued at the library, was disappearing. More families were coming to libraries than ever before, and some patrons were wondering where their old library was. Meeting the needs of multiple patrons in small spaces can be challenging, and it was critical that there be space at the Central Library dedicated to patrons and individuals who were looking for that quiet space. The TD Great Reading Room is the most traditional space in the library, where silence is a service and quiet and reflection are honored. It echoes traditional library reading rooms, such as the Rose Reading Room at New York Public Library and Bates Hall at Boston Public Library. The tables are made of white oak, crafted by Calgary company Mobius, and the surrounding shelves honor the history and tradition of libraries, with collection vignettes celebrating banned books, Indigenous writers, picture book illustrators, authors who have visited Calgary, and previous Calgary Public Library CEOs' favorite titles. This is a destination room in the building where students come to study, consultants come to work, and the community comes to read in a space where peace and quiet are honored and respected.

fig 27.6

TD Great Reading Room.
(Credit: Calgary Public Library.)

COMMUNITY COLLABORATION SPACE

During the significant community engagement the library conducted in 2012, free spaces to gather and meet were identified as a high priority. The new Central Library delivered with over 30 bookable spaces for the community in a variety of shapes and sizes. From a small four-person room with table and chairs, to a larger 10-person board-room-style setup, to a six-person room with more casual chairs and movable furniture, to a 50-person meeting room, to a 350+ person performance hall, the Central Library provides a wide variety of places for the community to host meetings, programs, and small groups. Additionally, some rooms are dedicated for same-day booking only, ensuring a wide variety of access for patrons. The library team also worked to ensure that access to these rooms was as self-service and seamless as possible, with an advance online booking system integrated with patron library card numbers that also facilitates self-serve access to the locked rooms and is supported by a digital kiosk at the entrance where patrons can find the meeting they were invited to and their meeting room. This self-serve booking system was tested and trialed at other community libraries, and as locations continue to be renovated, more small meeting rooms are being added at locations throughout the city, based on the significant use and demand for them at Central. Analysis of the booking and use of these rooms at Central after a year revealed that patrons from across the city booked these spaces, showcasing the use of the Central Library by the entire community.[5]

SERVICE ON THE FLOOR

With such a large building and so many different areas to explore, it was important to have a flexible staffing model, ensuring that staff could work collaboratively to effectively meet patrons' needs in all the different areas of this 240,000-square-foot building. First, it was important that patrons could find staff, and so a staff identifier team was initiated to test, trial, and make recommendations on what would be most effective. A bright blue vest was the top choice because it included different options for sizes and shapes, had large pockets, was easily washable, and looked good on everyone (figure 27.7). These bright blue vests were enormously successful because patrons could identify staff from across the large floors and seek out assistance. They were so successful, in fact, that in 2020 they were expanded system-wide for all Calgary Public Library public service staff at all locations. In addition to the staff identifiers, connection points (figure 27.8) were developed (to replace traditional service desks), where patrons could search titles on their own and also request help from staff. To make this effective, mobile technology was key. Staff were issued smartphones that allowed them to receive notifications of patrons requesting help at specific points, to connect with one another to redeploy staff from quieter areas of the building to busier ones, and to ensure building-wide communication in a variety of instances including security issues, the finding of lost children, and evacuations. This flexible and responsive staffing model has created an environment where staff are able to help patrons wherever they are and collaborate and connect when necessary.

fig 27.7

Staff identifiers.

(Credit: Neil Zeller.)

fig 27.8

Connection point.

(Credit: Calgary Public Library.)

These patron-centered services that have been highlighted are key to the success of the building, and why patrons return again and again to the Central Library. The library listened to patrons, identified target audiences and individual needs, and spent dedicated time observing, trialing, and testing in smaller locations to learn and guide decision-making at the Central Library. These broad concepts and the detailed approach to each aspect of the visitor experience (and the willingness to continue to learn and adapt) are foundational to the success of this new building.

Focus on Partnership and Inclusion

Collaboration is a core value of Calgary Public Library,[6] and one of the foundational approaches to the programming and outreach for the new Central Library and the system itself is a focus on partnership. Reach and inclusion can be expanded by working with organizations that have expertise in diverse fields, ensuring that the library is meeting a wide variety of community needs and is relevant in the lives of more members of the community. Areas such as career guidance, truth and reconciliation, and mental health support are demonstrated community needs, and it is through partnership that the library can best support the community with these needs.

CAREER GUIDANCE

Job Desk, offered in partnership with Bow Valley College, is a regular in-person program where patrons drop in to a dedicated space in the Central Library and receive help with their résumé, career advice, and interview support from experienced career practitioners. This is a demonstrated need in Calgary and Alberta that has been exacerbated by the COVID-19 pandemic and the related increase in unemployment numbers. This program quickly transitioned online during the pandemic to ensure these critical supports were available to the community for free through their library.

LIFELONG LEARNING

The public library offers the opportunity to connect with a wide audience, and one of the most successful and popular programs is the Think Big series events in partnership with the Hotchkiss Brain Institute and the University of Calgary. During Think Big programs, local university researchers highlight current topics of interest and local research that is paving the way for new discoveries. This partnership creates a higher profile for the university and makes research and science more accessible to the general community. A recent Think Big program focused on loneliness in the time of COVID-19.

TRUTH AND RECONCILIATION

The Indigenous Languages Resource Centre, the Elders' Guidance Circle (figure 27.9), and Indigenous Placemaking are critical components of the library's commitment to Truth and Reconciliation.[7] These spaces and programs offer opportunities for Indigenous and non-Indigenous community members to connect one-on-one with Elders, participate in Indigenous language classes, and learn about traditional ways of knowing and Indigenous history. The work toward Truth and Reconciliation is a key pillar of the library's strategic plan,[8] and it is work that must be done in collaboration with Indigenous communities. The library's Elders' Guidance Circle helps to shape the library's direction in this work and guide the library's approach. Indigenous placemaking, at the Central Library and other libraries throughout the system, offers opportunities for Indigenous people to see themselves and their stories and history in the library and allows non-Indigenous people to learn and gain appreciation and understanding of this rich history, culture, and perspectives.

fig 27.9

Elders' Guidance Circle.

(Credit: Calgary Public Library.)

COMMUNITY WELLNESS DESK

In response to the increasing mental health and addiction needs in the community from the impacts of the COVID-19 pandemic, Calgary Public Library, in partnership with Woods Homes, launched the Community Wellness Desk in fall 2020. Social workers were available on a drop-in basis at the Central Library for one-on-one consultations with individuals. This involved crisis response, library staff training, and referral and connection for patrons to ongoing mental health support.

These examples illustrate the many ways in which partnership allows the library to better respond to community needs, expand reach, and highlight resources and organizations for the betterment of the community as a whole.

Inspiring and Versatile Space Design

Calgary's Central Library, designed by Snøhetta and DIALOG, is an architectural marvel, highlighted by *Architectural Digest* as one of the world's most futuristic libraries.[9] The use of natural materials, biophilic design, and natural light is complemented with strong functionality and future-thinking features, such as raised flooring and open flexible spaces that allow for a broad variety of uses both now and in the future. This inspiring design is a significant part of what draws the community to the library because this public building, open to everyone, makes each individual who walks through the doors feel that they matter, and that they deserve beauty, dignity, and light.

BUILDING DESIGN FEATURES

There are four key building features that combine to create an experience of the building that amazes and inspires visitors: the archway, the oculus, the prow, and the curtain wall.

Visitors arrive at the building and enter under an archway, framed by a wood soffit of sustainably sourced western red cedar (figure 27.10). The form echoes a Chinook arch, a uniquely Calgary phenomenon when warm winds from the mountains signal a forthcoming increase in temperature, with clouds forming an archway in the western sky. Calgarians look to the west for breaks in the long winter months because Chinook winds mean melting snow and brief patio openings. This archway also connects the newly developing East Village to the downtown as a pedestrian thoroughfare.

fig 27.10

Welcome archway.
(Credit: Rob McMorris.)

The oculus stops visitors in their tracks when they enter the front doors. It is a central skylight that brings Calgary's famously sunny skies and natural light into all areas of the building (figure 27.11). Diffusing cloth panels soften the light and create beautiful shadows on the exquisite wood millwork surrounding the oculus. Patrons who spend the day experience the building in many different moods as the light shifts and new patterns emerge and the unexpected is highlighted by a sunbeam. In the winter, snowdrifts gather along the oculus and then slide off, revealing the sky. The oculus adds an element of beauty and playfulness to the building, bringing illumination to the numerous activities taking place inside.

fig 27.11

Shaikh Family Welcome Gallery and Oculus Skylight.
(Credit: Calgary Public Library.)

The prow (figure 27.12) is a destination in the building on all levels. It juts out over the mouth of the tunnel that encases the light rail transit (LRT) line, reaching out toward the river. Visitors gather on level 1M to watch the train enter or emerge from the tunnel below, and often meet at the Simmons Harvie Community Living Room on the fourth floor to enjoy the great city views.

fig 27.12

Simmons Harvie Community Living Room and Prow.

(Credit: Michael Grimm.)

The curtain wall for the Central Library is now an iconic image in Calgary. The geometric design is part of what makes the building so unique and inspired the library's rebranding and logo. The unique panels were manufactured by Ferguson Corporation, a Calgary-based company, and they have clear, glazed, or fritted finishes and support the LEED Gold designation of the building. They also create moments of surprise and delight through the Calgary Public Library Foundation Windows of Opportunity campaign, where the community could invest in the library and have chosen quotes or names added to the window mullions. The quotes do not interfere with the experience of the building and the design itself, but as the changing light hits, they offer moments of inspiration and delight, and sometimes levity.

These four key design features play a significant role in the community's experience of the Central Library and help to create an environment where visitors feel as though anything is possible.

BUILDING FUNCTIONALITY AND ACCESSIBILITY

A building must be functional as well as beautiful to truly achieve its potential. And a core tenet of functionality, particularly for a public space, is to be truly accessible. Public libraries are places for everyone in the community, and Calgary Public Library works hard to live up to that promise. Inclusion is both a core value and a strategic priority in Calgary Public Library's most recent strategic plan.[10] In order to deliver on this approach, the new Central Library was designed with accessibility as a priority. There were some site considerations that made accessibility more challenging, and a focus on overcoming these, and on both meeting and exceeding guidelines of the time (specifically the 2010 *Universal Design Handbook* and the 2008 Alberta *Barrier-Free Design Guide*), was foundational. The Central Library is built over the top of an LRT line and tunnel, which meant that the main entrance would be 17 feet above grade, necessitating a sloped walkway on the west side and an elevator on the east side. Additional accessibility features include tactile buttons in the floor and on handrails to indicate elevation changes; both gendered and everyone washrooms that meet Alberta building code standards; sloped interior walkways that connect levels 1 and 2; and glazing on the fourth floor railings toward the oculus and Shaikh Family Welcome Gallery, ensuring equitable views for everyone.

And yet, after the opening weekend with over 50,000 visitors in four days, there was criticism from the community regarding accessibility challenges. This criticism was seen by the library, the architects and designers, the project managers, and the construction team as an opportunity to listen and make improvements so this building could be even more accessible. Examples of improvements implemented since opening include the addition of intercom access at grade on the west side of the building; manual instead of "wave hand" auto operators for exterior doors; additional auto operators in various locations throughout the building, including on select single-stall washrooms and meeting rooms; and the addition of multiple self-checkout stations that are adjustable to accommodate a wide variety of heights and mobility devices. These learnings were also applied on a system-wide level, with the library completing an accessibility audit of the remaining 20 library locations in 2019 and identifying improvements that were completed throughout 2020 and continue to impact library renovations and future designs. This approach, and the subsequent improvements system-wide, enhanced the accessibility of the building and other community libraries to such a degree that, in fall 2020, the Central Library received a city of Calgary, Calgary Award, for Accessible Building Design.[11]

PROGRAMMING VERSATILITY

This is the people's library, and its success is driven by partnerships and community groups that have used the versatility of the form to bring their ideas to life. The open and welcoming design of the building made this possible, with raised flooring (power and data access basically anywhere you want it), a large welcome gallery and feature staircase, an incredible performance hall (figure 27.13), and highlighted by amazing public art. Some examples of events hosted by the library, in partnership with community groups and organizations, include the following:

- New Year's Eve 2018–2019 family celebrations, in partnership with the City of Calgary, featuring a family New Year's countdown by the mayor at 9:00 p.m., a children's dance party, live theater and performers, crafts and activities on all levels of the building, and over 7,000 visitors in three hours.

fig 27.13

Patricia A. Whelan Performance Hall.

(Credit. Calgary Public Library.)

- Canada Day 2019, in partnership with the City of Calgary, Calgary Municipal Land Corporation, Tourism Calgary, Fort Calgary, National Music Centre, and many other organizations, featuring performers, Indigenous drumming, crafts and activities, and over 10,000 visitors in five hours.
- Orange Shirt Day 2019, in partnership with the Society for Safe and Caring Schools, featuring Orange Shirt Day creator Phyllis Webstad, including thousands of students and community members and a building-wide round dance.
- Swearing-in ceremony for Calgary's new police chief, the first time a ceremony for this very public office has been held in a public building with the public welcome to attend, and including horses and a pipe band.
- Yoga at the Library on Sunday mornings, before the library opens to the public, in the Shaikh Family Welcome Gallery, below the oculus.
- Swingin' Sundays at the Central Library, where a local swing dance band comes to play, and professional dancers give swing dance lessons to whoever wants to join in.

Programs in partnership with the community ensure that the library is a place where visitors are continually surprised and delighted by what they encounter. These exceptional experiences result in repeat visits and increased interaction with the library, and future programming and ideas are inspired by what visitors encounter. When the community begins coming to the library, with ideas for programs and events that they want to host in the library space, that speaks volumes about the relevancy of the library to the community it serves.

COVID-19 SERVICE MODEL

The COVID-19 pandemic has challenged the world to rethink old paradigms and building design to support a safe community. The open and expansive Central Library has been well positioned to adapt to new service models that allow for physical distancing in new ways.

The most highly concentrated area for patrons and staff was in the CNOOC/Nexen Digital Commons, where most of the library's hard-wired computers were located. During the initial closure of libraries beginning in March 2020, the open and flexible space (and the raised flooring), allowed the library to distribute 40 computers and cubicles throughout the third floor, creating physical distancing for reopening.

Additionally, the multitude of seating areas, often separated by shelving and well spaced already, allowed the library to provide study space when reopened for many community members who were working remotely or studying online. The small meeting rooms were also sought after by community members seeking a space to participate in virtual meetings and interviews.

As the world continues to grapple with the impacts of the pandemic, as of the writing of this in mid-2021, libraries are continuing to change and adapt their building designs to create safe and welcoming spaces. Some of these impacts are anticipated to be long-term, including the following:

- The use and importance of outdoor spaces, in both temperate and non-temperate (like Calgary's) climates. Throughout the pandemic, outdoor spaces and activities have been determined to be much safer than indoor spaces. Libraries have often devoted more attention to the design of the inside of their buildings than to the outside, and this is anticipated to shift in the future, with the exterior of libraries becoming a more important component in library design.
- Individualized study space and meeting rooms are likely to become more and more important, as the virtual world continues, to provide space for virtual job interviews, meetings, and as spaces away from home as more people work remotely. We are hardwired as humans to want to be around other people, and the public library, with individual meeting rooms, allows people to be around other people while physically distanced and apart at the same time.
- Flexibility and versatility will be more critical than ever. This has always been the case with libraries because they are built to last for the long term. Finding ways to make adaptations easier in the future will

help ensure a building stands the test of time. Raised-access flooring, demountable partitions, and open spaces are all things that will allow libraries to continue to change and adapt for future services.

Moving Forward

At this time, libraries, and public libraries in particular, are more essential than ever for the community. As the COVID-19 pandemic creates greater divides among society, the library remains an equalizer. The human-centered, partnership-driven, and inclusive approach Calgary Public Library took when designing the new Central Library and that inspired the library's latest strategic plan (Calgary Public Library, "Potentials Realized"), has continued to drive further innovation and change to meet community needs. The library has continued to use this foundational approach when adapting programs, services, and library design in response to the pandemic, and the community continues to be engaged, connected, and inspired by the library to reach their potential.

Notes

1. Darren Krause, "'It's Meant for the Whole City'—New Central Library Data Shows Widespread Patron Use," LiveWire Calgary, December 20, 2019, https://livewirecalgary.com/2019/12/20/its-meant-for-the-whole-city-new-central-library-data-shows-widespread-patron-use/.
2. Wilder Davies, "Central Library, Calgary, Canada," in "World's Greatest Places 2019," *Time*, 2019, https://time.com/collection/worlds-greatest-places-2019/5654128/central-library-calgary-canada/; Elaine Glusac, "No. 20, Calgary, Canada," in "52 Places to Go in 2019," *New York Times*, 2019, https://www.nytimes.com/interactive/2019/travel/places-to-visit.html; Nick Mafi, "2/12: Calgary Library, by Snøhetta (Calgary, Canada)," in "The 12 Most Anticipated Buildings of 2018," *Architectural Digest*, 2017, https://www.architecturaldigest.com/gallery/most-anticipated-buildings-of-2018.
3. Calgary Public Library, *Early Learning Strategy* (Calgary, AB: Calgary Public Library, 2017), https://calgarylibrary.ca/assets/PDFs/2019/Early-Learning-Strategy.pdf.
4. Calgary Public Library, *Early Learning Centres at the Calgary Public Library* (Calgary, AB: Calgary Public Library, 2018), https://calgarylibrary.ca/assets/PDFs/2019/2018-Early-Learning-Centres-Report.pdf.
5. Krause, "It's Meant for the Whole City."
6. Calgary Public Library, "Potentials Realized: Calgary Public Library Strategic Plan 2019–2022," accessed January 14, 2021, https://calgarylibrary.ca/assets/PDFs/2020/2019-2022-strategic-plan-2020-initatives.pdf.
7. Calgary Public Library, "Indigenous Services," accessed January 14, 2021, https://calgarylibrary.ca/connect/indigenous-services/.
8. Calgary Public Library, "Potentials Realized."
9. Julia Eskins and Karen Burshtein, "Step Inside the World's 9 Most Futuristic Libraries," *Architectural Digest*, December 5, 2018, https://www.architecturaldigest.com/story/futuristic-libraries.
10. Calgary Public Library, "Potentials Realized."
11. City of Calgary, "2019 Calgary Award Recipients," 2019, accessed January 14, 2021, https://www.calgary.ca/ca/city-clerks/citizen-recognition-protocol/calgary-awards/2019-awards-recipients-bios.html (page discontinued).

28

CHAPTER TWENTY-EIGHT

A 21ST-CENTURY PROGRAM FOR THE LIBRARY

Serving the Broad Needs of the Community

SOHAIR F. WASTAWY

Qatar National Library, the world's newest national library, formally opened its doors in April 2018. During its grand opening celebration, the Dutch architect and the library designer Rem Koolhaas spoke of his craft, stating that "architecture very often attracts negative qualifications, it is incomprehensible, alien, intimidating, unnecessary, wasteful, commercial and of course the most common complaint—UGLY." Koolhaas went on to describe what architecture can really do, from "solving problems to creating a sense of community where none existed before, to being capable of embracing us, the moment, the world in spite of all its painful dysfunctionalities." He said that he hoped that his design "offers a new public space to the city, to welcome all and inspire all who enter."

Qatar is a country with an extremely diverse community, a wide range of literacy levels, and limited experience with libraries that necessitated an innovative approach to serve everyone. Qatar also lacked public libraries and places where the community of natives (350,000) and expats (2 million) can work and learn together. Designing library activities requires understanding not only community needs but also the physical environment that can affect the patronage of the members of the community. The long summer season with temperatures that often reach 50°C (122°F) necessitated the building of programs that motivate individuals to venture outside their homes in the summer months. Therefore, understanding the value of a community space as part of society's social infrastructure, as expressed in Eric Klinenberg's book *Palaces for the People*, becomes very important. Social infrastructure, as defined by Klinenberg, is "the physical places and organizations that shape the way people interact."[1]

For decades, shopping malls and coffee shops were the customary gathering places; however, these meeting places were divided along socioeconomic and nationality lines. In such an environment, the library set out to redefine what a public space is and worked to bring the best possible building features to attract the public and offer programs of value where the community feels a sense of ownership.

The library was in an unparalleled position to experiment with the function of the modern library, and from its very outset had the opportunity to create a community space and reinforce the relevance of libraries in today's society. Echoing Klinenberg, it had the opportunity to create a community space and reinforce the relevance of libraries in the digital age and the 21st century. Here, it is worth mentioning that the library came into being as part of the evolution of the Qatar Foundation, which was established in 1995 by the Emir of Qatar and his wife, Her Highness Sheikha Moza bint Nasser, who chairs the foundation and has been the driving force in creating Qatar's most advanced educational, scientific, and cultural institutions. The foundation established Education City, which as indicated by its name, includes educational institutions such as six branches of American universities, a Qatari university, and French and British colleges. Education City has grown to include basic education of all grades, a science and technology park, research facilities, a football stadium, a golf course, and cultural heritage institutions that include museums, galleries, and an equine center; all in all, 50 institutions within this Education City.

In 2011, Sheikha Moza sought to build a central library that can serve all the educational institutions within Education City, although each institution had its own library. She commissioned Rem Koolhaas, who was then building the foundation's headquarters. While Koolhaas went to work on a central academic/research library, Her Highness realized that the other institutions within Education City would also need a library and decided to modify the concept to include the public library portion. Shortly after, the drawings were modified for a third time to add the national library component. A tour of mixed-function libraries in Europe confirmed to her that the new paradigm of libraries is no longer about collections but rather about services to the community and the creation of a platform for all types of learning no matter what station in life the learners are.

The addition of national functions has led the library to be recognized by the state as a national entity and an Amiri decree (number 11 for 2018) was issued to declare the library's status, function, and governing structure. A spin-off from Qatar Foundation is currently underway.

Before we speak of what a modern library is, it's important to remind readers that the evolution of libraries began with their early adoption of information technology and the explosion of the web. Over the past 30 years, libraries began to fundamentally alter the way they offer services and the manner in which their buildings are used. This evolution showed considerably first on the public libraries front, followed by academic libraries, but hardly moved the needle for national libraries.

While altering old buildings remains challenging and costly, new buildings have better chances of articulating the profound transformation of libraries from the quite well-stocked places to the living room of the community to becoming the place where people come together to learn, be entertained, and enjoy each other.

Informed by the four-space model developed in 2012 by Jochumsen, Hvenegaard Rasmussen, and Skot-Hansen[2] many new libraries in Europe were built using the model's four distinct spaces (inspiration, meeting, learning, and performance) as important values for the modern library. The award-winning structures, such as Aarhus and Birmingham public libraries, coupled with their innovative services, enabled libraries to shift from focusing on transactional services to relational services in order to create more value for the users.

The Building

Qatar National Library was built as a tri-mission cultural institution. Its 45,000-square-meter (484,375-square-foot) building allows the space needed for a national collection, a public library, and a special library where the rare books collection is stored and exhibited. The building offers an array of spaces that allow quiet contemplation, active learning, performance, and inspiration.

Its design resembles two pieces of paper that are pulled apart and folded diagonally at the corners to create a shell-like structure, enclosing the open-plan interior (figure 28.1). Its low, slanting perspective and pale ochres blend into the terrain. The rippled glazing of the facade gives the space a lightness that is reflected in the white marble interior, and the glossy white origami-like ceiling amplifies the abundant natural light coming through the huge diamond-shaped glass walls made of self-supporting undulating glass panels. The clear light and open space blend seamlessly into the desert landscape beyond. Light is used as a design element as a metaphor for knowledge distinct from the darkness of ignorance.

fig 28.1

Qatar National Library, building exterior.

(Credit: Shadi Ghonim, courtesy of Qatar National Library, 2021.)

From the moment visitors enter the library, everything it has to offer opens before them (figure 28.2). The space is conceived as a single room; the books rise in graceful terraces, interspersed throughout with areas for studying, socializing, or curling up with a good book.

While the open platform design emphasizes librarianship values of openness, democracy, and equal access, it takes into consideration the distinct style of Qatar's natural environment and thus facilitates the emergence of a new architectural identity rooted in Qatari's historical adaptation to the austereness of its surroundings. It also observes the need for privacy, a key concern of Qatar's traditional architecture.

fig 28.2

Qatar National Library, Main Hall.

(Credit: Shadi Ghonim, courtesy of Qatar National Library, 2021.)

Other features, such as the prominent staircases and access ramps that traverse the tiers of shelving and their gradual elevation, add visual metaphor for the ascent to knowledge.

At the library's center sits the Heritage Library (figures 28.3 and 28.4), a six-meter-deep excavation that's reminiscent of an archaeological dig. It's faced with an earthy travertine, the color of the Qatari desert, suggesting the layers of history, the sediments of the nation's memory. Within this deep space, the display of rare books, manuscripts, and priceless artifacts evokes an atmosphere of the sacred vault. A blend of classical materials, such as marble for the Heritage Library, and modern materials, such as stainless steel for the general collection area, combine to emphasize the progression of knowledge from the past to the present.

fig 28.3

Qatar National Library, Heritage Library, aerial view.

(Credit: Shadi Ghonim, courtesy of Qatar National Library, 2021.)

fig 28.4

Qatar National Library, Heritage Library.

(Credit: Shadi Ghonim, courtesy of Qatar National Library, 2021.)

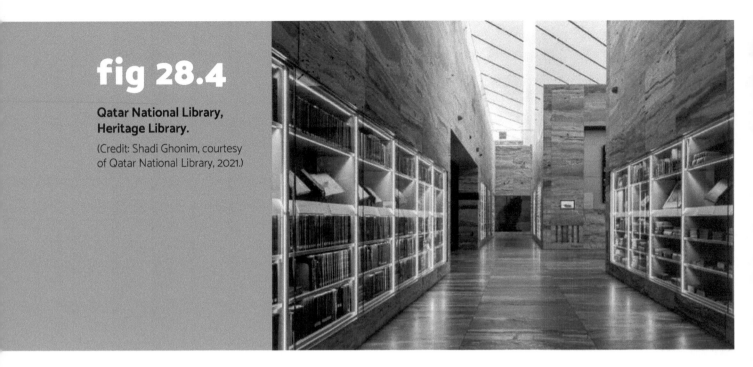

Crossing the open space high above is a single-span bridge, connecting the library's main book tiers and giving users a variety of routes around the building. The bridge is also a meeting space, with media and study rooms, reading tables, exhibition displays, a circular conference table, and a large multipurpose auditorium that is enclosed by a retractable curtain.

Toward the back of the space is the Children's Library, fitted with child-sized furniture in brightly colored modular spaces where reading, craftwork, and creative play happen. Toddlers have a soft-floor play area and a room to sit with guardians for story time and other activities.

The theater, which seats up to 400 and hosts concerts, lectures, panel discussions, and other events, is located on the perimeter of the library center. On the second floor, there is an auditorium with a 100-person capacity ideal for conference sessions, book clubs, interactive workshops, and presentations. The group study rooms hold up to eight people, and there are also 20 individual reading carrels. All of these spaces are freely available to the public and adaptable to community needs. This flexibility allows over 100 public events and activities every month. Individual reading carrels are used for research and writing, group study rooms and tables throughout the building foster collective learning, while the restaurant and café integrate social and study space.

Outside, a sunken patio provides light to the staff office space in the basement. The marble that is used to face the interior of the library is sourced in the Middle East, and the plantings in the sunken patio and the surrounding landscape have been designed to withstand the extreme heat and dry desert environment. The fountain—a cooling and traditional feature of the Islamic garden—that greets visitors outside the main entrance constantly recycles its water.

Technology

Technology has been intrinsically incorporated into the library space from the start. The library's book return system is built into the shelves themselves, and the assistive technology area is furnished with equipment and specialized software to enhance users' experience. Space has been reallocated to create the Digitization Centre and a cutting-edge, world-class Preservation and Conservation Centre. The Preservation and Conservation lab serves Qatar as well as all countries across the Middle East.

Other features include the self-checkout and return stations, media stations, and the people-mover system that transports users throughout the shelving tiers, making the collection easily accessible for all.

As users enter the library, two media walls by the main entrance welcome them, direct them to services, engage them in information games, and tell them about the day's events and activities.

There are more than 450 public computers throughout the building, and tablets in the shelving tiers help users find books as they browse the shelves. The Children's and Young Adults' Library also has dedicated digital resources such as tablets and educational software aimed at their respective target age groups to encourage learning in fun ways.

The library offers through its public workstations free access to thousands of digital resources for leisure, learning, and research, including e-books, academic journals, audiobooks, periodicals, and streaming video and music. Members can log in from anywhere to access these databases. Three computer labs for hands-on workshops and a comprehensive program of information literacy for all skill levels are available.

The Qatar Digital Library, another example of innovative programming, is offered as a free online platform for accessing digital heritage—visited by more than 1.2 million users a year, generating more than 10 million pages views. The Digitization Lab (figure 28.5) uses state-of-the-art technology to digitize materials from the Heritage Library and from Qatari government institutions, private citizens, and museums, increasing digital Arabic content by 4 million pages per year.

fig 28.5

Qatar National Library, Digitization Lab.

(Credit: Shadi Ghonim, courtesy of Qatar National Library, 2021.)

Building Pitfalls

Architects often create beautiful concepts and designs; however, some of their ideas may not be all that practical or accommodating to users' needs. As a result, it's absolutely critical that librarians and users be part of the design conversation. In general, there is no such thing as a perfect building. Somehow, there will be problems, such as a shortage of offices, let alone offices with windows, quiet places, and processing rooms. Libraries can live with some deficiencies, but most importantly, no building can achieve its full potential without the programmatic elements that enable the design to live up to and fulfill its purpose.

The opportunity to structurally correct a building is not often possible, but deliberate program planning can overcome some issues. A case in point at the Qatar National Library was the location of the Children's Library (figure 28.6), where children and their families have to cut across the building to reach that area. This was a situation that could not be resolved after the structure was completed. Some measures taken to improve the children's space included using other spaces for workshops, moving out staff offices to create a new space for toddlers, programing events outdoors when the weather allowed, and introducing the children to the Heritage Library through a special program. Reallocating space at a late stage was an intensive and expensive activity but necessary to create needed labs such as the digitization lab, the interactive learning spaces, and a secure reading room to serve the Heritage Library, which was built without one. These challenges required additional spending and delay of library operations with respect to these areas. On a different front, some of the built-in technology became dated right before the building opened.

fig 28.6

The Children's Library.

(Credit: Shadi Ghonim, courtesy of Qatar National Library, 2021.)

The modifications performed required the use of some of the spaces that were slated for general classroom use in order to create a reading room for the Heritage Library and a lab for assistive technology. Four study rooms were converted to studios to create interactive learning/maker space: a music room, a 3D printing lab, a photography studio, and a computer studio where design and editing software can be used.

How Programs Treated Cultural Norms and a New Paradigm

The combination of beautiful architecture with functional public space and effective programming can create the most comfortable places in a city, places that express richness and tradition and act as a setting for life to happen.

As mentioned earlier, some of the technology included large media walls. These walls aged in their novelty faster than expected. A series of 11 tall double-sided screens in the library's large open space were installed into the floor to display directional and general library information. With all such information available on the website and media walls, those screens were repurposed to create digital exhibitions that present relevant subjects and showcase the heritage collections (figure 28.7). The digital exhibition has created a great impact, and lectures and activities were built around these exhibits to add value and experiences for the users.

fig 28.7

Media walls/digital exhibition.
(Credit: Shadi Ghonim, courtesy of Qatar National Library, 2021.)

Programs

The challenge of building a library in a country where active libraries did not exist and where locals have the highest income per capita worldwide, and thus the ability to buy books and computing power in abundance, required a great deal of experimentation with programs. Added to this difficulty, no statistics about reading and information-seeking habits existed for the country. Introducing a new paradigm of a library where you can do academic research, use special collections, and find a sewing machine in the next room for a craft project required different kinds of conversations, assumptions, and risk-taking, as the traditional role of the library was all that was expected, as user surveys showed.

The library took a bold approach in creating activities and programs that cross the boundaries of education and socioeconomics. Programs addressed local culture, celebrated the diversity of the society, and changed the stereotype of the quiet reading place of the past. Regular concerts were held, school competitions were invited, exhibitions were mounted where library materials were presented next to objects privately owned by people from the community, and a focus highlighted programs for young adults and children (figure 28.8) as the generation that would grow with this cultural institution in their midst.

fig 28.8

Toddlers' reading program.
(Credit: Shadi Ghonim, courtesy of Qatar National Library, 2021.)

Many of the activities at the Children's and Young Adults' Library were designed to develop the habit of reading and to encourage learning through making. The library presented itself to each group as a place to pursue their dreams and aspirations.

It's vital that all users be able to access the resources equally, and as a result, the assistive technologies space offered for the first time in Qatar the tools for people with disabilities, supplementing the collection of Braille and large-print books in the case of the visually impaired. This was the first time any of these individuals had stepped into a library, and they never stopped coming. The Book Club for the Blind, which added the dimension of social interaction, such an enjoyable aspect of reading and learning, was well received and encouraged the users to establish new group activities.

Qatar has existed for a thousand years; it has become an independent country only in the past 50. Its citizens are diverse and cosmopolitan, and the library aimed to foster an understanding of the region's history and a sense of shared cultural identity. The Heritage Library fulfills this function through its offering of exhibitions, temporary displays, and outreach into local colleges and schools.

The four Innovation Stations (makerspace) had particular appeal to enterprising young creatives, and the library hosted workshops to introduce a range of technology tools. Musical instruments and recording equipment, 3D printers, electronics training kits, video, photography, and virtual reality hardware and software enabled them to create whatever they can imagine. It's important to mention that all the furniture is modular, and users were able to configure the spaces as they needed.

The library has set out to be as innovative in the digital sphere as it is in the physical. It began its digital exhibition with a data visualization display called "Information Is Beautiful" by data journalist David McCandless (https://informationisbeautiful.net).

Visitors' experience was guided by interactive maps, games, virtual postcards, and 3D object simulations.

In its role as a national library, the library is acting as a steward of Qatar's national heritage through collecting, preserving, and making available the country's recorded history. As a research library, it aims to foster and promote greater global insight into the history and culture of the Gulf region.

The library provides equal access for all Qatari residents to an environment that supports creativity, independent decision-making, and cultural development. As a new paradigm, the national library is one of the few that is a lending library with a Children's and Young Adults' Library incorporated into its function.

Before conducting user service evaluation, signs of success were apparent in the gate count and the heavy borrowing of both print and digital downloads of books and book chapters. The same high usage could be seen in statistics for program attendance in the library's first two years of existence.

fig 28.9

Qatar National Library, theater, Science Book Forum.

(Credit: Shadi Ghonim, courtesy of Qatar National Library, 2021.)

One of the programs that was geared to address the lack of good science education for Arab young adults, a Science Book Forum (figure 28.9), was established where science readings are the foundation of discussions with scientists all over the world about key topics.

The central performance space has given the library the opportunity to cooperate with other organizations, such as the Qatar Philharmonic Orchestra, the poetry club, and a playhouse, to cement agreement for a monthly performance that added a great deal to the sound and feel of the library. It was amazing to witness the sound of music filling the library while students and researchers carry out their work hundreds of meters away in the traditional and quiet study areas.

The library also embraced and encouraged talents through teaching and hosting experts to conduct workshops on a variety of topics, and performances meant to introduce the arts of the various international communities brought to the premises artists of Filipino, Indian, Syrian, and European origin in addition to many local artists.

Similarly, hosting international fairs, such as the Jaipur literature festival, and national competitions on robotics, chess, writing, and a great deal more has brought members of the community from all walks of life to the institution. The range of activities has the community encouraged, and their suggestions have presented new opportunities of engagement as well as protocol agreements with different organizations and ministries to help with the activities and funding. A proactive attempt has been made to open up all of these spaces to the public and utilize the public's ideas. The library continues to design its programs (100+/month) around the way the users want to use the building and its services.

Conclusion

With a rich history, early adaptation of technology, and undeniable value to society, libraries have been a cornerstone of many democratic and learned societies. It is therefore incumbent on national libraries and their parent organizations to rethink their roles and open up their buildings and collections to offer more services to the public. Indeed, one can easily say that the richness of national libraries is often underutilized and often limited to researchers, who are, by many measures, the smallest segment of the population. Sadly, many public libraries struggle with funding, and hundreds have closed their doors in developed and underdeveloped countries around the world.

National libraries are in a position to reimagine and advance their missions by serving the public on a much larger scale. Today, in addition to Qatar's National Library, examples of new national library buildings that include public access can be found around the globe in countries such as South Korea, China, and Singapore, with others in planning, for example in Canada.

Notes

1. Eric Klinenberg, *Palaces for the People: How Social Infrastructure Can Help Fight Inequality, Polarization, and the Decline of Civic Life* (New York: Crown, 2018), 5.
2. Henrik Jochumsen, Casper Hvenegaard Rasmussen, and Dorte Skot-Hansen, "The Four Spaces—A New Model for the Public Library," *New Library World* 113, no. 11/12 (2012): 586-597.

VIII

SECTION VIII

LOOKING AHEAD

TOM HICKERSON

JOAN K. LIPPINCOTT

LEONORA CREMA

Coeditors

As editors, we are inspired by the breadth of knowledge, depth of expertise, inspirational stories, and passion for libraries expressed by our authors. They have provided us all with principles for designing libraries, creative ideas for spaces and programs, and explorations of their institution's journey in developing new library spaces.

Their chapters chronicle a pivotal period in the evolution of academic libraries. For centuries, the library collection and the building in which it was housed were synonymous—bookstacks ordered in rows encircled by seats for individual readers, form following function. But around the turn of the century, with the introduction of new technologies and commons-like spaces for students and an array of campus partners, libraries transformed. This next generation of libraries evolved into dynamic social spaces and integrated service hubs where people do not just *go to find*, but *collaborate to create* knowledge: using new technology and productivity tools; taking part in classes and programs; gaining insights and skills to advance in research, learning, and career pursuits; and still with space for private reflection and assistance when it is needed. Open by design, these new libraries synergize their staff expertise in collaboration with student services, instructional designers, writing centers, research investigators, technologists, alumni offices, cultural organizations, and others. They act outwardly to build capacity across the campus and to engage with the diverse local and global communities that are increasingly vital to the academic mission. Libraries are now experiencing a moment of bold reinvention in which the full potential of their spaces is being revealed and the impact of these new capabilities is being realized.

In this, libraries are proving themselves outstanding assets for their institutions. At a time when colleges and universities will see parts of their mandate grow and others recede, the contemporary library is built to ease these transitions with flexibility at its core. For students, libraries are not only a welcoming home base but also experiential learning settings that equip them for academic and career success. For faculty, libraries provide spaces featuring powerful analytic, curatorial, and technical capacities supporting all parts of the research life cycle and catalyzing connections among disciplines. Like their institutions, libraries are dedicated to the public good, ensuring broad dissemination of knowledge and creating spaces for societal engagement in the life of the academy. And though the pandemic has accelerated the digital shift in many areas—libraries included, with their digital services driven to the foreground—it has also exposed a vast digital divide and, with it, libraries redoubling efforts as access enablers and equalizers.

Our recent collective experience of the pandemic has starkly reminded us that we are innately social creatures who depend on places of human connection for our health, happiness, resilience, and progress. And it is this that recommits us to libraries as an essential part of the academic and social fabric. The need for the physical facility, and with it a holistic suite of technology, programs, content, and expertise, will continue to be at the heart of planning for libraries in the future. We are grateful to our authors for sharing their experiences as signposts to that future.

As we turn to the next decades of this century, libraries are looking ahead to new space imperatives that include

- responding to social inequities by removing barriers to access, inclusion, and diverse representation in their collections, services, and built environments;
- developing spaces and programs that enable student success and a sense of belonging for all;
- being a locus for high-tech facilities and expertise, forging new partnerships with faculty, students, and offices of research to accelerate research outcomes;
- expanding hybrid, flexible program delivery in spaces and through virtual service channels, testing the library's capacity to engage with those who never use the physical facility, along with those who do;
- redesigning indoor environments to promote health and well-being, along with more creative, purposeful uses of outdoor space;
- navigating the changing balance between remote and in-person work for staff and users alike;
- ensuring environmental sustainability practices in planning for renovated and new buildings;
- making accessibility and universal design foundational elements of space planning; and
- incorporating AI and smart systems into building design, enabling functions and interactivity in ways still to be foreseen.

Through these and other changes, college and research libraries will continue to be trusted connectors to the shared knowledge upon which our collective success depends.

Our hope for readers of this book is that you have been inspired to renew your vision of libraries in the life of your campus and community. And our wish is that soon you will have an opportunity to realize that vision in your own place and keep on designing libraries in the 21st century.

A

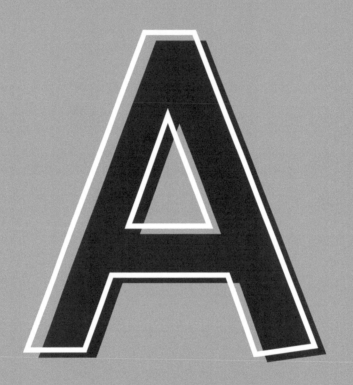

APPENDIX A

INTERVIEW WITH TOM HICKERSON

by CNI's

JOAN LIPPINCOTT

September 16, 2018

Note: This is an edited version of an interview of Tom Hickerson of the University of Calgary by Joan Lippincott of the Coalition for Networked Information at the 2018 Designing Libraries for the 21st Century Conference at the University of Calgary.

[Joan]: I'm Joan Lippincott from the Coalition for Networked Information, one of the organizers of the conference. Tom, in my view, the truly important projects where academic libraries have been redesigned or renovated have derived great strength from the vision that underlies the design. What are the ways that the Taylor Family Digital Library (TFDL) reflects your fundamental vision of libraries?

[Tom]: The first thing I'd say is that I see myself as a pragmatic visionary. I love great ideas, but I also think that we have to be committed to strategies that can realize those ideas. So importantly, it is to know your vision but also to realize it. The Taylor Family Digital Library was designed to support continuing change. I had seen the rapid evolution of library services and our role and knew that whatever we decided in 2007 was only going to be valid for 2007. So I've described this by saying, "You design for the library that you know now, you design for the library that you can imagine, and you design for the library that you cannot yet imagine." So what that means is that you actually have to build a fundamental infrastructure that will allow that building to evolve over time. And in the Taylor Family Digital Library, we did that by having raised flooring throughout the building, even in the museum. That was an 18-inch space that allowed us to put all of the electrical and networking under the floor, and so that allows us to have electrical outlets at every user seat in the building. And we also have over 50 percent demountable walls. Now that doesn't mean they're easily moved—they're not on wheels—but they're not load-bearing, so that, in fact, they really can be moved and so you really could create a very different structure in this building. And I would expect that to be the case in 20 years, in 2038, that the building would be quite different and supporting services and users in a very different way. The other thing that we focused on from day one was on users, on students and scholars. And Scott Bennett, former university librarian at Yale, had just published a terrifically important study, published by the Council for Libraries and Information Resources (CLIR) in 2003, in which he studied the 10 years of library growth immediately before that time. And what he found was that, in spite of the ideas that were thrown out, most of that growth had been focused on responding to collection growth. So I had the good fortune of having a new provost right at that point in time, Alan Harrison, arrive on campus almost simultaneously with me in 2006, so we came here to build this building. And he had just read Scott Bennett and was totally convinced, and so we were committed to making sure that collection growth never drove users out of the building. And in order to ensure that, we only installed space for 600,000 volumes in the building on day one, with the understanding that we would never increase that. And that, what was roughly two-thirds of the general collection that was in the main library at that point in time, would move to our high-density storage facility, which we were able to build at the very same time. I will say, today, there are fewer than 600,000 volumes in the building. Another focus was, I had a strong belief in the convergence of knowledge and culture. So I believe that libraries, archives, museums play an integrated role in supporting knowledge and understanding of artistic and scientific achievements, but, importantly, of the human experience. And those three areas fill that role in different ways, but they actually are such a rich combination together, and that we should support that to the degree we could. At that point in time, the university art museum reported to the position I held, but it had really not at all been integrated in the library. So we actually designed the TFDL with a full, functioning museum in the space and to offer students and scholars access to that broader cultural experience, to make the museum part of the instructional and research program of the library and of the university, not just an exhibition space. But, yet, at the same time, because it was a public exhibition space, it allowed us a new connection with the larger Calgary community. And the other really important thing from day one was the focus on knowledge creation. Information access is ubiquitous; it was then, and it's even more so today. But it's what we do to support the use of that information to create new knowledge. So we focused on technologies, we focused on collaborative spaces, we focused on expertise, and we also decided to invest in a 34.5 million pixel visualization studio, which was a very unusual decision at that point in time. But, in fact, that visualization studio has actually provided the first blueprint for the evolution of our functional support for the way research is done today, and I refer to this as a new synthesis. And this is where digital content and the analytical tools that support the analysis, creation, and dissemination of new knowledge are integrally related, and that we have to consider digital content and the analytical tools in combination.

[Joan]: And I think that many people here are so interested in bringing faculty back into the library, and that visualization studio at the outset was one of the most significant things for bringing faculty literally back into the library.

[Tom]: It was terribly important in and of itself because, one, there was actually not a 34.5 million pixel wall anywhere else on the campus, but it was particularly important for us because it brought people into the library from medicine and brought people into the library from medieval studies, it brought people in from architecture, and it very quickly built links with our Spatial and Numeric Data Services, where they were beginning to teach GIS to faculty and graduate students. And so that combination was a fervent initial mix for us, but it has evolved in a way that's absolutely essential today.

[Joan]: Tom, one of the lessons learned that we, the organizers, along with Greg Raschke, of the Designing Libraries Conference, hope to impart to all of you is that design is never complete, and we've heard that mentioned in a number of the presentations. So even newly opened libraries, meaning entirely new libraries, may need major or minor adjustments. What are some of the significant changes that have been made in the Taylor Family Digital Library since it opened?

[Tom]: Well, there are many, and probably some of them were corrections of thoughts that we had right off the bat. But the major changes have been substantial, and they're particularly meaningful, and the fact that we've been able to make them is terribly important. One of the important ones is the Graduate Research Commons. So the building is a wonderful space for students, but graduate students felt like we had not focused on them. So we have focused on them now, and we have a space where they can actually book, for a whole term, both a space and a locker where they can keep their materials and so forth, and only graduate students can enter the room. We developed this in association with the Graduate Student Association and with the Graduate Studies faculty on campus. I heard the reference earlier to microforms. We have moved all of our microforms and the equipment with which they were once used out of the building to the high-density library and turned that area into more student spaces and more technology spaces. We have created, as you just heard, a virtual reality and a one-button studio space. A particularly important move was that we moved the Research Data Center, which was in an adjacent building, into the library. And the Research Data Center is an outpost for a federal program from Statistics Canada that has confidential information about the general public of Canada, and one has to go through a very serious vetting process to be able to use that material. But our open Spatial and Numeric Data Services had compatible information, and it's publicly available. And what we realized was that for the people who were using the Statistics Canada information, there was this very closely interrelated data that they were not using, and in the workshops that it was introduced to them, they weren't hearing about all the kinds of data, and they weren't getting the kind of GIS and other analytical approaches. And so we actually created a space in the library to move them into the building immediately adjacent to Spatial and Numeric Data Services, in fact, to build a much closer relationship between those important areas of research support. We've created an audiovisual reformatting laboratory, and as those who went out to the new high-density library saw the other day, we're creating an audiovisual reformatting laboratory there, but we, in fact, first created one in the TFDL and started our work on the audiovisual content of the Capitol-EMI Music Archive, which we negotiated as a gift from Universal Music, officially announced in 2016, but which we had started in 2014. And we've had a good deal of support from the Andrew W. Mellon Foundation, and the reason for that is, one, because of the nature of the collection that we hold. Of the audio materials, 13,000 files are actual master files and production masters, not replicated anywhere else. Similar relationships in the video materials, and our libraries, our archives, and our museums are full of audiovisual material. Well, just our collection has 40 different formats in it, and, rapidly, those formats are becoming unusable. And so the Mellon Foundation sees this as actually an international crisis, since repositories are full of material that is increasingly unusable by the day. So we are developing an industrial model that we hope can be broadly replicated for converting material. We buy conversion equipment on eBay all the time, or wherever else we can find it, to move from one format to another, to create a body of material that can be preserved over time. And not just preserved, but actually made broadly accessible, because this material is really important. It's actually the record of the last half of the 20th century. In addition to that, you just heard a presentation about Lab NEXT. Lab NEXT was a very explicit outcome of the research project in identifying what today's researchers need. And so whether it is a perfect instance, and perhaps it isn't today, and hopefully we'll change it tomorrow, but it does respond to a vital need for multidisciplinarity and interdisciplinarity today, and those kinds of approaches to the grand challenges that society expects to see addressed in our universities.

[Joan]: I think many people here are worried about putting in high-tech facilities that may be out of date in a few years. So what strategies have you used to get the funding? Are you reallocating some of the library budget, are you getting funding from your VP for research, or your provost, or other places? Because a lot of your work, say, with the Mellon Foundation, I don't believe supports the actual reconfiguration of facilities; I may be incorrect there.

[Tom]: You're actually absolutely correct. So we're very fortunate and there has been a program on campus supported by the Office of the Provost, which we call FARCAR, which is a Facilities and Classroom Improvement Fund. We have been able to consistently apply to them for money to enhance particular areas for particularly vital purposes. And so not as much as we would have wanted, but about 50 percent of the Lab NEXT funding did come from those funds, and a number of the other areas in the building have similarly benefited. And then we are very fortunate that the Students' Union here at the University of Calgary is actually a very wealthy organization, in part because they support conferences like this, and so they have what they call "quality money," and we have been able to go to them for particular technology enhancements that gave more support for high-end animation and desktop creation, so we've been able to go there as well. I think we've been fortunate, and we have been oh so canny and oh so desperate all at the same time.

[Joan]: But also so visibly successful with your programs, and I think that's important, too, both for people who come into the library, for people who participate, and for the communications and outreach that you do.

[Tom]: I think Christie Hurrell's presentation gives you a good sense of how aggressive we are in trying to spread the word, and with the changing nature of research it's a complex environment, and before we started focusing on the multidisciplinary research needs of today, I had a sense that faculty didn't come into the library from many disciplines. In the process of our investigations, we found that, yes, indeed, they did come into the library, but they mostly went to Spatial and Numeric Data Services, they drew on the expertise, they drew on the data, and in fact, we were essential in their work, but they did not any longer take advantage of the traditional ways in which we have supported research. And so they all knew Peter Peller, who's the director of that program, but the traditional liaison network was really not a point in the new research environment where they were establishing those connections.

[Joan]: So this meant a lot to you in terms of the evolving role of the research library.

[Tom]: I think it's major. I referred to a new synthesis, and as I explained, I think that's the intersection of digital content and the analytical tools, and that one is not useful without the other. And as Christie referenced and showed you the diagram of the services that these scholars found most important going forward, they were areas in which we had strengths, but some of them were being envisioned to be applied in different ways. I had a discussion with Brian Moorman, who's an associate dean for research in the Faculty of Arts, and I was talking to him about the traditional ways that we in the library had supported research. And he turned to me, and it was without criticism and without sarcasm, and he just said it, he said, "But we don't do research like that anymore." So that's my new mantra, and I think it should be the mantra of everyone in the room. I think some of you are very aware of it. So what I would say about that is that, as Christie described, we're seeking to create a research platform. Research platforms are not a new concept, they're certainly in the STEM areas. There are those areas where you have a set of services that can be applied in multiple disciplinary focuses. And so, particularly in the neurosciences, in looking at everything from pre-birth problems to issues such as schizophrenia and depression, and then those that go right out into end-of-life problems, what they have created is an analytical layer that can support the research at each area of that spectrum, but by using the same functional capacity. So that's what we are trying to do for a range of areas. We're particularly focusing in areas where such research platforms don't exist. I mean, the great thing about libraries is that we're the neutral place and we'll support all of you. And some people come to us to a greater degree because they don't have labs and see that we can be their lab. But we need economies of scale; we cannot respond to these researcher needs in one-offs; we need to create this band of services. So what do I think, how do I think that matters for research libraries right now? I mean, it's not about tomorrow, this is right now! They so need these capacities that we may be the most logical place for them to receive this support. But if we don't support it, they will go elsewhere to develop it because they cannot do without it. So the Association of Research Libraries certainly has membership interest. Many have recognized this, and recently we created—and I was fortunate to have been actively involved in the creation of new criteria for research libraries in the 21st century—and identify the elements necessary to success. And in these new criteria, which were adopted unanimously by the membership—I mean, unanimity in ARL? But what they know is how important this is and that, in fact, libraries need a new role in the research ecosystem, and so several of the criteria specifically address the development of that new role. So what will happen if we don't? Our importance will be providing great learning spaces, but, in fact, the very same thing that those researchers need, our undergraduates are needing also. People are learning GIS at 19 years old, and they're learning VR at nine. So we're just behind the line, and if we do not develop in this way, our role in academic research will decline and our importance to our universities will be significantly diminished.

[Joan]: I am curious, what's your prediction? A percentage, a yes or no. Where do you think things are heading, broadly? I think it's great that ARL defined this set of characteristics, because it doesn't matter if you're in the organization or wanting to be or just not at all part of ARL, you can still use those same criteria as guideposts for where you want your library to be headed. But realistically speaking, do you want to venture a guess for where things are heading?

[Tom]: Well, first I want to agree with you that this is not about ARL libraries; this is about all libraries, but particularly in academia and where research is a vital function. I think we're significantly behind; this change has been going on for some time. It's not that we haven't recognized it, but what's happened in research is with the turn to society's grand challenges and this kind of multidisciplinary research. Suzanne Goopy, who spoke yesterday afternoon, she's a cultural anthropologist in the Faculty of Nursing and in the Community Health program, which is in medicine, and she's producing results that are about changing the protocols and the bus transportation routes of the city of Calgary. This is where we are today; this is what we all should be embracing; this is what's happening, and it's happening rapidly. And so an English professor and a computer scientist are involved in a common analysis of 150 years of science fiction literature. That's an everyday project today. I look at, proportionally, how fast we are progressing, it's not tremendous. But on the other hand, we are getting it. But when I talk about our getting it, and your question about money really speaks to this. I had a conversation with our colleague Greg Raschke from North Carolina State about the way we look at our collections budget as a budget to purchase and license content, irrespective of the analytical tools that will be essential to use that content, irrespective of the fact that over 50 percent of the material that people use is not what we purchase, is not what we license. And we have not embraced that world in thinking about how we manage our libraries. And if we don't do that, in spite of how damn smart we are, we won't be able to achieve at a fast enough rate. The nature of research will have changed again in five years, and we'll be a generation behind.

[Joan]: Tom, for my final question, most of you will probably not be aware that many years ago Tom and I were colleagues at Cornell University Libraries. Your role at that time was in special collections and archives. I find it fascinating that the span of what you've accomplished in your career is so much wider than that specialty, and I think our audience would be very interested in your role in documenting underrepresented groups and in making special collections and archives a signature program of the 21st-century library. Can you tell us a little bit about that, please?

[Tom]: I'd love to. I do think that a great deal of the information that we have managed in the past is now ubiquitous and that the collective collection, shared print, the HathiTrust, and so forth provides us access to a wealth of general collection materials. At the same time, rare and unique holdings are taking on a larger and larger importance, and in a different way than some of those reading rooms that we heard described earlier this morning, and that are terrifically compelling in instruction and research. I mentioned yesterday to some of the people touring the library about our numismatics collection, which is a very strong collection that's actually in our art museum, but it could be in our special collections. And it's such a powerful teaching tool. If you can put in the hand of a student a coin with the head of Cleopatra on it that was actually stamped by the Roman army when Mark Antony was in North Africa, what a view of society! How does that move a student from what happened on Facebook yesterday to all the Facebooks of history? It just introduces a tremendous impact on the mind going forward. So that's what teaching and research with special collections can do. But it also has a tremendous societal role. In the late 1980s at Cornell University, I was responsible for leading the initiation of the Human Sexuality Collection, which was the first focused effort by any academic institution in the US, certainly by any of the larger universities, to focus on documenting the social and political life of gay and lesbian individuals. And what I had seen over the years was how both our collecting and the way we described and promoted the material had marginalized women, had marginalized African Americans, and had marginalized Indigenous peoples. And we were going right on with that, and that, in fact, we had to change course, and that this was an opportunity to broaden the evidence and the record of a substantial component of society. And so when we did this, no one else had done it. It drew a lot of attention. It's the only time in my life that I received personal threats for my professional practice coming through the mail. Fortunately, it was real mail, not e-mail. Gosh, I would have hated that. But this was also right at the time that the AIDS epidemic hit, and it proved to be so important, and I'm going to tell one story, if I can get through it, of a man from North Carolina who had grown up in a rural area of North Carolina, had gone to New York City as a financial officer or a stockbroker and also became very active in the arts community in New York City. His firm fired him when they became aware that he was a gay man, and he contracted AIDS, and he had to return to his home in North Carolina. After hearing about our collection, he had a tremendous collection of art and records of his own experience about how he was treated with AIDS, which was horrifying in and of itself, in the medical environment, and he contacted me. I had newly hired a curator for the collection, and we flew down to, probably to Raleigh, we rented a car, and we drove out into the countryside, and we went to their home, where he and his sister, who was taking care of him, and where he had been living in a separate building on the property. And so we went out to where his collection was, and his sister and I carried him over our shoulders there, and we picked up the material, and we boxed it up and we hauled it to the plane and we flew it back to Ithaca, New

York. We contacted his sister on Monday of the next week, and she told us that he had died, and that he had stayed alive long enough for us to get his collection. So that's what the archival role can mean to individuals. But it is so powerful in the larger society and, obviously, has changed so much research and contributed to the elements of society today. At the same time, after coming here, I became a founding member, on behalf of the University of Calgary, of the board of the Military Museums, which is located near downtown, along Crowchild Trail. It's one of the two military history museums in Canada. And the University of Calgary has a library and an archives there, and I was fortunate to be able to raise private money to actually establish an exhibition gallery there as well. And so that collection is one of the great research collections, not just for military history, but for political history and social history. We chose to approach the collections, in terms of documentation, with a holistic approach, so the impact of warfare on society was included and not just the formal military experience but, in fact, how has that impacted society? How has that impacted civilian populations? Looking at the effect of terrorism, looking at the effect of internal civil wars. We created such a rich experience for the public and for researchers and for students to be able to understand the role of the military history of our society. And this is not political, this is professional. This is how we should be filling our professional role, by acquiring the records of important elements of society that might not be well documented or well understood or incorporated into the educational and research environment. And at the same time that we think about particular parts of society, we need to look at those parts of society that are oh so obvious, but because they're oh so obvious we may not be pursuing them. And that's the way I see the gift by Universal Music Canada of the Capitol-EMI Collection to the University of Calgary. It is a miracle that this collection exists. From 1949 to 2012, EMI became the major music industry giant worldwide, and this collection managed to survive through those years, through all the transitions in the music industry, through all the artists, through all the AR people, through all the concerts, and through the business operations, which were largely hidden. And so a collection of 5,500 boxes, over two million items, and as I mentioned, over 40,000 audiovisual and video tapes, recording Canadian artists like Anne Murray and Tom Cochrane, but also the original DAT tapes from the BBC sessions of the Beatles. The original disc from which the Rubber Soul vinyl albums were pressed, an album by David Bowie which was actually created in Quebec at a studio there but was never broadly distributed. So really remarkable material! But it's part of the culture, it's part of the social, it's part of the political, it's part of the industrial, it's part of gender roles, it's part of fashion. I would say that most of the people in the room have had some experience of the last half of the 20th century. What was more important across the spectrum of time than popular music? What does it tell us about our society and about the impact of popular music worldwide? We need to seize those opportunities to document and provide understanding and accessibility for materials that are the ubiquitous aspects of society. Once again, in developing the new criteria for ARL, this societal role is formally recognized for the first time. Yet, in fact, historically, libraries, archives, and museums have played this role over century after century after century in preserving, whenever possible, the record of diverse societies. And I'll tell you from a personal point of view, to have been able to enrich my career by involvement in playing this important societal role has been wonderful. I love it.

[Joan]: At the beginning of the interview, I talked about the importance of a vision for today's library. You've just heard such a vision, and the breadth of Tom's vision and his commitment to 21st-century libraries are truly remarkable. Thank you, Tom.

[Tom]: Thank you.

A video version of this interview is available at https://vimeo.com/297184427.

B

APPENDIX B

SALUTING JOAN K. LIPPINCOTT

Presented by

TOM HICKERSON

at the
Designing Libraries
VIII Conference

October 8, 2019
Atlanta, Georgia

Over the coming months, there will be many salutes to the accomplishments and contributions of Joan K. Lippincott. Clifford Lynch began this cascade of admiration and congratulation on the evening of September 6th with the first public announcement of her coming retirement from the position of associate executive director of the Coalition for Networked Information on January 1, 2020. It is now my honor to contribute to these accolades on behalf of Designing Libraries.

Joan Lippincott joined CNI in the fall of 1990, soon after the organization's inception under the leadership of founding director Paul Evan Peters, and she has played a critical role in shaping CNI's trajectory since the earliest days, making CNI an internationally recognized and highly influential organization. And within CNI's diverse mission, Joan has distinctly contributed in shaping the role of academic libraries in teaching and learning and scholarship.

I know little of Joan's childhood, but from the time she entered Vassar College, where she received her undergraduate degree in history with honors, she seems to have never paused, receiving an MLS two years later from the State University of New York at Geneseo. She spent the next four years as a reference and instruction librarian at the State University of New York at Brockport, followed by two years at Georgetown University, where she developed the library's first instruction program. She then moved to George Washington University, where she spent two years as the head of reference, including creating a credit course on library research skills for graduate students.

Joan then moved to Cornell University in 1982, where she really hit her stride. For six years, she was the head of public services at the Albert R. Mann Library. A seemingly independent library within the Cornell system [They definitely acted that way.], Mann Library created its own national reputation for innovation in library services, and Joan led in that development through an embrace of new technologies unusual at the time and a focus on electronic information as the medium of the future.

Just so she wouldn't be wasting any time while working at Cornell, Joan entered the doctoral program in educational administration at Cornell, completing 24 graduate credits. She later completed her PhD in educational policy, planning, and administration at the University of Maryland while working at CNI. Her dissertation is titled "Collaboration between Librarians and Information Technologists: A Case Study Employing Kolb's Experiential Learning Theory."

David Kolb, an American educational theorist, in the 1970s and 80s articulated a theory of holistic learning that accounted for how perception, emotions, and environment affected a learner. We have frequently seen Joan applying these same elements in her analysis and planning, a perfect illustration of how Joan's combination of deep knowledge and empirical observation have wonderfully equipped her for the evolving world of libraries and learning.

So it is not surprising that Joan has become an internationally recognized expert on student learning. If one looks at her publications, one will see she has often focused on aspects of the learning experience from two different directions. The first is emerging technologies, which aligns with her early embrace of digital information as essential to learning and knowledge creation, but it also reflects that CNI is a joint initiative of both EDUCAUSE and ARL. The second is spatial design, often addressed in combination with emerging technologies, but she increasingly focused her attention on architectural and environmental aspects of spatial design and began consulting broadly. It is in her growing concentration on spatial planning and architectural design that Joan and I renewed our association and why we are here together today.

As I noted, Joan spent six years at Cornell University. This is where our professional histories first crossed paths. During that period, I served as Cornell's chair of the department of Manuscripts and University Archives and then as assistant director of Olin Library. While our professional duties did not lead to collaborations, we knew each other and shared a mutual sense of professional respect, which later served as a foundation for Designing Libraries.

In the summer of 2006, I left Cornell and traveled to the University of Calgary, arriving along with a new provost, Alan Harrison, with the mission of building a new central library. Alan and I shared a common vision focusing on building spaces for student learning, emerging technologies, and knowledge creation, with the collection largely housed elsewhere. The Taylor Family Digital Library, incorporating the University Museum and the University Press, opened in the fall of 2011.

The building immediately drew professional interest, including that of Joan Lippincott, who decided that she wanted to see this building. But Joan, being Joan, immediately thought that others would want to see it also and asked herself if there was a way to combine the attraction of this new library with all of the new knowledge and creative dialogue that was underway regarding library space. And Joan, who has never had a good idea that she did not act on, contacted me immediately, and we agreed to meet during the ARL fall membership meeting in October. When we met there, Joan suggested that if I would hold a conference, she and CNI would help and support my doing so. I was excited by the prospect, and she told me that she would follow up with a fuller articulation. Joan has told me recently that she had confidence that I would prove a strong partner in this endeavor based on her knowledge of me at Cornell over 20 years earlier. So, remember, don't ever screw up in front of Joan Lippincott.

In November, Joan sent me her description of the envisioned symposium. She wrote:

> Libraries have been agile in adapting their collections and services to new technologies, but sometimes old physical facilities and outdated concepts of services hold academic libraries back from achieving their full potential in the digital age. The Taylor Family Library at the University of Calgary had a unique opportunity to rethink the library's physical space, technology infrastructure and delivery, and program of services. Participants will have an opportunity to experience the capabilities of the new facility through in-depth exposure to various aspects of the facility and services, and the symposium will enable participants to benefit from a wide variety of perspectives, including architects and designers, academic administrators, librarians, technologists, and outside experts.

We were soon joined by the wondrous Susan Nutter from North Carolina State University, where the remarkable Hunt Library would open in January of 2013.

The conference was first seen as a one-time occurrence, then two, then three, then four. Our intent was only to continue as long as there was attendee interest, because your engagement is the principal ingredient in conference success. Now, it is the eighth, and the ninth is scheduled. I am pleased to tell you that, although Joan and I are both going through professional transitions, we are committed, along with Greg Raschke, to continuing our involvement. And, like oh so many other initiatives that Joan has led, many, many people are responsible for its success, but Joan is always the SPARK!

Joan has achieved success in these efforts through her marvelous intellect, eloquent presence, astute organizational skills, and creative analysis of challenges and opportunities confronting libraries and higher education today and tomorrow. Her numerous presentations, articles and reports, institutional and professional consultations, and the many great conferences and other meetings that she has organized have combined to establish a remarkable record of achievement and impact. And all of this is augmented by her generosity of spirit and her personal counsel and assistance to so many in this profession. Our world just wouldn't be the same without Joan Lippincott!

C

APPENDIX C

REMEMBERING SUSAN K. NUTTER

GREGORY K. RASCHKE

The morning of Susan's memorial service, held several weeks after she died in March 2019, I was drinking a cup of coffee from a mug I received on a visit to Oxford University. Drinking from that mug I was able to reflect on how much Susan impacted my career, my life, and my professional outlook. After taking over as interim director for Susan upon her retirement, I spent many hours thinking about succeeding such a fantastic and legendary leader. What is the right approach to carrying forward the thousands of lessons she taught me and others while moving forward trusting our own instincts and approach? The morning of her memorial, looking at the mug from Oxford, my focus shifted from thinking about living up to her example to pure gratitude. I realized that the trip I took to Oxford to speak at the joint CNI/JISC conference the summer before was primarily due to Susan. The trip my wife and I took to Oxford University was a direct reflection of how much Susan influenced my life and career. Gratitude hit me in waves. Gratitude for hiring me at NC State. Gratitude for opening door after door to learn about and participate in the transformation of 21st-century libraries. Gratitude for her pushing and trusting me in a variety of roles. Gratitude for coming along for the ride in building the James B. Hunt Jr. Library. Gratitude for the countless hours she spent mentoring, guiding, and inspiring me. Gratitude for simply having known and worked with someone so extraordinary. And finally, gratitude for allowing me to participate in the Designing Libraries Conference. It was a conference, just like the buildings that have hosted the meetings, that blazed trails in bringing together librarians, architects, designers, and technologists in understanding and inspiring the transformation of library spaces and the organizations that build those spaces.

Designing Libraries is everything Susan loved. It pushes boundaries; challenges us to envision bold new ways to serve our users; brings bright, creative people together; and sets an ambitious agenda for the future of libraries. The conference enabled Susan to collaborate with her beloved colleagues Joan Lippincott and Tom Hickerson. It gave her a platform to connect with emerging leaders in librarianship and design, to both explore and inspire the future of libraries. Susan found inspiration in the future. One of her favorite questions was, "What's next?" She pursued that question with unflinching dedication and incredible creativity. As Craig Dykers, Snohetta's founding partner, said in memorializing Susan, "She made passion a verb rather than a noun." It is no surprise that tributes came in for Susan from all quarters, including from high-profile figures like Dykers and the namesake of the James B. Hunt Jr. Library, former North Carolina governor Jim Hunt. Two categories of tributors, though, stand out. Current and former employees, who had the opportunity to work with and learn from Susan, and former students. Both of those categories reveal two of her greatest passions, the future and people. Susan cared deeply about making NC State, North Carolina, and the world a better place. Not for herself, but for future generations. Her impact is felt most profoundly in the countless lives she touched and the countless more who will know NC State as a better university because of her work.

Susan, who served as our vice provost and director of libraries, retired in 2017 after a 30-year career as one of NC State's and the library world's most dynamic and influential leaders. She then passed away on March 25, 2019.

Susan was predeceased that December by her beloved husband, best friend, and creative colleague, Joe Anderson Hewitt, former vice provost and university librarian at the University of North Carolina at Chapel Hill.

A memorial service was held the following May at the Hunt Library, and to honor Susan, the Hill Library Color Wall and Conservatory were lit in purple—her favorite color—until after the memorial service. The libraries also created a memorial website (https://www.lib.ncsu.edu/remembering-susan) honoring Susan and her visionary career. Those who knew and worked with her were invited to celebrate her life by sharing thoughts, memories, and photographs of Susan on this site.

In memory of Susan, contributions continue to be made to the University Libraries' Susan K. Nutter Innovative Leadership Fund.

A Legacy of Leadership

Susan placed the libraries at the center of NC State's overall success. She set forth an ambitious vision and worked tirelessly to achieve it, transforming every aspect of the libraries along the way. Her many significant achievements ranged from building world-class research collections and spearheading the creation of the online library, to attracting and developing a uniquely talented and capable staff, to overseeing the design and realization of many beautiful and inspiring spaces for learning, collaboration, and discovery.

Opened in 2013, the award-winning Hunt Library—Susan's signature accomplishment—has become one of the region's most iconic buildings. With a distinctive, bold design and infused with engaging technology, it enables and reflects NC State's spirit of innovation and entrepreneurship. Susan also ensured that the university's first main library, the Hill Library, kept pace with Hunt through creative redesign and renovation of flexible, technology-rich learning spaces. These changes reinvigorated the very idea of a library's centrality to its campus community. The most recent renovation to the Hill Library, which Susan spearheaded, was completed in fall 2020.

While Susan's legacy is her embrace of emerging technologies and innovative scholarship as embodied in the Hunt Library, it was her ability to connect with students, faculty, staff, alumni, and colleagues that made her such a special leader. She dedicated herself fully to helping all libraries users succeed, and she lived and breathed that dedication every day, reaching out to them to learn about their needs and challenges and building an organization with the talent and agility to develop creative and responsive solutions.

Susan's many honors and awards include the Association of College and Research Libraries (ACRL) Hugh C. Atkinson Memorial Award (1999), the 2005 *Library Journal* Librarian of the Year, and the 2016 ACRL Academic/Research Librarian of the Year. Under her leadership, the NC State Libraries was the first university library to win the ACRL Excellence in Academic Libraries Award in 2000. In 2016, she accepted the IMLS National Medal for Museum and Library Service on the libraries' behalf from First Lady Michelle Obama in a White House ceremony.

Transforming the Libraries

From the time she arrived in 1987, Susan's vision for the libraries anticipated what users would need in the future. Having glimpsed the power of online resources through her early work at MIT, Susan immediately set out to build an online library at NC State. Today, the usage of the online library far exceeds that of the print collection. She also made the libraries one of the first research libraries with a learning technologies service to help faculty develop online courses, a scholarly communication center to advise on intellectual property in the digital age, and a digital library initiatives department developing innovative projects to revolutionize and enhance network-based services, access to collections, teaching, learning, and research.

In support of these innovations, Susan saw that she needed to build a staff that was agile enough to not only react to but also anticipate library users' ever-evolving needs. She recruited some of the profession's top talent through the NCSU Libraries Fellows Program, established in 1999. Considered one of the premier opportunities for new talent in academic libraries today, the program identifies the most promising new graduates in the field of library and information science and provides them with a unique opportunity to launch their career with challenging assignments and support for their professional development. To date, over 75 fellows have completed the program, over two-thirds of whom moved into permanent librarian positions here at the completion of their fellowship. Seven former fellows have been named *Library Journal* Movers and Shakers.

From the bustling Learning Commons at the Hill Library to the immersive visualization spaces at the Hunt Library, Susan gave NC State a world-class research platform with the power to transform teaching, learning, and research. She also built a highly motivated, expert staff that develops and delivers innovative services and is embedded in every aspect of the academic endeavor. Thanks to her leadership, the libraries truly embody NC State's "Think and Do" culture.

The Library of the Future—and a Crowning Achievement

During her interview here in 1987, when asked about her plans for the future of the libraries, Susan outlined a vision for building a library on Centennial Campus—a creative "nexus" for the emerging community of students, faculty, researchers, and corporate and government partners. In 2013, her dream was realized in a way that was more extraordinary than anyone could have imagined.

Now universally acknowledged as "the library of the future," the Hunt Library is a signature building for the university. Its bold design echoes its bold purpose—to welcome all members of the NC State community to learn, experiment, collaborate, and create. This library has enlivened an international dialogue about the place and purpose of academic libraries in the 21st century.

The Hunt Library has been recognized nationally with some of the most prestigious awards for libraries and architecture. Notable recognition includes the 2014 American Institute of Architects (AIA) Educational Facility Design award, the 2013 AIA/ALA Library Buildings Award, and the 2014 Stanford Prize for Innovation in Research Libraries.

Always Looking Ahead

Although the Hunt Library is what will come to many people's minds when they remember Susan's legacy, her career at the libraries ultimately adds up to an overarching idea. She was always asking the question, "What's next?" Even while focused on the needs of current NC State students and faculty, Susan was driven to anticipate the needs of the students and faculty five or ten years in the future. She knew that as soon as an institution like an academic library holds still or rests on its laurels, it loses relevance. The student body changes substantially every year. Faculty come and go. Rather than just reacting to change and constantly chasing the needs of those the library served, she wanted to be out in front, with the resources already in place to meet those needs. She was proud of what she accomplished at the libraries, but she didn't much care to dwell on the past. She was always looking forward, toward building the best library and assembling the best team for the future.

Susan Nutter's legacy remains alive today, both within and beyond the libraries, manifest in a dynamic organization that is always asking, "What's next?" and challenging others in librarianship, information technology, and higher education to do the same.

Biographies

B I O G R A P H I E S

ABOUT THE EDITORS AND CONTRIBUTORS

About the Editors

H. Thomas Hickerson's career includes international leadership in library and museum administration, archives and special collections, technology innovation, and library building design. As an archivist, he guided the Cornell University Library's archives and rare book programs, serving as President of the Society of American Archivists (SAA) and on the International Council on Archives Executive Board. As a technology innovator, he created campus and international collaborations using emerging technologies to expand access to diverse academic and cultural holdings. In 2006, Tom became Vice Provost at the University of Calgary with a mandate to lead the design of a new model for university libraries. The $205M project to build the Taylor Family Digital Library led to broad recognition and to his founding role in the Designing Libraries for the 21st Century Conference series. His professional leadership includes serving on the Board of the Association of Research Libraries and as President of the Canadian Association of Research Libraries. He is a Cornell University Librarian *Emeritus* whose recognitions include being named an SAA Fellow and Computerworld Honors Program Laureate for "the use of information technologies for the benefit of society."

Joan K. Lippincott (BA, MLS, PhD) is Associate Executive Director *Emerita* of the Coalition for Networked Information (CNI), a joint program of the Association of Research Libraries (ARL) and EDUCAUSE. At CNI, Joan provided leadership for programs in learning spaces, teaching and learning, digital scholarship, ETDs, and assessment. She served on the boards of the Networked Digital Library of Theses and Dissertations (NDLTD), the New Media Consortium (NMC) and on the advisory board for the *Horizon Report.* Joan was the editor of the *EDUCAUSE Review* E-Content column and was chair of the Association of College & Research Libraries' (ACRL) New Publications Board, and served as a member of the ACRL task force that produced the Framework for Information Literacy for Higher Education. She served on the advisory boards of the Learning Spaces Collaboratory and the Learning Space Toolkit project. Joan has consulted with many academic libraries on their space renovation projects and has been on the planning committee for the Designing Libraries for the 21st Century conference since its inception.

Leonora Crema (BA, MA, MLS) is a Librarian *Emerita* at the University of British Columbia. She has exercised a leading role in the design of two new buildings on the UBC campus, the Walter C. Koerner Library and Library PARC, as well as numerous space renovations. Leonora's roles at UBC have included serving as Associate University Librarian for Client Services, AUL for Planning and Community Relations, and Director of External Relations for the Irving K. Barber Learning Centre. Active in professional associations, including as a past President of the British Columbia Library Association, she speaks regularly on topics such as service innovation and library space design. Her career recognitions include a national award for innovation from the Canadian Association of University Business Officers, and a Council of Prairie and Pacific University Libraries award for outstanding contributions to the consortium. Leonora has been an invited speaker and mentor at library leadership institutes, drawing upon her experiences in coaching early career professionals.

Our Contributors

Kristin Antelman is the University Librarian at the University of California Santa Barbara. Prior to coming to UCSB in 2018 she was University Librarian at the California Institute of Technology (Caltech) and prior to that Associate Director for the Digital Library at North Carolina State University from 2002-14. While at NCSU, Kristin was one of the architects of the James B. Hunt Jr. Library technology program and a contributor to several Designing Libraries conferences. She has published several articles on open access, including "Leveraging the Growth of Open Access in Library Collection Decision Making" (2017) and "Do Open Access Articles Have a Greater Research Impact?" (2004) At the University of California, she is active in the development of strategies to advance the transition to open access.

Kineret Ben-Knaan is the Research and Assessment Librarian at the University of Miami. In this role, Kineret supports the achievement of the University of Miami Libraries' strategic goals by developing data-driven assessment activities related to services, collections, technology, and physical spaces. She engages in querying and analyzing data to gain new insights and works collaboratively with members of the libraries' leadership and management teams to inform data-driven decisions. Kineret received her master's in information science from Bar-Ilan University, Israel, and obtained her BA and MA, both in art history, from Tel Aviv University, Israel. She also holds a certificate of business analytics from Cornell University and is a Microsoft Certified Data Analyst Associate.

Janette Blackburn, FAIA, and **Carole Wedge**, FAIA, are architects at Shepley Bulfinch, one of the nation's leading design firms. They represent a collaborative team whose passion for library design is expressed throughout their chapter. The firm's work includes libraries for Ringling College of Art and Design, Virginia Commonwealth University, Salem State, and Johns Hopkins, as well as Princeton's Firestone Library with Frederick Fisher Partnership and Austin's Central Library, a joint venture with Lake Flato Architects. Janette is a Principal in Shepley Bulfinch's education practice. Her library design work is recognized internationally and informed by a deep understanding of library environments and their advancement of community learning and engagement. As a Principal at Shepley Bulfinch, Carole's work in both leadership and design capacities is noted for its success in strategically positioning her clients for the future. Using a collaborative approach, Carole works with organizations to find creative, flexible solutions that anticipate and embrace change. Both Janette and Carole have been recognized as Fellows in the American Institute of Architects for their contributions to architecture and society.

John Brosz is the Data Visualization Coordinator in Libraries and Cultural Resources at the University of Calgary where he provides data visualization support, consultation, and training to scholars and students from a variety of areas across campus. From 2017-20 he was the Project Coordinator for the Academic Research and University Libraries: Creating a New Model for Collaboration Project funded by The Andrew W. Mellon Foundation and led by Thomas Hickerson. John has a PhD in computer science where he was involved in research in the areas of information visualization, computer graphics, and human-computer interfaces.

Mimi Calter is the Vice Provost and University Librarian at Washington University in St. Louis. Prior to joining Washington University, Mimi served as Deputy University Librarian for Stanford Libraries, where she was responsible for operations and the implementation of strategic projects across library departments, with special focus including capital project implementation, organizational development for the libraries, and copyright issues at both the library and university level. She holds an MBA and MLIS from Drexel University and an MA from the University of Pennsylvania. She is also a birder and will often be found outside the library watching whatever is flying by.

John Danneker is the Director of the Learning Services Department at the University of Washington Libraries in Seattle—a role which includes administrative leadership for Odegaard Undergraduate Library—and a member of the Research and Learning Services portfolio leadership team. As a department, Learning Services supports the whole student by deepening learning related to inquiry and the critical use of information and celebrates learning occurring both inside and outside of the formal classroom. The department's four units—Curriculum Support, Instructional Design/Online Learning, Undergraduate Student Success, and Access and Building Services for Odegaard—partner closely with in-building academic support offices for writing/rhetoric and learning technologies, in addition to collaborating with many other units in the Libraries and across campus. Professionally, John is interested in creating supportive learning environments through both personnel and physical spaces and in employing limited capacities in a sustainable way to embrace strategically-chosen initiatives.

Steve Dantzer enjoyed a 35-year career in facility management and capital program oversight. Prior to his retirement in 2015, Steve was the Associate Vice President (Facilities Development) at the University of Calgary, where he led a multi-disciplinary team responsible for managing the process of effective design and construction within the university's facilities, utilities, and sites. The architects, engineers, and project management professionals in this unit had oversight of almost a billion dollars' worth of new building and renovation projects. Prior to the University of Calgary's building boom, his responsibilities included directing the university's Campus Infrastructure department, which comprised the operations, maintenance, property management, leasing, and construction work units. Steve was previously Director of Physical Resources at Trent University in Ontario and was Manager of Administrative Services for the City of Peterborough, Ontario. Steve holds a degree in Industrial Design from Carleton University in Ottawa, Ontario.

Patrick Deaton, AIA, is the Associate Director for Learning Spaces and Capital Management at the North Carolina State University Libraries. He is responsible for overseeing the design, construction and furnishing of all Libraries facilities, including the James B. Hunt Jr. Library and the D. H. Hill Jr. Library. Patrick was a member of the core team for the Learning Space Toolkit project. He is a frequent conference speaker, including several Designing Libraries for the 21st Century conferences. He is a former Association of Research Libraries Leadership Fellow (2013-15). Patrick received his architectural training at the University of Virginia and Princeton University. Prior to joining the Libraries in 2009, he was an architect in private practice and designed several major library and higher education projects. He occasionally serves as a design consultant for public and academic libraries.

Catherine DeRose is a technical writer. Prior to that, she was the Program Manager for Yale University's Digital Humanities Lab, where she provided project consultations, taught workshops on data analysis and visualization, and directed the Digital Humanities Teaching Fellowship program. She also held an appointment as a Lecturer in Yale's Department of Statistics and Data Science. Catherine received her PhD in English from the University of Wisconsin-Madison.

Ameet Doshi joined Princeton University Library as Head of the Donald E. Stokes Library in 2021 and has held previous positions at the Georgia Institute of Technology and University of North Carolina, Wilmington. He earned a master's in public administration (MPA) from the University of North Carolina, Wilmington and an MLIS from the University of Tennessee. As Head of the Stokes Library, Ameet supports the School of Public and International Affairs (SPIA), the Office of Population Research, and Princeton students, faculty and researchers exploring policy-related topics. Ameet has served on the American Library Association's Center for the Future of Libraries advisory board and is a reviewer for the *Journal of Learning Spaces* and *Performance Measurement and Metrics*. His research interests include computational social science, library and learning spaces, and science and technology policy. In 2022, he co-authored a paper in the *Proceedings of the National Academies of Sciences* about the use of open access science by the American public.

Elliot Felix founded and leads brightspot strategy, a Buro Happold Company. Brightspot is a consultancy on a mission to create more engaging and equitable student experiences by transforming college and university spaces, support services, staffing, and systems. Elliot is an accomplished strategist, facilitator, and sense-maker who has helped transform over 90 colleges and universities including Carnegie Mellon University, Georgia Tech, MIT, North Carolina State University, New York University, McGill University, Stanford University, University of Michigan, University of Minnesota, and University of Virginia.

Andrew Frontini (BArch, OAA, LEED AP BD+C, FRAIC) is a Toronto-based architect with a long history of designing award-winning public architecture. He is particularly passionate about the design of libraries and has worked with academic and public librarians across Canada and the US to help them reimagine the ever-evolving essence of the library. Andrew serves as the design director for the Toronto and Ottawa studios of Perkins&Will where he leads a design culture with a strong social agenda. He uses bold material expressions and considered responses to context to create spaces around which communities form. By maintaining a design philosophy that is open and collaborative, Andrew never stops learning, producing, and evolving. His designs for universities, municipalities, library systems, and commercial clients have been published internationally. Andrew is a graduate of the University of Waterloo School of Architecture. He shares his passion for design through exhibitions, published articles, and speaking engagements.

Harriette Hemmasi was appointed Dean of the Library at Georgetown University in the summer of 2018. Previously, Harriette served as the University Librarian at Brown University, the Executive Associate Dean at Indiana University, and the Associate University Librarian for Technical and Automated Services at Rutgers University. Harriette began her library career as a Music Librarian at Rutgers after receiving a master's in library and information science from the University of California Berkeley and a master's in music from Indiana University. The focus of her leadership is advocating for and advancing the role of the academic library through the use of digital tools and methodologies to enhance access, use, dissemination, and preservation of all forms of scholarly communication in support of innovative approaches to teaching, learning, and research.

Joel Herndon is the Director of the Center for Data and Visualization Sciences (CDVS) at Duke University Libraries where he leads a library data science program providing support for data visualization, data curation, data management, digital mapping, and computational research support for the Duke community. Joel's research focuses on how universities can improve data sharing and data science initiatives through partnerships, training, infrastructure, and project support.

Peter Leonard is Assistant University Librarian for Research Data Services at Stanford University Library. He was the founding Director of Yale University's Digital Humanities Lab from 2015 to 2022. He received his BA in art history from the University of Chicago and his PhD in Scandinavian literature from the University of Washington. Peter was a postdoctoral researcher in text-mining at UCLA, supported by a Google Digital Humanities Research Award. During 2007-8, he was a Fulbright Scholar at Uppsala University in Sweden.

Joseph Lucia is Dean of Libraries at Temple University. Under his leadership, in 2019 the university completed construction and began operation of the world-class Charles Library, notable for its unique design by architects Snøhetta and local partners Stantec. Prior to serving as Dean at Temple, Lucia served as University Librarian at Villanova University for 11 years. During his tenure at Villanova, Falvey Library won the 2013 ACRL Excellence Award in the University category. Before assuming his post at Villanova in 2002, Lucia served as Director for Library Technology & Access within Information Resources (a merged library and computing support organization) at Lehigh University in Bethlehem, Pennsylvania. While at Lehigh, Lucia taught creative writing in the English Department from 1995 through 2002. In addition to his professional work, he is an active amateur musician with a current solo project called Sounds from Upstairs audible on Soundcloud at https://soundcloud.com/jlucia

Mary Ann Mavrinac (BA, BEd, MLS, EdD) is the Vice Provost and Andrew H. and Janet Dayton Neilly Dean, University of Rochester Libraries. Prior to this, she was chief librarian at the University of Toronto Mississauga, where she led from vision to occupancy a new, award-winning academic library, the Hazel McCallion Academic Learning Centre, which opened in 2006. Previously, she was head, The D. B. Weldon Library, Western University. Her interests and research focus on library as place, leadership and change, strategic planning, and mentoring—topics about which she is frequently invited to speak. Mavrinac was the 2010 President of the Ontario Library Association. In 2014, she was honored with the Ontario College and University Library Association's Lifetime Achievement Award. She served on the board of the Association of Research Libraries from 2013-19, elected as President in 2017-18.

Brian Mathews is the Associate Dean for Innovation at the Carnegie Mellon University Libraries. He previously served in leadership roles at Virginia Tech, Georgia Tech, and University of California Santa Barbara. Brian is fascinated with the psychology of physical environments and explores this theme in his book *Encoding Space: Shaping Learning Environments that Uunlock Human Potential.* Brian was a columnist for *American Libraries* and a blogger for the *Chronicle of Higher Education* often writing about the future of libraries and his pragmatic experiments with new tools and approaches. Brian's work at the CMU Libraries involves developing an innovation management system to help propel the libraries forward with new services, spaces, and engagement opportunities. He earned an MLIS from the University of South Florida in 2000.

Sarah Meilleur (BA, MLIS) is the CEO of Calgary Public Library. She led the design thinking, completion, and launch of Calgary's new Central Library that saw over two million visitors within the first year. Sarah is a recognized speaker at international conferences, has lectured at Harvard University on library design, and has worked as a consultant for library systems and architectural firms. Sarah completed her undergraduate degree at the University of Calgary and her MLIS degree at the University of Western Ontario. She believes in supporting the community through volunteering and has served on the Calgary Heritage Authority, the Cultural Leadership Council, and the Social Wellbeing Advisory Committee. Sarah is passionate about the ways in which public libraries transform lives, and she works to foster curiosity, innovation, inclusion, and fantastic visitor experiences.

Liz Milewicz heads the Digital Scholarship & Publishing Services department and co-directs ScholarWorks: A Center for Scholarly Publishing at Duke University Libraries. Her team, including interns from regional library school programs and Duke graduate students, partners with the Duke community on digital research, teaching, and publishing projects and provides training and consulting in digital approaches to scholarship. She helped to plan and launch The Edge: The Ruppert Commons for Research, Technology, and Collaboration, a space for project teams to pursue interdisciplinary, data-driven, and digitally reliant research. Currently Liz also co-leads Project Vox, a digital publication and educational initiative that seeks to reform and diversify philosophy instruction.

Kelly E. Miller is Associate Dean of Learning and Research Services at the University of Miami Libraries. She previously held positions at UCLA Library and University of Virginia Library. A 2013 graduate of the Leading Change Institute and a former Council on Library and Information Resources (CLIR) Postdoctoral Fellow in Academic Libraries, she focuses on the transformation of library spaces and services in support of the educational mission. She has published articles in *EDUCAUSE Review*, *portal: Libraries and the Academy*, *Archive Journal*, and other journals, and she has presented on library space projects at such conferences as the Society of College and University Planning, EDUCAUSE Learning Initiative, and Designing Libraries. She earned a PhD and MA in slavic languages and literatures at the University of Michigan, and a BA in Russian and English from Stetson University.

James L. Mullins retired from Purdue University January 1, 2018, and holds the title of Dean *Emeritus* of Libraries and Esther Ellis Norton Professor *Emeritus* after serving since 2004 as Dean of Libraries. Prior to Purdue, he held library administrative positions at Indiana University, Villanova University and the Massachusetts Institute of Technology (MIT). His education was completed at the University of Iowa with a BA and MALS and a PhD from Indiana University. During his career he was active in the American Library Association, IFLA and the Association of Research Libraries. In 2018, he founded Prior Art Documentation Librarian Services, LLC as a consulting service to patent attorneys to meet their requirement for authentication and proof of public access to books, journal articles, theses, etc. for patent cases appearing before the Patent and Trademark Board and the Federal District Court. He presently resides in Williamsburg, Virginia.

Catherine Murray-Rust retired in 2020 as Dean of Libraries at Georgia Institute of Technology. Prior to Georgia Tech, she served as Dean of Libraries at Colorado State University, Associate University Librarian at Oregon State University, and Associate University Librarian at Cornell University. She worked in special libraries after earning her library degree at the University of London. For more than 40 years, she has been a change agent, reimagining library services and collections to meet the needs of the community. Now, she focuses on telling encouraging stories and offering practical advice about how to help libraries and library workers thrive in the future.

Roxane Pickens is Director of the Learning Commons at University of Miami Libraries, and she also directs the American Studies Program in the College of Arts and Sciences at UM. Her current research and teaching interests include interdisciplinarity and cultural literacies in library settings, teaching with primary resources, diversity/equity/inclusion in academic spaces, American Studies, African American literature/culture, US identity construction, and the rhetorical dimensions of ethnic festive/expressive culture. She received her MA and PhD in American studies at the College of William and Mary, and a BA in American studies from the former Newcomb College of Tulane University.

Gregory K. Raschke is the Senior Vice Provost and Director of Libraries at North Carolina State University where he leads a system comprised of two main libraries, three branches, and over 200 FTE staff. He leads partnerships and strategic efforts in pursuit of its vision—to make the Libraries NC State's competitive advantage. He served for over a decade as the Associate Director for Collections and Scholarly Communication with the Libraries where he led programs to build, manage, and preserve the Libraries' extensive general and special collections. Greg served on the leadership team that envisioned, planned, and implemented the award-winning James B. Hunt Jr. Library. His undergraduate and graduate degrees are from the University of Illinois at Urbana-Champaign.

Carli Spina is an associate professor and the Head of Research & Instructional Services at SUNY's Fashion Institute of Technology in New York City. She has an EdM from the Harvard Graduate School of Education, an MLIS from Simmons College, and a JD from the University of Chicago Law School. She specializes in accessibility, Universal Design, user experience, and copyright. She is the author of a book entitled *Creating Inclusive Libraries by Applying Universal Design* and regularly teaches courses and workshops on accessibility and Universal Design.

Shan C. Sutton is Dean of University Libraries and Katheryne B. Willock Endowed Chair at the University of Arizona. His prior positions include Associate University Librarian for Research and Scholarly Communication at Oregon State University, and Associate Dean and Head of Special Collections at the University of the Pacific, where he curated the John Muir Papers and the Dave Brubeck Archive. Sutton's primary areas of focus as an administrator are open access, innovative learning spaces, and the integration of library services throughout faculty research workflows. Sutton holds a master's degree in library science from the University of Arizona, and a master's degree in humanities from Wright State University. His humanities thesis, an anthropological and comparative religion study of the Grateful Dead, was published in the book *Deadhead Social Science: You Ain't Gonna Learn What You Don't Want to Know* (Altamira Press, 2000).

John E. Ulmschneider retired as *Emeritus* Dean and University Librarian at Virginia Commonwealth University in 2020 after guiding the growth and maturation of VCU Libraries for over 20 years. Under his leadership, VCU Libraries in 2018 became the first US academic library to join the Association of Research Libraries in over 15 years. ACRL recognized VCU Libraries with the 2018 ACRL Excellence in Academic Libraries Award, and Mr. Ulmschneider with the 2020 ACRL Academic/Research Librarian of the Year Award. Mr. Ulmschneider inspired and guided the 2014–16 expansion and renovation of James Branch Cabell Library, subsequently recognized with the 2016 Library Journal New Landmark Libraries Award. Through December 2022, he is Program Director for the Association of Research Libraries Leadership Fellows Program. Mr. Ulmschneider is an alumnus of the University of Virginia, the UNC-Chapel Hill School of Information and Library Science, and the National Library of Medicine Associates Program, and was honored as a UNC-CH SILS Distinguished Alumnus in 2011.

Sohair Wastaway was the founding Executive Director of the Qatar National Library, the Dean of Libraries at Florida Institute of Technology, Illinois State University, Illinois Institute of Technology, and the first chief librarian of the Library of Alexandria, Egypt. Dr. Wastawy also worked as a lecturer in Saudi Arabia, Egypt, and the US respectively. She serves as a member of professional association boards and is the recipient of many awards and honors including a Fulbright scholarship. She is also an international consultant for library buildings and management. Dr. Wastawy received her BA, MA, and completed work towards her PhD thesis in linguistics at Cairo University, Egypt, a master's degree in library and information science from The Catholic University of America, Washington DC, USA, and a doctorate degree in library and information management from Simmons College, Massachusetts, USA.

Brittany Wofford is the Librarian for the Nicholas School of the Environment at Duke University Libraries, providing research support and instruction to the Earth and Climate Sciences and Environmental Sciences and Policy divisions and connecting users to library staff and resources. Previously, she was the Coordinator for The Edge. She is passionate about creating programs to support graduate student learning and skill-building across schools and departments.

David Woodbury is the Department Head for Learning Spaces & Services at the North Carolina State University Libraries. He manages technology-rich learning spaces at Hunt and Hill libraries: makerspaces, digital media labs, virtual reality exploration rooms, and collaborative computing areas. David helps lead the innovative teaching and learning program and supports several key library initiatives, including efforts to increase cocurricular workshops and promote technology lending offerings. On campus and at conferences, he is regularly invited to present on developing informal learning spaces and the thoughtful application of emerging technologies in academic libraries.